Forensic Investigation of Smart Digital Devices

As digital ecosystems advance toward pervasive connectivity, smart devices have become embedded in the operational, social, and economic fabric of modern life. While this integration enhances productivity and accessibility, it generates unprecedented volumes of heterogeneous electronic data and expands the attack surface for cybercrime. The complexity, proprietary architectures, and distributed nature of these technologies simultaneously present profound challenges for contemporary forensic practice. *Forensic Investigation of Smart Digital Devices: A Hands-On Guide* offers a rigorous and comprehensive examination of these challenges. Across thirteen systematically structured chapters, the book provides an in-depth exploration of forensic methodologies for a wide spectrum of device classes, including IoT infrastructures, smartphones, embedded chips, unmanned aerial vehicles (UAVs), social robots, gaming consoles, smart wearables, mobile applications, and autonomous vehicles. Each chapter translates theory into actionable investigative workflows using validated tools, documented case studies, and reproducible techniques. Addressing both current technologies and emerging frontiers, the book integrates discussions on artificial intelligence (AI), machine learning (ML), computer vision (CV), and advanced computational paradigms, highlighting their transformative role in modern digital forensic analysis. This guide equips forensic investigators, cybersecurity specialists, law enforcement personnel, legal professionals, and academic researchers with the methodological rigor and applied skills required to conduct thorough and reliable forensic investigations. Through practical examples and hands-on exercises, it bridges the gap between theory and practice, offering a valuable resource for strengthening cybersecurity and combating cybercrime in the era of smart connected technologies.

Dr. Farkhund Iqbal is a Full Professor and Director of the Advanced Cyber Forensics Research Laboratory (ACFRL) at the College of Technological Innovation, Zayed University, United Arab Emirates. He holds a Master's degree (2005) and a Ph.D. (2011) in Computer Science and Software Engineering from Concordia University, Montreal, Canada. He has over 15 years of teaching and research experience. Dr. Iqbal believes in a student-centered, engaging, and collaborative teaching and learning environment where students are equipped with the knowledge, skills, and competencies required to meet the emerging needs of society. His research focuses on the use of Artificial Intelligence, Machine Learning, Service Robotics, and Data Analytics techniques to meet the challenges in the domain of digital security, cybercrime investigation and digital forensics, healthcare, and smart city. He has over 200+ refereed publications and more than 5600 citations and h-index:39 (on Google Scholar). He is ranked among the top 2% of researchers worldwide in 2025, according to the Stanford and Elsevier global researcher ranking. He is the lead author of multiple books and a recipient of several prestigious awards. He has served as chair and co-chair for numerous IEEE/ACM conferences and workshops and has been a guest editor and reviewer for multiple high-ranking journals. Dr. Iqbal is an Adjunct Professor in the School of Information Studies at McGill University, Montreal, Canada, and an Associate Graduate Faculty member in the Faculty of Business and Information Technology at Ontario Tech University, Toronto, Canada.

Forensic Investigation of Smart Digital Devices
A Hands-on Guide

Dr. Farkhund Iqbal

CRC Press
Taylor & Francis Group
Boca Raton London New York

CRC Press is an imprint of the
Taylor & Francis Group, an **informa** business

Designed cover image: Shutterstock ID: 1508063537

First edition published 2026
by CRC Press
2385 NW Executive Center Drive, Suite 320, Boca Raton FL 33431

and by CRC Press
4 Park Square, Milton Park, Abingdon, Oxon, OX14 4RN

CRC Press is an imprint of Taylor & Francis Group, LLC

© 2026 Dr. Farkhund Iqbal

ISBN: 978-1-041-07830-2 (hbk)
ISBN: 978-1-041-08203-3 (pbk)
ISBN: 978-1-003-64425-5 (ebk)

DOI: 10.1201/9781003644255

Typeset in Sabon
by SPi Technologies India Pvt Ltd (Straive)

Contents

Acknowledgments

I would like to thank Niyat Habtom Seghid and Zainab Khalid of Zayed University, United Arab Emirates, for their continuous editorial support, including structuring and formatting the content, such as figures, images, tables, and other related materials. Special thanks are extended to Faouzi Kamoun from the Esprit School of Business, Tunisia, for his motivation and valuable suggestions. I also gratefully acknowledge the support of renowned research scientists in cybersecurity and digital forensics, including Prof. Mourad Debbabi, Dean of the Gina Cody School of Engineering and Computer Science at Concordia University, Canada; Prof. Benjamin Fung, Canada Research Chair in Data Mining for Cybersecurity (McGill University, Canada); Prof. Patrick C. K. Hung (Ontario Tech University, Canada); and Aine Mac Dermott, Senior Lecturer (Liverpool John Moores University, UK), for their intellectual input and professional support on the core themes of this book.

AI usage

Napkin AI was used to design and generate a small number of diagrams that appear within the book. These diagrams were created specifically to help explain and clarify key concepts discussed in the text—they are not decorative or illustrative in nature. Additionally, GPT-4 was used minimally to assist with proofreading select sections of the manuscript for clarity and grammar.

Chapter 1

IoT forensics

The Internet of Things (IoT) refers to a vast ecosystem of interconnected physical devices embedded with sensors, software, and communication capabilities that allow them to collect, transmit, and sometimes act on data autonomously. Common examples include smart home appliances, wearable devices, Unmanned Aerial Vehicles (UAVs), Electric Vehicles, surveillance systems, industrial sensors, and smartphones (see Table 1.1). These devices continuously generate vast amounts of real-time data, making them integral components of modern digital environments. The term IoT was first coined in 1999 by a computer scientist, Kevin Ashton, who described it as *"a system where the Internet is connected to the physical world via ubiquitous sensors"* [1]. IoT is a vast network that connects devices that have a (1) Radio Frequency Identification (RFID) sensor, (2) Operating System (OS) and software applications, (3) memory, and (4) Internet Protocol (IP) address using which they can gather and share data/information on the Internet [2]. Unique Identifiers (UIDs) associated with these smart digital devices are used to transfer data over the network without the requirement of *Human–Human* (HH) or *Human–Computer* Interaction (HCI).

In the realm of cybercrime investigations and digital forensics, IoT devices have emerged as vital sources of digital evidence. They can provide valuable metadata such as timestamps, geolocation, user interactions, environmental readings, and communication records that may help reconstruct incident timelines, identify perpetrators, or validate testimonies. Nonetheless, the forensic examination of IoT devices presents significant challenges, including data volatility, hardware and software diversity, proprietary protocols, and restricted access. Addressing these complexities requires tailored methodologies and robust forensic tools to preserve the integrity and legal admissibility of collected evidence.

The IoT landscape is constantly changing, with new devices appearing on a daily basis. Over the years, the field of IoT has evolved with the convergence of embedded systems, ubiquitous computing (ubicomp), cloud computing, and Machine Learning (ML). This chapter takes a deep dive into understanding the concept of IoT and why we need IoT forensics. A holistic

DOI: 10.1201/9781003644255-1

1

Table 1.1 List of common IoT devices and their components

IoT device type	Common operating systems (OS)	Common firmware	Common file systems
Smartphone	• Android • iOS • Blueberry • Symbian • HarmonyOS • Sailfish OS • LineageOS • Ubuntu Touch • Tizen	• Android Open Source Project (AOSP) firmware • Bootloader firmware • iOS firmware • Qualcomm Snapdragon firmware • Samsung Exynos firmware	• FAT32 • ext4 • HFS+ • APFS (for iOS)
Wearable Devices	• Wear OS by Google • watchOS • Fitbit OS • Tizen (Samsung wearables) • Garmin OS • Zepp OS	• Nordic Semiconductor firmware • ARM Cortex-M-based firmware • STM32 firmware • ESP32 firmware	• FAT32 • ext4 • YAFFS2
Unmanned Aerial Vehicles (UAVs)	• Dronecode • PX4 • ArduPilot • DJI Flight Control Systems • Custom Linux-based OS	• Betaflight firmware • PX4 firmware • ArduPilot firmware • Cleanflight firmware • DJI Naza firmware	• FAT32 • ext4 • squashfs
PCs	• Windows • macOS • Linux (Ubuntu, Fedora, Arch, etc.)	• BIOS • UEFI firmware • Intel ME firmware • AMD PSP firmware	• NTFS • ext4 • APFS (for macOS)
Smart Toys	• Android Things • Embedded Linux • Proprietary OS	• VTech firmware • Hasbro firmware • Fisher–Price firmware	• FAT32 • ext4

Device Type	Operating Systems	Firmware	File Systems
Gaming Consoles	• PlayStation OS • Xbox OS • Nintendo Switch OS	• PlayStation firmware • Xbox One firmware • Nintendo Switch firmware	• FAT32 • exFAT • ext4
Smart Cameras	• Android • Embedded Linux • RTOS-based systems • Proprietary systems for cameras • VxWorks	• Ambarella firmware • Hisilicon firmware • Novatek firmware • Hikvision firmware	• FAT32 • JFFS2 • YAFFS2
Smart Thermostats	• Embedded Linux • Proprietary OS • Android Things • OpenWRT	• Proprietary thermostat firmware (e.g., Honeywell, Nest) • RTOS-based firmware • ESP8266 firmware	• FAT32 • JFFS2
Smart Appliances	• Embedded Linux • Tizen (Samsung appliances) • Android-based OS for smart appliances • RTOS-based systems	• Proprietary appliance firmware (e.g., LG ThinQ, Samsung SmartThings) • ESP32 firmware	• ext4 • JFFS2 • FAT32
Smart Health Monitors	• Wear OS • Tizen-based (Samsung health devices) • RTOS • Proprietary medical OS	• Nordic Semiconductor firmware • Qualcomm Snapdragon Wear firmware • Real-time health monitoring firmware	• ext4 • FAT32
Electric Vehicles	• Automotive Grade Linux (AGL) • QNX Neutrino RTOS • Android Automotive OS • Tesla OS (Linux-based custom OS)	• ECU firmware • CAN bus firmware • Tesla Autopilot firmware • Bosch Vehicle Control Unit (VCU) firmware	• FAT32 • ext4 • NTFS
Smart Assistants/ Speakers	• Alexa OS (Fire OS-based) • Google Cast OS • Android Things • Embedded Linux	• Alexa firmware • Google Cast firmware • Tizen firmware • Linux-based custom firmware	• ext4 • FAT32

IoT forensics framework is illustrated, along with the enumeration of challenges one may face when performing IoT-specific digital investigations.

1.1 CYBERCRIME INVESTIGATION AND DIGITAL FORENSIC PROCESS

Digital forensics is a critical field that involves the identification, preservation, analysis, and documentation of digital evidence in a legally admissible manner. In our increasingly digital world, where vast amounts of information are stored and transmitted electronically, digital forensics plays a crucial role in investigating a wide range of incidents, from cybercrimes and data breaches to intellectual property theft and fraud. Essentially, it is the process of uncovering and interpreting the digital traces left behind after a digital event, providing investigators with valuable insights into what happened and who might be responsible.

The digital forensic process typically follows a structured methodology to ensure the integrity and admissibility of evidence. It is often summarized as:

1. **Identification:** Recognizing and defining the scope of the digital crime. This involves determining the crime committed, scale of damage, systems and data affected, the criminal behind the crime, and associated digital evidence.
2. **Preservation:** This is *critical*. Evidence must be collected in a way that prevents it from being altered or destroyed. This often involves creating forensic copies of data (bit-by-bit duplicates) and using write-blocking tools to prevent accidental changes to the original data. Chain of custody documentation is also crucial, meticulously recording who handled the evidence and when.
3. **Analysis:** Examining the collected data to reconstruct events, identify perpetrators, and uncover relevant information. This often involves using specialized forensic tools to search for keywords, analyze file structures, recover deleted data, and interpret log files.
4. **Documentation:** Creating a detailed and accurate record of the entire investigation process, including the evidence collected, the analysis performed, and the findings. This documentation is essential for legal proceedings.
5. **Presentation:** Presenting and reporting the findings in a clear and understandable way, whether in a written report or testimony in court.

Digital evidence, the subject of forensic examination, is far more diverse than simply files on a hard drive. It encompasses any data stored or transmitted digitally. This includes, but is not limited to: Files (documents, images, videos, audio recordings, spreadsheets, databases), email and messaging data (including deleted messages, which often leave recoverable traces in system files or server logs), system logs (detailed records of computer and network activity, crucial for reconstructing timelines, and identifying unauthorized access), network traffic (captured data packets revealing communication patterns, protocols used, and potential malicious activity), deleted data (often recoverable through specialized techniques, demonstrating intent or hidden actions), metadata (data about data, such as file creation dates, author information, device identifiers, geolocation tags, and camera settings), memory dumps (snapshots of a computer's RAM, potentially containing valuable information about running processes, encryption keys, and malware remnants), mobile device data (call logs, text messages, contacts, photos, app data, location history, and even health data from wearables), and, as this book highlights, data from Internet of Things (IoT) devices. The increasing prevalence of IoT devices, from smart home appliances to industrial sensors, expands the scope of digital forensics significantly, introducing unique challenges due to the heterogeneity and limited capabilities of these devices.

Several key principles underpin digital forensics. *Integrity* ensures that the evidence is not altered or tampered with during the investigation. *Authenticity* verifies that the evidence is what it is claimed to be. *Accuracy* demands that the investigation and analysis are conducted with precision and thoroughness. *Admissibility* requires that evidence is collected and handled in a way that makes it legally admissible in court. Finally, *reproducibility* dictates that the investigation process should be repeatable by another qualified forensic examiner, ensuring the reliability of the findings.

Despite its importance, digital forensics faces numerous challenges. Encryption can make data inaccessible without the decryption key. Anti-forensics techniques, employed by sophisticated criminals, aim to hide their digital tracks. The sheer volume of data on modern devices can make investigations time-consuming and complex. Cloud computing, where data are stored remotely, presents challenges in terms of access and legal jurisdiction. And, as this book will effectively point out, IoT devices, with their diverse nature and interconnectedness, introduce a whole new set of forensic challenges. These devices often have limited storage, processing power, and logging capabilities, and data may be scattered across multiple devices and networks, demanding specialized forensic techniques and tools. The evolving landscape of technology constantly presents new hurdles for digital forensic investigators, requiring ongoing adaptation and innovation in methods and tools.

1.2 WHY IoT FORENSICS

Over the past few years, IoT has grown to a level where we can connect anything, equipped with just an embedded chip, with a seamless Internet connection. However, the progression of IoT is accompanied by serious concerns about the security and privacy of user data [3]. Such hyper interconnection between the smart digital devices creates many opportunities for criminals and red hats to exploit user data in a multitude of ways and agendas. IoT devices are now used as tools for committing digital crimes and exploiting data. Smart devices like CCTV cameras, drones, smart watches, health monitoring devices, etc., can also work as spy machines over users. In one such account, smart camera vulnerabilities were reported by the users of Google Nest Hub and Xiaomi Mijia. They claimed to have received still images from random people's smart homes while streaming content from their smart cameras by Xiaomi to a Google Nest Hub [4]. Another study by research experts at the University of Texas at San Antonio (UTSA) reported that smart bulbs based on infrared properties can be exploited by sending commands to other smart devices in the IoT ecosystem via infrared light emitted by the smart bulbs [5]. Such incidents are not only affecting individuals but also governments, inter-governmental organizations, and non-governmental organizations. Crime has always been a part of human history, but its nature is changing now. With advancements in IoT technology, things have become much easier for criminals and hackers raising security and privacy concerns related to extensive networks and each connected node.

1.2.1 IoT forensics as a defense

The question arises: Why do we need IoT forensics? The answer lies in the fact that every digital device in this world is somehow prone to a security breach. Consequently, IoT has been an interesting topic among forensic researchers. Given the shifting cybercrime landscape, it becomes imperative to formulate and standardize digital investigation methodologies, frameworks, and tools for forensic investigators in order to extract digital evidence and establish some form of accountability should a breach occur in these ever-changing networks. Every end node/smart device and connection on the network can come under scrutiny when forensic investigations are performed. IoT forensics is more complex and multifaceted than traditional device forensics because of the exponential number of end nodes and networks involved; safe to say it is a cumbersome job.

For a postmortem of any digital event in the IoT environment, we need object-driven forensic frameworks [6]. These frameworks must include data preservation and analysis of sensors, data stored on all the concerned end devices, platforms, and networks. IoT forensics is an amalgamation of different types of digital forensics, like device (hard drive) forensics, memory forensics, network forensics, cloud forensics, etc. Memory or Random Access Memory (RAM) in IoT devices is comparatively smaller, and data are forwarded/discarded as soon as possible. Over the network, data transfers are usually in an encrypted form. The data are usually processed (and stored) in a cloud environment, in servers located in different regions around the world. This makes IoT forensics a bit of a challenging task.

1.3 IoT FORENSICS MODELS

When it comes to IoT, traditional forensic methodologies need to cater for the distributed and heterogeneous nature of the IoT infrastructures and individual devices. In general, digital forensics is performed through either (1) static analysis or (2) dynamic analysis models, which are also applicable in IoT forensics.

1. **Static analysis** examines the contents of a particular file on a disk. It parses data, detecting anomalies and identifying patterns, characteristics, and artifacts.
2. **Dynamic analysis** examines target data/files *live*, in action (or when detonated in a virtual environment deliberately for the purpose of analysis). Open network connections and running processes are the source of information in this case. Rather than depending on signatures to identify dangers, the file is assessed based on what it performs when executed.

1.3.1 Forensic layers in IoT

IoT infrastructure consists of different types of end nodes or smart digital devices, networks, and servers/cloud. Consequently, forensic analysis of IoT environments is carried out by considering all components (or layers) involved.

1. **End nodes/devices** are the foremost sources of evidence to be considered in an investigative scenario. Forensic analysts usually gather data from the local memory, storage space (hard drive), software, application level, firmware, APIs, and other related controllers of the IoT device. IoT sensors and RFIDs that collect and store data in the device may also be considered. In addition, in case there are any externally connected devices, such as flash (USB) drives, they are also analyzed for potential clues and evidence.
2. **Networks** are another important source of evidence. The network can be a significant source of evidence because it can provide network log data, etc. The network topology has a great impact on the forensics process. For example, it is easier to analyze a Local Area Network (LAN) compared to a Wide Area Network (WAN). Other common network topologies in IoT networks include Metropolitan Area Networks (MAN), and Personal Area Networks (PAN).
3. **Cloud/server** environments use virtualization to provide on-demand, scalable Computer-as-a-Service (CaaS) and other facilities. Cloud servers also store user-related data and are, therefore, a source of evidence during the forensics process.

1.3.2 Forensic analysis phases

Once analysis components/devices are identified, a general and standard-ized forensic analysis process is adopted. According to the Digital Forensic Investigation Model (DFIM), the process can be divided mainly into four phases [7]. First, data are acquired as part of the *data collection* step. This will include imaging the storage and memory of end devices, capturing net-work traffic, or acquiring cloud data. Secondly, in the *preservation* phase, the acquired data are stored/preserved properly, as per standard practice, for further analysis. The third step, analysis, entails an in-depth *examina-tion and analysis* of the acquired data in search of incriminating evidence and supporting clues. Finally, the results are detailed in the *reporting* phase. Some standards have an additional presentation phase as well, which per-tains to the presentation of results to the court. Figure 1.1 shows a general schema for IoT Forensics.

1.4 IoT FORENSICS METHODOLOGIES

IoT forensics can be performed using the general four-step digital foren-sics process as discussed previously, that is, collection, preservation, anal-ysis, and reporting. However, extensive research efforts in academia have resulted in streamlined IoT-specific frameworks. Kebande and Ray claim to present one of the first generic frameworks for IoT, a holistic Digital Forensic Investigation Framework (DFIF-IoT) that complies with ISO stan-dard 27043 [8]. It consists of (1) proactive, (2) IoT forensics, and (3) reactive processes. The proactive process emphasizes preparing the IoT environment for potential incidents, covering scenario definition, evidence source iden-tification, and evidence preservation. IoT forensics involves extracting evi-dence from cloud, network, and device-level contexts. The reactive process handles the actual investigation stages, including initialization, evidence acquisition, and analysis. The framework's potential to integrate with exist-ing models and its adherence to standardized processes are highlighted as its advantages.

The Forensic State Acquisition from the Internet of Things (FSAIoT) framework proposed by Meffert et al. focuses on collecting the current states of IoT devices [9]. It includes a centralized Forensic State Acquisition Controller (FSAC) and three modes: FSAC to IoT device, FSAC to cloud, and FSAC to controller. These modes enable state acquisition. The FSAIoT framework is implemented using openHAB due to its comprehensiveness, vendor neutrality, and open-source nature. The FSAC, based on openHAB, ensures forensic soundness, logs date/time, and maintains secure storage and integrity of collected IoT state data. A proof of concept was conducted, involving IoT devices like door and motion sensors, an IP camera, and a nest thermostat. The framework successfully acquired device state data for analysis, showing the feasibility of the approach in IoT forensics.

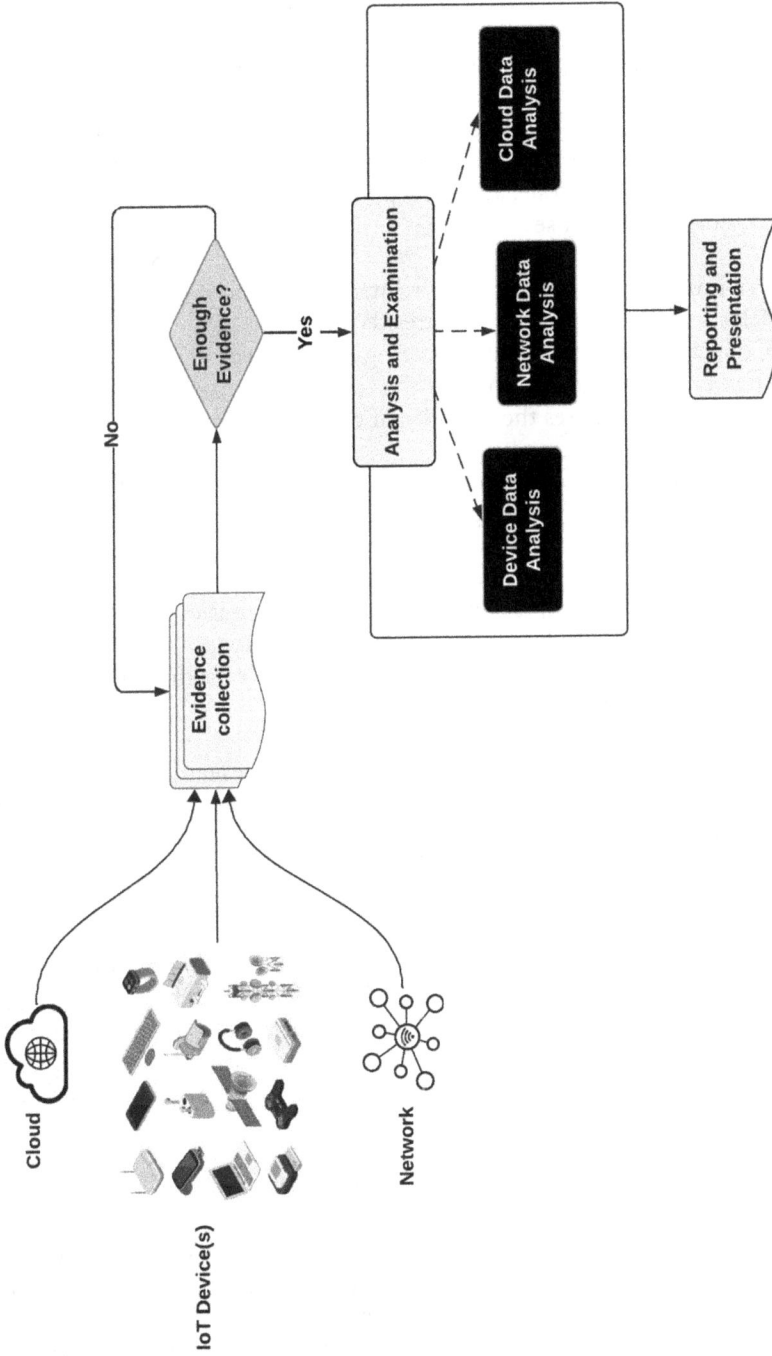

Figure 1.1 A general schema for IoT forensics.

Qatawneh et al. introduced a Digital Forensics Investigation Model (DFIM) tailored for the IoT environment [7]. The DFIM presents a comprehensive model for investigating IoT-related crimes, focusing on validation, evaluation, and review processes to improve the accuracy and effectiveness of IoT forensics. It identifies two main types of systems within IoT: (1) general-purpose systems (e.g., computers, servers) and (2) special-purpose systems (e.g., handheld devices, embedded systems). DFIM encompasses three zones: Cloud zone, fog zone, and perception zone.

The DFIM consists of seven stages:

1. **Pre-investigation** collects crime-related information, validates requests, selects investigators, and prepares data zones.
2. **Collection and evaluation:** Investigators collect evidence, which is then evaluated for relevance to the crime.
3. **Preservation** ensures the integrity of collected evidence using one-way hash algorithms.
4. **Examination and analysis** where collected evidence is analyzed and matched to the crime using specific algorithms.
5. **Information sharing** allows the sharing of evidence among investigators and data zone providers.
6. **Report and documentation** generate a final forensics report detailing investigation procedures, analysis, and conclusions.
7. **Final review:** The investigation authority reviews the report before submitting it to the court.

The proposed model aims to ensure the availability, authentication, integrity, authorization, non-repudiation, and confidentiality of evidence at different stages. It enhances investigation accuracy, performance, data reduction, openness, and transparency. The DFIM addresses limitations in existing investigation models, adds validation, evaluation, and review stages, and introduces the concept of data zone providers.

The forensic investigation framework for IoT (FIF-IoT) is another model for the forensic analysis of IoT devices [10]. The framework uses the public digital ledger to point out the criminal activities that occur inside the IoT ecosystem. Three types of interactions are considered to store data. They include things-to-things, things-to-cloud, and things-to-human interactions.

1.5 KEY COMPONENTS OF IoT DEVICES

In the field of IoT forensics, certain key components of IoT devices are critical during investigations, as they contain valuable data and insights used to reconstruct events, identify anomalies, or trace malicious activity. These primary components, mainly SD card, firmware, filesystem, and operating system (OS), provide a wealth of information, aiding investigators in understanding how the device was used, the nature of the data it handled, and whether it was compromised (refer to Table 1.2). The thorough examination of each component is essential for a successful forensic analysis, offering clues that help piece together the device's operations and security status.

Table 1.2 Key components of IoT devices

Component	Types	Forensic relevance	Common devices
OS	• Linux (Ubuntu, Fedora, Raspbian) • Windows IoT • FreeRTOS • Contiki • TinyOS • Mbed OS • Apple OS (iOS/macOS) • Console OS (PlayStation OS, Xbox OS) • Drone OS (PX4, ArduPilot) • Metaverse OS (customized Android versions, specialized VR platforms)	• Logs of system and network activity • Security configurations and breaches • Installed applications and user management	• Computers • IoT Devices • Consoles • Drones • VR Devices
Firmware	• Bare-metal firmware • RTOS-based firmware • Linux-based firmware • Proprietary firmware • Drone firmware (e.g., Betaflight, OpenPilot)	• Control device operations • Show evidence of tampering or unauthorized changes • Integrity checks for security breaches	• IoT Devices • Industrial Controls • Drones • Consumer Electronics
SD Card	• Standard Capacity (SDSC) • High Capacity (SDHC) • Extended Capacity (SDXC) • Ultra Capacity (SDUC)	• Storage of logs, sensor data, and configurations • Recovery of deleted files • Evidence of device usage and data handling	• Cameras • Smartphones • Drones • Portable Media Players
Filesystem	• FAT32 • NTFS • ext2/ext3/ext4 • HFS+ • YAFFS2 • JFFS2 • Btrfs • APFS (Apple File System)	• File access, creation, and deletion logs • Recovery of deleted data • User activity and system operation insights	• Network Attached Storage • Smartphones • Embedded Systems • Desktops and Laptops

Firmware: As the embedded software controlling the device's hardware, firmware follows specific instructions to operate the device. Forensic analysis of firmware is vital because it may contain evidence of tampering or modifications indicative of malicious actions. This analysis is particularly crucial when checking firmware updates that could either secure vulnerabilities or introduce new risks. Investigators look to extract version information, assess integrity violations, and compare current firmware against official versions to detect alterations.

Filesystem: The filesystem organizes and manages the data stored on the device, encompassing user data, system logs, configurations, and potentially sensitive information such as encryption keys or credentials. The forensic analysis of the filesystem is pivotal as it allows the recovery of deleted files, access to logs, and the uncovering of hidden data. By examining the filesystem's structure, forensic experts can trace user activities, including commands executed, files manipulated, and interactions with external systems, all of which are crucial for understanding the scope of any breach or misuse.

Operating System (OS): The operating system manages the IoT device's resources and applications, providing a layer of software essential for the device's operations. Investigating the OS offers insights into how the device operates, the security mechanisms employed, and any signs of compromise. The OS reveals crucial information about installed applications, active processes, network activity, and security settings. Through this analysis, forensic experts can identify vulnerabilities, detect suspicious behaviors, and uncover unauthorized access or malware infections.

SD Card: Commonly utilized for external storage in IoT devices, SD cards hold crucial data including logs, sensor data, configuration settings, and sometimes backup copies of the device's operations. These elements are indispensable for forensic investigators as they reveal usage patterns, user interactions, and records of data transmission. The information extracted from SD cards helps to track the lifecycle of the device's operations, detect unauthorized access, and understand unusual behaviors. Analyzing SD cards can provide a detailed timeline of events, assisting in correlating them with other forensic artifacts.

By delving deep into these components, forensic investigators can gain significant insights into an IoT device's operations, uncover evidence of malicious activity, and effectively reconstruct events leading up to and following an incident. Each component provides unique data points that, when integrated, offer a comprehensive view of the device's state and operational integrity, making them indispensable in IoT forensic investigations.

This integrated approach ensures a thorough understanding of the device's functionality and security, providing a solid foundation for legal and security responses.

1.6 KEY CHALLENGES

IoT forensics is a very complex process due to the large volumes of data and multiple forensic layers involved. Each step poses unique challenges that make it difficult to collect, preserve, and analyze digital evidence effectively. Some of the key challenges in IoT forensics include:

1. **Heterogeneous and Resource-Limited Ecosystem:** IoT environments consist of a wide variety of devices with different hardware, software (OSs), communication protocols, and data formats. This diversity complicates the standardization of investigation processes and tools [11]. Most IoT devices have limited processing power, memory, and storage capacity [12]. This makes it challenging to run resource-intensive forensic tools directly on these devices and necessitating external resources for analysis.
2. **Scale Evidence Management Challenges:** IoT systems can involve massive numbers of devices spread across various locations. Investigating such large-scale deployments requires specialized tools and techniques to efficiently collect and analyze evidence from numerous sources. Moreover, securing the chain of custody is critical, as evidence integrity must be maintained with records of who, when, and where contacted the evidence. Many IoT devices are designed with minimal consideration for forensic analysis and lack built-in logging mechanisms, tamper-resistant storage, or other forensics-friendly features needed for preserving digital evidence.
3. **Data Acquisition and Processing Complexities:** IoT devices generate voluminous real-time data streams requiring specialized capture techniques to ensure timely analysis. Data are often encrypted (hindering access without proper keys) and fragmented across different locations, which complicates timeline reconstruction and can lead to false negatives and false positives due to limited information. Time synchronization issues between devices further complicate establishing a coherent timeline of events [13].
4. **Network Evidence Challenges:** IoT devices often communicate with each other and external systems, leaving traces of evidence in various locations requiring network forensics expertise for investigating networked evidence. Network topology significantly impacts analysis difficulty, as forensic analysis is easier in LAN environments but

becomes considerably more complicated in complex MAN and WAN topologies, where forensic analysis becomes rather complicated, and many tools fail to function properly with large network log data.

5. **Governance and Jurisdictional Issues:** Determining ownership of IoT devices and their data presents challenges, especially with shared devices or multiple users. Cross-border jurisdiction issues commonly arise in global IoT deployments. Authentication and authorization problems make it difficult to establish the authenticity and integrity of device interactions, especially when dealing with compromised devices or unauthorized access.

6. **Standards and Adaptability Concerns:** The absence of standardized IoT forensic procedures, tools, and protocols makes it challenging to ensure consistency and interoperability across investigations. IoT ecosystems are continuously evolving with new devices, protocols, and technologies, requiring investigators to constantly update their approaches to effectively investigate emerging threats.

Addressing these challenges requires a multidisciplinary approach that combines expertise in digital forensics, IoT technologies, cybersecurity, and legal aspects. As the IoT landscape continues to evolve, researchers and practitioners are working to develop specialized techniques, tools, and best practices to overcome these challenges and conduct effective investigations for smart digital devices in IoT environments. Figure 1.2 illustrates some of the challenges faced in IoT forensics.

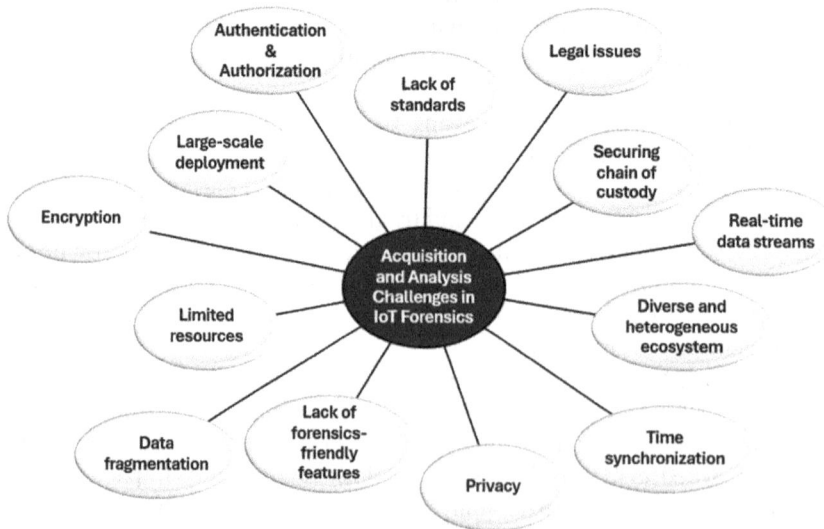

Figure 1.2 Challenges in IoT forensics.

1.7 OPPORTUNITIES IN IoT FORENSICS

While IoT forensics indeed encounters a multitude of challenges, as explored in the previous section, these challenges also signify a myriad of avenues for exploration aimed at resolving these pressing issues. Given that IoT operates within a distributed framework and encompasses a diverse array of interconnected smart digital devices, the task of erasing all traces of evidence becomes significantly arduous for criminals. Forensic investigators may grapple with the intricacies of analyzing extensive datasets, but there exists a robust likelihood that crucial evidence remains intact. This is primarily due to the decentralized nature of IoT, where data are often shared across a network of devices rather than being confined to a single unit.

In contrast to traditional digital forensics, IoT introduces a wider array of potential evidence sources. The sheer volume of data that smart digital devices in IoT generate can be immense, with even seemingly inconsequential devices like smart toys proving invaluable in the forensic process. Additionally, the convergence of evidence from diverse devices can synergistically contribute to the creation of a comprehensive and holistic view of a collective event

Figure 1.3 consolidates the discussions presented throughout this chapter by providing a comprehensive taxonomy of IoT forensics, including device types, investigative models, forensic phases, analytical layers, and associated tools.

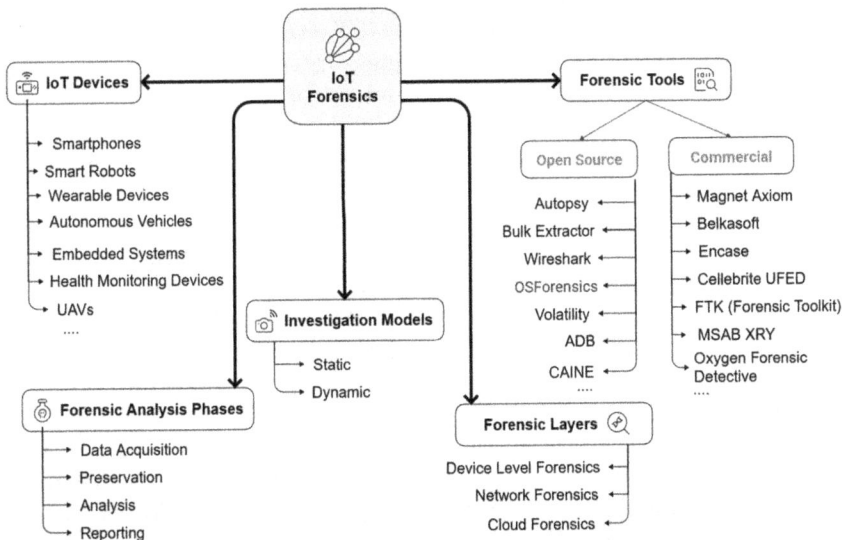

Figure 1.3 Detailed taxonomy of IoT forensics.

END OF CHAPTER QUESTIONS

1. How does the heterogeneity of IoT devices affect the standardization and effectiveness of forensic investigations? Provide examples to illustrate your answer.
2. Discuss how the principle of reproducibility in digital forensics can be challenged in the context of volatile IoT environments.
3. Evaluate the impact of decentralized data storage (e.g., cloud and fog layers) on the chain of custody in IoT forensic investigations.
4. What are the ethical dilemmas associated with forensic data acquisition from personal IoT devices like smartwatches or fitness trackers?
5. Compare and contrast static and dynamic analysis models in the context of IoT forensics. Which is more applicable and why?
6. How do time synchronization issues across IoT devices influence the accuracy of forensic timelines?
7. In what ways could the absence of built-in logging mechanisms hinder forensic investigations? Propose strategies to overcome this challenge.
8. Critically assess the strengths and limitations of the DFIF-IoT framework in handling IoT forensic cases involving both cloud and device-level evidence.
9. What role does firmware analysis play in detecting unauthorized activities in IoT ecosystems?
10. How could blockchain or distributed ledger technologies enhance the integrity and auditability of IoT forensic processes?
11. Describe how a forensic investigator could validate the authenticity of evidence collected from a compromised smart home device.
12. Analyze the potential risks of relying on third-party forensic tools in investigations involving proprietary IoT ecosystems.
13. How would you design a logging mechanism for a resource-constrained IoT device to support future forensic investigations?
14. Discuss how machine learning might assist in filtering and correlating massive data streams generated by IoT devices during forensic investigations.
15. Propose a policy framework that balances user privacy with the need for forensic access to IoT data in criminal investigations.
16. Evaluate how forensic readiness can be integrated into the IoT product lifecycle. What stakeholders should be involved?
17. What are the implications of cross-jurisdictional evidence collection in global IoT deployments? Suggest solutions to mitigate legal conflicts.
18. Explain how the concept of "digital traceability" in IoT forensics could evolve in future smart environments with AI-driven automation.
19. You are investigating a case involving a compromised smart thermostat. Outline the forensic methodology you would employ to analyze the device, including any tools you would use.

20. Imagine you have found suspicious data on an IoT fitness tracker. What are the potential avenues of investigation, and how might these data be relevant to a larger case?

21. A law enforcement agency receives a report of unauthorized access to a smart security camera system. Describe how you would approach the investigation and what types of data you would prioritize.

22. While investigating a home automation system, you find multiple logs indicating unusual activity. Explain how you would analyze these logs and what insights you hope to gain from them.

23. You encounter a smart appliance that was remotely accessed without authorization. What steps would you take to secure the device and preserve evidence?

24. Given a smart health device transmitting encrypted telemetry via LTE, how would you isolate, intercept, and decode relevant forensic evidence? Include both network and device-level tactics.

25. How can forensic investigators acquire and analyze evidence from an IoT device's firmware? What types of forensic insight can this analysis reveal?

26. Discuss how the architecture of an IoT device (e.g., firmware, OS, SD card, filesystem) influences the type and depth of digital forensic evidence that can be collected.

27. How does limited memory and storage in IoT devices complicate the preservation and extraction of digital evidence? What strategies might help mitigate these constraints?

28. In the context of the forensic analysis process (collection, preservation, analysis, reporting), how would you apply these phases to a compromised smart thermostat?

29. What is the role of metadata in IoT forensics, and how might forensic analysts extract and utilize metadata from an IoT environment?

30. How does the dynamic and distributed nature of IoT networks affect the chain of custody and integrity of evidence during an investigation?

31. Compare and contrast static and dynamic analysis models as they apply to IoT forensics. In what scenario would each be most effective?

32. What types of logs or traces might an investigator look for on the filesystem of an IoT device, and what tools could be used to analyze them?

33. What are the specific forensic challenges associated with extracting evidence from the cloud component of an IoT infrastructure?

34. Discuss how forensic analysis differs when targeting an end-node device versus analyzing the cloud or server layer in an IoT forensic investigation.

35. How would a forensic expert verify whether the operating system on an IoT device has been compromised or altered?

36. What technical procedures can be used to analyze data stored on an IoT device's SD card? What kinds of evidence might this component provide?
37. What forensic value does RAM (volatile memory) hold in IoT devices, and how can these data be captured before it is lost?
38. How does time synchronization (or lack thereof) between IoT devices complicate forensic timeline reconstruction? What can be done to align events accurately?
39. What are the implications of proprietary protocols and vendor-specific hardware for IoT forensics, particularly in terms of tool compatibility and evidence accessibility?

REFERENCES

[1] Silica, A., "Avnet: Quality electronic components & services," www.avnet.com, Feb. 11, 2018. https://www.avnet.com/wps/portal/silica/resources/article/interview-with-iot-inventor-kevin-ashton-iot-is-driven-by-the-users/

[2] Ambrosin, M. et al., "On the feasibility of attribute-based encryption on internet of things devices," IEEE Micro, vol. 36, no. 6, pp. 25–35, Nov. 2016, doi: 10.1109/mm.2016.101

[3] Zarpelão, B. B., Miani, R. S., Kawakani, C. T., and de Alvarenga, S. C., "A survey of intrusion detection in internet of things," Journal of Network and Computer Applications, vol. 84, pp. 25–37, Apr. 2017, doi: 10.1016/j.jnca.2017.02.009

[4] CISOMAG, "Xiaomi security camera bug shows other homes' camera feeds," CISO MAG | Cyber Security Magazine, Jan. 03, 2020. [Online]. Available: https://cisomag.eccouncil.org/xiaomi-security-camera-bug-shows-other-homes-camera-feeds/

[5] "Smart light bulbs can hack your personal information," gulfnews.com. [Online]. Available: https://gulfnews.com/technology/smart-light-bulbs-can-hack-your-personal-information-1.1571846229201

[6] Alaba, F. A., Othman, M., Hashem, I. A. T., and Alotaibi, F., "Internet of things security: A survey," Journal of Network and Computer Applications, vol. 88, no. 88, pp. 10–28, Jun. 2017, doi: 10.1016/j.jnca.2017.04.002

[7] Qatawneh et al., "DFIM: A new digital forensics investigation model for internet of things," Journal of Theoretical and Applied Information Technology, vol. 97, p. 24, 2019.

[8] Kebande, V. R. and Ray, I., "A generic digital forensic investigation framework for internet of things (IoT)," IEEE Xplore, Aug. 01, 2016. [Online]. Available: https://ieeexplore.ieee.org/document/7575885

[9] Meffert, C., Clark, D., Baggili, I., and Breitinger, F., "Forensic state acquisition from internet of things (FSAIoT)," In Proceedings of the 12th International Conference on Availability, Reliability and Security, Aug. 2017, doi: 10.1145/3098954.3104053

[10] Hossain, M., Karim, Y., and Hasan, R., "FIF-IoT: A forensic investigation framework for IoT using a public digital ledger," In 2018 IEEE International Congress on Internet of Things (ICIOT), Jul. 2018, doi: 10.1109/iciot.2018.00012

[11] Alenezi, A., Atlam, H., Alsagri, R., Alassafi, M., and Wills, G., "IoT forensics: A state-of-the-art review, challenges and future directions," In *Proceedings of the 4th International Conference on Complexity, Future Information Systems and Risk*, 2019, doi: 10.5220/0007905401060115

[12] MacDermott, A., Baker, T. and Shi, Q., "Iot forensics: Challenges for the Ioa era," In *2018 9th IFIP International Conference on New Technologies, Mobility and Security (NTMS)*, 2018, pp. 1–5, doi: 10.1109/NTMS.2018.8328748

[13] Servida, F. and Casey, E., "IoT forensic challenges and opportunities for digital traces," *Digital Investigation*, vol. 28, pp. S22–S29, Apr. 2019, doi: 10.1016/j.diin.2019.01.012

Chapter 2

Forensic analysis methods for IoT devices

Smart digital devices, with smartphones as the most ubiquitous example, offer a gateway to a diverse array of applications. These applications span from entertainment and gaming to lifestyle, photography, social media, and Instant Messaging (IM). However, these devices are being exploited for a variety of online crimes, ranging from disseminating slander and engaging in cyberstalking to perpetrating bullying. The surge in cybercriminal endeavors has, in turn, given rise to the emergence of new digital forensics sub-disciplines, exclusively dedicated to researching and crafting tools essential for extracting evidence from smart digital devices [1]. Smart digital devices, as integral parts of the IoT, amass substantial volumes of private, sensitive, and usage-related data. Consequently, digital forensic investigations delve into the digital artifacts stored, processed, or transmitted by these devices.

Challenges, however, in the forensics of smart digital devices arise due to the absence of standardized evidence-gathering interface ports and specialized forensics equipment. Privacy and security concerns within the smart digital devices realm, coupled with potential safety risks to human life stemming from inadequate technical controls surrounding data collection, processing, and storage, have also come to the forefront [2]. As we navigate the complex smart digital device environment, challenges emerge in terms of data extraction procedures and techniques. Collaboration between the digital forensics sector and the vendors responsible for creating and developing these devices is vital to advancing the field [3]. The dynamic generation of digital evidence, coupled with growing confusion and uncertainty regarding its extraction and analysis, underscores the urgency of such collaboration. The type of device in use, its price point, and its security features all play a role in the feasibility of forensic investigation.

In addition, the evolving sophistication of hacker tools and exploit kits further complicates the matter. Amidst these shifts, the digital forensics industry also faces challenges ranging from complexity and consistency, data volume, and unified time-lining of evidence to varying time zones and the diverse hardware and software of the myriad digital devices in circulation [3]. The ability to conduct effective digital forensic analysis of smart

DOI: 10.1201/9781003644255-2

digital devices becomes a pressing issue. This chapter details the considerations necessary for smart digital devices throughout the various forensic analysis phases.

2.1 CONFISCATION

The conventional method of conducting computer forensics involves shutting down the suspect's device, transporting it to a laboratory, extracting the hard disk, and capturing images of the confiscated device for further analysis. This process is time-consuming, and considering the importance of timely justice, it is often more preferable to initiate some form of on-site triage or preliminary investigation. In fact, such an approach might even lead to confessions when the suspect is confronted with evidence of their wrongdoing on the spot.

Forensic examination environment boot media can be utilized in three main ways in these cases:

- Supplying *known-good* binaries for analyzing the system in real time.
- Performing an analysis of the device at the location without disassembling it or imaging its hard disk.
- Using the suspect's hardware to examine the disk, especially when specialized or legacy hardware is unavailable for imaging specific hard disks.

Through these investigative methods, the suspect's device is employed to probe the activities that occurred on it. During the investigations, the integrity of Electronically Stored Information (ESI) must be maintained through forensically sound collection practices.

Several key principles underscore the argument that smart digital devices require the capability for digital forensic analysis:

- Legal authorities possess proper authorization or warrants for confiscation.
- Law enforcement can commence a study of smart devices once seized.
- Adhering to essential procedures such as preparation, identification, collection, and customization during processing.
- Evaluating investigation risks, identifying physical evidence, determining device capabilities, and locating necessary tools for analysis.
- Examining Wi-Fi connections, geolocation data, storage, camera data, and other relevant device areas during forensic analysis.

Overall, the effectiveness of current forensic tools/technologies in gathering and processing ESI from smart digital devices is lacking. Even when tools are available, discrepancies in artifact storage among different models of smart devices can pose challenges. Forensic professionals frequently encounter hurdles due to hardware variations, device alterations, resource limitations, and anti-forensic techniques [4].

2.2 ACQUISITION

During evidence gathering, the forensic investigator proceeds with creating a *duplicate copy* of the original material. The forensic investigator initiates the setup, conducting a thorough scan of the device. This step helps the examiner determine the nature of data that needs to be acquired from the stored sources. The investigator focuses on methods for *logical* or *physical* acquisition, aiming to access ESI within the smart device. Ensuring the integrity of the evidence is paramount at this juncture; the investigator verifies that both the original and duplicate copies match through *hash verification*.

It is important to acknowledge that modern devices come equipped with robust security features like encryption to prevent unauthorized access. This poses a significant challenge for forensic investigators, as gaining access to the device can be the most arduous aspect of the acquisition process. While techniques like brute force attacks may be employed to bypass security measures, many smart gadgets incorporate advanced security protocols that thwart such attempts and restrict data access. For instance, Apple wearables implement restrictions on passcode attempts, triggering a factory reset and data deletion after numerous unsuccessful tries.

When dealing with devices that require and store passkeys, it is imperative to follow specific steps to safeguard the device's data. This involves carefully removing the battery and placing it in an evidence bag for preservation purposes.

Before initiating logical and physical acquisition, the suspected smartphone must undergo a comprehensive scan using established methods. These methods encompass both hardware and software-based approaches to bypass any device blocks that rely on authentication mechanisms such as passwords. Techniques like Joint Test Action Group (JTAG)[1] and flasher boxes can help bypass authentication mechanisms. Additional methods include specific attacks tailored to particular devices, such as unlocking Android-based devices by cooling them to sub-zero temperatures and disconnecting and reconnecting the battery with precise timing [5]. Remote acquisition of live forensic memory images can also be performed using tools like EnCase Enterprise, ProDiscover IR, X-Ways Capture, and FTK Imager Lite [6]. An innovative approach involves using ColdBoot to extract RAM images by exploiting the temporary data retention nature of DRAM.

Figure 2.1 shows the standard procedure for evidence acquisition, where a write-blocker is used to ensure data integrity during imaging via a forensic workstation or dedicated imager.

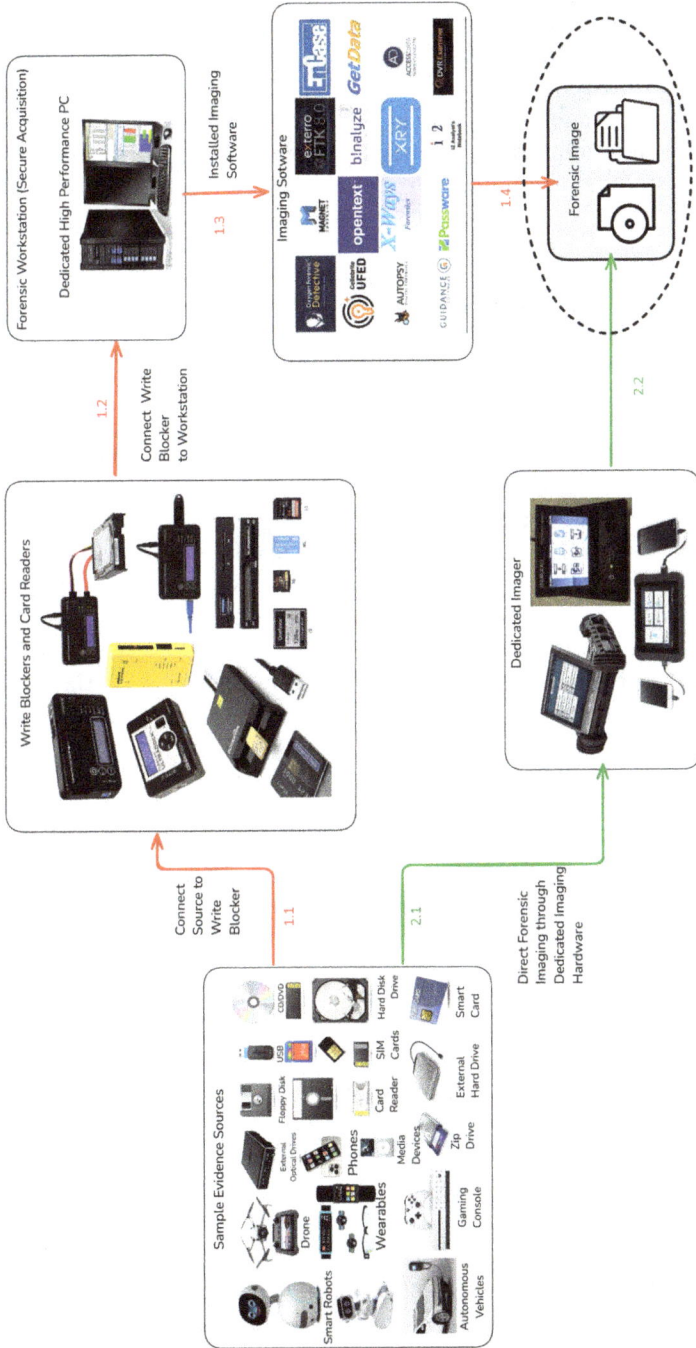

Figure 2.1 Digital evidence acquisition process using a write blocker with a workstation or a dedicated forensic imager.

2.2.1 Manual acquisition

Manual extraction is probably the most straightforward technique compared to others since it involves a tester directly operating the device under scrutiny by using its input interface (such as keypads and buttons), while documenting the content displayed on the device's screen [7]. However, there may be questions raised about its admissibility in court, unless a strict chain of custody is maintained by methods such as taking a video of the analyst interacting with the suspect device.

2.2.2 Logical acquisition

Logical extraction involves enabling the examiner to obtain files and directories residing within the system. It achieves this by facilitating the extraction of logical storage objects via the wired or wireless interfaces of the device. However, this method does not grant access to unallocated areas. During acquisition, the forensic examiner should take note of the acquisition method used and any potential alterations that might have occurred on the device while data are collected. In the majority of anticipated acquisitions, the industry-standard approach of logical extraction is employed. This method offers a higher level of abstraction for system data structures, which, in turn, aids in the extraction and presentation of evidence through forensic tools. Forensic examiners need to comprehend both the external and internal components of the device to effectively investigate using this approach.

The logical data collection approach involves using specialized tools to obtain user data. This can be accomplished by connecting the device to a forensics workstation via cable or wireless connections. This strategy generally yields information comparable to that acquired through manual data collection but in an automated manner. Before data can be extracted using this method, preparatory steps are necessary. While the initial steps can vary based on the specific device, in most cases, the Software Development Kit (SDK) must be installed. This SDK provides forensic investigators with access to the device's hardware and software at the manufacturer level. This method is valued for its reliability, speed, simplicity, and forensic integrity. However, it is important to note that although this method can retrieve a significant amount of data, a comprehensive forensic examination requires the recovery of deleted and corrupted files. Unfortunately, this technique is unable to recover erased data and files that have been compromised.

The Android Debug Bridge (ADB) is a versatile command-line tool designed for facilitating communication with devices. This tool streamlines a range of device operations, including app installation and debugging. Furthermore, it grants access to a Unix shell, which can be utilized to perform diverse actions on a device, including a logical acquisition [8]. However, it is important to note that to avail this access, the Android OS must be rooted. The process commences with rooting the device, a step that often proves pivotal in investigations as evidence tends to be scattered across memory blocks.

2.2.3 Sparse acquisition

Another acquisition method is the sparse acquisition technique, which plays a significant role in capturing even the deleted artifacts of smart digital devices. Unlike logical acquisitions, which target only the filesystem, sparse acquisition also gathers fragments of unallocated (deleted) data. The sparse acquisition technique is used during static acquisitions in RAID systems or on systems where the suspect's lack of technological proficiency necessitates the use of intricate anti-forensic measures. With the continuously increasing number of devices in active use, the potential for smart digital devices to hold crucial digital evidence is ever-expanding. However, the specifics regarding how, where, and for how long such evidence is stored often remain unclear.

2.2.4 Physical acquisition

The physical data collection method involves creating a bit-by-bit clone of all data stored on a device, including hidden/deleted files. This technique is executed either by connecting with the smart digital device through a cable or by removing its storage cards and copying the entire file system. Forensic experts commonly employ this approach across a range of investigative scenarios, as it balances extraction speed, user-friendliness, and data volume. Irrespective of whether data are allocated within a file system, physical data collection ensures its extraction. To perform physical acquisition, direct access to the device's flash memory is required. This method grants a forensic analyst entry to unallocated space and all data on the device, including erased files. Physical acquisition also employs techniques like hex dumping/ JTAG extraction. There are two types of physical acquisition:

1. **Hardware-Based Physical Acquisition:** Hardware components are removed from the device and then forensically imaged. This method does not require root access.
2. **Software-Based Physical Acquisition:** The software acquisition does not cause any harm to the memory but requires root privilege. Tools like Smart Phone Forensic System Professional (SPF Pro) can be used to conduct software-based acquisition.

The primary goal of physical extraction is to comprehend the configuration and structure of file systems and media storage on mobile devices, particularly focusing on hidden data. Leading commercial forensic tools such as Cellebrite UFED Touch, Encase Smartphone Examiner, and XRY can execute this process effectively.

During the investigation, law enforcement officers seeking images scrutinize files from designated locations and subject them to distinct analysis processes:

Log analysis: This process involves auditing log files from the smart digital device's OS to identify potentially malicious behavior based on recognized patterns. The aim is to comprehensively review data to establish the context of user activity. This process uses standardized, normalized terminology to generate reports and statistics from a diverse environment. Some IM applications, including WhatsApp, store images on the device by default. However, some configurations may save logs in cloud storage, adding complexity to log analysis.

File name analysis: File names from acquired images are compared against a predefined list of keywords. This list commonly includes terms and phrases frequently associated with the distribution of illicit images. Suspicious files with varying attributes like extensions, sizes, signatures, and associated properties can be detected using this analysis.

Smart device site analysis: This analysis aims to determine the precise location of the user during a potential criminal act. It relies on data from the device's GPS, along with records of SMS messages, phone calls, and downloads from the device's history. Service providers for smart devices often retain copies of these records.

There are many forms of analysis to be performed on the acquired device images, which will be detailed later in the chapter.

2.2.4.1 Rooting and jailbreaking

Physical acquisition of smart digital devices requires processes known as *rooting* and *jailbreaking*. These procedures involve obtaining root access to the device's OS, effectively bypassing the limitations imposed by vendors. These limitations are intended to prevent users from switching providers and to restrict unauthorized access to perform investigative actions. When an iPhone is jailbroken, Apple's restrictions are removed, allowing the installation of apps from any developer, various tweaks, iOS themes, and unrestricted content. This process also grants the ability to uninstall pre-installed iOS apps. It is important to note that rooting/jailbreaking does come with risks. By bypassing some of Android's/Apple's security measures, the device becomes more vulnerable to viruses and unauthorized data intrusions. To mitigate these risks, it is recommended to secure the rooted/jailbroken device with a reputable VPN and a comprehensive security suite. While there is a common perception that Apple devices and applications offer better security and privacy compared to competitors like Android, it is crucial to understand that no system is completely immune to threats. Although the iOS ecosystem incorporates architectural decisions that inherently enhance their resilience against malware, such as the restriction on side-loading software, the potential for data breaches and misuse still remains [9].

When it comes to other smart digital devices, the rooting methods may slightly differ for each device or even each model/version. Consequently, it becomes too complicated a task dealing with distinct models and figuring out rooting and jailbreaking nuances for each one.

2.2.4.2 Chip-off technology

The chip-off physical extraction method, as defined by the National Institute of Standards and Technology (NIST), entails physically removing the flash memory chips, referred to as a chip-off, for subsequent examination. Chip off is a hardware-based physical extraction. It was utilized as part of a forensic study by Nintendo to extract and decrypt data from the NAND memory chip of the 3DS console. This approach provides access to vital information, including the plaintext user passwords, deleted photos, contact details, friends' information, Internet browsing history, and serial numbers. However, due to the manner in which many established methodologies and software tools are designed, they are often more suited for conventional digital forensics tasks. This presents challenges for digital forensic practitioners when dealing with IoT devices.

In certain situations, a chip-off procedure might be the preferred initial step, although typically only after exhausting all other forensic extraction options, such as JTAG. Such instances arise when preserving the exact memory state on the evidence device is of utmost importance. Given the wide array of chip types employed in smart digital devices, this method poses greater technical complexity. The procedure involves heating and dislodging the memory chip, making it both costly and necessitating expertise at the hardware level. Successful chip-off extraction necessitates comprehensive training, as inadequate techniques can irreversibly damage the memory chip, rendering all data irretrievable. The chip-off technique is applicable to extracting data from nearly any device that utilizes flash memory, be it NAND, NOR, OneNAND, or eMMC.

2.3 ANALYSIS AND EXAMINATION

Forensic investigators must exercise utmost caution during the analysis of smart digital devices. Acquisition conducted while the device is operational can inadvertently lead to changes in system logs and user data, posing a serious risk of losing critical information. Additionally, viewing user content while the device is active could unintentionally alter metadata, potentially erasing valuable evidence sources. The investigation continues to delve into the OS features of the device through analysis. This stage aims to extract data from the knowledge acquired about device OS functionalities.

The objective is to examine all evidence to ascertain the presence of a crime, legal requirement, or policy violation. Once this analysis is complete, the evidence is prepared for presentation and stored securely in a designated database for evidence retention [4].

Furthermore, criminals are actively seeking ways to conceal illicit activities, often resorting to encrypting removable storage devices or entire hard drives. This emerging practice halts the analysis altogether. Fortunately, recent research indicates that encryption keys used for volume/disk encryption are frequently retained in the device's memory (RAM) for the duration of their requirement, especially when the encrypted device is mounted. Memory forensic tools like Memorize can be employed to extract these keys from live memory dumps. Apart from encryption keys, these open-source tools can retrieve various other forensically relevant and sensitive information, such as registry data, DLLs, and login credentials like usernames and passwords. Additionally, traces of sensitive data like email logins and passwords might guide researchers further. It is worth noting that encryption software often leaves residual information, and physical drives generate temporary files or functional copies [5].

With an increasing array of devices processing, sharing, and storing data, forensic analysts must collaborate with manufacturers to update procedures and techniques for data extraction and analysis. Trusted forensic analysis tools are essential for precise storage data validation and analysis. Challenges such as full hard disk encryption, user account switching, and the utilization of cloud services as supplementary evidence sources alongside physical drives pose additional hurdles for forensic investigations. When possible, employing a forensic tool to analyze individual system partitions and perform keyword searches for pertinent data within images is advisable.

A write blocker is used to protect the evidence from any unintentional changes, constituting a specific form of *live analysis* [10]. However, the capacity of forensic technologies to effectively extract and parse evidence from images on smart digital devices appears to be constrained. Consequently, the most pragmatic approach to forensic analysis often entails performing a live analysis. In executing this approach, a cautious effort is made to minimize any manipulation or tampering with the evidence. If adjustments are modest, well-documented, and repeatable, the evidence maintains its admissibility in a court of law.

By conducting a live analysis of a smart device, an investigator can access various facets of a user's profile, including play history, achievements, messages exchanged, and a comprehensive record of completed activities with corresponding timestamps. This capability aids investigators in chronologically aligning events, establishing connections between relevant evidence, and highlighting their temporal sequence. Additionally, network artifacts such as IP addresses, default gateways, and primary and secondary DNS records can be collected. However, these efforts might prove cumbersome if the user's account is not configured for automatic console logins.

In terms of *network analysis*, tools such as Wireshark and NetworkMiner are employed to capture network traffic, unveiling details like open ports, hostnames, OS, and active sessions. Depending on the smart device's application, network communication might be encrypted or transmitted in a proprietary protocol, beyond NetworkMiner's parsing capabilities. A thorough examination of network traffic helps in uncovering additional artifacts.

Considering user data storage options beyond local hard disks, like cloud services, requires forensic investigators to broaden their investigative scope, which consequently elevates associated risks.

2.4 REPORTING AND PRESENTATION

The final phase, *presentation*, encompasses the consolidation of factual outcomes and the effective communication of these findings to the appropriate audience. Three foundational principles underpin the argument that smart digital devices necessitate the capability for digital forensic analysis:

1. **Pre- and post-analysis of device:** This involves assessing the device before and after analysis to determine the extent to which forensic evidence can be retrieved from linked smart devices.
2. **Alteration of smart digital devices:** Understanding how a smart digital device has been tampered with.
3. **Expansion of IoT devices:** The proliferation of IoT devices, such as smart devices that store information in the cloud, presents opportunities for malicious actors to exploit cybersecurity vulnerabilities for illicit or ethically objectionable activities.

To support the prosecution of cybercrimes, investigators must possess the ability to conduct forensic analysis and extract ESI from smart devices [4]. Most smart digital devices available in the market lack a standardized interface for data extraction. Consequently, an established forensic framework for efficiently extracting ESI using Standardized Operating Procedures (SOPs) has been lacking.

An example of evidence can be observed in a list of paired Bluetooth devices, wherein a smart watch linked to an Apple iPhone is highlighted. This evidence includes crucial data entries such as name, address, resolved address, Universal Unique Identifier (UUID), last seen, and last connection timings. This focus extends to the Apple iPhone's watch application, where a wealth of data, including Nike Plus and GPS data, could potentially serve as future evidence.

Staying up-to-date with forensic techniques compatible with the diverse array of smart devices, each operating on distinct systems like Google's Android, Apple's iOS, RIM's Blackberry OS, and more, presents a challenge for forensic examiners. This challenge is exacerbated by the swift evolution of new devices. As new models emerge more rapidly than forensic tools, one tool might not universally support all devices and OSs. This can result in the need for multiple tools to access all data on a single device due to the scarcity of forensic acquisition tools and accessories.

2.5 DIGITAL FORENSIC TOOLS

Forensic tasks, once thoroughly studied and practiced, are automated using forensic tools and utilities. A range of forensics tools exists that aid a forensic analyst during acquisition, preservation, analysis, and reporting phases of IoT device forensics. It is pertinent to note that tools developed specifically for a device, say a smartphone, can possibly be utilized for other IoT devices as well, given they are compatible. This applies especially if the IoT device's OS is the same as one of the smartphone OSs, such as Android (or a different flavor of the same OS).

Table 2.1 lists a detailed summary of some prominent tools employed in IoT forensics.

In addition to forensic tools, it is likely that cutting-edge technologies may be utilized to make the job easier. Forensic analysts encounter volumes of data during the IoT forensics processes; one way to tackle such volumes is by using Artificial Intelligence (AI) or ML technologies, which help process and analyze the data for reporting.

Forensic analysis of IoT devices challenges investigators to move beyond conventional approaches and adopt adaptive, context-aware strategies. Acquisition methods must be chosen deliberately, balancing technical feasibility with evidentiary integrity. More than just collecting data, IoT forensics requires interpreting fragmented, volatile, and often indirect evidence within complex environments. This chapter underscores the need for methodological precision and investigative flexibility—both of which are essential as IoT ecosystems grow more autonomous, encrypted, and diverse.

Table 2.1 Common forensic tools employed in IoT forensics

Forensic phases	Tools	Unique features
Acquisition	FTK Imager	GUI-based, supports both disk imaging and live memory capture on a device to retrieve passwords or other data saved in the active device's memory. https://www.exterro.com/ftk-imager
	DumpIt	Open-source, command-line tool, fast memory dump creation for Windows (x86, x64, and ARM64). https://www.magnetforensics.com/resources/magnet-dumpit-for-windows/
	Magnet Axiom	User-friendly GUI, integrates with other Magnet products for a seamless workflow. Used for RAM acquisition. https://www.magnetforensics.com/resources/magnet-dumpit-for-windows/
	Magnet ACQUIRE	Free tool, GUI-based, supports a wide range of mobile devices. https://www.magnetforensics.com/resources/magnet-acquire/
	Oxygen Forensics	Commercial tool, comprehensive device support, advanced analysis features, GUI-based. Enables the extraction, analysis, and interpretation of digital evidence from various electronic devices, including smartphones, computers, and cloud services. https://oxygenforensics.com/en/
	MSAB XRY	Commercial tool with a GUI, extensive smartphone support, and advanced data retrieval features. The tool is a data retrieval program used for smartphones to recover information. https://www.msab.com/product/xry-extract/
	MOBILedit	Commercial tool, GUI-based, supports a wide range of mobile devices, including data recovery and management tools. https://www.mobiledit.com/
	Kismet	Open-source, command-line tool, broad wireless device support. Originally a Wi-Fi network detector, Kismet expanded to support various wireless devices, making it useful for IoT device detection and analysis. https://www.kismetwireless.net/

(Continued)

Table 2.1 (Continued)

Forensic phases	Tools	Unique features
Device Forensics	EnCase	Commercial tool, robust GUI, extensive feature set for data recovery and analysis. Used globally to collect, preserve, and analyze digital evidence from diverse sources. https://www.opentext.com/products/encase-forensic
	Sleuth Kit Autopsy	Open-source digital forensics platform that includes modules for IoT device analysis. Particularly useful for post-incident extensive file system analysis. https://www.sleuthkit.org/
	CAINE	Open-source, Linux-based, and command-line tool that provides a range of tools and features to assist investigators in tasks like data recovery, disk imaging, analysis, and reporting. https://www.caine-live.net/
	Radare2	Open-source, command-line tool, powerful for reverse engineering and binary analysis of firmware and software on IoT devices. https://rada.re/n/
	IDA Pro	Commercial tool, industry standard, advanced decompiler, and GUI. Widely used for reverse engineering purposes, IDA Pro can assist in analyzing the firmware and software of IoT devices. https://hex-rays.com/ida-pro/
	Ghidra	Open-source software reverse engineering framework developed by the NSA that can help in analyzing binary files, including firmware in IoT devices. https://ghidra-sre.org/
	Binwalk	Open-source, command-line tool, specialized in firmware analysis (analyzing and extracting files from firmware images). Binwalk can help uncover hidden data within IoT devices. https://github.com/ReFirmLabs/binwalk
	Blacklight	Commercial tool, GUI, strong capabilities in Mac and iOS forensic analysis. Used to analyze and examine digital devices, providing investigators with the means to recover and interpret digital evidence, such as files, artifacts, and system data. https://themarkup.org/blacklight
	Elcomsoft iOS Forensic Toolkit (EIFT)	Commercial tool, GUI, specialized in iOS devices, includes jailbreaking capabilities. Can acquire data as well as analyze it. iPhones having 64-bit (iPhone 6 and more advanced versions) need jailbreaking first to acquire data. https://www.elcomsoft.com/eift.html

Memory Forensics	Volatility	Open-source, command-line tool, extensive plugin support for various memory formats. Typically used for memory analysis, Volatility can also be applied to analyze the memory of IoT devices for signs of compromise. https://www.volatilityfoundation.org/
	Bulk Extractor	Open-source, command-line tool, efficient processing of large datasets. Employs specialized algorithms to identify and extract items like email addresses, credit card numbers, URLs, and other potentially relevant data. https://www.kali.org/tools/bulk-extractor/
	Registry Recon	Commercial tool, GUI, focused on comprehensive registry analysis and reconstruction. Aids in uncovering artifacts, user activities, and system configurations stored within the Windows Registry, providing insights crucial for investigating and understanding a system's history and potential security incidents. https://arsenalrecon.com/products/registry-recon
Network Forensics	Nmap	Open-source, command-line tool with extensive network scanning capabilities assisting in discovering and mapping devices, services, and vulnerabilities on a network. https://nmap.org/
	Wireshark	Open-source, GUI, supports deep packet inspection for various protocols. A network protocol analyzer that can capture and dissect the traffic between IoT devices and networks, aiding in the identification of potential security breaches. https://www.wireshark.org/
	NetworkMiner	Open-source, focuses on file extraction and artifact identification from captured network traffic. https://www.netresec.com/?page=NetworkMiner
	Cain and Abel	Freeware, GUI, versatile in password cracking and network analysis. Though primarily a password recovery tool, it can also be used for network monitoring and analyzing IoT device traffic. https://sectools.org/tool/cain/

(Continued)

Table 2.1 (Continued)

Forensic phases	Tools	Unique features
	Snort	Open-source, command-line tool, highly configurable with extensive rule sets. Can be configured to monitor network traffic for suspicious activities and potential IoT device attacks. https://www.snort.org/
	Fiddler	Freeware, specialized in HTTP/HTTPS traffic analysis. A web debugging proxy tool that can be useful for monitoring and analyzing traffic between IoT devices and web servers. https://www.telerik.com/fiddler
Cloud Forensics	UFED Cloud Analyzer	Commercial tool, GUI, specialized in cloud data analysis. UFED cloud analyzer is another tool that collects the metadata information from the acquired user data. https://cellebrite.com/en/ufed-cloud-analyzer-5/
	FROST	Open-source, command-line tool, tailored for cloud forensics. Gathers API calls from virtual users. https://www.sciencedirect.com/science/article/pii/S174228761300056X
	Docker Forensics Toolkit	Open-source, command-line tool, specialized in Docker container forensics. Extracts and analyzes the data from the host system. https://github.com/docker-forensics-toolkit/toolkit

END OF CHAPTER QUESTIONS

1. What is the chip-off method as defined by the National Institute of Standards and Technology (NIST)?
2. Which type of data can be extracted using the chip-off method from a NAND memory chip in devices like the Nintendo 3DS?
3. Why is chip-off extraction often considered a last resort in forensic investigations?
4. What factors increase the technical complexity of chip-off extraction in smart digital devices?
5. List the types of memory from which data can be extracted using the chip-off method.
6. Why does the chip-off method present challenges in digital forensics when applied to IoT devices?
7. Why is tool compatibility across different device operating systems essential in IoT forensics?
8. In scenarios where encryption keys cannot be recovered, what alternative artifacts or indirect digital traces could be used to establish criminal intent or user behavior from the inaccessible data segments?
9. How does the absence of standardized evidence-gathering ports in smart digital devices influence the forensic acquisition strategy, and what adaptive approaches must forensic practitioners take?
10. Evaluate the impact of security features such as automatic data wiping and passcode attempt restrictions (e.g., on Apple devices) on the feasibility and timing of physical or logical acquisition.
11. Compare the reliability, scope, and legal admissibility of manual acquisition versus logical acquisition in smart digital device forensics. Under what conditions might one be preferred over the other?
12. Given the use of logical acquisition via SDKs and tools like ADB, what are the potential forensic limitations of relying solely on SDK-provided APIs for data extraction?
13. Discuss how root access changes the forensic landscape in Android-based smart digital devices. How does rooting both empower and complicate forensic investigations?
14. Explain the specific technical steps and conditions necessary for initiating sparse acquisition. In what investigative scenarios would this method be more beneficial than logical or physical extraction?
15. What are the primary risks to evidence integrity when performing live acquisition or analysis on an active device, and how can these be mitigated?
16. Assess the use of chip-off extraction in modern forensic practice. What are the circumstances under which chip-off is not only justified but critical?

17. Describe the role of JTAG and flasher boxes in bypassing authentication mechanisms. How do these techniques differ in terms of hardware interaction and data access?

18. How can investigators verify that evidence retrieved via hardware-based physical acquisition (e.g., hex dumping, chip-off) has not been altered during extraction?

19. In the context of encryption, how does the retention of decryption keys in RAM present both an opportunity and a risk during forensic acquisition?

20. How might memory forensic tools like Memorize be leveraged during a live analysis session to extract critical evidence that would be unavailable after shutdown?

21. How does forensic site analysis utilize geolocation data, SMS, and app activity to reconstruct user behavior, and what technical challenges might arise in correlating these data sources?

22. What are the key differences between hardware-based and software-based physical acquisition techniques, particularly in relation to rooting requirements and data comprehensiveness?

23. How can anti-forensic techniques such as storage encryption, data obfuscation, or deletion affect the success of sparse and physical acquisition methods? Provide technical countermeasures.

24. Analyze how the lack of tool compatibility across different versions of iOS, Android, and proprietary OSes challenges the universality of forensic toolkits. What technical solutions might improve adaptability?

25. Evaluate the forensic value of Bluetooth-paired device metadata (e.g., UUID, connection history) in building circumstantial cases. How can these data be retrieved and validated?

26. Given the growing volume and volatility of smart digital device data, how can forensic workflows be optimized using techniques like selective partition analysis, pre-analysis scanning, and AI-assisted filtering?

27. In live forensic acquisition of active smart digital devices, what forensic techniques or tools can be applied to differentiate system-generated metadata changes from examiner-induced ones during volatile memory extraction?

28. In smart device site analysis, how would you technically correlate disparate temporal artifacts (e.g., app usage logs, geolocation pings, SMS timestamps) to construct a coherent activity map across devices with unsynchronized clocks?

NOTE

1 The JTAG technique requires connecting to the standard Test Access Points (TAPs) on a device and instructing the device to transfer the memory to an integrated chip.

REFERENCES

[1] Hung, P. C., Kanev, K., Iqbal, F., Mettrick, D., Rafferty, L., Pan, G. P., Huang, S. C., and Fung, B. "A study of children facial recognition for privacy in smart tv," In *International Symposium Computational Modeling of Objects Represented in Images* Sep. 2016, pp. 229–240. Springer, Cham.

[2] Yankson, B., Iqbal, F., and Hung, P. C. "4P based forensics investigation framework for smart connected toys," In *Proceedings of the 15th International Conference on Availability, Reliability and Security*, Aug. 2020, pp. 1–9.

[3] MacDermott, Á., Lea, S., Iqbal, F., Idowu, I., and Shah, B. "Forensic analysis of wearable devices: Fitbit, Garmin and HETP Watches," In *2019 10th IFIP International Conference on New Technologies, Mobility and Security (NTMS)*, Jun. 2019, pp. 1–6. IEEE.

[4] Iqbal, F., Yankson, B., Alyammahi, M. A., AlMansoori, N., Qayed, S. M., Shah, B., and Baker, T.. "Drone forensics: Examination and analysis," *International Journal of Electronic Security and Digital Forensics*, vol. 11, no. 3, pp. 245–264, 2019.

[5] Iqbal, F., Marrington, A., Hung, P. C., Lin, J. J., Pan, G. P., Huang, S. C., and Yankson, B. "A study of detecting child pornography on smart phone," In *International Conference on Network-Based Information Systems*, Aug. 2017, pp. 373–384. Springer, Cham.

[6] Al Shehhi, H., Asad, I., & Iqbal, F.. "A forensic analysis framework for recovering encryption keys and BB10 backup decryption," In *2014 Twelfth Annual International Conference on Privacy, Security and Trust*, Jul. 2014, pp. 172–178. IEEE

[7] Mahalik, H., Tamma, R., and Bommisetty, S., *Practical Mobile Forensics*, 2nd edition. Packt Publishing Ltd, 2016.

[8] *Android Debug Bridge (ADB): Android studio: Android developers*. Android Developers. https://developer.android.com/studio/command-line/adb

[9] Shah, M. U., Rehman, U., Iqbal, F., Wahid, F., Hussain, M., & Arsalan, A. "Access permissions for apple watch applications: A study on users' perceptions," In *2020 International Conference on Communications, Computing, Cybersecurity, and Informatics (CCCI)*, Nov. 2020, pp. 1–7. IEEE.

[10] Khalid, Z., Iqbal, F., Kamoun, F., Hussain, M., & Khan, L. A. "Forensic analysis of the Cisco WebEx application," In *2021 5th Cyber Security in Networking Conference (CSNet)*, Oct. 2021, pp. 90–97. IEEE.

Chapter 3

Smartphone forensics

The most important consumer invention of the 21st century is the smartphone; it has become an indispensable part of our lives. Almost 8.6 billion smartphone subscriptions worldwide were estimated in the year 2019, and 1 billion in the year 2000 [1]. Consequently, smartphones are now a vast repository that contains the most sensitive and private user data. Malicious actors target these data for monetary gain, which is why there is a need for smartphone forensics frameworks and tools that can retrieve user data (artifacts) for attribution. This chapter details the need for smartphone forensics, standard methods for data extraction and analysis for different smartphone OSs, and the challenges an examiner may face during the forensics process.

3.1 SMARTPHONE FORENSICS: AN OVERVIEW

Smartphone forensics deals with the retrieval of digital evidence from smartphones. Smartphone forensics complies with the general forensic framework (discussed in Chapter 2), which has four phases: (1) confiscation/seizure, (2) data acquisition, (3) data analysis, and (4) reporting and presentation [2]. Confiscation is a technical step that requires proper handling of the smartphone. Smartphones are mostly confiscated in Faraday bags that isolate them from radio or electromagnetic waves [3]. For example, if the confiscated smartphone is in a powered-on state, a criminal can easily send a wipe command via a Bluetooth connection or Wi-Fi access point to erase data, in which case a Faraday bag can help retain important evidential information. The data acquisition process is critical as well; examiners can adopt different acquisition methods according to their requirements. Some acquisition tools require a communication vector for evidence collection; other collection techniques may involve installing a bootloader before the extraction step. Smartphones usually show a dynamic behavior, hence making it challenging for forensic examiners to perform articulative analysis during the analysis phase.

The general smartphone forensics framework is illustrated in Figure 3.1.

DOI: 10.1201/9781003644255-3

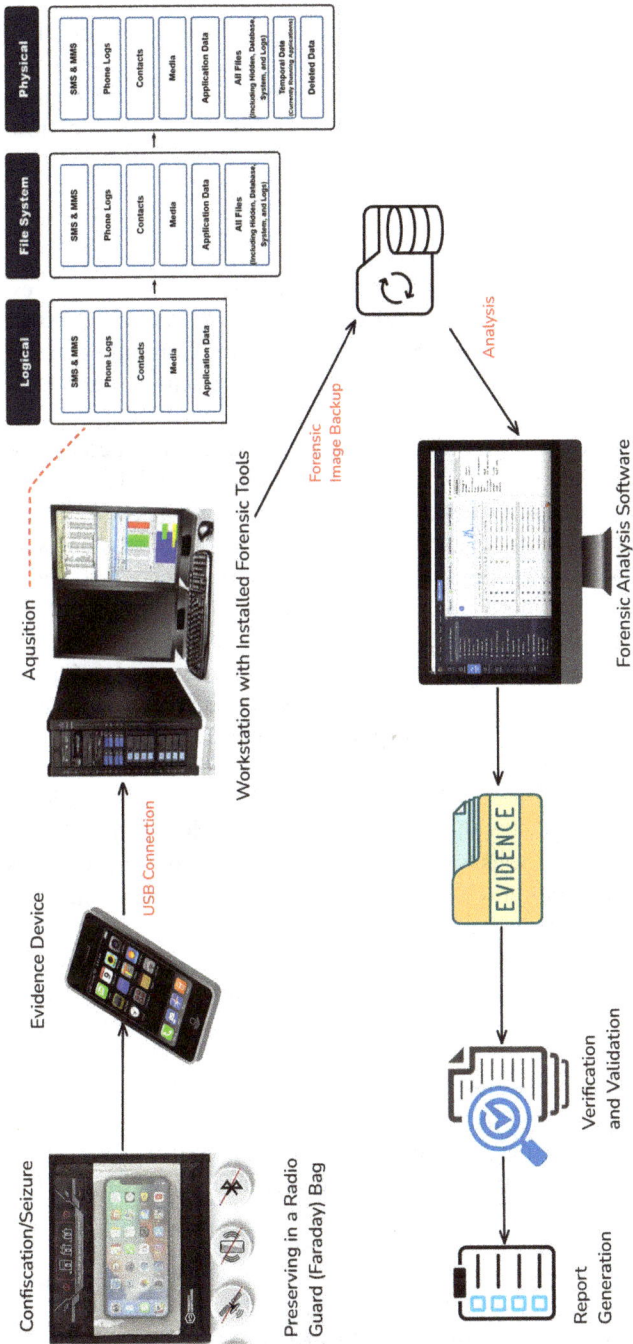

Figure 3.1 General framework for smartphone forensics.

3.2 SMARTPHONE COMPONENTS

Smartphones have various components such as Subscriber Identity Module (SIM) card, Secure Digital (SD) card, etc., that are of interest to forensic investigators; they contain imperative evidential information regarding digital crimes, including but not limited to call history, SMS, location history, emails, personal photos, and videos, etc.

3.2.1 SIM card

A **SIM card** is a basic component of a smartphone, which activates it using stored information about the telecommunication service, network, user identity, etc. [4]. The Global System for Mobile Communications (GSM) standard, which allows text, voice, and data to be sent through cellular networks, ushered in a telecommunications revolution that has had a profound impact on our lives. The industry has seen a dramatic increase ever since the European Telecommunications Standards Institute (ETSI) announced its GSM 11.11 specifications of the SIM-ME interface in the 1990s. It began with the suggestion that the smartphone be divided into two parts: A removable SIM, which houses all subscriber information related to the network, and a Mobile Equipment (ME), which is the remaining part of the smartphone. The demand for SIM cards has been rising annually around the world and is predicted to surpass the previous record of 5.4 billion shipments made in only one year in 2015. In reality, the SIM card is a miniature computer with a CPU, Input/Output (I/O) interface, and both volatile and non-volatile memories. These elements come together primarily to calculate answers to the problems put forth. Through a serial I/O connection, the SIM card communicates with the smartphone that sends commands to the SIM card and receives responses. Its RAM manages how programs are executed. A ROM that manages the OS's workflow, user authentication, data encryption, and other programs is also included.

Given its extensive use, SIM cards store a wealth of user data. There are a number of identifiers associated with a SIM card and other information that may be interesting:

- International Mobile Subscriber Identity (IMSI)
- Service Provider Name (SPN)
- Mobile Subscriber Identification Number (MSIN)
- Mobile Station International Subscriber Directory Number (MSISDN)
- Mobile Country Code (MCC)
- Mobile Network Code (MNC)
- Last Dialed Numbers (LDN)
- Local Area Identity (LAI)
- Temporary Mobile Subscriber Identity (TMSI)

Better communication is possible with Universal Mobile Telecommunications Service (UMTS). USIM cards are used with 3G technology. While standard SIM cards provide network access, USIM cards have their built-in mini-computer, enabling them to handle multiple mini-applications and support video calls, provided the device and network are compatible. Integrated algorithms enhance security, preventing unauthorized access to the phone line. Additionally, USIM cards employ stronger encryption keys for data exchanges compared to SIM cards. Moreover, USIMs store significantly larger phonebooks, capable of storing a multitude of detailed contacts, which may include email addresses, photographs, and multiple phone numbers.

3.2.1.1 SIM card: an important evidence source

Currently, off-the-shelf technologies are typically designed to let examiners analyze the smartphone as a whole, ignoring the fact that some crucial information may reside in smaller modules like the SIM card. No doubt data on a smartphone are still very important, as it plays a direct (or indirect) role in crimes. Smartphones may store data including call history, text messages, emails, Web pages, and images, among other things. The majority of the current study focuses on looking for crucial indicators in a smartphone, that is, calls dialed and received with timestamps, and caller ID numbers. However, a SIM card is also an important reserve for useful forensic data on contacts, SMSs, call records, location data, and a list of all the network towers to which they have lately linked, login credentials for social networking accounts and bank accounts, and deleted communications as well. An investigator can get help from open-source and for-profit technologies to retrieve pertinent data from SIM cards. In early 2016, call detail records (CDRs) from a SIM card played a crucial role in a murder investigation. The records showed that the phone was active at the time of the crime and, due to the suspect's frequent SIM card switching, the police were able to trace another 23 mobile phones linked to the case. In another incident, fraudsters used smartphone information to illegally transfer funds from bank accounts. The scammer carried out a *SIM-swap* scheme, replacing an existing SIM card with a new one, which allowed the victim's mobile number to be taken over and used to access the original post-paid subscriber's online bank account for unauthorized transactions.

Heat, flame, dust, soil, moisture, stains, or magnetic fields do not harm the data on SIM cards. Therefore, it is unaffected by the environment. Scratches and striations do not render the SIM card unreadable; only physical damage can render a SIM unusable. Also, to make it practically impossible for a stranger or a criminal to take sensitive information easily with the help of a SIM card reader, SIM cards should not be thrown away entirely. Even unreadable SIM cards can still be read by inserting a new SIM card with an EEPROM chip or by coupling it to the appropriate probes.

3.2.1.2 SIM card: physical structure and file system

The International Organization for Standardization (ISO) and the International ElectroTechnical Commission (IEC) jointly maintain the ISO/IEC 7816 standard, which specifies the physical dimensions of SIM cards. This standard is divided into 15 parts, of which parts 1 and 2 provide a detailed description of the physical properties of identity Integrated Circuit Cards (ICCs; SIM Cards are one type of ICC). The ISO/IEC 7816 standard was adopted by manufacturers, who thereafter produced full-size, mini, micro, and nano SIM cards. The earliest SIM cards made were full-size, which is the size of a credit card. The full-size SIM card was replaced by the mini-SIM, which was around one-third as big after gradually getting smaller over time. The micro-SIM and nano-SIM are the smallest sizes available today. For Machine-to-Machine (M2M) applications, SIM cards may also be integrated into hardware in the form of an embedded Universal ICC (eUICC).

The EEPROM contains the hierarchical tree-structured SIM card file system, which is used to store information like text messages, network service settings, names, and phone number entries, etc. As previously discussed, three different file types are included in the file system's anatomy: Master Files (MF), Dedicated Files (DF), and Elementary Files (EF), as shown in Figure 3.2. The root of the file system is the MF. DF are the child directories of the MF, such as the DF (DCS1800), DF (GSM), and DF (Telecom), which hold information about services and carriers, and the networks they operate on.

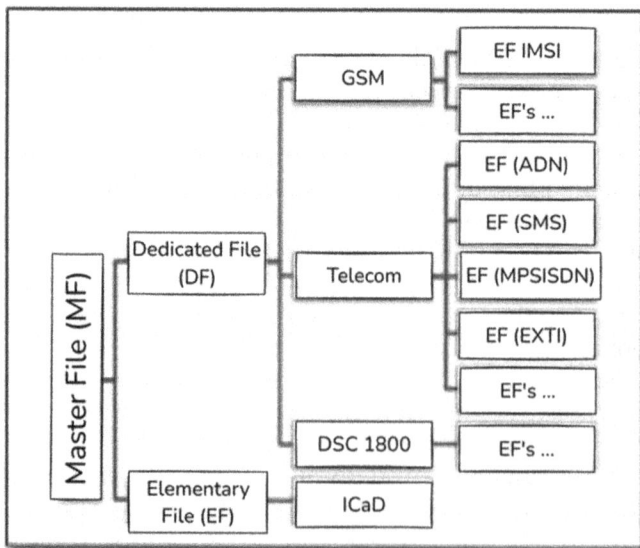

Figure 3.2 SIM card file system hierarchy [4].

Additionally, EF includes the actual data in several formats, organized as a series of data bytes, a series of fixed-size records, or a series of fixed-size records used repeatedly. All files have headers but only EFs have data.

3.2.1.3 SIM card security

SIM cards have built-in security mechanisms established using Card Holder Verification (CHV1 and CHV2). These two parameters limit access to users who have active verification PINs. Other features restrict different smartphone users' access to the GSM network by giving each group a unique Access Control Class (ACC). By using a cipher key to authenticate the SIM on the smartphone network and a cipher key sequence number, encryption is used to prevent tampering and assure data security. The SIM card also contains other data on the GSM cellular network architecture, such as a phase identifier. The introduction of SIM cards, ciphering, voice telephony, international roaming, call forwarding, and SMS services was all part of Phase 1 of the delivery of GSM services. Since most data, including that related to financial, educational, and social platforms, are communicated via smartphones, it is crucial to safeguard SIM cards by using PIN codes, KC, and ACC, to prevent SIM swapping attacks. Data security depends heavily on SIM security. Users risk losing everything if a thief steals or clones a physical copy of their SIM card, including bank information.

3.2.1.4 Forensic analysis and SIM card applets

To retrieve SIM card data, it is mounted in a common smart-card reader, which allows logical access. The SIM card's contents are kept in a collection of files as binary data. Data are retrieved by forensic tools and then examined.

Applets are quick programs that the UICC's SIM cards (mostly GSM) use. Additionally, the applets are designed to perform tasks like browsing the Internet, sending SMS, and making calls. As additional optional fundamental files, Service Provider Name (SPN) and Service Dialing Numbers (SDN) express the name of the GSM network service provider and the distinct services it offers (i.e., customer care number). According to the standard, any fields with variable lengths should have the remaining digits set to the hexadecimal digit F. Temporary Subscriber Identity (TMSI) is a temporary identifier that is transferred between the smartphone and the adjacent local network. To prevent signal fading when a subscriber changes location, the TMSI is immediately updated, enabling the level of mobility offered by GSM cellular networks. Subscribers can communicate via messages sent and received over the cellular network using SMS. Since SMS data also include the time, date, sender's phone number, and the message status in addition to the text of the exchanged messages, it is regarded as forensically relevant evidence (i.e., read, unread, sent, etc.). Even more significant are deleted texts since they may include content that warrants further investigation. Although a message's reference is marked as free space until fresh data can overwrite it, the data included in the message are not immediately wiped when it is deleted. Numerous manufacturers create their smartphone handsets to automatically use their internal storage because of the SIM's restricted storage capacity. To explicitly choose which storage to utilize depends on the user settings and phone software. SMS data, such as the location of the operator's short message switching center, message lifetime/timeout, and coding format, are contained in the elementary files known as SMS, Short Message Service Parameters (SMSP), and Short Message Service Status (SMSS). In-depth analysis of the speech and data communication fields yields location information. Each Location is identified by its unique identification number, which is called Location Area Information (LAI). The LAI will be stored in the SIM card to receive service from the nearest phone tower. The Location Area Identifier (LAI), which is made up of the Mobile Country Code (MCC), Mobile Network Code (MNC), and Location Area Code (LAC), as well as the Routing Area Code (RAC) and Routing Area Information, is part of Location Information (LOCI). When a SIM card is examined, forensic investigators can get a basic notion of where the SIM card has been geographically, which is a huge plus.

3.2.1.5 SIM card artifacts

One can determine which services (such as SMS and FDN) are allocated and activated in the SIM and which are not by using the SIM Service Table (SST) basic file. The Preferred Languages (PL) variable is used to specify language preferences for menu interaction. Additionally, the SIM card may include two Group Identifiers: GID1 and GID2. Only the GSM Service Provider modifies these two parameters to designate a collection of SIM cards for specific associations and applications. Another service-provider-specific term is Emergency Call Code, which can be used to establish an emergency call, for example, to 999 in the event of threats. The PLMN Search Period (HPLMN), which the Service Provider additionally configures, specifies how frequently the smartphone device should look for the home network (the range is between 6 minutes and 8 hours). Preferred Network List (PLMN), which is controlled by the service provider, enables users to choose a network to connect to while roaming abroad from a pre-configured list. On the other hand, Forbidden Networks (FPLMN) are networks that a phone is not allowed to connect to. In the GSM cellular standard, a Broadcast Control CHannel (BCCH) is a pattern that carries system information messages on the identity and configuration of the base transceiver station. The content of the cell broadcast messages that a subscriber would receive from the Service Provider partners (preferred networks) is specified by the Cell Broadcast Message Identifier (CBMI). Forensic investigators can utilize location data to determine where a phone was last used and to pinpoint a suspect's past locations or the scene of an incident. Due to the smartphone manufacturers' default settings, which restrict saving SMS data to SIM cards and instead use the phone's internal memory, SMS data are essential in forensic investigations but is not stored.

3.2.1.5.1 Integrated Circuit Card Identifier

This Integrated Circuit Card Identifier (ICCI), which can be up to 20 digits long, is primarily composed of two parts: The Issuer Identification Number (IIN) and the Account Identification Number (AIN). The following explanation applies to the issuer identification: In addition to a three-digit Issuer Identifier Number, the first two numbers are set aside for the Major Business Identifier (MII), which in this case is 89 for the SIM telecommunications industry (refer to Figure 3.3). The Account Identification Number is made up of six digits for the individual SIM number, four numbers for the manufacture month/year, two digits for the configuration code, and finally a checksum digit for error detection.

- 89 is considered the Major Industry Identifier.
- 971 as the Country Code (i.e., United Arab Emirates).
- The Issuer Identifier (12) belongs to Etisalat.
- The Individual Account Identification number, which includes the SIM number, Configuration code, and month/year of manufacturing, is 212696410287.
- The checksum, which is determined from the remaining 19 digits, is 7.

A solid data source from a forensic perspective is the ICCID, which is permanently engraved on the SIM to uniquely identify the chip across the globe and cannot be altered or updated afterward. Additionally, after obtaining a search warrant for the logs of a specific suspect or victim, investigators could get in touch with the service provider identified by the ICCID using the Issuer Identifier to request the logs for additional examination.

3.2.1.5.2 International Mobile Subscriber Identity

The International Mobile Subscriber Identifier (IMSI), a 15-digit number, is primarily used for signaling and messaging over a GSM network. The IMSI is constructed similarly to the ICCID, with the Mobile Country Code (MCC) including three digits, the Mobile Network Code (MNC) being two

ICCID: 89971122126964102877
8 9 9 7 1 1 2 2 1 2 6 9 6 4 1 0 2 8 7 7

Figure 3.3 Example of Integrated Circuit Card Identifier (ICCI).

IMSI: 424021445434857														
4	2	4	0	2	1	4	4	5	4	3	4	8	5	7

Figure 3.4 Example of International Mobile Subscriber Identifier (IMSI).

to three digits, and the remaining digits identifying the Mobile Subscriber Identity Number (MSIN) being an allotted sequential serial number (MSIN), as shown in Figure 3.4.

Following are several possible interpretations of the IMSI:

- United Arab Emirates' MCC is seen here.
- The Mobile Network Code, which is the Emirates Telecommunications Corporation, is denoted by the number 02 (Etisalat).
- The Mobile Subscriber Identification Number is represented by the remaining digits (1445434857).

3.2.1.5.3 Mobile Station International Subscriber Directory Number

The Mobile Station International Subscriber Directory Number (MSISDN), which has a maximum of fifteen digits, is assigned to a subscriber to accept calls but is not indicated to or from a device. Each MSISDN that a subscriber has relates to the subscriber's whole phone number, including the MCC. In general, the MSISDN is composed of an MCC with a maximum of three digits, a National Destination Code (NDC) with a maximum of three digits, and a Subscriber Number (SN) with a maximum of ten digits (refer to Figure 3.5). In contrast to ICCID and IMSI, MSIDSN is an optional elementary file (i.e., an Optional EF is not required to be saved on the SIM card itself) (which are mandatory fields). A similar application called Own Dialing Number enables smartphone customers to find out their phone numbers by dialing a specified numeric code. MSISDN contains the following information:

- 971 represents the MCC (United Arab Emirates).
- 50 identifies the National Destination Code (Smartphone by Etisalat).
- 5682881 refers to the Subscriber Number.

MSISDN: +971505682881											
9	7	1	5	0	5	6	8	2	8	8	1

Figure 3.5 Example of Mobile Station International Subscriber Directory Number (MSISDN).

It is important to note that, in addition to the ICCID, the information included in the SIM (i.e., MSISDN) might be changed at a later time. As a result, the validity of such evidence is occasionally questioned in a court of law.

3.2.1.5.4 Abbreviated Dialing Numbers

Abbreviated Dialing Numbers (ADNs) are the subscriber's saved contacts list on the SIM card. On the other hand, Last Numbers Dialed (LND) refers to the most recent number the subscriber phoned. A SIM can store additional digits from ADN and LND into the dialing extensions EXT1 and EXT2 elementary fields, although its capacity limits the number of contacts it can hold. ADNs are very important since they can be used to identify connections and relatives of the owner of a smartphone or to tie an unidentified phone to a suspect or victim. However, some contemporary smartphones (particularly the iPhone 4S) use ME storage in place of the SIM card itself to store these numbers.

3.2.1.5.5 Fixed Dialing Numbers

Fixed Dialing Numbers (FDN) are comparable to those fields in that they both contain a phonebook that can only be accessed if a particular mode is turned on. This might be applicable, for example, in the case of a company SIM card that limits outbound calls to only those numbers that have been preconfigured to prevent employees from spending company resources on personal calls. Along with the related mobile equipment and subscriber settings, the aforementioned parameters are also bundled in a set known as Capability Configuration Parameters (CCP).

3.2.2 Memory chip, SD card, and eMMC

Apart from SIM cards, another component of the smartphone that can be of value is the main *memory chip*. Its extraction procedure, however, is difficult and expensive and needs a lot of care and experience. The memory chip is detached from the device by *de-soldering* it. Even a small mistake at this point can lead to a damaged memory chip. Raw data recovered using this method need to be parsed and interpreted manually or via tools. Another problem with this method is that smartphones have different types of memory chips that vary in size, circuit, etc., so it is difficult to have their specific memory card readers available at the time of forensic analysis.

SD cards are used to extend the memory of the mobile device. SD cards can easily be removed and can be inserted into another device to extract the data. The problem arises when it is secured with a password/encryption. In that case, a key/passphrase is required to bypass the security.

The **eMMC** is also a kind of external (non-volatile) storage device; its performance is comparable with SD cards. It provides extended storage from 1GB to 512 GB. The forensic analysis of these chips can provide useful information related to the crime under investigation.

3.3 EVIDENCE EXTRACTION USING MURPHY'S MODEL

Detective Murphy designed a more comprehensive version of the general smartphone forensics framework discussed earlier [5]. She elaborated a nine-step process:

1. **Intake:** During the evidence intake phase, examination requests are managed, often involving the completion of request forms and intake paperwork. These documents serve to record critical information, including the chain of custody, ownership details, and the nature of the incident related to the smartphone. A pivotal aspect of this phase is establishing specific examination objectives.

2. **Identification:** During this stage, a broad assessment of the smartphone's characteristics is conducted. This includes considering the legal authority under which the examination is conducted, determining the purpose of the forensic examination, identifying the smartphone's make and model, examining any external or removable storage, and considering other potential evidence.

   a. Legal Authority: Forensic investigators must adhere to legal jurisdiction and procedures, such as obtaining a warrant for smartphone seizure.

   b. Forensic Examination Objective: Clearly documenting the purpose of the forensic examination helps determine the required depth of analysis and appropriate tools. For example, Wireshark or Nmap may be suitable for network data analysis, while the Sleuth Kit Autopsy tool is preferable for memory analysis.

   c. Smartphone Model: Knowing the smartphone's make and model is crucial for forensic analysis, as different models may have unique features or connectors.

   d. Identification of External Storage: Some smartphones support external memory cards like SD cards, which must be acquired and subjected to traditional forensic analysis.

   e. Consideration of other Evidence: Investigators should also anticipate biological or fingerprint evidence before seizing the smartphone to prevent contamination.

3. **Preparation:** The preparation phase encompasses in-depth research on the specific mobile device slated for examination, the selection of suitable tools for the examination, and the setup of the examination

machine to ensure the presence of all required equipment, cables, software, and drivers necessary for the examination.

4. **Isolation:** Ensuring the isolation of the smartphone is vital due to its connectivity to various networks and communication services. Placing the smartphone in airplane mode is a common practice, but this may require unlocking the phone if it is pin/pattern locked. Additionally, some phones may maintain Wi-Fi connections in airplane mode. Therefore, placing the smartphone in a signal-blocking bag is often the safest option.

5. **Processing:** After securely seizing the device, the next step involves the acquisition and examination/analysis of data. Physical acquisition, which extracts raw data from the device in an OFF state, is typically the preferred method. If physical acquisition fails, alternative methods like manual/logical acquisition or filesystem acquisition, chip off, and sparse acquisition can be considered. After acquisition, analysis using appropriate tools is performed.

6. **Verification:** The investigator must verify the integrity of the extracted data by comparing it to the data on the smartphone. This can be accomplished by calculating hash values for both sets of data.

7. **Documentation:** A comprehensive report detailing the entire evidence extraction process is generated. This report should include information on the methodology, the purpose of evidence extraction, details about the smartphone, its state, and the tools used for acquisition.

8. **Presentation:** Findings from the forensic phase are documented in a clear and concise manner to ensure that results can be easily understood and repeated.

9. **Archiving:** The final step in evidence extraction involves archiving evidence to ensure data integrity throughout court proceedings and for future reference.

3.4 SMARTPHONE HETEROGENEITY AND THE FORENSICS PROCESS

Multiple heterogeneous factors, such as variance in models, OSs, and third-party applications, play a pivotal role in the process of data acquisition and examination/analysis when dealing with smartphones. Smartphone OSs still continue to evolve significantly across the spectrum, incorporating a multitude of novel features with each passing day. These OSs wield direct influence over how forensic examiners can access smartphones. For example, the Android OS grants terminal-level access, a capability not extended by iOS. The diversity introduces certain nuances in each step of the forensics analysis framework for each smartphone model and OS, which need to be considered with utmost sensitivity for accurate and reliable forensic results.

3.4.1 Android phone forensics

Android OS sees the most widespread use in smartphones. Due to the diversity of Android devices, versions, and customizations, forensic investigators encounter a myriad of challenges. To extract data, they often rely on a combination of logical and physical acquisition methods. However, most Android smartphones need to be rooted for full access to its storage. Once data are acquired, forensic experts delve into file system analysis, scrutinizing directories, databases, and cache files. They employ tools like ADB and open-source forensic software, such as Autopsy and ALEAPP, to parse data from various sources like call logs, SMS messages, app data, and GPS location information. Overcoming security measures like device encryption and screen locks requires advanced techniques, such as brute force attacks or exploiting vulnerabilities. The continually evolving Android ecosystem necessitates forensic analysts to stay updated on the latest OS versions and security mechanisms, making Android forensics both a technically intricate and dynamically evolving discipline.

3.4.2 iOS phone forensics

Compared to Android, iOS is a more secure OS. Apple's commitment to user privacy and device security poses formidable obstacles for forensic experts. Logical acquisition methods, such as iTunes backups or iCloud synchronization, can yield substantial data but may not provide access to all information. Physical acquisition, on the other hand, is limited due to Apple's Secure Enclave and data encryption, which require techniques like jailbreaking to circumvent. The examination phase involves the parsing of various data sources, including the SQLite databases where iOS stores a multitude of information, such as call logs, messages, contacts, and app data. Forensic tools like Cellebrite and Magnet AXIOM assist in parsing these data. Additionally, investigators need to navigate complex artifacts like the iOS keychain, which securely stores sensitive information, and the handling of encrypted backups that require brute force or dictionary attacks to unlock. Staying current with iOS updates and security measures is essential in iOS forensics, where technical expertise and adaptability are key to successful investigations.

3.4.3 Windows phone forensics

Windows smartphone forensics, while increasingly rare due to the platform's waning popularity, involves the technical examination of digital evidence from smartphones running the Windows OS. This field requires expertise in data extraction, analysis, and recovery techniques specific to the Windows platform. Forensic analysts typically use specialized tools to access data on these devices, leveraging methods like JTAG or chip-off forensics for physical acquisition when necessary. They analyze data stored in databases, proprietary file formats, and system directories, aiming to extract information such as call logs, text messages, emails, and app data. As with other smartphone platforms, Windows demands an understanding of device encryption, security features, and file structures, making it a technically involved discipline that may be encountered in legacy cases or specialized scenarios.

3.5 CHALLENGES IN SMARTPHONE FORENSICS

Smartphone forensics presents several challenges due to the complexity and security features of modern smartphones. It requires skilled professionals equipped with up-to-date tools and a thorough understanding of legal and ethical considerations to overcome some of the recurrent challenges and effectively extract and analyze digital evidence. These challenges arise for several reasons, including the dynamic operating systems of smartphones [6]. The following discussion addresses challenges specific to smartphone forensics, in addition to those already discussed in Chapter 1.

3.5.1 Hardware heterogeneity

The diversity of smartphone hardware poses a common challenge for digital forensics examiners when dealing with smartphones. Paying close attention to the smartphone's hardware is crucial (particularly when it comes to preserving the eMMC memory chip and microSD card). The market is saturated with a multitude of smartphone variants and versions. Since the inception of the iPhone, there have been over two dozen different versions available. Other platforms, such as Windows phones and Android devices, offer even greater diversity. These variations can make it challenging for examiners to carry out the forensic process. For instance, with such an extensive array of smartphones available, identifying the actual manufacturer, version, and model of a phone by visual inspection alone can be quite daunting. One possible method is to remove the battery to access this information, but doing so can potentially jeopardize volatile data integrity.

3.5.2 Evolving smartphone operating systems

Smartphone OSs (e.g., iOS, Android, SymbianOS, BlackberryOS, Windows) frequently receive updates, introducing new security features and changes in data storage. Forensic tools must keep pace with these updates to remain effective. In addition, sometimes criminals use a special *feature phone*, designed for customers having exclusive software and user interface. So, it becomes harder for a forensic analyst to investigate such phones for data extraction and preservation.

3.5.3 Smartphone platform security

With the advancement in technology, the security of user data has become a central debate among technology experts. Smartphone users are concerned about the security of their data. Therefore, manufacturers are adding strong security features to smartphones to protect users' privacy. Although these security features are a good add-on for smartphone users, these features are also creating difficulties for forensic investigators during the forensic process, especially during the acquisition. Encryption is an example. The investigator needs to decrypt user data to extract it from the mobile device [7].

3.5.4 Dynamic nature of evidence and lack of resources

Smartphones and their applications are dynamic in that the user data may be altered or stored/moved (intentionally or unintentionally). For example, WhatsApp can be accessed using many devices, and hence, the data can be altered, erased, or moved using the access feature of the app. Also, data stored in cloud services like iCloud or Google Drive can be challenging to access and extract due to security measures and the need for proper legal authorization.

There are a lot of different manufacturers and variants of smartphones. Each has different hardware, OS, file system formats, and other features. A single tool might not be comprehensive enough for forensic analysis. Availability of multiple tools for data acquisition and analysis is a preferable scenario. However, choosing the right tool is also a crucial step. This applies not only to the software tools but also to the hardware, like cables, etc. Some smartphones require C-cables, others require micro-USB Type-B cables, or iOS pin8, etc.

3.6 PRACTICAL FORENSIC ACQUISITION OF SMARTPHONES

This section demonstrates practical approaches to smartphone forensic acquisition using industry-standard tools. We will explore a logical acquisition method for iOS device, showcasing step-by-step procedures for data extraction and analysis.

3.6.1 Logical acquisition of iOS device using MOBILedit acquisition tool

Here, we will demonstrate how to use MOBILedit Forensic Tool, version 9.2.0.25909, which is a forensic imaging and analysis tool built for mobile phones. MOBILedit Forensic is a powerful tool used in smartphone investigations to acquire and analyze data from mobile devices. It supports a wide range of devices, including iPhones and Android phones, and can extract various types of data such as contacts, messages, call logs, photos, videos, app data, and more. The tool also provides options for creating backups, including iTunes backups for iOS devices, and generating detailed forensic reports.

Let us acquire an iPhone 14 running iOS 17.4.1 using the MOBILedit Acquisition Tool:

1. Connect the device to a workstation using a USB cable and launch MOBILedit Acquisition Tool. The device should appear in the list of connected phones.

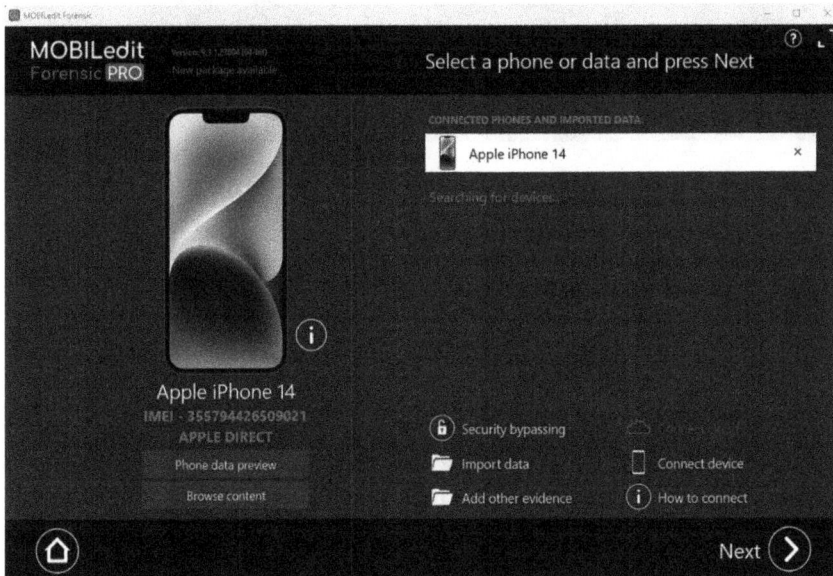

Figure 3.6 Choosing the source.

2. Select the Acquisition Method
   - Select the iPhone 14 from the list of connected devices.
   - Choose the Logical Acquisition method, which is non-intrusive and suitable for extracting a wide range of data from iOS devices.

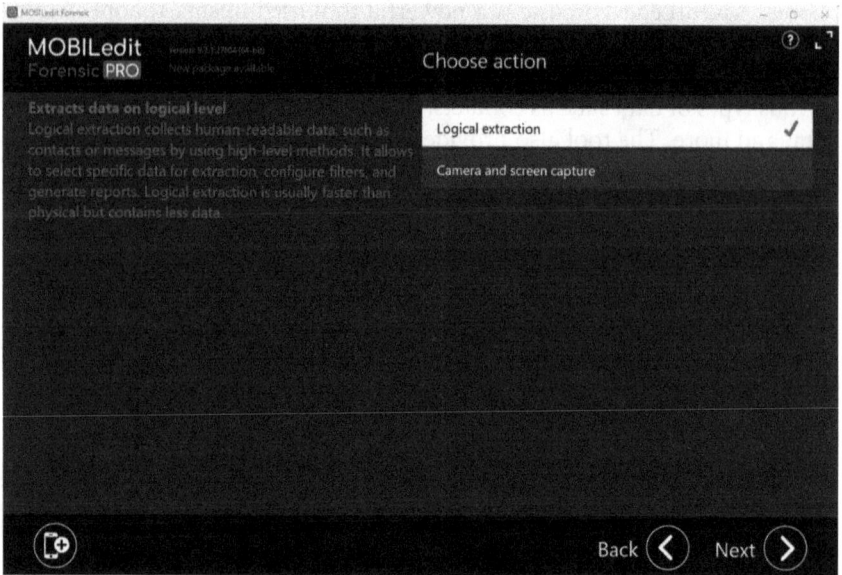

Figure 3.7 Choosing the acquisition method.

3. Specify the Data to Extract
   - Select the types of data you want to extract, such as contacts, messages, call logs, photos, videos, app data, and more.
   - Enter relevant case information such as the case number, investigator name, and description.

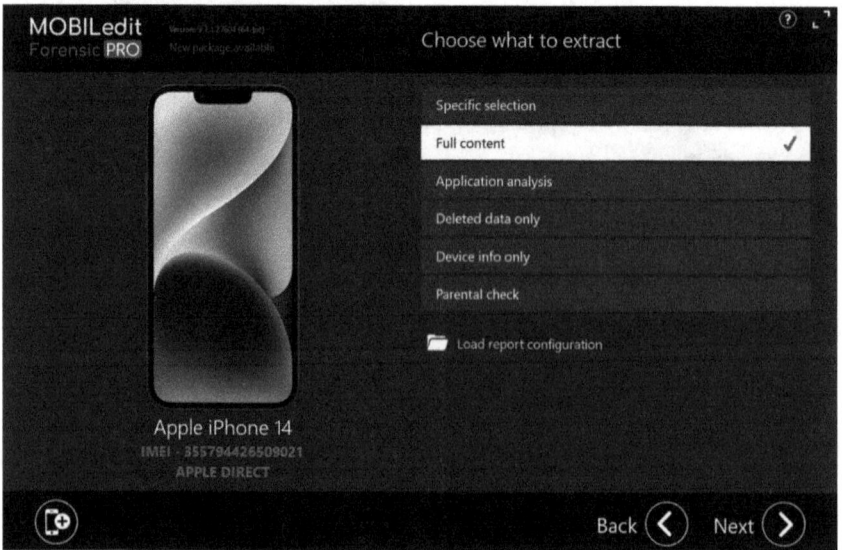

Figure 3.8 Selection of specific device content.

4. Choose the Output Format and Destination
- Specify the output formats (e.g., MOBILedit proprietary format, CSV, HTML) and the destination for the acquired data.
- If prompted, confirm the creation of an iTunes backup. This ensures a comprehensive acquisition by capturing data stored in the iTunes backup files.

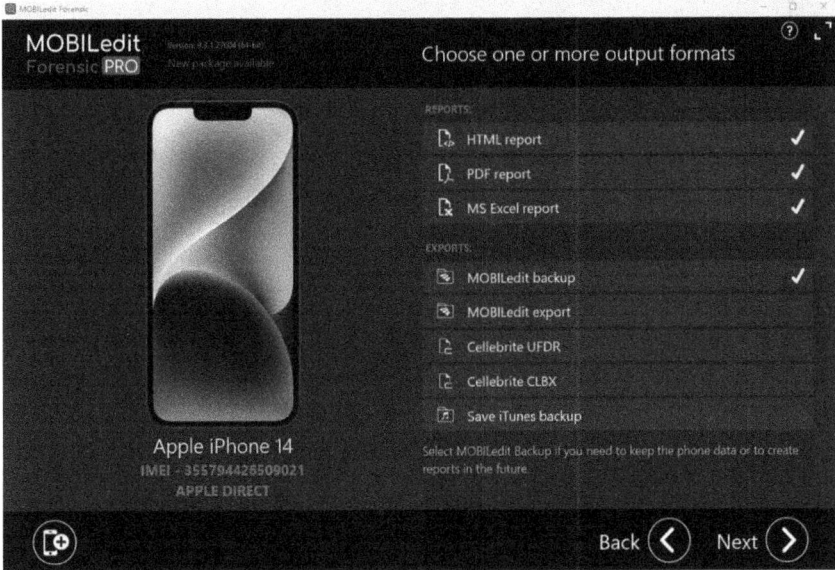

Figure 3.9 Choosing output formats.

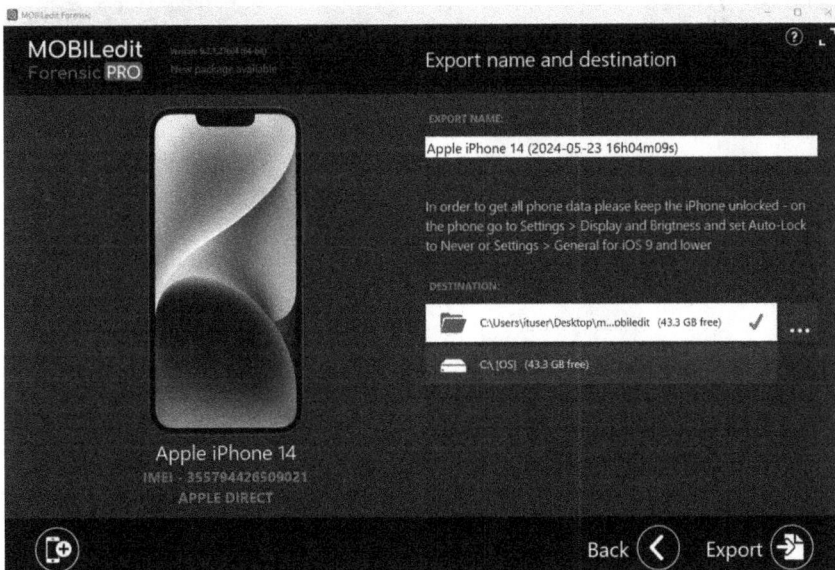

Figure 3.10 Selecting image destination.

5. MOBILedit enables creating an iTunes backup if the device is not rooted. If you want to include a backup, confirm the notification on the window.

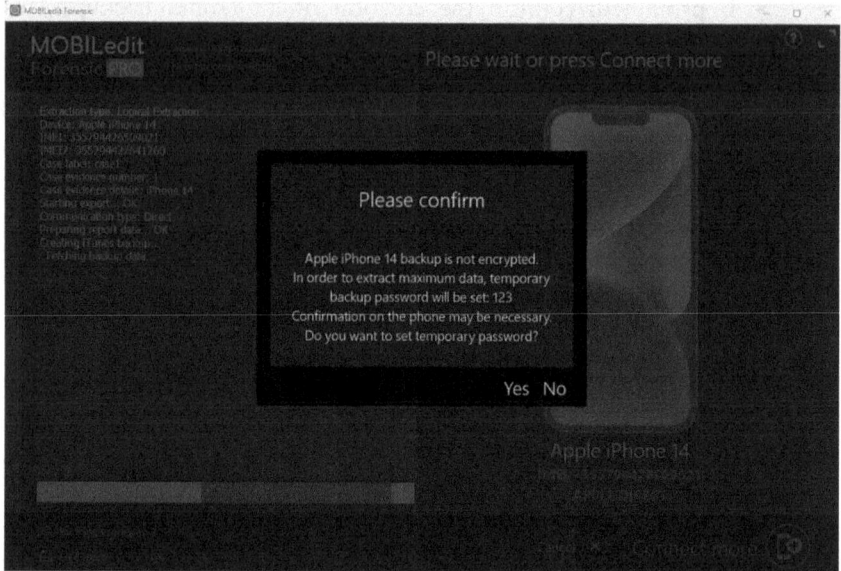

Figure 3.11 Confirming iTunes backup.

6. Review the settings and start the acquisition process. Wait for the task to finish successfully.

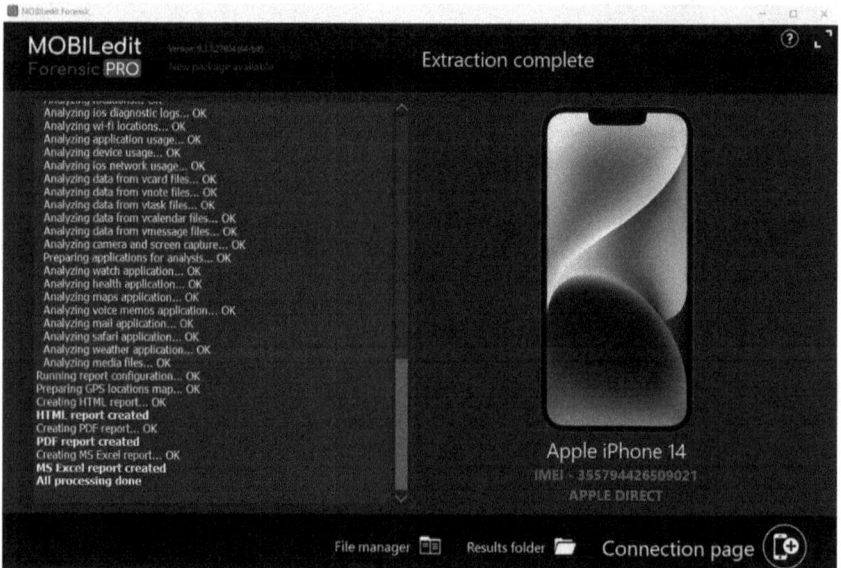

Figure 3.12 Confirming complete extraction.

7. You will find your device's logical image in the folder you chose in the previous step. A report of the extracted data is displayed.
8. Analyze the Acquired Data
   - Use MOBILedit Forensic to load the acquired data and perform a detailed analysis.
   - The tool provides various features to search, filter, and examine the data, including keyword searches, timeline analysis, and data visualization.

Post-acquisition analysis

- The backup and acquired data can be analyzed manually or by using other mobile forensic tools for more detailed investigation and reporting.

END OF CHAPTER QUESTIONS

1. How does the diversity of smartphone models and operating systems impact the forensic process?
2. Why is it essential for forensic analysts to stay updated on the latest smartphone operating systems and security measures? Discuss the implications for successful investigations.
3. In the context of smartphone forensics, how do evolving operating systems pose challenges to investigators? Provide examples of security features that complicate data extraction.
4. What are the primary components of a smartphone that are of interest to forensic investigators? Explain the relevance of each component.
5. You are investigating a case involving a missing person in a remote area. The only item found at the scene is a damaged smartphone with no SIM card but with an embedded eMMC chip. Describe how you would proceed with evidence extraction, what challenges you would expect, and how you would mitigate potential data loss.
6. Why is the SIM card often overlooked in smartphone forensic investigations, and what specific types of evidence can it offer that internal storage cannot?
7. Explain how the physical structure and hierarchical file system of a SIM card (MF, DF, EF) impact the forensic process of evidence retrieval.
8. What challenges do smartphone OS heterogeneity and frequent updates pose to forensic tool reliability, and how should forensic practitioners adapt?
9. Discuss how Murphy's model enhances the procedural robustness of smartphone forensics compared to traditional four-phase models.
10. What are the forensic benefits and limitations of logical acquisition compared to physical acquisition in the context of modern smartphones?

11. Why is proper isolation of a smartphone (e.g., through airplane mode or Faraday bags) essential during seizure? What are the consequences of failure in this step?

12. Describe how encrypted backups and secure hardware elements like Apple's Secure Enclave impact forensic analysis. What approaches exist to mitigate these limitations?

13. Given the risk of data alteration in apps like WhatsApp that sync across devices, how can a forensic investigator ensure the integrity and originality of extracted data?

14. Explain why understanding the specific make and model of a smartphone is crucial before initiating any forensic procedure. Provide examples of how this affects tool and cable selection.

15. What is the forensic significance of Location Area Identifier (LAI) data in SIM cards, and how can it be used to construct movement patterns in an investigation?

16. A suspect's smartphone was seized in a powered-on state while connected to Wi-Fi. The examiner was not equipped with a Faraday bag at the scene. What are the immediate technical risks involved, and what alternative steps can be taken to isolate and preserve evidence in such a situation?

17. You are leading a multi-agency investigation involving a corporate espionage ring. A smartphone was seized that has data encrypted at rest and protected with a biometric lock. Discuss the forensic options for bypassing or defeating security without compromising the evidentiary chain of custody.

18. Suppose you have an iOS and an Android device from two co-conspirators. Both devices are suspected to contain synchronized communication evidence. Outline how you would synchronize and correlate data from these heterogeneous systems during forensic analysis.

19. Discuss the forensic implications of the difference between ICCID, IMSI, and MSISDN when linking a suspect to a particular device and mobile account, especially when multiple numbers and SIM swaps are suspected.

20. You are analyzing the smartphone of a person accused of financial fraud. How would you prioritize forensic analysis between internal phone storage and SIM card data? Justify your approach with reference to artifact types and legal traceability.

21. A criminal group uses SIM swapping to gain unauthorized access to victims' online bank accounts. What forensic artifacts from the smartphone and SIM card can help confirm such attacks? How would you structure your investigation?

22. A high-profile white-collar crime investigation involves executives using jailbroken iPhones and rooted Androids to hide evidence. You are given full resources. Describe a structured forensic acquisition and analysis plan, considering the risks and validation steps at each stage.

23. In a politically sensitive murder case, a smartphone confiscated from the victim has location data inconsistencies between SIM card LAI logs and app-based GPS logs. Discuss how you would resolve the inconsistency and determine the most forensically reliable source.

24. How would you handle the forensic investigation of a smartphone with an embedded eUICC (embedded SIM), considering it cannot be physically removed? What tools and strategies would be required?

25. Examine the data below extracted from the telephony.db database using a database browser. Identify and list as many forensic artifacts as possible. For each artifact, explain its forensic significance and discuss how it may be relevant in an investigation.

```
New Database   Open Database   Write Changes   Revert Changes   Undo   Open Project   Save Project   Attach Database   Close Database
Database Structure   Browse Data   Edit Pragmas   Execute SQL
Table: carriers
```

_id	name	numeric	mcc	mnc	carrier_id	apn	user	server	password	proxy	port	mmsproxy	mmsport	mmsc	authtype	type	current	protocol
1	Google Fi - Tm	310260	310	260	-1	h2g2	none	*	none					http://mmsc1.g-mms.com/mms/wapenc	-1	default,supl,mms,fota,cbs	0	IPV6
2	Google Fi - Tm	310260	310	260	-1	h2g2									-1	ia	0	IPV6
3	Google Fi - Tm	310260	310	260	-1	ims	none	*	none					http://localhost/mmsc	-1	ims	0	IPV6
4	Google Fi - Tm	310260	310	260	-1	h2g2-T									-1	dun	0	IPV6
5	Google Fi - Sp	310120	310	120	-1	n.nv.iepsn								http://mms2.g-mms.com	-1	default,supl,mms,ims,cbs,ia	1	IPV4V6
6	otasn	310120	310	120	-1	otasn								http://mmsn2.g-mms.com	-1	fota	1	IPV4V6
7	Google Fi - Sp	310120	310	120	-1	nv.pamsn									-1	dun	1	IP
8	Google Fi - Sp	310120	310	120	-1	n.nv.iepsn								http://mms2.g-mms.com	-1	default,supl,mms,ims,cbs,ia	1	IPV4V6
9	otasn	310120	310	120	-1	otasn								http://mmsc2.g-mms.com	-1	fota	1	IPV4V6
10	Google Fi - Sp	310120	310	120	-1	nv.pamsn									-1	dun	1	IP
11	Google Fi - 3HK	45403	454	03	-1	h2g2											1	IPV4V6
12	Google Fi - 3UK	23420	234	20	-1	h2g3.pmvno									-1			IPV4V6
13	Google Fi - USCC	311580	311	580	-1	h2g2.odma								http://mmsc1.uscc.net/mmsc/90t3	3	default,mms,hipri,fota	1	IPV4V6
14	Google Fi - USCC	311580	311	580	-1	h2g2-T								http://mmsc1.uscc.net/mmsc/90t3	-1	default,mms,hipri,fota,ia		IPV4V6
15	Google Fi - USCC	311580	311	980	-1	h2g2-T								http://mmsc1.uscc.net/mmsc/90t3	-1	dun		IP
16	Google Fi - SAT	23210	232	10	-1	h2g2.pmvno									-1			IPV4V6

26. You suspect a deleted SMS stored in SIM card memory may hold critical case information. However, the data appears overwritten or partially corrupted. Explain the forensic recovery process for such deleted SIM artifacts.

27. During the intake phase of a forensic investigation, why is it essential to define examination objectives clearly? How would misdefining these objectives affect the validity or admissibility of the evidence?

28. You are given two conflicting versions of app usage logs: One from logical extraction using ADB, and the other from an encrypted iTunes backup. Discuss how you would validate the authenticity and timeline accuracy of both datasets.

29. In an international investigation, a device with foreign SIM data (e.g., MCC 971, MNC 02) is seized. What steps would you take to contact the foreign telecom provider, interpret SIM records, and validate jurisdictional admissibility of such data?

30. A deceased individual's phone contains group identifiers (GID1/GID2) and preferred roaming lists (PLMN). Explain how these can assist in profiling the user's affiliations and movement patterns during a multi-country investigation.

31. What are the legal and forensic implications of mounting a SIM card in a common reader versus using a proprietary forensic tool? How do these choices affect chain of custody and evidentiary admissibility?

32. Given a device that was suspected to have communicated critical information via applets (e.g., USIM-based Java cards), outline the technical and procedural steps to extract and interpret these applet logs during forensic analysis.

33. You are tasked with presenting smartphone forensic findings in court where metadata and timestamps are being challenged by the defense. How do you defend the reliability of your acquisition and timeline reconstruction process?

34. Critically evaluate how Murphy's nine-step model enhances the reliability, reproducibility, and legal robustness of smartphone forensic investigations compared to traditional four-phase models.

35. Discuss how the hierarchical structure of a SIM card's file system affects the process of data retrieval during a forensic examination.

REFERENCES

[1] "Mobile subscriptions worldwide 1993-2021," *Statista*. [Online]. Available: https://www.statista.com/statistics/262950/global-mobile-subscriptions-since1993/#:~:text=The%20total%20number%20of%20mobile

[2] Yusoff, Y., Ismail, R., and Hassan, Z., "Common phases of computer forensics investigation models," *International Journal of Computer Science and Information Technology*, vol. 3, no. 3, pp. 17–31, Jun. 2011, doi: 10.5121/ijcsit.2011.3302

[3] Lennox-Steele, A. and Nisbet, A., "A forensic examination of several mobile device Faraday bags & materials to test their effectiveness," pp. 34–41, 2016, doi: 10.4225/75/58a550b153635

[4] Ibrahim, N., Naqbi, N. A., Iqbal, F., and Alfandi, O., "SIM card forensics: Digital evidence," *Proceedings of the Annual ADFSL Conference on Digital Forensics, Security and Law*, Daytona Beach, FL, 2016. https://commons.erau.edu/adfsl/2016/thursday/3

[5] Murphy, C. A., "Developing process for mobile device forensics." [Online]. Available: https://sansorg.egnyte.com/dl/lpIZSVtbFu

[6] Thing, V. L. L., Ng, K.-Y., and Chang, E.-C., "Live memory forensics of smartphones," *Digital Investigation*, vol. 7, pp. S74–S82, Aug. 2010. doi: 10.1016/j.diin.2010.05.010

[7] Fukami, A., Stoykova, R., and Geradts, Z., "A new model for forensic data extraction from encrypted mobile devices," *Forensic Science International: Digital Investigation*, vol. 38, p. 301169, Sep. 2021, doi: 10.1016/j.fsidi.2021.301169

Chapter 4

Embedded chips

Embedded chips are specialized microchips designed to perform specific functions within electronic devices. Unlike general-purpose processors, these chips are often integrated directly into a system to manage tasks like storage, communication, or security operations [1]. They are typically found in a range of devices, from personal gadgets to industrial equipment, where their compact size, low power consumption, and specialized functions make them indispensable.

Embedded chips are critical components of modern technology, powering everything from mobile phones and smart cards to thumb drives and authentication devices. Their importance comes from their ability to facilitate secure data storage, enable user authentication, or manage the internal workings of a system.

4.1 RELEVANCE IN DIGITAL FORENSICS

In digital forensics, embedded chips serve as key sources of evidence. As embedded systems are responsible for handling sensitive and mission-critical data, the information they store can be vital in forensic investigations. Whether examining a smartphone's SIM card, a USB drive used for data transfer, or a smart card used in banking transactions, embedded chips may contain logs, metadata, communication records, and more, all of which can be analyzed to uncover digital evidence [2].

Some key aspects embedded chips are relevant in forensic investigations include data storage, where many embedded chips store user-generated content, system logs, or transactional data. Recovering this information can help investigators trace back to key events or understand device usage. Even when users delete files or records from devices, forensic tools can often recover this data from embedded chips, helping investigators uncover hidden or lost information [3]. Additionally, embedded systems often come with security features designed to detect tampering or unauthorized access. Forensic investigators may analyze these logs to determine if and when an embedded chip was compromised or altered. Furthermore, many devices

DOI: 10.1201/9781003644255-4

with embedded chips track authentication events or access logs, which can provide crucial evidence in cases involving unauthorized system access or breaches.

Embedded chips can be found in a wide range of devices, including smart cards, SIM cards, thumb drives (USB drives), removable media, SD cards, memory sticks, TransFlash (microSD cards), and authentication sticks. Each of these devices plays a distinct role in digital ecosystems, but they all share the potential to hold valuable forensic evidence that can be crucial in digital investigations. In the next section, we will explore some of the most common types of embedded chips in more detail, examining their specific features and forensic importance.

Figure 4.1 provides standard process flow for investigating digital devices with embedded chips.

4.2 SMART CARD FORENSICS

A smart card is a small, wallet-sized plastic card embedded with a microchip that can either store information or, more commonly, perform processing tasks. These microchips, which may contain a microcontroller (complete with a processor, memory, and input/output interfaces) or simply a memory chip, allow smart cards to handle more complex operations than traditional magnetic stripe cards, making them a powerful and versatile tool in a wide variety of applications [4].

Smart cards operate either via contact or contactless communication methods. Contact smart cards have metal contacts on their surface that come into physical contact with a card reader to facilitate data exchange. These are commonly used in credit/debit cards and government-issued ID cards. Contactless smart cards, on the other hand, use radio frequency identification (RFID) or near-field communication (NFC) to communicate wirelessly with a card reader when in proximity. Contactless cards are popular in modern applications such as public transportation systems and mobile payment systems (e.g., Apple Pay, Google Pay). Today, smart cards have evolved into a critical part of both public and private sectors. From banking systems to telecommunications (in the form of SIM cards) and access control systems, these cards have become indispensable for secure identity verification, data storage, and transactions. Their flexibility in function—ranging from simple memory storage to sophisticated cryptographic computations—makes them ideal for high-security environments [5]. Their dual ability to store data and perform complex processing tasks allows them to serve multiple roles, from authenticating users in secure networks to facilitating transactions and storing sensitive information.

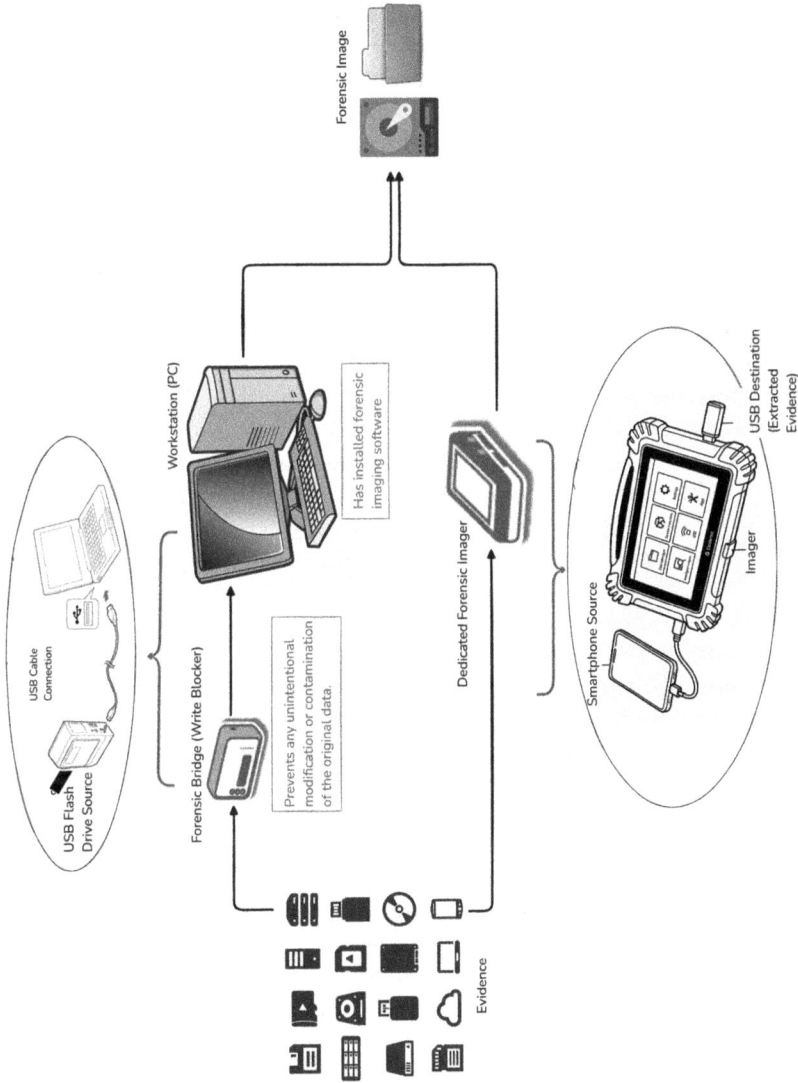

Figure 4.1 Forensic investigation process for various digital devices.

4.2.1 Forensic relevance of smart cards

As digital technology continues to permeate all areas of modern life, smart cards have emerged as critical tools not just for everyday use but also as key artifacts in digital forensic investigations. The unique role of smart cards in securing sensitive information, facilitating identity authentication, and logging transactions makes them a vital source of forensic data. They can provide a wealth of information in investigations involving financial crimes, cyber fraud, identity theft, and unauthorized access, among others.

In the context of digital forensics, smart cards are often scrutinized for several reasons. Firstly, they are employed in environments that require high levels of security. Whether used for financial transactions, secure access control, or telecommunications, smart cards hold encrypted data that are crucial to unraveling the flow of events in a forensic investigation. In many cases, smart cards act as the primary means of authentication, controlling access to various systems. As a result, investigators can uncover vital information such as access logs, credentials, and encrypted communication keys, which are crucial in understanding how a system was compromised or misused.

Smart cards are also frequently used for authentication in multi-factor authentication (MFA) systems, where the possession of the card itself is combined with other factors, such as a password or biometric data. These cards play a vital role in access control systems, where they log the identity of users, the time of access, and the locations of entry points. In forensic investigations, these logs can be instrumental in identifying who accessed secure areas or systems at specific times, establishing a timeline of events, or even pinpointing a suspect in an investigation.

In the case of financial investigations, smart cards such as debit cards, credit cards, and prepaid cards can hold transactional data that link suspects to financial activities. Forensic examiners can retrieve logs that record purchases, withdrawals, or other financial activities. These logs provide not only transaction amounts but often timestamps and geographic data, helping investigators map out the physical movements of individuals or track fraudulent activities. A specialized type of smart card, known as a SIM card (Subscriber Identity Module), is used in mobile devices to authenticate users to cellular networks. In telecommunications forensics, SIM cards can provide essential information about a suspect's mobile identity, call records, SMS history, and geolocation data. These data are particularly valuable in cases involving criminal communications, where investigators seek to tie individuals to specific calls or messages. The forensic extraction of call logs, text messages, subscriber information, and network access data from a SIM card can often provide direct links between suspects and criminal activities.

A notable case involving smart card forensics occurred during an ATM fraud investigation in Europe, where criminals used "shimming" devices to steal data from chip-enabled smart cards. These devices, placed inside ATMs, captured data between the card and the ATM terminal [6]. Forensic analysts recovered encrypted transaction logs from the smart cards, then used forensic software to decrypt and analyze the data. This allowed law enforcement to trace the transactions, leading to the identification of the criminals responsible. The use of specialized forensic tools, such as hardware device readers and decryption algorithms, was critical in recovering the data necessary for prosecution.

4.2.1.1 Legal and investigative relevance

Smart cards hold immense legal importance due to their use in highly regulated industries such as banking, healthcare, and telecommunications. The regulated nature of these industries means that data stored on smart cards are often subject to laws and policies governing data retention, privacy, and security. In forensic investigations, this means that smart card data can serve as legally admissible evidence when obtained and analyzed correctly. In cases involving fraud, embezzlement, or money laundering, forensic investigators can examine the data stored on smart payment cards to uncover transaction histories, track money flows, and link suspects to illegal activities. This can include analyzing encrypted payment logs, ATM withdrawals, or point-of-sale transactions.

Additionally, smart cards are frequently used as part of identity verification systems in both physical and digital environments. In forensic investigations, data from smart cards can provide proof of identity, help verify or refute claims of impersonation, and determine whether someone had legitimate access to sensitive data or areas. For example, an individual using a cloned or stolen smart card to gain unauthorized access to a secured system can be linked to the card through forensic analysis, offering proof of malicious intent. Smart cards are also utilized in cybersecurity for tasks such as digital signatures and secure login authentication. In cases of security breaches, forensic investigators may retrieve data from smart cards to uncover login attempts, tampered credentials, or altered security tokens. This can help identify how the breach occurred, which accounts were compromised, and which data may have been stolen or tampered with.

In industries or environments where physical security is paramount, smart cards are often used to control access to sensitive areas. Forensic analysis of smart card data can provide a log of entries and exits from these areas, helping to establish a timeline of events or identify unauthorized individuals. For example, in an investigation into corporate espionage or theft, forensic experts might analyze smart cards used by employees to enter and exit secure buildings or rooms, allowing them to determine who was present at the time of the incident.

During forensic investigations, the type of data extracted from a smart card depends on the card's specific use and architecture. Most smart cards, especially those used in ID verification or SIM cards, store personal identification numbers (PINs), subscriber identities (IMSI, ICCID), and biometric templates (in the case of multi-factor authentication). Many smart cards retain logs of authentication events, such as login attempts, successful verifications, and failed PIN entries. These logs can help forensic investigators establish when a card was used, how often, and whether it was involved in any suspicious activity.

For smart payment cards, forensic investigators can retrieve transaction histories, including timestamps, merchant data, and transaction amounts. This type of evidence is valuable in tracking financial fraud, reconstructing events, and identifying patterns of illegal activity. Smart cards often store cryptographic keys, which are used for encryption, digital signatures, or secure communication. In forensic investigations, access to these keys may allow investigators to decrypt data or verify the authenticity of digital signatures in cases involving fraud, tampering, or document forgery. In systems where smart cards are used for physical access control, forensic investigators can retrieve logs of entry attempts, detailing the time and location of access. This is particularly useful for identifying unauthorized access to restricted areas. SIM cards, as a specialized form of smart card, store mobile subscriber data, call logs, SMS records, and geolocation information, all of which are crucial in criminal investigations, particularly in cases of terrorism, drug trafficking, or cybercrime.

4.2.2 Challenges in using smart cards as forensic evidence

Despite their wealth of information, using smart cards as forensic evidence is not without its challenges. These include:

1. **Encryption and Security Features:** Smart cards are designed with robust security mechanisms to prevent unauthorized access. This can include PIN protection, encryption of stored data, and tamper-evident mechanisms. In some cases, these security features can make it difficult for forensic investigators to access data without specialized tools or legal authority to bypass protections.

2. **Anti-Forensic Measures:** Some smart cards, particularly those used in highly sensitive environments, are equipped with self-destruct mechanisms that wipe data if unauthorized access is detected. Investigators need to carefully handle such cards to avoid accidentally triggering these measures and losing crucial evidence.

3. **Legal Considerations:** Given the sensitivity of the data stored on smart cards, investigators must often comply with strict legal protocols to ensure the admissibility of evidence in court. Unauthorized extraction or mishandling of smart card data can render the evidence inadmissible, compromising the investigation.

4.2.3 Smart card physical structure and file system

Smart cards are much more than simple pieces of plastic with a chip embedded in them. Their physical structure and file system architecture are meticulously designed to ensure security, durability, and functionality across different applications. Understanding the physical components of a smart card, as well as how data is structured within it, is crucial for forensic investigators. This knowledge aids in identifying potential entry points for forensic data extraction and analyzing the types of information that might be stored on a card.

At a high level, the structure of a smart card can be broken down into three key components:

1. *The Card Body*: The card body itself is usually made of PVC, polyester, or polycarbonate. The outer body of the smart card may also include visual identifiers, such as logos, cardholder names, or chip locations. In some cards, printed barcodes or QR codes may also exist, which can be used for further identification or tracking purposes.

2. *The Embedded Microchip*: The heart of a smart card is its microchip, which is either a microcontroller or a memory chip, depending on the card's function. This chip may be visible externally, particularly in contact smart cards, where a metallic contact plate is exposed. In contactless cards, the chip is typically embedded deeper within the card body and communicates wirelessly. The chip consists of several components, including the central processing unit (CPU), which executes cryptographic algorithms and handles input/output operations, the read-only memory (ROM), which stores the card's operating system, and the random access memory (RAM), which is used for temporary storage during the execution of tasks [4].

3. *Antenna (for Contactless Cards)*: In contactless smart cards, an RFID antenna is embedded within the card. This antenna allows the card to communicate wirelessly with external readers via radio frequency or near-field communication (NFC). The antenna can be a forensic point of interest, particularly in determining how and when a card communicated with external systems or devices.

4.2.3.1 Smart card file system

Smart cards contain a structured file system similar to a typical computer's file system, but much simpler and more secure. Defined by the ISO/IEC 7816 standard, this system outlines how data are stored, accessed, and protected on the card. The smart card file system is typically hierarchical and consists of three main types of files: The Master File (MF), Dedicated Files (DFs), and Elementary Files (EFs). The Master File acts as the root directory and contains the entire structure of the card, serving as a container for all sub-files and applications present on the card. Forensic investigators usually start their analysis at the MF level, mapping out the card's data structure. Access to the MF reveals key details about the card's contents, such as the types of applications stored, including banking applications or ID credentials.

Dedicated Files are subdirectories under the Master File, each representing a logical grouping of data related to a specific application. For example, in a SIM card, separate DFs might exist for SMS storage, call logs, and network information. Forensic investigators often analyze these DFs to target specific areas of interest, such as recovering SMS messages or logs of communication with mobile networks. Accessing a DF frequently requires specialized authentication mechanisms, such as PIN codes or cryptographic keys.

Elementary Files reside within DFs and store the actual data. EFs can contain different types of data, such as binary data, transparent data, or structured data. Transparent EFs store raw data in a sequential manner, much like a binary file, often used for storing public key certificates or basic configuration data. Linear Fixed EFs are designed for record-oriented storage, where each record has a fixed length, often used for storing access logs, transaction records, or authentication attempts. Cyclic EFs, on the other hand, are designed to store cyclic records, with new records overwriting old ones when storage limits are reached. In SIM cards, call logs and SMS records are often stored in cyclic EFs. These files are particularly valuable in forensic investigations, as they provide a continuous history of data that can be linked to specific user actions over time.

The structure of a smart card's file system provides multiple entry points for forensic analysis. For example, investigators can target specific Elementary Files to retrieve transaction logs, authentication attempts, or encrypted certificates. Accessing Dedicated Files can reveal application-specific data, such as SMS history, call logs, or network authentication records in a SIM card. A key forensic technique is the *cloning of a smart card*, which involves creating an exact replica of the card's data structure for analysis without risking damage to the original card. This process allows forensic investigators to explore the card's file system safely, analyze file structures, and extract critical evidence without altering or triggering the card's security features.

4.2.4 Forensic analysis of smart cards

The forensic analysis of smart cards presents unique challenges due to their robust security measures, proprietary architectures, and specialized file systems. Nevertheless, smart cards often contain crucial data that can serve as valuable evidence in digital investigations. Given their widespread use in financial transactions, secure identification, and access control systems, forensic investigators frequently need to extract and analyze the data stored on these devices. Forensic analysis of smart cards can be broken down into several critical stages, including data acquisition, authentication bypassing, data decoding, and analysis of specific artifacts. Each stage requires specialized knowledge and tools to ensure that evidence is gathered securely, effectively, and in a forensically sound manner.

4.2.4.1 Identification and initial handling

The first step in smart card forensic analysis is identifying the type of smart card and ensuring that it is handled correctly to preserve the integrity of the data. Smart cards come in various forms, such as SIM cards, banking cards, and access control cards, each requiring a slightly different forensic approach. During the initial inspection, investigators must confirm whether the card is a contact or contactless card. Contact cards have a visible chip on their surface, while contactless cards may lack any visible chip and rely on wireless communication through RFID or NFC. Some cards may be hybrids, supporting both forms of communication.

Handling precautions are crucial in smart card forensics. Investigators should use anti-static gloves, avoid exposing the card to extreme temperatures, and ensure that the card is not placed near devices emitting electromagnetic interference. This is especially critical for contactless cards, as accidental NFC or RFID reader interaction could potentially alter the stored data.

4.2.4.2 Data acquisition

Once the smart card has been identified, the next phase is data acquisition. This involves creating an exact copy of the data stored on the smart card, typically referred to as cloning the card. The process must adhere to the chain of custody and follow best practices to ensure that the data remain unaltered.

4.2.4.2.1 Cloning the smart card

The purpose of cloning is to create a bit-for-bit copy of the card's contents, which can be analyzed without damaging the original card. Cloning is particularly useful in cases where repeated access to the card may trigger security mechanisms that wipe or alter the data. The first step in cloning involves connecting the smart card to a forensic card reader or writer. For contact-based cards, the reader makes a direct connection to the card's chip, while contactless cards require an RFID/NFC reader. These devices extract data from the smart card and store it in an image format, such as .bin, .img, or .iso. Specialized software tools such as CardPeek, SIMclone, or PySim facilitate the data extraction process by allowing forensic investigators to interact with the card's file system, Dedicated Files, and Elementary Files.

After the cloning process, it is crucial to verify the integrity of the data image. Hashing algorithms like SHA-256 or MD5 can be used to generate a unique hash value for both the original card and its cloned image. The hash values must match to ensure that the cloned data are an exact replica of the original. This process ensures that any evidence gathered from the cloned image can be considered valid and has not been altered during acquisition.

4.2.4.2.2 Authentication bypassing and accessing protected data

Smart cards implement multiple layers of authentication mechanisms to protect sensitive data. These mechanisms may include PIN codes, PUK codes, cryptographic keys, or challenge–response authentication protocols. In many forensic cases, investigators need to bypass these authentication methods to access protected files and records. For example, many smart cards, particularly SIM cards and banking cards, require a PIN (Personal Identification Number) for access. If the correct PIN is not entered after several attempts, the card may lock and require a PUK (Personal Unlocking Key) code to regain access.

In some forensic investigations, brute force attacks may be used to guess the PIN code, though this can be risky as many smart cards will lock or wipe data after a certain number of failed attempts. There are also specialized forensic tools, such as MOBILedit Forensic and SIMCon, that can attempt to bypass or recover PINs using known vulnerabilities in the smart card's security protocols. For more advanced smart cards, such as those used for secure access and encryption (PKI-based smart cards), data are protected with cryptographic keys. Extracting data from these cards often requires specialized hardware and software to bypass encryption. Techniques like side-channel attacks, including power analysis or timing attacks, can some-times be employed to extract cryptographic keys from smart cards by ana-lyzing the power consumption or timing variations during operations. Once the cryptographic keys are retrieved, they can be used in combination with forensic decryption tools, such as ElcomSoft Distributed Password Recovery, to unlock encrypted data stored within the smart card.

4.2.4.2.3 Analyzing smart card data and artifacts

Once access to the smart card is gained, forensic investigators can begin to examine the data and artifacts stored within. The types of data available for analysis will vary depending on the card type, its intended function, and the applications it supports. Some common data types stored on smart cards include:

1. **Personal Identification Data:** Smart cards used for identification (e.g., national ID cards, driver's licenses) often contain personally identifi-able information (PII), such as names, addresses, dates of birth, and biometric data. Forensic analysis of these cards can reveal user iden-tity and usage history.

2. **Transaction Logs:** In banking smart cards, forensic investigators can extract transaction history records, which may include details of purchases, withdrawals, balance checks, and account interactions. These logs are often stored as binary records or encrypted text files within the card's file system.

3. **Access Control Records:** Smart cards used for physical or digital access control (e.g., building access cards, secure system logins) may store records of login attempts, time stamps, and access locations. These logs can be critical for investigations involving unauthorized access or security breaches.

4. **SMS and Call Logs:** In the case of SIM cards, investigators can recover SMS messages, call logs, and network registration data. These records are often stored in cyclic elementary files (EFs), meaning that older records may be overwritten by newer ones. However, forensic tools can recover deleted data from these areas in certain cases.

In addition to the primary data, forensic investigators are often interested in other artifacts stored on smart cards. Encryption keys are a major focus, as they are used to secure data and communications. Investigating encryption keys stored on smart cards can provide access to otherwise inaccessible records or services. Authentication artifacts, such as tokens or certificates used for secure communications, are also valuable in cases involving secure communications, VPN access, or digital signatures. Timestamps embedded within logs or files can be used to establish a timeline of card usage, identifying when, by whom, and where the card was used—crucial information for reconstructing events in forensic investigations.

4.2.5 Tools for smart card forensics

Forensic analysis of smart cards requires specialized tools capable of interacting with the card's file system, bypassing security protocols, and extracting artifacts without altering the card's data. These tools include both hardware (e.g., card readers) and software platforms designed for data extraction and analysis (see Table 4.1).

4.3 THUMB DRIVES (USB DRIVES)

Thumb drives, also known as USB flash drives, are portable data storage devices that allow users to store and transfer a variety of file types, including documents, photos, videos, software, and system backups. Their portability and plug-and-play capabilities make them highly convenient for users who need to carry data with them, making data transfer between computers or devices quick and easy. Thumb drives are also widely used for data backup, allowing users to archive critical files and protect them from

Table 4.1 Software and hardware tools for smart card forensics

Tool name	Type	Functionality	Key features	Usage
Omnikey Reader	Hardware	Interfaces with contact and contactless smart cards	Supports multiple card types (e.g., SIM cards, banking cards) and RFID/NFC communication	Used for reading and accessing data from smart cards via contact or wireless protocols.
Gemalto Smart Card Reader	Hardware	Reads contact and contactless smart cards	Compatible with a variety of smart cards and RFID/NFC standards	Ideal for forensic data acquisition from smart cards with advanced encryption mechanisms.
CardPeek	Software	Reads and analyzes smart card data, including SIM and banking cards	Provides access to smart card file systems and supports elementary and dedicated file extraction	Used to interact with the smart card's file system and retrieve data like SMS or transaction logs.
SIMCon	Software	Extracts and analyzes data from SIM cards	Recovers call logs, SMS, and service provider information	Commonly used for telecommunications forensics to recover data from SIM cards.
PySim	Software	Clones and interacts with SIM card data	Cloning capability and support for GSM SIM cards	Used in cloning SIM cards and extracting personal identification data (IMSI, ICCID, etc.).
ElcomSoft Distributed Password Recovery	Software	Unlocks encrypted data stored within smart cards	Supports password recovery and decryption of PKI-based cards	Used for decrypting secure data in encrypted smart cards, such as banking and government ID cards.
Proxmark3	Hardware	Analyzes RFID and NFC communications from contactless smart cards	Offers support for analyzing and capturing RFID communications; highly portable	Ideal for capturing data from contactless smart cards used in transportation and mobile payments.

potential system crashes or data loss. Additionally, one of the most significant functions of thumb drives is their ability to be configured as bootable devices, enabling users to install or repair operating systems directly from the drive. This feature proves especially useful for IT professionals and computer technicians who often need to perform system repairs or installations in various environments. These versatile functionalities make thumb drives indispensable tools in both personal and professional settings. Furthermore, thumb drives are non-volatile, meaning they retain data even when not powered, which ensures the long-term preservation of information. Using flash memory technology, a form of solid-state memory, thumb drives offer high-speed data transfer and greater durability than traditional magnetic storage media. These attributes, combined with their small size and durability, have revolutionized how data are stored and transported, making them ideal for diverse applications. Consequently, thumb drives are often targeted in digital forensic investigations due to their ability to store a wide range of evidence, including documents, media files, logs, and encrypted data. Their non-volatile nature, high speed, and flexibility in storing encrypted or hidden data make them key devices in many cybercrime cases, requiring meticulous forensic analysis to uncover potentially incriminating information.

4.3.1 Importance of thumb drives as forensic evidence

Thumb drives play a critical role in forensic investigations due to their potential to contain digital evidence. They are often used for both legitimate and illicit purposes, storing critical files that may have been deliberately transferred or hidden. The portability of thumb drives makes them ideal for transporting data, but it also makes them vulnerable to misuse in criminal activities such as intellectual property theft, illegal data storage, or the distribution of malware.

One of the most common uses of thumb drives in criminal activity is data exfiltration, where an individual uses the device to steal sensitive or proprietary information from an organization. In addition, thumb drives are frequently used for storing illegal media, such as pirated content or explicit materials, due to their small size and discrete nature. Another critical use of thumb drives in criminal activities is the distribution of malware, viruses, or ransomware. These devices can easily spread malware, especially in cases of insider threats or targeted attacks, making them a significant tool in cybercrime.

Furthermore, thumb drives may serve as a means of evidence concealment. Criminals often store critical information, such as financial records, communication logs, or incriminating documents, on these devices, effectively hiding data outside of traditional computer systems. Forensic experts often analyze thumb drives to recover deleted files, examine file system timestamps, or uncover hidden encrypted partitions, all of which can provide direct links between a suspect and criminal activity [3].

4.3.2 Physical structure and storage technology of thumb drives

A thumb drive consists of several key components that enable it to function as a portable storage device. These include:

- *USB Connector*: The interface through which the drive connects to a computer or other device. The most common versions are USB 2.0 and USB 3.0, with the latter offering faster data transfer speeds.
- *Flash Memory Chip*: The storage unit where data are written and retrieved. Thumb drives use NAND flash memory, which is non-volatile and can store data even when the drive is unplugged from a power source.
- *Controller*: A small processor embedded in the thumb drive that manages the data flow between the USB interface and the memory chip. It controls how data are read from and written to the flash memory.
- *Capacitor and Crystal Oscillator*: These components help regulate the power supply to the thumb drive and maintain a consistent clock signal for data transfer operations.

Thumb drives use flash memory, which operates using an electronic storage method without moving parts. This technology is much faster and more reliable than traditional hard disk drives, which use mechanical spinning parts. Flash memory writes data in blocks and erases data in sectors, making it highly durable but sometimes complex for forensic recovery, especially in cases involving deleted files or damaged sectors.

4.3.3 Forensic analysis of thumb drives

Forensic analysis of thumb drives involves retrieving and examining the stored data to uncover evidence related to criminal activity or civil disputes. Thumb drives present unique challenges and opportunities in forensic investigations due to their size, capacity, and potential for portability.

- **Logical Analysis:** Involves accessing the visible file system of the thumb drive to retrieve intact files. Logical analysis may include examining file names, timestamps, and directory structures to uncover evidence of when and how files were accessed or modified.
- **Physical Analysis:** This method involves creating a bit-by-bit copy of the thumb drive (a forensic image) to recover deleted, hidden, or corrupted files. Physical analysis goes beyond the file system to recover data from the drive's memory sectors, including slack space and unallocated space where remnants of old files may exist.

- **File Carving:** When files are deleted from a thumb drive, the associated data may not be entirely removed. File carving techniques allow forensic experts to recover these deleted files by analyzing the drive's raw data and piecing together file fragments based on file signatures.

4.3.4 Forensic artifacts

Thumb drives store a wide array of digital artifacts that can be critical to forensic investigations. Metadata such as file creation, modification, and access times can provide a detailed timeline of events, offering insights into user activity leading up to a crime [3]. Forensic tools enable experts to recover deleted files, even after users attempt to erase them. In addition, thumb drives often contain encrypted files or partitions, which may require specialized decryption techniques to access and analyze. These encrypted sections can store sensitive information that plays a crucial role in building a case.

In some instances, hidden partitions are deliberately created to conceal sensitive data. Forensic investigators must identify and access these hidden areas, which are not visible to the typical user, to retrieve potential evidence. These concealed partitions can contain incriminating documents, communication logs, or other critical data essential for establishing the connection between the suspect and illegal activities. Files and documents stored on thumb drives, such as contracts, spreadsheets, or incriminating documents, can directly link suspects to unlawful actions. Additionally, malware and other malicious executables stored on thumb drives can help trace the origin of a cyberattack or virus distribution [2].

The analysis of metadata, including file creation and modification timestamps, is essential for establishing a clear timeline of user activity and determining when files were accessed or altered. System logs stored on thumb drives can also provide important information, such as details on which devices the drive was connected to and the specific times of these connections. Forensic experts meticulously analyze partition information, recovering partition tables and investigating hidden or encrypted sections of the drive for any evidence that may otherwise go unnoticed [3].

4.3.5 Challenges in thumb drive forensics

Several challenges complicate forensic analysis of thumb drives. One significant obstacle is the wear-leveling mechanism used in flash memory. Wear leveling is a process that distributes writes evenly across the memory cells, extending the lifespan of the device. However, this mechanism can complicate data recovery, as wear leveling may overwrite deleted data or scatter file fragments across the drive.

Another challenge is data encryption. Many modern thumb drives come with built-in encryption mechanisms that protect the data from unauthorized access. Forensic investigators must obtain the encryption keys or use sophisticated decryption software to access this data. Physical damage to the thumb drive also presents difficulties, as standard forensic tools may be unable to retrieve data from a damaged device. In such cases, advanced techniques like chip-off analysis, where the flash memory chip is physically removed and analyzed directly, may be required.

4.3.6 Tools for thumb drive forensics

Forensic investigators rely on various tools to extract and analyze data from thumb drives. These tools are designed to create forensic images of the drive, recover deleted files, and analyze the drive's file system. One of the most widely used tools is FTK Imager, which creates bit-by-bit copies of thumb drives and other storage devices. This tool allows investigators to recover deleted files and examine file metadata, including timestamps and file paths. Another popular tool is Autopsy, an open-source forensic tool with a graphical interface for analyzing storage media. It can extract data from thumb drives, recover deleted content, and analyze the file system for evidence. EnCase is a comprehensive forensic tool capable of creating forensic images, analyzing thumb drives, and recovering a wide range of artifacts such as documents, executable files, and metadata.

ProDiscover is another tool used to analyze thumb drives. It allows investigators to create forensic images, recover deleted data, and analyze file system structures. Lastly, USB Detective is a specialized tool for extracting artifacts related to USB activity on a computer. It helps investigators determine when a specific thumb drive was connected to the system, which files were accessed or transferred, and provides valuable insights into USB usage patterns.

4.3.7 Thumb drive forensics—real life case: breaking a child exploitation ring

In July 2022, U.S. law enforcement successfully prosecuted two men in Oklahoma for their involvement in distributing child sexual abuse material (CSAM) [7]. The investigation began when law enforcement received a tip about suspicious online activity linked to the BitTorrent network, where CSAM was being shared. The suspects, Timothy Gregston and Earl Morrow, were eventually tracked down, and during a search of their homes, investigators discovered several thumb drives.

Forensic examiners conducted a detailed analysis of the thumb drives using tools like FTK Imager and EnCase. Despite the suspects' efforts to delete the files, forensic tools were able to recover thousands of illegal images and videos. Investigators also analyzed the metadata of the recovered files, including timestamps, to establish when the files were accessed and distributed. The forensic imaging of the thumb drives allowed investigators to create exact replicas, which were used in court without damaging the original evidence.

In addition to the digital content, investigators found encrypted folders on the thumb drives, which were cracked using specialized decryption software. This revealed additional CSAM material, further incriminating the suspects. Both men were sentenced to significant prison terms [7]. The thumb drives were central to the investigation, providing irrefutable evidence of the crimes committed.

4.4 TRANSFLASH CARDS FORENSICS

TransFlash cards, also known as microSD cards, are a miniature version of SD cards designed for compact and portable devices. Introduced initially as a storage solution for mobile phones, TransFlash cards have become integral to various consumer electronics, including cameras, tablets, and wearable devices. Their small size, combined with substantial storage capabilities, makes them a versatile choice for users requiring high-capacity data storage in a compact form. Understanding the structure, use, and forensic relevance of TransFlash cards is crucial for investigators dealing with digital evidence.

TransFlash cards utilize the same flash memory technology as standard SD cards, allowing them to store data persistently without power. They were developed to meet the growing demand for storage solutions in increasingly smaller devices, providing users with an efficient way to expand the memory capacity of their gadgets. The physical dimensions of TransFlash cards are significantly smaller than those of regular SD cards, typically measuring 15 mm x 11 mm x 1 mm, which makes them particularly suited for mobile applications where space is limited.

TransFlash cards can be used with various devices through adapters that convert them to standard SD card sizes, ensuring compatibility across different platforms. Their ability to hold substantial amounts of data, ranging from a few gigabytes to several terabytes, makes them attractive for users looking to store high-resolution photos, videos, applications, and other data-intensive files.

4.4.1 Importance of TransFlash cards as forensic evidence

TransFlash cards are increasingly encountered in digital forensic investigations due to their widespread adoption in smartphones and portable electronic devices. As these cards often store a wealth of personal and sensitive information, they can serve as crucial evidence in investigations involving identity theft, cybercrime, and other illicit activities. For example, in cases of cyberbullying or harassment, investigators may retrieve messages, photographs, or videos stored on a TransFlash card that could substantiate claims or provide critical insights into user behavior.

Moreover, the compact nature of TransFlash cards often leads individuals to use them for discreet storage of illicit materials, including illegal photographs or sensitive information. Forensic analysts must be proficient in recovering data from these small storage devices, as users may believe that removing a TransFlash card from a device eliminates their digital footprint. However, forensic techniques can often reveal hidden or deleted data, providing essential insights into a case.

4.4.2 Physical structure and file systems of TransFlash cards

The physical structure of TransFlash cards consists of a tiny circuit board containing flash memory chips and a controller, all housed within a durable casing. This design is essential for protecting the internal components, as TransFlash cards are often exposed to varying environmental conditions due to their use in portable devices.

Like SD cards, TransFlash cards utilize various file systems, with FAT32 being the most common for lower-capacity cards, while exFAT is used for larger capacities. The file system determines how data are organized, stored, and accessed, and influences the forensic recovery process. Understanding the file system employed on a TransFlash card is critical for forensic analysts, as it guides the methodologies used in data recovery and analysis.

4.4.3 Forensic analysis of TransFlash cards

The forensic analysis of TransFlash cards follows similar principles to the analysis of larger SD cards. The first step involves creating a forensic image of the card to preserve the original data. This imaging process ensures that any examination of the card's contents does not alter the original evidence.

After obtaining a forensic image, analysts explore the file structure to identify active and deleted files. Forensic tools designed for data recovery can extract remnants of deleted data, revealing files that users may have believed were permanently erased. In addition to recovering files, analysts can examine metadata associated with the data stored on the card, which can provide vital context regarding file creation and modification dates.

Given the prevalence of mobile devices that utilize TransFlash cards, investigators must also be aware of the various applications that may have stored data on these cards. For example, social media apps, messaging platforms, and multimedia applications can all leave traces of user interactions on the card, providing valuable insights into user behavior and activities.

During forensic examinations, various artifacts may be recovered from TransFlash cards. These artifacts can include not only user-generated content, such as images, videos, and documents but also remnants of deleted files and hidden data. Investigators often analyze these artifacts to reconstruct user actions and establish connections to specific events or individuals.

Additionally, data remnants may include application caches or temporary files that can provide further context regarding user interactions with specific applications. Understanding these artifacts is crucial for forensic analysts, as they can help build a comprehensive timeline of user activities and intentions.

4.4.4 Tools for TransFlash card forensics

Forensic analysts utilize a variety of specialized tools for examining TransFlash cards. Some commonly used tools include FTK Imager, which allows for the creation of forensic images and supports file recovery; Autopsy, an open-source platform for comprehensive digital investigations; and EnCase, a widely recognized commercial tool offering a suite of forensic capabilities.

In addition to these general forensic tools, investigators may employ mobile forensic tools specifically designed to extract and analyze data from mobile devices that utilize TransFlash cards. These tools enable forensic analysts to recover data from applications, user interactions, and other relevant information that may reside on the card.

4.4.5 TransFlash card forensics—real life case: uncovering a drug syndicate

In 2022, law enforcement agencies in South America broke up a major drug trafficking syndicate, thanks to forensic analysis of TransFlash (microSD) cards. These cards were found in the burner phones used by the traffickers to communicate securely. During the raid, investigators seized several TransFlash cards, which were encrypted to prevent easy access.

Forensic experts used specialized decryption tools to unlock the files stored on the cards, which contained detailed communication logs, transaction records, and contact information for buyers and suppliers. Forensic analysis also revealed deleted messages that linked the traffickers to specific drug shipments. The recovered data helped authorities trace the flow of drugs through multiple countries and led to the arrest of key figures within the organization. The ability to recover encrypted and deleted data from TransFlash cards was pivotal in this case, as the traffickers relied heavily on these devices to conduct their operations without leaving a trace. Forensic analysis of these small but powerful storage devices provided law enforcement with the evidence they needed to bring down the syndicate.

4.4.6 Legal considerations in TransFlash card forensics

Conducting forensic analysis on TransFlash cards necessitates strict adherence to legal and ethical standards to ensure the evidence remains admissible in court. Maintaining a chain of custody is critical to establish the integrity of the evidence, and thorough documentation of the forensic examination process is essential for presenting findings in legal proceedings.

When accessing data on TransFlash cards, investigators must also be aware of data privacy laws, particularly if the cards contain sensitive or personal information. In many cases, obtaining a search warrant may be necessary to access the data stored on the card, emphasizing the importance of legal compliance in digital forensic investigations.

4.5 AUTHENTICATION STICKS FORENSICS

Authentication sticks, also known as hardware security tokens or USB security keys, are specialized devices designed to enhance the security of digital systems by enabling two-factor authentication (2FA) or multi-factor authentication (MFA). These sticks are typically small USB-based devices that provide a physical layer of security, requiring the user to have physical access to the stick in order to authenticate their identity, often in conjunction with a password or biometric data. Due to their role in securing sensitive systems and data, authentication sticks can be valuable pieces of forensic evidence in investigations involving digital crimes, unauthorized access, or fraud.

Authentication sticks are designed to prevent unauthorized access to digital accounts or systems by requiring physical possession of the stick in addition to the user's password or other credentials. Popular brands include YubiKey and Google Titan, both of which follow open standards like FIDO2 and U2F (Universal 2nd Factor). These devices have gained widespread adoption for securing online accounts, protecting sensitive data, and ensuring that only authorized users can gain access to specific systems or applications.

Authentication sticks often work by generating cryptographic keys, which are used to authenticate the user's access to a system. When the stick is plugged into a computer or mobile device, it communicates directly with the system and completes the authentication process. This process adds an extra layer of security, as even if an attacker obtains a user's password, they cannot access the system without the corresponding hardware token.

4.5.1 Importance of authentication sticks as forensic evidence

Authentication sticks are increasingly encountered in digital forensic investigations due to their widespread use for securing online accounts and sensitive data. Their forensic significance lies in the critical insights they provide regarding access control and user authentication events. In the context of a digital crime investigation, the presence of an authentication stick can help establish a direct link between a user and specific login events, which is essential in cases of unauthorized access, fraud, or identity theft. For instance, if an organization experiences a cybersecurity breach, investigators can analyze the authentication sticks associated with compromised accounts to determine whether they were used legitimately or if they were involved in unauthorized access attempts. By examining the authentication logs generated by these devices, investigators can ascertain when and where the sticks were used, correlating this information with other digital evidence, such as system logs or user activity records. This correlation can help piece together a timeline of events leading up to the breach.

Moreover, authentication sticks are often used in high-security environments, such as financial institutions, government agencies, and corporate networks. The data stored within these sticks can provide insights into user behavior, access patterns, and potential insider threats. For example, if an employee's authentication stick is discovered at a crime scene, it could imply their involvement or connection to the incident, warranting further investigation.

4.5.2 Physical structure and cryptographic functions

Authentication sticks generally have a compact, durable design that includes a small printed circuit board housed within a plastic or metal casing. Internally, these sticks contain cryptographic processors that generate and store private keys used in the authentication process. The sticks also feature contact points for connecting with USB ports or other interfaces, such as NFC (Near Field Communication), for mobile authentication. The cryptographic function of these sticks is central to their use. When inserted into a computer or device, the stick uses public-key cryptography to authenticate the user. The stick stores a private key, while the corresponding public key is used by the service or system being accessed. This exchange ensures that authentication only occurs if the correct private key is present in the device. This cryptographic exchange is secure and does not transmit sensitive information, which makes it difficult for attackers to intercept and misuse authentication data.

4.5.3 Forensic analysis of authentication sticks

The forensic analysis of authentication sticks involves several steps, each crucial for ensuring the integrity of the evidence and the reliability of the findings. The analysis process typically begins with the creation of a forensic image of the stick. This imaging process aims to preserve the original state of the device while allowing analysts to work with a copy to minimize the risk of data alteration. Once a forensic image is created, investigators can explore the contents of the stick to identify the stored cryptographic keys, user account associations, and any login event records. Forensic tools designed for digital investigations can facilitate this analysis by extracting and interpreting the data stored on the device.

Key aspects of the forensic analysis of authentication sticks include:

- **Creation of a Forensic Image:** The first step involves creating a bit-for-bit copy of the authentication stick to ensure that the original evidence remains intact and unaltered.
- **Data Extraction:** Forensic tools are used to extract cryptographic keys, login logs, and other relevant data from the forensic image of the device.
- **Log Analysis:** Investigators analyze the authentication logs generated by the stick, which detail usage events, timestamps, and associated devices. This helps establish a timeline of user actions.
- **Correlating Evidence:** By cross-referencing the data obtained from the authentication stick with other digital artifacts, such as system logs or network traffic, investigators can build a comprehensive understanding of user behavior and access events.
- **Identifying Anomalies:** Analysts look for unusual patterns or discrepancies in the data that may indicate misuse, such as unauthorized access attempts or failed login events.
- **Vulnerability Assessment:** Forensic analysis may also include an examination of the device for potential security flaws or signs of tampering, which could provide insights into how the security of the authentication system was compromised.

One of the primary objectives during forensic analysis is to uncover how the authentication stick was used in connection with specific user accounts. Investigators may review the logs generated by the stick, which typically document each authentication attempt, along with timestamps and associated devices. By analyzing these logs, forensic analysts can correlate authentication events with other digital evidence, such as network traffic logs or system access records, to build a comprehensive timeline of user actions and events leading up to a potential security breach. Moreover, forensic investigators may examine the stick for potential vulnerabilities or security flaws. For example, if the stick is compromised, it may store unauthorized cryptographic keys or exhibit signs of tampering. Identifying these anomalies can provide additional insights into how the security of the authentication system was breached and whether any sensitive data was exfiltrated.

While the device itself may not store extensive amounts of user data, it is often used in conjunction with a broader forensic investigation, where the authentication stick's role in enabling access or securing data becomes part of the overall picture. Its use in MFA also means that it can serve as corroborating evidence in cases involving identity theft or hacking.

4.5.4 Authentication stick forensic artifacts

Authentication sticks store a range of digital artifacts that are critical for forensic analysis, including cryptographic keys, user account associations, and login event records. These artifacts provide investigators with insight into the specific accounts that the stick has been linked to and the services it has authenticated. Cryptographic keys, for example, are integral to the authentication process. The stick stores private cryptographic keys that, when matched with their corresponding public keys, verify legitimate access to systems or networks. Additionally, authentication systems often generate logs documenting when and where the stick was used. These logs allow investigators to analyze login events, helping them identify the frequency, timing, and location of the authentication stick's use.

Another valuable set of artifacts includes metadata, such as device usage history or associations with specific systems or applications. This metadata can be instrumental in tracking a user's activities and identifying patterns of behavior. When these artifacts are analyzed alongside other digital evidence, such as network logs or system records, they provide a comprehensive view of the device's usage, enabling investigators to reconstruct a detailed timeline of events and actions taken by the user. This multi-faceted approach allows for a more complete forensic analysis, aiding in the detection of unauthorized access or malicious activities [8].

4.5.5 Forensic tools for authentication stick forensics

Several tools are available for analyzing authentication sticks. These tools focus on extracting cryptographic keys, reviewing login logs, and analyzing associated metadata. Some of the key tools used in authentication stick forensics include:

- *FTK Imager*: A common tool for creating forensic images of digital devices, including authentication sticks.
- *YubiKey Manager*: Specifically designed for YubiKey devices, this tool allows forensic analysts to retrieve information about the stick's configuration and usage.
- *EnCase*: A comprehensive forensic tool that can be used to analyze artifacts from authentication sticks as part of a broader forensic investigation.
- *Cryptographic Key Extractors*: Specialized tools for retrieving and analyzing cryptographic keys stored on the device.

Investigators often use a combination of these tools to ensure a thorough analysis of the authentication stick, enabling them to identify the cryptographic details, usage patterns, and associated accounts or systems.

4.5.6 Challenges in authentication stick forensics

One of the main challenges in analyzing authentication sticks is the robust security mechanisms they employ. Since these devices are designed to protect sensitive data, they often use encryption to safeguard information, making it difficult for forensic analysts to extract usable data without the appropriate decryption keys. Moreover, if an authentication stick is physically damaged or corrupted, recovering data can become even more challenging.

Additionally, authentication sticks may not store extensive user data beyond their cryptographic keys and logs. Therefore, investigators often need to rely on corroborating evidence from the systems or accounts the stick was used to access. Nevertheless, the presence of an authentication stick can serve as vital evidence in cases involving unauthorized access, confirming that a user had the physical means to authenticate themselves to a system. Moreover, the rapid evolution of authentication technologies and the proliferation of different devices can make it challenging for forensic analysts to keep pace with the latest developments. New authentication protocols, security standards, and device configurations continuously emerge, necessitating ongoing training and adaptation for forensic professionals.

4.5.7 Legal considerations in authentication stick forensics

Conducting forensic analysis on authentication sticks requires strict adherence to legal and ethical standards to ensure that the evidence remains admissible in court. Investigators must maintain a chain of custody to establish the integrity of the evidence, documenting every step taken during the analysis process. This documentation is crucial for demonstrating that the evidence has not been altered or tampered with.

Additionally, when accessing data on authentication sticks, investigators must be aware of data privacy laws, particularly if the sticks contain sensitive or personal information. In many jurisdictions, obtaining a search warrant may be necessary to access the data stored on the stick, emphasizing the importance of legal compliance in digital forensic investigations.

Failure to adhere to these legal considerations can result in the dismissal of evidence in court, undermining the entire investigation. Therefore, digital forensic professionals must prioritize legal and ethical compliance throughout the analysis process, ensuring that all actions taken are justified and documented.

END OF CHAPTER QUESTIONS

1. You have seized a smartphone that contains both a SIM card and an SD card. Discuss the order in which you would extract data from these components and explain your rationale.

2. A forensic investigator discovers a thumb drive during an investigation. Discuss the steps the investigator should take to ensure data integrity during the acquisition process.

3. What are the challenges associated with extracting data from eMMC storage in smartphones?

4. Identify and explain two primary differences between thumb drives and SD cards in terms of forensic analysis.

5. In what ways do the various encryption methods used in removable media (e.g., SD cards, thumb drives) impact the forensic analysis process?

6. Evaluate the implications of using proprietary data formats on the forensic analysis of smart cards and their applications.

7. How does the dynamic nature of data stored in cloud environments complicate the forensic examination of embedded chips?

8. Examine the role of authentication sticks in digital forensics and discuss how their unique features can aid or hinder investigations.

9. What considerations should a forensic examiner make when determining the best method for extracting data from removable media, considering variations in hardware and software?

10. Discuss the potential impact of rapid advancements in embedded chip technology on current forensic methodologies and tools.

11. What methods can forensic investigators use to analyze the data stored on a USB drive that has been encrypted using hardware-based encryption?

12. What are the primary security features found in Smart Cards that complicate forensic analysis?

13. You are investigating an insider data exfiltration case at a financial institution. A smart card and an encrypted thumb drive were recovered from the suspect's desk. How would you determine whether these devices were used in the breach, and what forensic approach would you take to validate your findings?

14. A forensic team encounters a smart card that is PIN-locked and may have a self-destruct trigger after several failed attempts. What acquisition strategy should they follow to preserve evidence without triggering data loss?

15. Compare and contrast the forensic procedures, challenges, and tools required for analyzing an encrypted TransFlash (microSD) card versus an authentication stick used in MFA.

16. You are tasked with investigating a cybercrime case where the primary suspect has used a hardware authentication stick (e.g., YubiKey) to access multiple secured systems. What forensic artifacts would you target, and how would you correlate them with system-level logs?

17. During a child exploitation case, a thumb drive is recovered with signs of formatting. Discuss the techniques and tools you would employ to recover deleted data and assess whether it had been deliberately wiped using anti-forensic methods.

18. In a breach of a restricted research lab, logs indicate access via a smart card. However, the suspect claims their card was cloned. What forensic steps would you take to verify whether the card used was original or a clone?

19. Explain how the file system hierarchy of a SIM card (MF, DF, EF) influences the prioritization and scope of data extraction during forensic analysis. Provide examples of forensic targets within each file type.

20. A national ID smart card is suspected of being used to sign falsified digital contracts. How would you conduct a forensic examination to validate whether the smart card's cryptographic signature was used, and what legal precautions must be considered?

21. You are examining an SD card suspected of storing malware that was used to compromise hospital equipment. What unique forensic considerations does this scenario involve in terms of evidentiary integrity and chain of custody?

22. Discuss the legal and procedural importance of cloning a smart card before analysis. What risks does direct access pose, especially with tamper-evident or self-destruct mechanisms?

23. How would the presence of wear-leveling algorithms in a thumb drive complicate recovery of deleted files, and what forensic techniques can help mitigate this issue?

24. You are investigating a case of espionage where encrypted TransFlash cards were discovered hidden in common objects. What strategies would you employ for secure extraction, decryption, and attribution?

25. A forensic examiner encounters a thumb drive with hidden partitions containing suspected stolen corporate documents. Explain how hidden volumes are detected and analyzed for legal admissibility.

26. Compare the forensic relevance and volatility of cryptographic keys stored on an authentication stick versus SMS-based 2FA data stored on a SIM card.

27. You are asked to train new digital forensics investigators. Design a comparative module explaining the differences in forensic acquisition and analysis between contact-based and contactless smart cards.

28. What challenges arise when forensic tools are incompatible with proprietary smart card architectures? Discuss how reverse engineering or protocol analysis can assist in such cases.

29. In an investigation involving multiple USB thumb drives, some contain bootable partitions. How does this affect forensic procedures and the potential scope of evidence?

30. A whistleblower claims their secure authentication stick was cloned and misused to access classified files. How can you forensically verify or refute the claim?

31. How do encryption standards used on smart cards and authentication sticks affect data recovery in forensic analysis? What methods can be used to legally access encrypted content?

32. A suspect's SIM card contains references to multiple IMSIs and LAIs, raising questions about SIM swapping. How would you construct a forensic timeline of SIM activity and link it to device behavior?

REFERENCES

[1] Wolf, M. *Computers as Components: Principles of Embedded Computing System Design*. 3rd edition. Morgan Kaufmann, 2022.

[2] Carrier, B. *File System Forensic Analysis*. Addison-Wesley, 2005.

[3] Nelson, B., Phillips, A., and Steuart, C. *Guide to Computer Forensics and Investigations: Processing Digital Evidence*. Cengage Learning, 2018.

[4] Hendry, M. *Smart Card Security and Applications*. 4th edition. Artech House, 1997.

[5] Taherdoost, H., Sahibuddin, S., and Jalaliyoon, N. "Smart card security: Technology and adoption," *International Journal of Security (IJS)*, vol. 5, no. 2, pp. 13–22, 2013. https://www.cscjournals.org/manuscript/Journals/IJS/Volume5/Issue2/IJS-84.pdf

[6] Krebs, B. *How Cyber Sleuths Cracked an ATM Shimmer Gang*, 2021. https://krebsonsecurity.com/2021/06/how-cyber-sleuths-cracked-an-atm-shimmer-gang/

[7] DOJ. *Two Men Sentenced in Child Pornography Cases*. U.S. Department of Justice, 2022. https://www.justice.gov/usao-ndok/pr/two-men-sentenced-child-pornography-cases

[8] Kim, D., and Solomon, M. *Fundamentals of Information Systems Security*. Jones & Bartlett Learning, 2019.

Chapter 5

Unmanned aerial vehicles (UAVs) forensics

A new generation of Unmanned Aerial Vehicles (UAVs) with information gathering, storage, and processing capabilities emerged as a result of advancements in embedded systems, nanotechnologies, sensor technologies, image processing, and navigation systems. Drones, often termed UAVs, are small, pilotless aircraft that are flown remotely via a Ground Control Station (GCS). Drones can capture both images and video sequences within a specific region, transmitting them to a remote server for storage and subsequent processing. Many cutting-edge technologies, such as high-resolution zoomable cameras, wireless RF antennas, recording devices, etc., are combined in the complex construction of drones. Depending on the device's requirements, sensors can take the shape of a camera, a GPS sensor, or a temperature sensor, among other variations. All these features elucidate the reasons why several organizations have integrated the use of drones into their services. Drones can be used practically everywhere to conduct reconnaissance, gather data, deploy resources, and carry a variety of payloads. The gathered information may be kept locally on the device or saved to an SD memory card. Drones make it possible for users to carry out tasks that would have previously been challenging due to physical access limitations or barriers. Drones have been widely used in the market, mostly to decrease manual labor and increase process efficiency in both commercial and non-commercial applications, such as recreation, education, law enforcement, and national security, to name a few. Drone technology is now used for sophisticated military and meteorological purposes. Small UAV toys, which can capture live movies and photographs, are also available today from a variety of toy merchants for a few hundred dollars. Most people view drones as either *toys* or *weapons*, two quite different forms of pilotless aircraft. It is either a little, insect-like device flying over parks or beaches viewing aerial panoramas, entering difficult-to-access locations, or it is a big plane spying on people and carrying a weapon. Drones can be grouped into four categories, according to the Center for a New American Security[1]:

DOI: 10.1201/9781003644255-5

1. **Hobbyist drones** are flown for leisure or other pastimes. They are readily available for a modest price and do not need formal infrastructure or training to operate (e.g., the DJI Mavic).
2. **Commercial and military drones** of a medium scale need institutional infrastructure and training. They are primarily employed by the military for payload delivery, reconnaissance, and surveillance purposes.
3. **Big military-focused drones** need military infrastructure and education. These drones are only used for military purposes.
4. **Stealth combat drones** contain very advanced technologies that are inaccessible to non-indigenous manufacturers.

Drones are continually evolving with respect to hardware, software, and networks. They come in a variety of shapes, sizes, and technical configurations with a range of features and capabilities. The camera, lithium batteries, and sensors are supported by sophisticated gimbals. Developers/vendors have improved recognition software that enables them to lock onto targets and follow them around, find and avoid obstacles, and automatically return to their launch location before running out of battery. These drones create a tremendous amount of vital data that reveals usage patterns and performance since they are outfitted with such cutting-edge capabilities.

In 2014, almost two million units were sold worldwide, and this number is rising quickly [1]. Nearly 90% of all drone sales globally fall under the second category, *military drones*. Business Insider (BI) Intelligence projected drone sales worth $12 billion in the United States by 2021.[2] Major players in the consumer market include (1) DJI, (2) 3D Robotics, and (3) Parrot. The Chinese company DJI, which holds 76.8% of the market, is the world leader in drone manufacture for commercial and recreational use, according to industry research group Drone II. The DJI Phantom 4 has a total weight of three pounds and can travel at least four miles without losing its video stream or remote controls. The DJI S900, the Phantom's bigger sibling, has a maximum payload of just less than seven pounds, while the Phantom can only carry a little over one pound when flying. Other businesses, such as Intel (3.7%), Yuneec (3.1%), and Parrot (3.1%), compete for the remaining market share. Vendors continually add new features, improving performance and energy economy, as well as smaller size, lighter weight, and improved usability to their UAV product lines.

UAV use is expanding as they become more economical, which opens the door to commercial exploitation. Anyone willing to pay around $2000 for one can probably fly over a prison yard and deliver a sizable package of illegal contraband to their friends inside. The DJI Phantom III has been used to drop bombs and conduct remote surveillance already [2]. Examiners need an in-depth understanding of drones' forensic techniques and the capabilities of existing tools to successfully extract the information needed for investigations. Primarily, forensic techniques should enable analysts to connect a drone to its owner as part of attribution/non-repudiation. This is a challenging task due to the proliferation of different drone types, the absence of drone security standards, the variations in drone components, structures, and storage media, and, finally, the need for appropriate forensic tools that enable investigators to uphold the integrity and chain of custody of their evidence. Another pertinent issue is the secure confiscation of a drone that is being flown inside a prohibited airspace. Targeting the radio controller-drone communication is appropriate in this situation; it is practical to attack the drone by interfering with the GPS signal. Controlling the flying drone becomes difficult when using a device that jams the GPS signal, and if it is flying in windy conditions, it may crash ultimately. The final query deals with the scenario of discovering a drone in an unapproved location. If forensic investigators can link the suspect's Command and Control (C&C) device, that is, the GCS, to that particular drone, they may be able to prove the suspect is guilty of the crime. He may, therefore, be held responsible for his actions.

5.1 UAV COMPONENTS AND MODELS

In the initial stages of developing robust forensic methodologies and workflows, it is essential for forensic investigators and researchers to understand where to locate crucial pieces of both physical and digital evidence. To achieve this goal, it is worth noting that a standard small Unmanned Aircraft System (sUAS or drone) comprises various essential components that can be found across diverse geographical locations [3, 4]:

1. The drone itself: Housing a radio transceiver module, CPU, internal flash memory, flight controller chip (potentially capable of data logging), multiple sensors (such as optical image sensors, gyroscopes, accelerometers, velocity sensors, magnetometers, GPS sensors, etc.), compass, batteries, collision avoidance detectors, spectrometers, spectrophotometers, wireless router, optionally attached camera, removable SD card, engines, QR code, serial and model numbers, and even small solar panels and carried payloads.
2. The battery charging system.
3. A radio controller, often a smartphone equipped with a specialized flight navigation application, acting as a remote controller. More advanced drones might be operable through First Person View (FPV) terminals or video goggles to provide telepresence.
4. An optional Wi-Fi range extender.
5. An optional laptop, possibly used for configuring other components.
6. A ground-level server or remote cloud environment, facilitating the transfer and storage of captured data.

All of these components can serve as physical evidence during a forensic investigation. There are different models of drones available on the market. Notable commercial manufacturers and their commonly encountered models include:

- DJI: Mavic series (e.g., Mavic Air 2, Mavic Mini 2), Phantom series (e.g., Phantom 4 Pro), Inspire series (e.g., Inspire 2), Spark, Matrice series (e.g., Matrice 300 RTK), and DJI FPV.
- Parrot: Anafi, Bebop 2, Disco, and Mambo.
- Autel Robotics: EVO series, including EVO Lite+, EVO Lite, and EVO 2.
- Yuneec: Typhoon series (e.g., Typhoon H Pro) and Mantis series (e.g., Mantis Q).
- Skydio: Skydio 2.
- PowerVision: PowerEgg X.

5.2 DRONE FORENSICS ANALYSIS METHODS

Drone forensics falls within the domain of smartphone and wireless forensics, which are components of the broader field of digital forensics. To protect public safety, studies have been conducted in the area of drone forensics, but further effort is needed to develop tools and standardized procedures that may help investigators in drone-related crimes. Inquiries must be addressed if a crime is committed, and a drone is found at the scene: Can we establish ownership? Can the drone be connected to the crime? What tasks, such as flight take-off information, in-flight information, and landing information, has the drone performed? What data can be gathered from that particular drone to assist law enforcement in attributing it to its owner? [5]. In addition, during the drone forensic analysis, questions may concern the data that are saved inside the drone, including how, what, who, and where. The following are the key inquiries that must be addressed:

1. How could the information be gathered and recorded?
2. Is it possible to extract flight data?
3. Can the media files be recovered?
4. How can the drone's ownership be established?

Investigations require the extraction of forensic data related to drone ownership (controller's identification, serial number, Android ID, etc.), flight path history (including takeoff location, flight attitudes, speed, flight duration, and distance covered), activated onboard sensors, photographic and video recordings, log files, system files, timestamps, and more. The primary aim is to substantiate the digital non-repudiation requirements by corroborating ownership evidence with indications of deliberate usage. Key discrete digital repositories within the drone, including:

1. Embedded operating systems and associated file systems and firmware,
2. Digital image files from the onboard camera and linked thumbnails or EXIF optical sensor metadata,
3. Digital video files from the onboard camera,
4. Telemetry data,
5. Flight trajectory details extracted from the flight controller chip and GPS coordinates.

Figure 5.1 illustrates the main drone-related evidence sources used in forensic investigations.

Extraction of the enumerated artifacts from UAV devices is difficult since they do not use a standardized data storage or file system. An analyst may start by locating the serial number of the drone. The authority might contact the DJI representatives to identify the owner of the aircraft using its serial number. The serial number is visible inside the drone's body. A DJI aircraft must be registered and linked to a specific account to take flight; thus, it is crucial to keep in mind that the serial number can be used by DJI officials to determine who the drone's owner is.

The drone's battery is uniquely identified by a serial number. The GCS's serial number is unique. The OS will identify the drone as removable media when using a USB cord to attach it. The location where the media files were collected can be determined by looking at each media file and the EXIF data that is integrated into the files.

Analysts may determine the precise location by putting the numbers on a map after determining the longitudes and latitudes. Since there is no clear/standardized way to extract the flight logs either, the drone may be identified as detachable storage when it is connected to a PC.

There are different kinds of drones, and each kind is unique in the ways that it can be connected to another drone. Some may use a direct USB cord and certain protocols like File Transfer Protocol (FTP), Telnet, and others. The rights given for accessing the drone also vary from vendor to vendor, and in many cases, access is limited to the system files or the media folder. As a result, since there are currently no consistent methods for conducting drone acquisition, each drone needs to be treated individually.

To hijack the drone, the investigator must first determine how the drone and the GCS communicate. The chip-off and JTAG techniques could also be used. Consequently, this method can aid in more effectively reading the data in the event of a damaged drone.

A study of the DJI Phantom III by Clark et al. [2] offered detailed insights into its proprietary file structures. Additionally, a forensically sound open-source tool called DRone Open source Parser (DROP) was developed based on their findings. DROP parses encrypted and encoded DAT files extracted

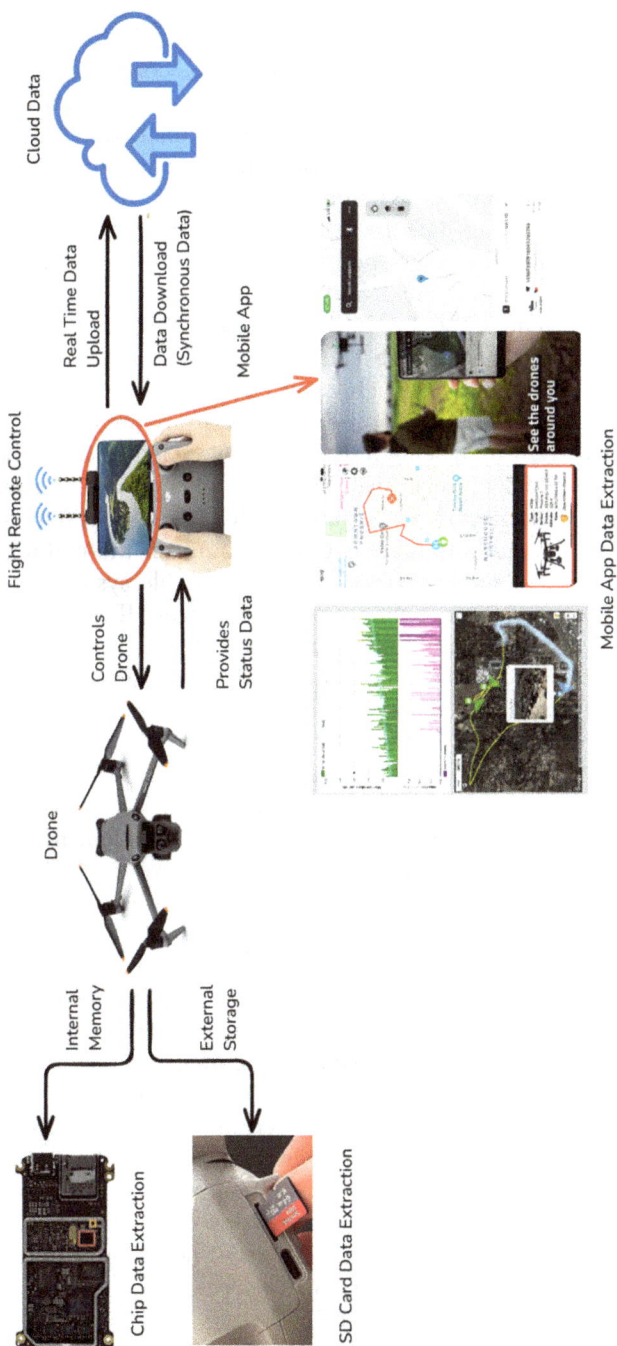

Figure 5.1 Primary sources of evidence in drone forensics.

from the drone's non-volatile internal storage. These DAT files contain valuable data, such as GPS locations, battery status, flight time, and more. The authors also shared initial findings about TXT files, which are also encrypted, and proprietary files found on the mobile device controlling the drone. These TXT files hold essential information. By extracting data from both the controlling mobile device and the drone itself, the research successfully established correlations and linked users to specific devices based on extracted metadata. Notably, the findings highlight that the optimal method for forensically acquiring data from the tested drone involves manually extracting the SD card by disassembling the drone. Importantly, the study cautions against turning on the drone during data acquisition, as doing so can alter data by generating new DAT files and potentially deleting stored information if the internal storage is full.

Bouafif et al. highlighted the significant challenges in the field of drone forensics, particularly through an in-depth case study involving the Parrot AR drone 2.0, thereby enhancing researchers' awareness of these challenges [3]. They introduce a comprehensive procedure for conducting drone forensic investigations, offering valuable guidance for future research endeavors in this domain. The authors present novel findings in the realm of drone forensics, showcasing the capability to access the file system via FTP or serial connections and retrieve the controller's Android ID, which can serve as a crucial tool in establishing ownership of the drone.

In addition, forensic analysts can employ tools like DroneShield,[3] which can be used to trace a drone back to its pilot when seizing a drone that is in an active state. Other tools, like the DroneGun jammer[4] (in RF-only mode), might cause the drone to return to its starting place, making it possible to trace the person operating it. Additionally, DroneGun can be used to shoot drones out of the air, which makes it simple for law enforcement to seize the device and carry out the necessary investigation.

5.2.1 Evidence extraction and analysis

Forensic investigators and researchers need to know where to seek relevant parts of (logical and physical) forensic evidence as a first step in creating sound forensic procedures and workflows. The owner of the drone, the history of its flight path (including the launch location, flight attitudes, flight time, and distance traveled), the onboard sensors that have been activated, the data they have been collecting, and the reason for the flight are some of the main artifacts.

With the objective of confirming the ownership of the drone and proof of its intentional use to validate the requirements of non-repudiation, the general methodology followed during drone forensics is:

1. **Confiscation:** Confiscate the UAV aircraft and make sure it is turned off to prevent data tampering from a distance. Based on fingerprint and DNA data, consider using conventional forensic criminal

investigation techniques to determine ownership. Make sure to keep these materials safe throughout the investigation.

2. **Acquisition:** Access and catalog the numerous artifacts and digital storage devices, including those found on the detachable SD card. The manufacturer, serial number, model number, MAC address, payload, and QR code of the drone are only a few examples of physical proof. To ensure the integrity of the digital forensic evidence and thereby verify that the onboard data collected is forensically certified, caution must be taken.

3. **Analysis:** Examine the different digital artifacts and evidence-containing files, including firmware, thumbnail images, EXIF metadata, Linux file systems, registry settings, active/hidden files, and mount files, to retrieve the evidence.

To produce factual data to support or refute a theory in a court of law, civil action, or other proceeding, drone forensics adheres to a strict scientific process of acquisition and analysis. The process of acquiring data for the first phase starts with the seizure, imaging, or collection of digital evidence to record questionable media, network activity, and logs. A replica (forensic) image of the original media evidence is made and verified when digital media are gathered.

JPEG photos have embedded information called EXIF data (Exchangeable Image File). Some of the tools, such as Autopsy, E3:Universal, ProDiscover, and Encase, are better at parsing and displaying EXIF data than others. Date, timestamp, file source, GPS, altitude, altitude reference, latitude, longitude, and other types of EXIF data are a few examples. This information might be useful in pinpointing the location and time of the photo shoot.

It is also important to note that the drones rely on the connected smartphone or smart controller for a reference time; if the time system on the smartphone were changed, the files the drones made would reflect the new timestamp.

5.2.2 Ground control station evidence

A drone is an aircraft that is operated remotely. It can record photos and video sequences of a specific area and send them to a distant server for archival and later analysis. The server can be placed in a secure cloud environment or co-located with the GCS. Typically, a handheld device like a radio controller, a smartphone, or a tablet is used to control the drone. Analysis of its forensic image can start after the duplicate image of the evidence is made. Evidence is gathered to reconstruct events or actions and present facts to the concerned party. Collecting relevant flight route information, identifying the drone's owner, and extracting relevant metadata linked to capture images or videos are done. A summary of the key forensic investigation results is given finally, together with an explanation of the techniques used to derive the findings. These might be used to support or refute explanations and assertions made.

What can be done to connect the suspect phone to the flying drone when law enforcement suspects someone of operating a drone in a prohibited area? The serial number of the remote controller used to control the drone may serve as the link between it and the ground control station (i.e., smartphone).

Once the remote controller's serial number has been located, the number will likely be kept in one of the application files for the app. The application files for the DJI GO application can be extracted using any smartphone acquisition tool. There is a clear connection between the drone and the smartphone. The *pilot.plist* file stores the serial number of the linked radio controller. Open the *com.dji.pilot.plist* file and extract the DJICModelName, where the C stands for the "controller," using any plist viewer. The smartphone under investigation can be used to operate the drone after determining the radio controller's serial number. Therefore, the owner of the phone must be able to describe how he is related to the drone that was found at the crime site.

The investigator must concentrate on the program files linked to the Freeflyight3 application used to control a Bebop Parrot drone when working with the device controlling the drone. The flight data are kept in the application files associated with the Freeflight3 application, much like the internal storage of a drone.

The files may be located in any of the following locations, depending on whether the controlling device is an Android or iOS smartphone:

1. /data/data/com.parrot.freeflight3/files/academy on Android
2. iOS: Documents/academy/com.parrot.freeflight3/Applications

The flight data is saved in *pud* format, just like the drone, including the file's related metadata.

The GCS has direct access to the drone's internal storage for the drone's media files (pictures and movies). Any media file can be downloaded or deleted by the user using only their smartphone. By gaining access to the media folder, the media files can be found.

The *com.parrot.freeflight3.plist* file needs to be reviewed to connect the GCS to the concerned drone. The file is located at:

1. Data/data/com.parrot.freeflight3/shared prefs on Android
2. Application/com.parrot.freeflight3/Library/Preferences on iOS

The Bebop Parrot drone may be operated without a controller by utilizing just the GCS. As a result, it is reliant on the drone's Wi-Fi network, which does not demand authentication to connect. Due to its reliance on this unprotected Wi-Fi network, it is open to de-authentication attacks, which could lead to another device stealing control of the drone.

5.2.3 External storage (SD CARD) evidence

SD (Secure Digital) cards are compact, portable flash memory devices that have become ubiquitous in digital storage, particularly in devices such as digital cameras, smartphones, tablets, and various portable gadgets. Their small form factor, combined with varying capacities from a few megabytes to several terabytes, makes them ideal for a wide array of applications, including the storage of multimedia files, applications, and documents. Because of their versatility and accessibility, SD cards are frequently encountered in digital forensic investigations, where they can house critical evidence, including user data, communications, and media files. Understanding the structure, importance, and forensic analysis of SD cards is essential for investigators.

As non-volatile memory devices, SD cards retain their data even when not powered, making them a reliable option for long-term storage. This characteristic is particularly valuable for portable devices that may be switched off or disconnected from power sources. SD cards come in various formats, including standard SD, SDHC (Secure Digital High Capacity), and SDXC (Secure Digital Extended Capacity), each offering different storage capacities and features tailored to specific use cases.

The fundamental operation of an SD card involves a controller interfacing with flash memory chips to manage data storage and retrieval. SD cards are designed for ease of use, allowing users to insert them into compatible devices for quick data transfer. This functionality often leads to them being overlooked in traditional digital forensic investigations. However, their role as a data storage medium means that they can contain significant amounts of information, often critical to investigations, including potentially incriminating data that users believe is deleted or hidden.

SD cards can be invaluable in criminal investigations due to the wealth of information they can contain. Users often utilize these devices to store a variety of data, including photographs, videos, documents, and communications, all of which may serve as vital evidence in a case. For instance, in investigations involving illegal activities such as drug trafficking or cybercrime, SD cards may contain multimedia evidence or documents that establish timelines, motives, or connections between suspects. Moreover, the compact nature of SD cards allows individuals engaged in illicit activities to conceal them easily, making thorough searches for these devices essential. Investigators must be diligent in identifying and analyzing SD cards during their inquiries, as even seemingly insignificant storage devices may hold critical evidence that could influence the outcome of a case.

5.2.3.1 SD card: physical structure and file system

The physical structure of SD cards consists of a small circuit board embedded with flash memory chips and a controller, all encased in a protective plastic shell. This structure is designed to withstand the rigors of everyday use while safeguarding the internal components. Understanding the architecture of SD cards is crucial for forensic analysts as it informs the methods employed during data recovery and analysis.

SD cards support various file systems, which dictate how data are organized and stored. Common file systems include FAT16 and FAT32, typically used for cards with lower capacities, and exFAT, preferred for SDXC cards. The choice of file system has implications for forensic analysis, as different systems offer varying capabilities for data recovery. For instance, FAT32 has limitations on file sizes, which can affect the retrieval of larger files, while exFAT supports larger volumes and file sizes, enhancing the possibilities for data extraction from high-capacity cards.

Understanding the file system in use is essential for forensic examiners, as it determines the appropriate techniques for recovering data. If the file system becomes corrupted or damaged, forensic tools may be required to reconstruct the file system or recover fragmented data, ensuring that investigators can access relevant information.

5.2.3.2 Forensic analysis of SD cards

Forensic analysis of SD cards typically follows a systematic process, beginning with the preservation of evidence and followed by data extraction, recovery, and analysis. The key steps involved in SD card forensics include:

1. **Imaging the SD Card:** As with any digital storage device, forensic examiners must create a bit-by-bit copy of the SD card's contents. This forensic image ensures that the original data remain untouched, preserving the integrity of the evidence. This step is critical, as SD cards, especially those using flash memory, can be easily overwritten if accessed improperly.
2. **Examining the File System:** Once an image is obtained, examiners analyze the file system to identify active and deleted files. Even if files have been deleted by the user, remnants of those files may still exist on the SD card. Tools such as file carving software can be used to recover partial or fully deleted data.
3. **Analyzing Metadata:** The metadata stored in files on SD cards is often just as important as the files themselves. Metadata can provide timestamps, geolocation data, device information, and other critical details that help reconstruct a suspect's activities.
4. **Recovering Deleted or Corrupted Data:** SD cards, especially those using wear-leveling techniques, can pose challenges for data recovery. Wear leveling spreads data across different sectors of the memory to prolong the lifespan of the card, which can result in fragmented or overwritten data. Forensic tools such as EnCase or Autopsy can help in recovering data from such devices, even when files have been fragmented or the card's file system is corrupt.

5. **Extracting Encrypted Data:** In cases where SD cards are encrypted, investigators may need to bypass encryption mechanisms to access the data. This may involve decrypting the SD card through passwords, brute-force techniques, or leveraging vulnerabilities in the encryption scheme, if applicable.

While this section focuses specifically on SD card forensics, the overarching forensic investigation process for various embedded digital devices, including SD cards, USB drives, and SIM cards, is discussed in Chapter 4, along with a visual representation of the standard investigative workflow.

5.2.3.3 SD card: forensic artifacts

During forensic investigations, SD cards can yield a wide array of digital artifacts that provide insights into user activities. These artifacts can include not only user files, such as photographs, videos, and documents, but also remnants of deleted data that may still exist on the card. The presence of metadata associated with these files can reveal crucial information about the file's origin, including when it was created and modified, as well as any geolocation data that may link the user to specific locations or events.

Additionally, system files and logs stored on SD cards may provide context regarding how the card was utilized within a device. Understanding these artifacts is key to reconstructing a timeline of events and drawing connections between suspects and criminal activities. Embedded device forensics is discussed in more depth in Chapter 4.

5.2.3.4 Legal considerations in SD card forensics

Conducting forensic analysis on SD cards necessitates adherence to strict legal standards to ensure that the evidence is preserved and admissible in court. Maintaining a clear chain of custody is essential to establishing the integrity of the evidence. Proper documentation of the examination process, including any interactions with the SD card and the tools used, helps bolster the credibility of the findings. Moreover, forensic investigators must be cautious when dealing with encrypted or password-protected SD cards. In many cases, law enforcement, mindful of data privacy laws, may especially need to obtain a search warrant to access the data stored on the card, emphasizing the importance of legal compliance throughout the forensic process.

5.3 CASE STUDY—DJI PHANTOM 3

The DJI Phantom 3 drone is a sophisticated drone widely used for professional photography, videography, and recreational flying. Due to its advanced features and capabilities, the Phantom 3 can store a wealth of data that may be crucial in a forensic investigation.

The DJI Phantom 3 drone has multiple storage components that can hold significant amounts of data. For a comprehensive forensic acquisition, three primary sources need to be imaged:

1. **Internal Memory of the Drone:** Built into the drone itself, and is used to store system files, configuration data, flight logs, and some user data. This memory is essential for understanding the drone's operational history and settings.
2. **External Memory of the Drone:** Consists of a removable microSD card. This card is used to store larger amounts of user data, such as high-resolution photos and videos captured during flights.
3. **Control Device:** Could be a smartphone, tablet, or dedicated remote controller. This device communicates with the drone and can store significant amounts of related data.

These sources collectively provide a comprehensive view of the drone's operations and user interactions. The following acquisition process will involve creating forensic images of each of these components using OSForensics.

5.3.1 Forensic acquisition using OSForensics

In this section, we demonstrate how to perform a forensic acquisition using OSForensics.

1. **Forensic Imaging of Drone Internal Memory**
   - Power off the DJI Phantom 3 drone and disconnect it from any network connections to prevent data alteration.
   - Connect the drone to your forensic workstation using the appropriate cables.
   - Open OSForensics on your forensic workstation.
   - Navigate to *Acquire > Create Image* to start the acquisition process.
   - Select the internal memory of the DJI Phantom 3 as the source.
   - Specify the destination for the acquired image, choosing the appropriate format (e.g., E01).
   - Enter relevant case information such as the case number, investigator name, and description.
   - Start the acquisition process and allow OSForensics to create a bit-by-bit copy of the internal memory.
   - Verify the integrity of the acquired image by comparing hash values.
2. **Forensic Imaging of Drone External Memory**
   - Safely remove the microSD card from the DJI Phantom 3.
   - Connect the microSD card to your forensic workstation through a write blocker.

- Open OSForensics and navigate to *Acquire > Create Image*.
- Select the external memory as the source.
- Specify the destination for the acquired image, ensuring the appropriate format and case details are entered.
- Start the acquisition process and create a bit-by-bit copy of the external memory.
- Verify the image integrity by comparing hash values.

3. **Forensic Imaging of Drone Controller Device**
   - Identify the control device used with the DJI Phantom 3.
   - Connect the control device to your forensic workstation using the appropriate cables.
   - If the control device is a smartphone or tablet, use OSForensics to perform a logical or physical acquisition, depending on the device's capabilities.
   - Navigate to *Acquire > Create Image* and select the control device as the source.
   - Specify the destination for the acquired image, enter the case details, and choose the appropriate format.
   - Start the acquisition process to create a bit-by-bit copy of the control device's data.
   - Verify the integrity of the acquired image by comparing hash values.

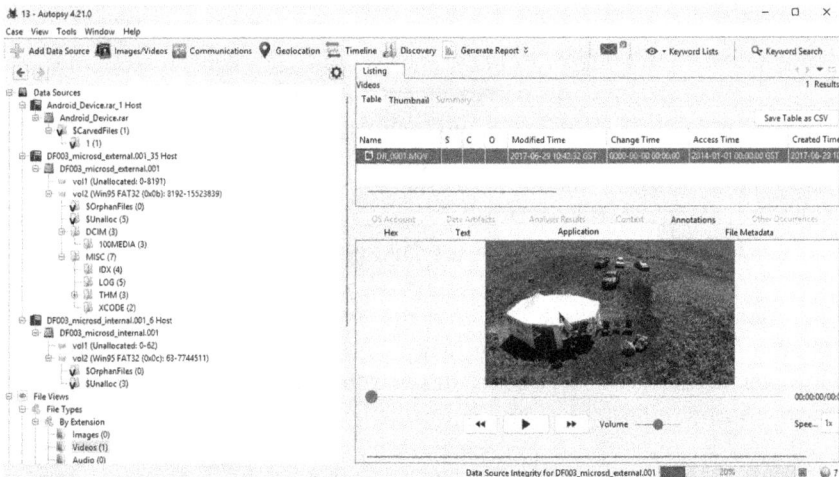

Figure 5.2 Forensic imaging results of DJI Phantom 3—internal, external, and control device.

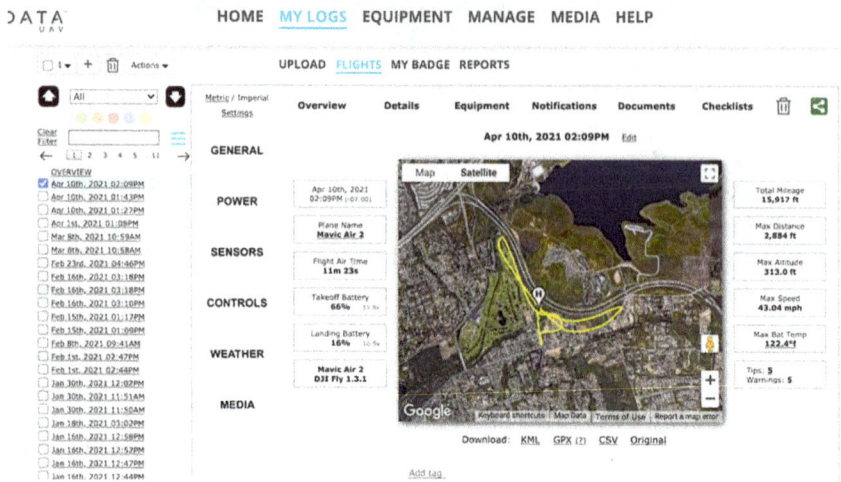

Figure 5.3 DJI Phantom 3 flights details from AirData website.

4. **Analyzing the Acquired Images**
   - Load the acquired images into OSForensics for detailed analysis.
   - Use the tool's features to search, filter, and examine the data, including file carving, timeline analysis, and keyword searches.
   - Focus on extracting relevant evidence such as flight logs, user activity, and media files.
   - Tools such as FTK Imager and DatCon software are pivotal for parsing .*DAT* files, converting them into readable formats like CSV. These records offer detailed insights into flight activities, including timestamps, altitudes, speeds, and GPS coordinates, vital for reconstructing drone movements. Additionally, these files contain angular measurements and command data received during flights, providing comprehensive information for forensic analysis.

5.4 CHALLENGES IN DRONE FORENSICS

Forensic investigators and researchers must use standard investigation frameworks and technologies to make UAV forensics easier and efficient. However, due to the unique combination of its hardware and software containers, drone forensics is posed with significant challenges:

1. Small Unmanned Aerial System (sUAS) parts, such as servers, radio controllers, and drones that make up the physical evidence in a forensic inquiry, can be dispersed around the scene in different locations. Furthermore, it can be challenging to establish a reliable forensic link between a confiscated drone and its accompanying radio controller to determine ownership [6].

2. The remote controller is typically required to access the flight data through the onboard flight controller chip, and Law Enforcement Agencies (LEAs) and forensic investigators are unlikely to have access to the remote controller. Additionally, the flight information that is taken from the flight controller chip is often encrypted. Thus, the absence of the remote controller makes forensic investigation more difficult.

3. Data acquisition, or getting a forensic image of onboard drone media, may not always be easy or doable.

4. Regulation, safety, privacy, security, and the hazy business model environment are only a few of the difficulties brought on by the quick development of drones for civilian use.

5. Identification of drone owners is challenging because some are operable without registering the owner's name, address, and other crucial identifying information.

6. Drones may use a variety of file systems. More than five different file system types can be found on a single UAV aircraft, some of which cannot be identified with current commercial forensic software. Software, hardware, and firmware for the onboard drone are not yet standardized and differ between vendors. For instance, neither a uniform format for flight data nor a de facto standard protocol for flight controllers exists at the moment. Users can also improve a drone's capabilities by adding new parts or by altering it using Software Development Kits (SDKs), which are made available by the majority of drone manufacturers.

7. Drones mainly rely on RAMs; therefore, they can only retain the information they store there while they are powered up. Also, data persistence may be an issue since, in contrast to traditional digital forensics, it is less clear where the data came from and where it is stored [7]. However, some sensor data can be configured to be posted on file-sharing or social networking websites, uploaded to a secure server located in a private or public cloud, or both. To fully comprehend everything related to the drone, digital investigators must put up greater effort.

8. Commercial drones that lack data logging features on their flight controls.

9. The forensic investigation may be compromised if a suspect uses the controller to remotely erase media files from the drone or do a full factory reset.

10. The handset controller's GPS location, as well as GPS data about the drone's flight path, are both saved in the drone as GPS data. With the aid of GPS spoofing software, both types of GPS data can be altered or prevented from being captured, obscuring the real drone's flight path or the location of the phone during the flight.

11. In some circumstances, obtaining a forensic image of a flying UAV camera's content without endangering its integrity may not be simple or even viable. For forensic imaging, several drones include USB ports that prevent direct access to the physical disk. Due to this, forensic

investigators must conduct a remote forensic imaging technique using wireless connections. It can be challenging for the investigator to simply plug in a forensic device and extract the digital evidence from some embedded data storage containers (such as the recorded flight data stored in the flight controller chip). The OS files and information may not be included in the forensic picture due to probable access restrictions, requiring the forensic analysts to connect to the UAV through Telnet and use conventional commands to view system folders and configuration files.

12. When a case is filed before a court, it is essential to be able to locate and produce proof of illegal drone usage. The data extraction procedure can be difficult because there are numerous types of drones, each with a unique set of technological components, features, and capabilities. Although it is challenging for the law to keep up with the developments in drone technology and the surrounding environment. To protect personal property rights and public safety, drone use is not yet controlled. Information now available from the majority of nations indicates government efforts to create regulations that can regulate the frequent use of drones by civilians. There are multiple parties with interests in this process: end users drone manufacturers, software providers, and governments at the federal, state, and local levels are just a few. Law enforcement can act by seizing the drone if it crashes inside a crime scene. This suggested method can be used by law enforcement to de-authenticate the drone, take control of it, and seize it if it is in midair. The correct legal and forensic best practices for seizure should be followed in both situations. This means that the confiscation was carried out by law enforcement with the necessary warrants or the proper authority. Law enforcement can examine the drone after it has been seized.

END OF CHAPTER QUESTIONS

1. Discuss how forensic investigators can use UAV telemetry logs to reconstruct the flight path of a drone. Include considerations regarding the accuracy of timestamps, GPS data, and altitude measurements.
2. Analyze how Wi-Fi and radio frequency (RF) signal interference can impact drone communications and the forensic examination of drone activity in cases of suspected signal jamming or hijacking.
3. In a drone forensics case where encryption is used for communication between the drone and its controller, describe the steps you would take to decrypt the transmitted data and verify the integrity of the evidence collected.
4. Explain how chain-of-custody is maintained in a forensic investigation involving drone hardware and data, and discuss the potential pitfalls if these procedures are not strictly followed.

5. Analyze how forensic investigators can use RF spectrum analysis to detect drones operating in sensitive areas without physically recovering the drone itself. What limitations exist with this approach?

6. Discuss the legal challenges associated with recovering and using encrypted telemetry and flight logs from commercial drones in forensic investigations. How do privacy laws impact the process?

7. A suspect's drone was recovered after it allegedly collided with critical infrastructure. How would you approach extracting evidence from the drone's onboard sensors (e.g., gyroscope, accelerometer, barometer) to establish the exact cause of the collision?

8. Suppose a drone was used in a high-profile case involving illegal surveillance. After retrieving the drone, what forensic techniques would you employ to validate its camera usage at specific times and locations, and what challenges might you encounter?

9. Investigators found a drone that has been submerged in water for an extended period. Explain the forensic recovery process for electronic components, and detail the challenges associated with data recovery from water-damaged drones.

10. A drone's collision with a private property has left its flight logs inaccessible due to a corrupted memory card. What advanced data recovery techniques could you employ to retrieve the necessary evidence, and how would you ensure its admissibility in court?

11. In a case where a drone was flown illegally in a restricted airspace, investigators suspect the use of third-party software to bypass geofencing restrictions. How would you approach the forensic analysis of both the drone and the pilot's control device to confirm this suspicion?

12. A drone crash occurred during an active investigation, and there are suspicions that the drone was remotely hacked mid-flight. Describe your approach to verifying the integrity of the drone's control system and wireless communication logs to determine if a cyber-attack occurred.

13. You are asked to investigate the unauthorized use of a DJI drone in a restricted urban airspace. Explain how you would approach identifying the drone's owner using onboard artifacts and control device data. Discuss the forensic tools and steps required.

14. Discuss the technical and evidentiary challenges of acquiring encrypted flight logs from a confiscated drone. How would you preserve integrity and ensure admissibility of data when using tools like DROP or OSForensics?

15. In a drone-related vandalism case, the onboard SD card appears corrupted. Describe your forensic recovery process, the tools you would employ, and how you would validate any recovered artifacts in court.

16. During an international cyber-espionage investigation, a UAV with proprietary firmware and unknown file systems is found. How would you reverse-engineer its storage and extract useful forensic artifacts?

17. A recreational drone crashes into critical infrastructure, and the suspect claims GPS spoofing caused the crash. Describe how you would forensically determine whether the drone was manipulated mid-flight.
18. Compare forensic acquisition and analysis workflows for three components: Internal drone memory, SD card storage, and the Ground Control Station (GCS). Which presents the greatest evidentiary challenge and why?
19. You are investigating a high-profile surveillance operation involving a DJI Phantom 3. How would you use camera metadata, flight trajectory, and app-based controller data to confirm surveillance intent and identify the pilot?
20. Describe the legal and ethical concerns in using RF-based drone interception tools (e.g., DroneGun, DroneShield) during forensic seizure. How do such methods affect the chain of custody and evidentiary handling?
21. In a case where a drone is found mid-mission with unknown payload, what forensic steps would you take to safely analyze its physical components and correlate them with digital findings?
22. A commercial drone is suspected of having been modified using SDKs. Explain how you would detect, analyze, and validate such software or hardware modifications during forensic examination.
23. Describe how forensic investigators can leverage EXIF metadata from drone-captured images or videos to reconstruct suspect behavior and establish location or time-based patterns.
24. Discuss how fragmented drone parts (e.g., camera, controller, motors) recovered from a crash site can be linked forensically to reconstruct the device's flight behavior and ownership.
25. What are the forensic limitations of current commercial tools in acquiring drone data from multiple file systems (e.g., Linux, FAT32, proprietary)? How can investigators overcome these constraints?
26. A drone's onboard storage contains both DAT and TXT encrypted logs. Detail a multi-step process for decrypting and analyzing these files, and discuss how they can be used to establish operator intent.
27. How would you construct a comprehensive forensic timeline involving a drone, a smartphone controller, and cloud storage logs to validate a suspect's involvement in aerial surveillance?
28. The GPS logs on a drone and the control app show inconsistent locations. Discuss how you would investigate this discrepancy and whether GPS spoofing or sensor malfunction is more likely.
29. Outline a forensic acquisition strategy for a flying drone that must be seized without altering onboard data. What are the risks and what hardware/software precautions would you use?
30. In a smart city surveillance breach, several drones with similar configurations are discovered. Explain how forensic markers (e.g., MAC address, firmware ID, controller pairing ID) help distinguish individual drone identities.

31. Critically evaluate the effectiveness of using drone forensic evidence in criminal proceedings. What safeguards must be in place to defend the evidence chain, interpretation accuracy, and tool reliability?

32. You are investigating a drone-aided burglary in a smart city. The drone, a smartwatch, and a smart home security system were all operational in the timeframe. Discuss how you would collect, synchronize, and analyze evidence across these heterogeneous IoT systems to establish the suspect's physical presence and intent.

33. During a corporate data breach investigation, a UAV was used to intercept wireless communications. The drone was recovered alongside a Raspberry Pi and an SD card. Design a forensic methodology to analyze these devices and determine whether data exfiltration occurred.

34. Describe a scenario where data from a smart home assistant (e.g., Alexa), a drone's camera footage, and an owner's smartwatch collectively contribute to solving a physical assault case. What are the forensic integration and validation challenges?

35. Explain how the flight controller, firmware logs, and environmental sensors on a drone could collectively help determine whether a crash was accidental or caused by operator negligence or tampering.

36. The following is flight data from an internal memory of a DJI drone exported from DatCon software. The outputs are exported as CSV, Event Log File, and Config Log File (as shown in the screenshots). Examine each of the three files and mention in general terms what type of information these files include and give detailed description of specific details you could note from the provided information on how they correlate and would help in an investigation.

NOTES

1 https://www.cnas.org/.
2 https://www.businessinsider.com/drone-technology-uses-applications#:~:text=Insider%20Intelligence%20expects%20sales%20of.
3 https://www.droneshield.com/.
4 https://www.droneshield.com/products/dronegun-tactical.

REFERENCES

[1] Clarke, R. and Bennett Moses, L. "The regulation of civilian drones' impacts on public safety," *Computer Law & Security Review*, vol. 30, no. 3, pp. 263–285, Jun. 2014, doi: 10.1016/j.clsr.2014.03.007

[2] Clark, D. R., Meffert, C., Baggili, I., and Breitinger, F., "DROP (DRone Open source Parser) your drone: Forensic analysis of the DJI Phantom III," *Digital Investigation*, vol. 22, pp. S3–S14, Aug. 2017, doi: 10.1016/j.diin.2017.06.013

[3] Bouafif, H., Kamoun, F., and Iqbal, F., "Towards a better understanding of drone forensics," *International Journal of Digital Crime and Forensics*, vol. 12, no. 1, pp. 35–57, Jan. 2020, doi: 10.4018/IJDCF.2020010103

[4] Yousef, M., Iqbal, F., and Hussain, M., "Drone forensics: A detailed analysis of emerging DJI models," In *2020 11th International Conference on Information and Communication Systems (ICICS)*, pp. 066–071, 2020, Apr., IEEE.

[5] Al-Room, K., Iqbal, F., Baker, T., Shah, B., Yankson, B., MacDermott, A., and Hung, P. C. "Drone forensics: A case study of digital forensic investigations conducted on common drone models," *International Journal of Digital Crime and Forensics (IJDCF)*, vol. 13, no. 1, pp. 1–25, 2021.

[6] Bouafif, H., Kamoun, F., Iqbal, F., and Marrington, A. "Drone forensics: challenges and new insights," In *2018 9th IFIP International Conference on New Technologies, Mobility and Security (NTMS)*, Feb., 2018, pp. 1–6. IEEE.

[7] Horsman, G. "Unmanned aerial vehicles: A preliminary analysis of forensic challenges," *Digital Investigation*, vol. 16, pp. 1–11, 2016.

Chapter 6

Social robot forensics

Social robots are IoT devices capable of interacting with humans and serve as useful tools for day-to-day tasks. These robots use IoT technology to provide varying functionality and rely on *supervised learning* to customize their utilization of the IoT to various people and environments. Their development has resulted in the replacement of human labor in various industries with applications in public spaces such as assisted living, medical facilities, and airports. Robots are now thought to be prepared to interact with us at work, home, and public settings because of technological breakthroughs and innovations in AI. Web service capabilities, AI and ML analytics and predictions, device data synchronization across platforms, and interaction with other IoT devices and services are some of these robots' important characteristics.

A robot designed to imitate the human body is called a *humanoid*. For example, its design can be utilized for functional tasks like interacting with tools and environments created by humans, as well as experimental tasks like researching bipedal locomotion, etc. Similarly, social robots are described as mobile, autonomous devices built to communicate with people. This interaction entails demonstrating social behaviors such as recognizing, following, and helping their owners in conversation.

Some estimates predict that worldwide spending on robotics, and humanoids, will grow to $188 billion per annum [1]. The use of social humanoid robots is a technological advancement that has recently attracted notice in the literature. Since their commercialization, social robots have gained popularity as useful tools to help people with daily tasks. People's abilities to complete daily tasks steadily decline as they get older. Therefore, there is a critical need for research on the advantages provided by humanoid robots. Humanoid robots typically engage with humans as natural social partners, with elements including voice, gestures, and eye-gaze referring to the users' social context and data. The way anthropomorphic robot users interact with them suggests that people are more accepting of robots. For instance, previous studies indicate that an embodied humanoid robot is considerably more likely to gain consumers' trust than a disembodied interactive kiosk. The study of how to comprehend, design, and assess robots for use by or

DOI: 10.1201/9781003644255-6

interaction with people from a social-technical standpoint is known as Human-Robot Interaction (HRI).

Social (companion) robots, such as Pepper, Buddy, Miko, Lynx, Misty Robotics' Misty II, Amazon Astro, and ASUS's Zenbo, are devices that comprise a physical humanoid robot component that connects through a network infrastructure to online services that enhance traditional robot functionalities. Robots can typically be controlled via smartphone controllers that can communicate commands after establishing a connection with them. Popular social robots like Zenbo can carry out basic tasks around the house. They aim to make household chores for a family comfortable and simple to complete. Additionally, they are made to communicate with young people, adults, and senior citizens. For instance, they can show pictures and read children's favorite stories. Additionally, they can be used to operate household appliances and carry out surveillance functions. These robots contain sensors that can detect falls or communicate with other family members to aid. Their ability to adapt to the environment and more human-like behavior make them suitable for families.

Additionally, Zenbo is simple to access on cell phones, and users may use the built-in camera to record occurrences. For instance, such events might serve as a reminder for doctor appointments, workout plans, and meditation sessions. Additionally, social robots are capable of carrying out more general duties, including handling video conversations, smart home controls, social media interactions, and interactive communication.

As a potential incursion on the communication lines between humans and social robots is regarded to be one of the simplest attack vectors due to the use of *open communication networks*, social robots are particularly vulnerable to cyberattacks. For instance, an Amazon Echo (an Alexa-enabled speaker) was seized in a murder investigation in 2015 because it was believed to have gathered information that could have verified the involvement of the primary suspect [2]. It is believed that social robots' forensic analysis needs a comprehensive and varied approach due to the sophisticated capabilities of such devices. A social robot can be a rich source of sensitive data about individuals and environments, delivering additional information during a crime scene investigation. In the case of social robots, exploration and experimentation into the multiplicity of devices and prospective evidence types are required, much like in the case of UAV drones, because current forensic procedures were created for a different generation of evidence sources, such as one-unit/singular smartphones and desktop client devices.

6.1 ROBOT OPERATING SYSTEM

Different technological ecosystems, such as hardware, firmware, and OSs, make up robots' OSs. A shared feature of the social robots that are now on the market in the healthcare industry is their Android-based OS, albeit this may not always be the case.

Zenbo, Pepper, and Sanbot humanoids can link to many smart home devices and offer features that appeal to people of all ages. These particular humanoids all run on the Android OS. Large-scale connectivity is provided by real-time monitoring based on the data gathered from the connected devices. We now have the chance to create programs that can adapt to the many needs of contemporary society, thanks to the ongoing advancements in humanoid robotics and human interaction. Non-invasive sensors make it possible to gather and use the information that is retrieved, which concurrently increases the necessity to protect personal information.

Images, cloud data, GPS data, databases, files, and network logs can all be included in the data produced by Robot OSs (ROSs). The maximum output from ROS is what a forensics examiner is looking for, such as the most recent memory dump, cached files, and deleted files or images.

6.2 FORENSIC METHODOLOGY

Different types of evidence sources are catered to by current forensic procedures for robots. In contrast to IoT, where objects of forensic interest may not always be available or accessible, it is assumed that they will be available and accessible. In a changing regulatory environment, a new era of best practices and digital forensics methods is needed to concurrently validate and use physical and digital evidence. When identifying evidence at crime scenes using IoT, numerous interconnected and dependent devices may be used, and the order of processing may need to be prioritized. For extending and developing applicable use cases and digital forensic procedures, it is essential to comprehend how investigators may be presented with crime scenes in the future. A general forensic methodology followed to perform forensic analysis of robots may consist of the following steps:

Data generation	1. Factory reset the ROS
	2. Acquire the initial forensic image from the device
	3. Install applications on the chosen devices
	4. Initial setup
	5. Operate the robot
Data acquisition	6. Acquire the final forensic image from the robot.
	7. Use the hashes from previous acquisitions to identify changes and extract useful artifacts.
Data analysis	8. Analyze robot artifacts and related applications' data

6.2.1 Zenbo robot

ASUS Zenbo robot is an IoT device running on a well-known OS, that is, Android version 6.0.1. To perform device-specific forensics, an investigative scenario involving the use of the Zenbo Robot, Zenbo Master app, and Zenbo App Builder, two applications that interact with the device, needs to be analyzed. This may entail performing a set of controlled experiments that involve several scenarios, each one referring to a specific usage scenario (e.g., initiating and receiving video calls, sending voice commands, getting alert reminders, using storytelling mode, etc.) during which a typical record of user activities has taken place. These activities enable the forensic analyst to generate data to forensically examine the social humanoid Zenbo robot, examine the companion app (XXXXX), and examine the companion network. Details of the investigative scenario and stages of methodology are described below.

Zenbo Master is an application developed by AsusTek Computer Inc. and is available on both Google Play and App Store. Through this program, Zenbo's owner and any connected family members and friends can communicate with the robot remotely. Features include making and receiving video calls, speaking to the robot, receiving alerts for events like reminders and emergencies, taking and viewing images that are kept on Zenbo, and more. ASUS does not offer a different web console for managing Zenbo's settings.

ASUSTek also created the *Zenbo App Builder* visual development platform to give customers an interface for quickly creating their applications that can utilize Zenbo's features, like movement expressions. App Builder is available as an application for Android and iOS as well as through a web browser. By connecting the robot and device to the same Wi-Fi access point and then turning on the Zenbo App Builder app on the robot, the produced applications, which have the extension *ZBA*, can be copied to Zenbo over the Internet. This indicates that Zenbo App Builder is accessible on both the robot and the developer's devices.

It is important to note that Zenbo App Builder permits media upload as part of the created apps. When an app is produced using a browser, executable files, and other non-media files can be added; however, this is not possible when an app is developed for iOS or Android unless the file extensions are changed. Another point to note is that, unlike smartphone app development using Zenbo App Builder, generating the app through a regular browser does not require ASUS login information.

6.2.1.1 Analysis tools

A variety of tools can be used to perform analysis of the data found in humanoid social robots and IoT devices. Mature solutions that are used by professional forensic examiners are a best practice. Open-source tools such as Autopsy and OSForensics, as well as commercial solutions such as AccessData FTK Imager, Magnet Axiom, and Cellebrite UFED Touch, are some examples of tools that may be utilized.

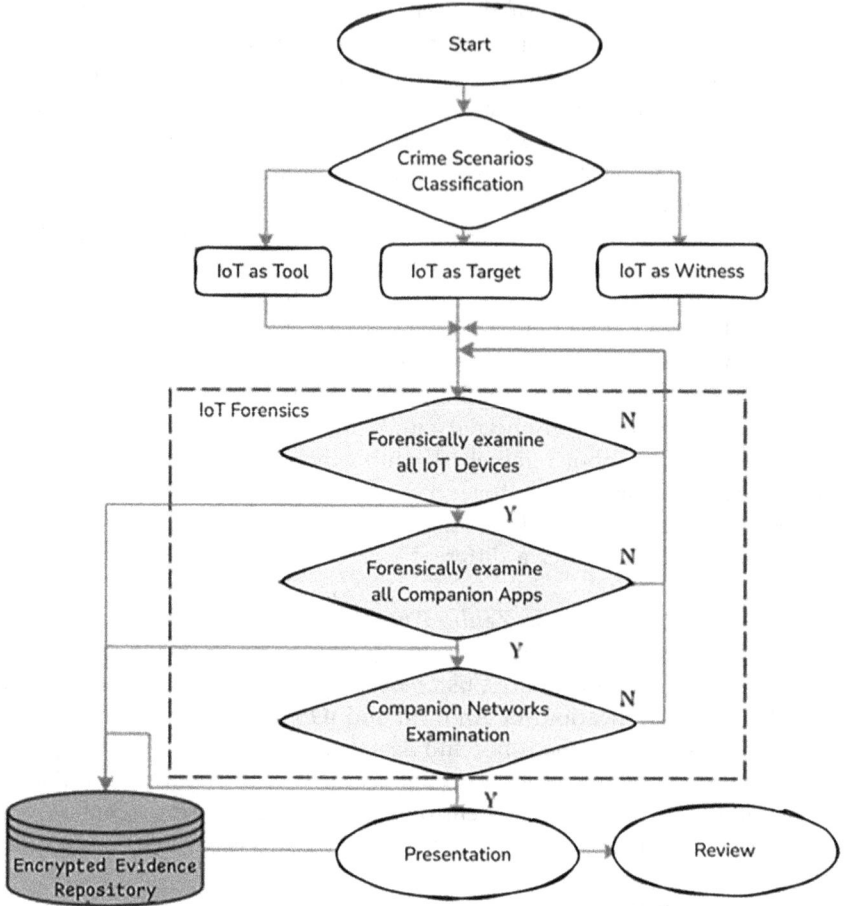

Figure 6.1 Forensic methodology.

The stipulated forensic methodology is illustrated in Figure 6.1 while Figure 6.2 provides forensic acquisition methods for sample social robots using specific methods/tools.

6.2.1.2 Practical forensic acquisition of Zenbo with ADB

Android Debug Bridge (ADB) is a forensic tool used to investigate Android devices. Let us use this tool to acquire the forensic image of the Zenbo robot.

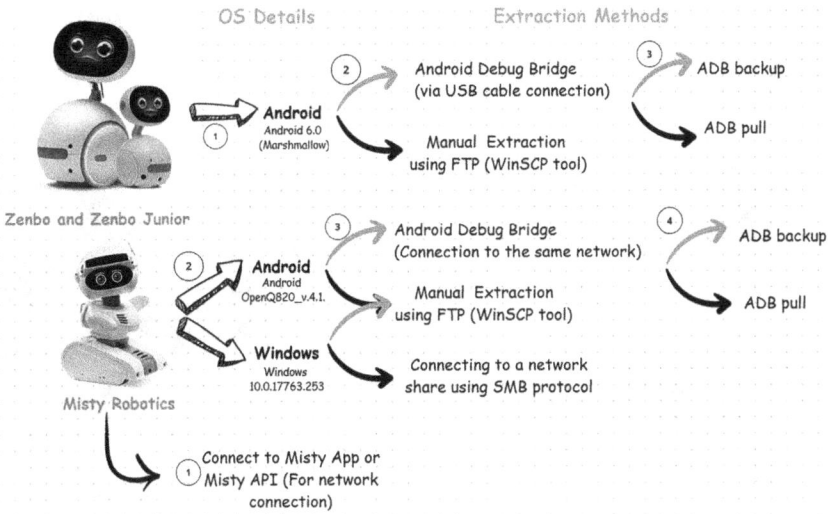

Figure 6.2 Forensic acquisition methods of Social robots.

1. Connect Zenbo to a workstation using a USB cable and use the *adb devices* command to see the list of connected Android devices.

Figure 6.3 ADB list of connected devices.

2. After confirming the right device is connected, access the shell and list the device directories using the *adb shell* and the *ls* command, respectively.

Figure 6.4 Accessing the Shell.

3. Try accessing the root directory if permissions allow. If not, get the backup of the device using the command *adb backup*.

```
shell@ASUS_ZENBO:/ $ whoami
shell
shell@ASUS_ZENBO:/ $ su
/system/bin/sh: su: not found
127|shell@ASUS_ZENBO:/ $
```

Figure 6.5 Trying to access the root directory.

```
PS C:\Users\ituser\Downloads\platform-tools_r34.0.5-windows\platform-tools> ./adb backup
-apk -shared -all -f zenbo_backup.ab
WARNING: adb backup is deprecated and may be removed in a future release
Now unlock your device and confirm the backup operation...
```

Figure 6.6 Getting a Zenbo backup.

4. Use the *adb pull* command if you want to retrieve specific directories/paths one by one to the local system. Include a specific directory path to save the pulled content.

```
adb pull /data C:\Users\ituser\Desktop\zen\data
adb pull /cache C:\Users\ituser\Desktop\zen\cache
adb pull /config C:\Users\ituser\Desktop\zen\config
adb pull /etc C:\Users\ituser\Desktop\zen\etc
adb pull /init C:\Users\ituser\Desktop\zen\init
adb pull /proc C:\Users\ituser\Desktop\zen\proc
adb pull /root C:\Users\ituser\Desktop\zen\root
adb pull /sbin C:\Users\ituser\Desktop\zen\sbin
adb pull /sys C:\Users\ituser\Desktop\zen\sys
adb pull /system C:\Users\ituser\Desktop\zen\system
adb pull /vendor C:\Users\ituser\Desktop\zen\vendor
adb pull /sdcard C:\Users\ituser\Desktop\zen\sdcard
adb pull /init.rc C:\Users\ituser\Desktop\zen\init.rc
adb pull /init.environ.rc C:\Users\ituser\Desktop\zen\init.environ.rc
adb pull /init.zygote32.rc C:\Users\ituser\Desktop\zen\init.zygote32.rc
adb pull /init.zygote64_32.rc C:\Users\ituser\Desktop\zen\init.zygote64_32.rc
adb pull /init.recovery.x2_cht_hr.rc C:\Users\ituser\Desktop\zen\init.recovery.rc
adb pull /selinux_version C:\Users\ituser\Desktop\zen\selinux_version
adb pull /sepolicy C:\Users\ituser\Desktop\zen\sepolicy
```

Figure 6.7 Pulling files to local workstation.

5. Optional: Use the *df* command to display information about total space and available space on a file system.

```
shell@ASUS_NICOLA_C1:/ $ df
Filesystem           Size     Used     Free   Blksize
/                   923.2M    5.0M   918.2M    4096
/dev                948.9M   48.0K   948.8M    4096
/sys/fs/cgroup      948.9M    0.0K   948.9M    4096
/sys/fs/cgroup/memory: Permission denied
/mnt                948.9M    0.0K   948.9M    4096
/system               3.4G    2.9G   480.8M    4096
/cache               94.4M    1.3M    93.1M    4096
/config               3.9M   48.0K    3.8M    4096
/factory              3.9M  732.0K    3.1M    4096
/storage            948.9M    0.0K   948.9M    4096
/sys/fs/cgroup/cpuset: Permission denied
/data                10.5G    1.7G     8.8G    4096
/mnt/runtime/default/emulated: Permission denied
/storage/emulated    10.5G    1.7G     8.8G    4096
/mnt/runtime/read/emulated: Permission denied
/mnt/runtime/write/emulated: Permission denied
1|shell@ASUS_NICOLA_C1:/ $
```

Figure 6.8 Zenbo file system.

6. Optional: Use direct commands such as *mount* or *cat* **** to display the contents of a file inside adb.

```
shell@ASUS_NICOLA_C1:/ $ mount
rootfs / rootfs ro,seclabel,size=945348k,nr_inodes=236337 0 0
tmpfs /dev tmpfs rw,seclabel,nosuid,relatime,mode=755 0 0
devpts /dev/pts devpts rw,seclabel,relatime,mode=600 0 0
proc /proc proc rw,relatime 0 0
sysfs /sys sysfs rw,seclabel,relatime 0 0
selinuxfs /sys/fs/selinux selinuxfs rw,relatime 0 0
binfmt_misc /proc/sys/fs/binfmt_misc binfmt_misc rw,relatime 0 0
debugfs /sys/kernel/debug debugfs rw,seclabel,relatime 0 0
none /acct cgroup rw,relatime,cpuacct 0 0
none /sys/fs/cgroup tmpfs rw,seclabel,relatime,mode=750,gid=1000 0 0
none /sys/fs/cgroup/memory cgroup rw,relatime,memory 0 0
tmpfs /mnt tmpfs rw,seclabel,relatime,mode=755,gid=1000 0 0
none /dev/memcg cgroup rw,relatime,memory 0 0
none /dev/cpuctl cgroup rw,relatime,cpu 0 0
none /dev/cpuset cgroup rw,relatime,cpuset,noprefix,release_agent=/sbin/cpuset
pstore /sys/fs/pstore pstore rw,seclabel,relatime 0 0
none /sys/firmware/efi/efivars efivarfs rw,relatime 0 0
/dev/block/dm-0 /system ext4 ro,seclabel,relatime,data=ordered 0 0
/dev/block/by-name/cache /cache ext4 rw,seclabel,nosuid,nodev,noatime,
/dev/block/by-name/android_config /config ext4 rw,seclabel,nosuid,nodev,noatim
/dev/block/by-name/android_factory /factory ext4 rw,seclabel,nosuid,nodev,noat
adb /dev/usb-ffs/adb functionfs rw,relatime 0 0
tmpfs /storage tmpfs rw,seclabel,relatime,mode=755,gid=1000 0 0
```

Figure 6.9 Using the "mount" command to display file contents.

6.2.1.3 Forensic analysis of Zenbo using autopsy

Another tool well-suited for the forensic examination of robotic assistants is Autopsy. Let us undertake a forensic analysis using this tool, focusing on a Zenbo home assistance robot. Autopsy is a comprehensive digital forensics platform that facilitates analysis of data from various devices, including specialized robots like Zenbo. To begin the forensic process with Autopsy, connect Zenbo to your forensic workstation. Launch the Autopsy application and follow the structured steps provided below:

1. Create a new case and fill out the new case information.
2. Add a data source. Autopsy supports multiple types of data sources, including disk image, local disk, and logical files.

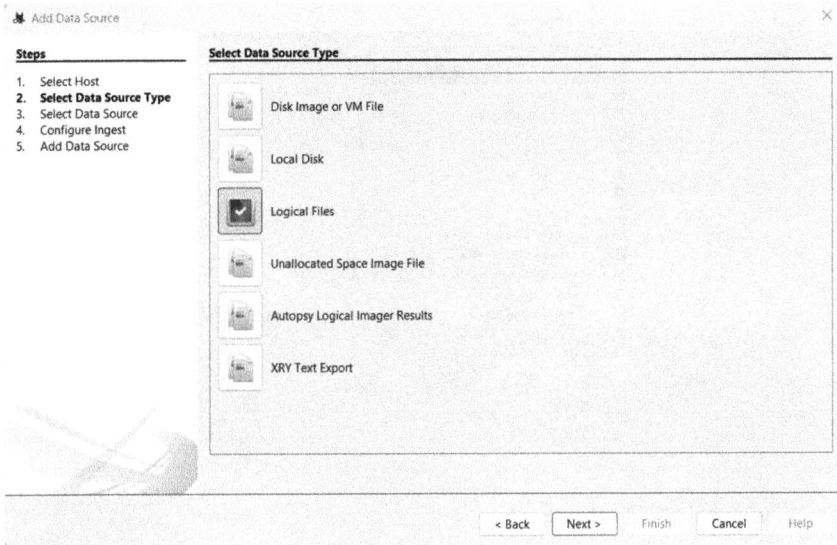

Figure 6.10 Selecting type of data source.

3. Select the data source path.

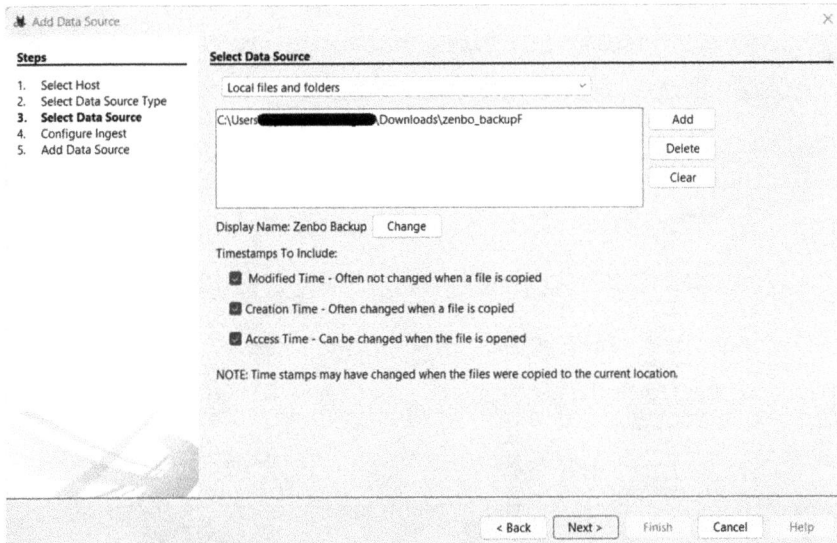

Figure 6.11 Attaching the image data source.

4. Next, you will be prompted with a list of ingest modules to enable.

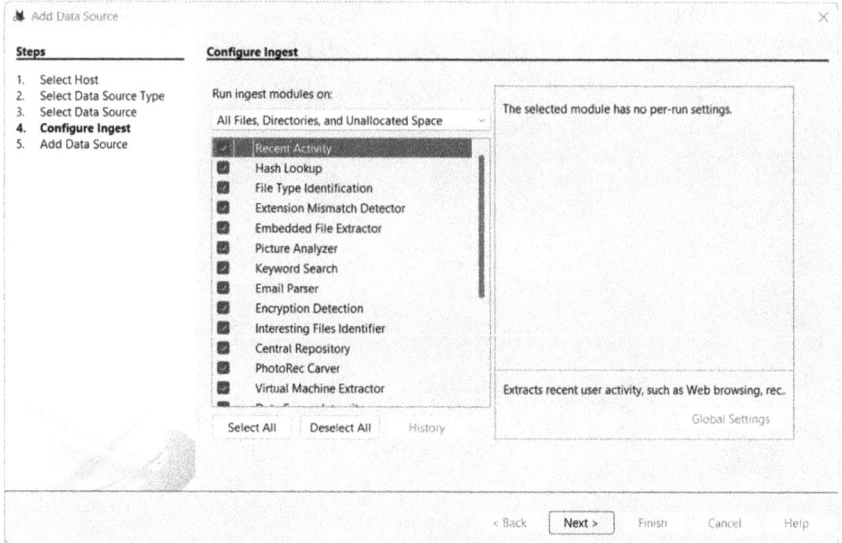

Figure 6.12 Selecting ingests.

5. Proceed and complete adding the data source. The tree on the left-hand side of the main window is where you can browse the files in the data sources in the case and find saved results from automated analysis (ingest).

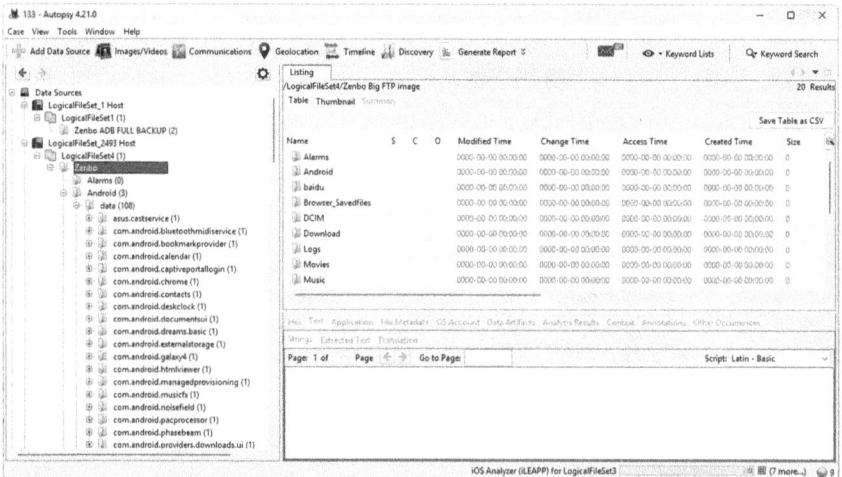

Figure 6.13 List of installed packages in Zenbo ready for analysis.

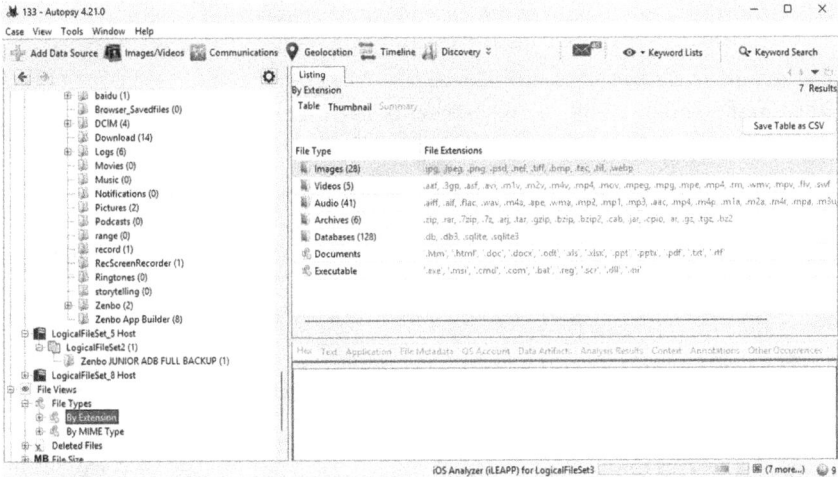

Figure 6.14 Examining file types by extension.

6. Generate a final report based on selected tags or results.

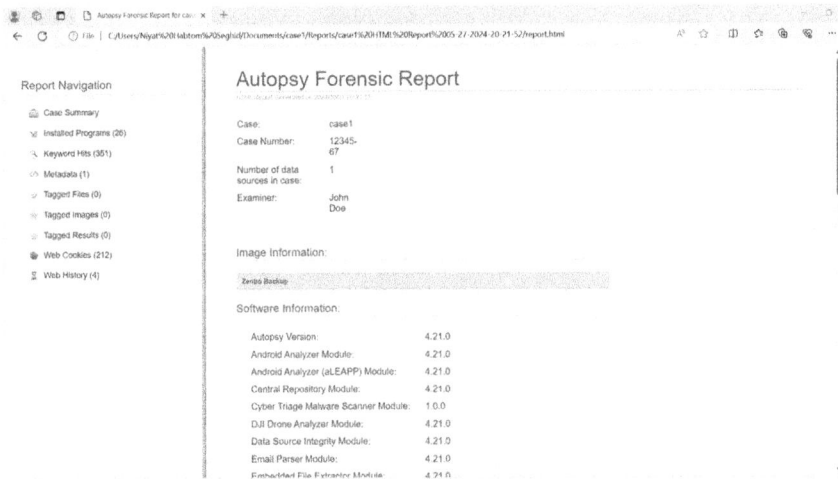

Figure 6.15 Final report.

6.2.2 Forensic artifacts

6.2.2.1 Zenbo master application

The primary mechanism for remote communication with Zenbo at the moment is thought to be Zenbo Master. The database file *asusRobot-Videophone.db* contains data from the Zenbo Master, the user, and

Table 6.1 Artifacts extracted from the Zenbo Master app package

Filename/Directory	Artifacts
asusRobotVideophone.db	• User profile, user ID, relationship, and user profile picture • Call logs • Information about Zenbo linked to the app • Logs of speak-out commands • Notifications sent to Zenbo Master from the Zenbo robot
share_pref, 2E8585D2-AF18-4AE88E7B-A25CB4B71EF5.xml	• Server offset time.
SHARE_PREF.xml	• Gmail account used to configure the Zenbo Master app • Configured the name for the Zenbo robot
zenboImageVersion2E8585D2-AF18-4AE8-8E7B-A25CB4B71EF5	• Robot version number.
allSpace2E8585D2-AF18-4AE88E7B-A25CB4B71EF5	• Total storage space available on Zenbo.
useSpace2E8585D2-AF18-4AE88E7B-A25CB4B71EF5	• Space used on Zenbo. This is indicative of the last time the app was connected to Zenbo.
zenbo_language.xml	• The main language configured on the app indicates the main language of the user.
com.asus.robot.avatar_preferences.xml	• Whether the user is an admin or a normal user.
battery, 2E8585D2-AF18-4AE88E7B-A25CB4B71EF5.xml	• Shows the battery level of the Zenbo robot recorded at the time when the app was last connected to Zenbo.

interactions with the Zenbo robot, according to an analysis of the contents of the package.

Table 6.1 summarizes the artifacts extracted from the Zenbo Master package.

6.2.2.2 Zenbo application builder

No files, databases, or other information about the applications that were created on the device can be retrieved. Despite data being copied to Zenbo through the Internet, the retrieved data are not linked to any IP addresses of the user's smartphone. Therefore, even if a smartphone were seized by an investigator, there would be no way to connect it to the robot's imported applications. This implies that we are unable to corroborate a suspect's involvement in downloading malware from their smartphone in circumstances where it has been discovered on Zenbo; at least this is the case in the current version of the robot and applications.

6.2.2.3 Zenbo—the robot

6.2.2.3.1 User call logs

Information on users of robots is kept in the package *robot.asus.com.robotprofileprovider*. The administrator can add this information by using the voice command feature. During the investigation, knowledge of family and friends might be quite helpful. The database file *asusRobot.db*, notably the table *user profile*, contains a list of all contacts. This database contains information about each user that was set up on the Zenbo robot, and the field *related* indicates the nature of the connection to the robot's owner or primary user. Additionally, this database file contains the *relative's* profile photo, which can be used to positively identify the relative. These colleagues' birthdays, email addresses, gender, and whether they are admin or regular users of the Zenbo robot are among the other information that may be discovered about them.

The list of all calls made to and from Zenbo was located in the table of *call logs*. The only parties to which calls can be made are the robot and an application. As both files should include the same information, a comparison of the call log data retrieved from this table with the data from the Zenbo Master's database, *asusRobotVideophone.db*, can reveal whether data were altered. While the customer ID with whom the call originated can be determined by reading information from the *cus id* field, the call's origin or the individual's IP address cannot be determined.

6.2.2.3.2 Calendar and to-do list

Analysis of the calendar and to-do list items (which Zenbo uses to remind users of scheduled activities) can help reconstruct user activity in an investigation. Such details can be found in the package *com.asus.robot.reminder 1.0.0*.

6.2.2.3.3 Voice commands

When the Zenbo robot hears vocal orders, it confirms them with a voice response before acting. The robot's analysis reveals that default text files with the prefix *AsrSet* are saved in the location */sdcard/Logs/DS* and contain default data. The user's vocal commands are not recorded in any way. However, *Record********TtsInfo.txt* files, where stars stand in for the year, month, and day, are thought to be helpful. One of these files is created every day and is stored in the */storage/self/primary/Logs/DS* directory. Each file also contains all of the responses that Zenbo provided in response to the user's voice instructions. Since Zenbo does not provide timestamps for each voice response, it is impossible to arrange the responses in reverse chronological order.

6.2.2.3.4 Storytelling

One of Zenbo's features is storytelling for kids, where the robot narrates pre-written tales. It was possible to retrieve artifacts from this functionality, including various JavaScript files for each tale as well as image, video, and audio files. When one of the stories was deliberately altered to operate and activate the camera or audio recording to enable unauthorized video and/or audio monitoring of Zenbo's immediate surroundings, it is one of the situations in which this artifact can prove to be significant. The path */system/media/storytelling* is where you can find the storytelling artifacts.

6.2.2.3.5 System apps

On Zenbo, various apps have been installed, some of which give users access to the robot's primary features, while others offer system features that can only be accessed by the robot. Android devices are one of the most frequently targeted platforms by cybercriminals due to their popularity. Third-party applications can be installed quite easily, making them particularly vulnerable to outside attacks; for this reason, it is crucial to list installation artifacts. The application's findings are as follows:

1. System-related apps (APK files) can be found in the */system/app* directory and enable Zenbo to carry out essential system operations. If these programs are malware-infected, analysis can reveal that information. The timestamp of extracted apps in our studies did not match the app installation time since we used a logical acquisition; instead, it matched the moment the package was pulled from the robot.
2. APK files for applications that are intended to be used by the system in the background, such as those for Google backup, uploading logs, and changing system configurations, can also be found in the */system/priv-app* directory.
3. The database file *frosting.db*, from package com.android.vending 17.9.17, offers a list of all installed packages with their real installed paths, whereas the first two locations stated above supply the raw APK files. A screenshot from this database file is shown in Figure 6.16.

PK	APK Path
jackpal.androidterm	/data/app/jackpal.androidterm-1/base.apk
com.google.android.tts	/data/app/com.google.android.tts-2/base.apk
com.asus.robot.storytelling	/system/app/RobotStoryTelling/RobotStoryTelling.apk
com.android.providers.telephony	/system/priv-app/TelephonyProvider/TelephonyProvider.apk
com.asus.robotframework.robotposmanualset	/system/app/RobotPosManualSet/RobotPosManualSet.apk
com.android.providers.calendar	/system/priv-app/CalendarProvider/CalendarProvider.apk
com.asus.zenbohichannel	/system/app/ZenboHichannel/ZenboHichannel.apk
com.android.providers.media	/system/priv-app/MediaProvider/MediaProvider.apk
com.asus.robotframework.sampling	/system/app/Sampling/Sampling.apk

Figure 6.16 Installed packages.

6.2.2.3.6 Miscellaneous artifacts

In addition to system event logs, diagnostic logs, kernel logs, and ASUS server debugging logs, several log files can be detected and recognized. This information provides a distinctive collection of data that enables the robot's actions to be identified, along with the times at which they were carried out. This can be used to accurately depict the sequence of events that took place over a certain period.

The DCIM and download directories contain the majority of the media content, the same as on other Android smartphones. Images and movies shot by the robot or stored on it are kept in DCIM, whilst data obtained from the Internet are kept in the download directory. It is important to note that it is advised to examine the media files' metadata because it contains a useful source of data for forensic investigators.

To source a specific photo back to Zenbo based on the image qualities, it may be helpful to recover the built-in camera profile and settings. With a Zenbo camera, for instance, we can see the camera resolutions and supported picture sizes. If we have an image that does not match the acquired sizes, we can rule out Zenbo as the source of that image. The findings on the supported font types on Zenbo are comparable in that a piece of writing using an unsupported font type may likewise be disregarded as a source on Zenbo.

Table 6.2 summarizes all sources of data and possible artifacts recovered from the Zenbo robot.

6.2.3 Misty II robot as a case study

The Misty II robot from Misty Robotics incorporates two operating systems, Android and Windows, which are hosted on separate processors. This dual-system configuration presents unique challenges and opportunities for forensic examination. This case study explores the approach to forensic analysis of such a sophisticated robotic platform.

In the context of forensic investigations, Misty II operates with a dual-processor setup: An 820 processor for Android and a 410 processor for Windows. Each system serves distinct functions and interacts differently with network environments and external devices, necessitating a bifurcated approach to forensic analysis. The investigation involves the Misty II robot, the Misty Robotics SDK, and the Misty Companion App. The SDK allows developers to create custom skills (programs) for Misty, which can significantly alter how Misty behaves and interacts. The Companion App facilitates remote interactions with Misty, such as command sending, monitoring, and data retrieval. The investigation covers scenarios including:

1. Command execution via voice and app.
2. Data transmission and storage processes.
3. User interaction logs during navigation tasks.
4. Image and voice data handling and storage.

Table 6.2 Artifacts extracted from Zenbo robot

Filename/Directory	Artifacts
BlocklyEngine. dbZenboScriptFolderPlace folder	Details about apps imported on Zenbo
robot.asus.com.robotprofileprovider	Zenbo users' call details
com.asus.robot.reminder	Information about activities scheduled by the user
/sdcard/Logs/DS	Zenbo's default responses in a text format
/storage/self/primary/Logs/DS	Zenbo's responses to commands
/system/media/storytelling	Details on the robot's storytelling feature
/acct/cpuacct.usage /acct/cpuacct.stat /acct/cpuacct.usage_percpu	CPU-related details like the robot's running time and processing details.
/system/etc/fonts.xml /system/etc/fallback_fonts.xml	Font-related data, like the supported fonts.
/system/etc/camera_ddr.sh /system/etc/camera_profiles.xml /system/etc/camera_realsense.gmin. xml /system/etc/camera_realsense.xml	Camera profiles and settings.
/system/etc/audio_effects.conf /system/etc/audio_policy.conf	Audio-related configurations and profiles.
/system/etc/event-log-tags	The file holds all the tags that can be seen in event logs and that correspond to specific events.
/system/etc/permissions	Hardware and software features of Zenbo. For example, "android.hardware. bluetooth" has Bluetooth features.
/sdcard/Logs/last_kernel_logs	All the messages of the kernel.
/sdcard/Logs/UploadRecord.txt	It holds a date and time value that gets updated every 24 hours. It may be related to syncing to the server.
com.android.documentsui	Database "recent.db" has timestamps of when apps were last used.
com.google.android.apps.photos	Databases "gphotos0.db" and "local_trash. db" show details about where photos are stored and also the location of deleted photos.
com.android.providers.settings	Robot settings like screen brightness, dim screen setting, auto time detection, notification setting when a new Wi-Fi access point is available, and whether the USB mass storage is enabled on the device.

6.2.3.1 Challenges and considerations

- Complexity of Dual-System Management: The necessity to manage and synchronize forensic processes across two distinct operating systems adds a layer of complexity to the investigation.
- Ensuring Data Integrity: Maintaining the integrity of data during forensic extraction is crucial. Techniques such as checksums and detailed logging are implemented to preserve the original state of data.
- Security Analysis: Given Misty II's connectivity capabilities, identifying security loopholes through meticulous network traffic analysis is critical to understanding potential exploitation vectors.

6.2.3.2 Practical forensic acquisition of Misty II

The Misty II robot, as described, employs dual operating systems. This sophisticated arrangement necessitates a detailed forensic methodology to access, extract, and analyze data across these distinct environments. The following description outlines the procedures and forensic relevance of data artifacts that can be recovered from Misty II's complex file system.

Forensic access to the Android system can be achieved using the Android Debug Bridge (ADB), which facilitates a direct connection to Misty II after enabling USB debugging. This setup allows investigators to use commands like *adb pull* for retrieving specific files and *adb backup* for a complete backup, thereby capturing a wide range of data, including user interactions, application data, and system logs. This mirrors traditional forensic approaches used in mobile device analysis, ensuring procedural consistency and reliability. Connection via IP and use of ADB facilitates access to the root directory and subsequent data extraction, following standard procedures applicable to Android devices.

Accessing the Windows environment can be done using the SMB protocol to establish a network share from Misty II to the forensic workstation. Utilizing this protocol, forensic analysts can access the file system on the Windows processor directly, enabling a comprehensive examination of the files and directories in this location. The method is also conducive to extracting large volumes of data, including system configurations, user documents, and event logs, which are critical for a full forensic analysis and hidden directories.

6.2.3.3 Artifact extraction and their forensic implications

In the Android environment, interaction logs located in */data/data/com.mistyrobotics.sdk/logs/* provide detailed records of user commands, essential for reconstructing user interactions and identifying any anomalies or unauthorized commands. Additionally, application data stored in */data/data/com.mistyrobotics.companionapp/shared_prefs/* include XML files that reveal user settings and preferences, offering insights into the user's configuration of the robot.

In the Windows environment, the *C:\Windows\System32\winevt\Logs* directory is particularly valuable as it contains logs that record system events, security-related events, and operational errors, which are vital for identifying security incidents and system malfunctions. The *C:\Users\<User Profile>\Documents* directory holds user-created files, providing a window into the content interaction and creation by the user.

END OF CHAPTER QUESTIONS

1. Discuss the relevance of Robot Operating Systems (ROS) in forensic investigations. How does it affect data acquisition and analysis?
2. In a controlled forensic experiment, Zenbo is used to send voice commands and reminders. Describe how you would generate and analyze data from these activities for forensic investigation purposes.
3. A forensic examiner needs to acquire data from the Zenbo App Builder, including uploaded media and executable files. Explain the process of accessing and analyzing this data.
4. Reflect on the ethical considerations that arise when investigating humanoid robots used in healthcare or assisted living environments. How should forensic investigators balance privacy concerns with the need for thorough investigations?
5. You are investigating a data leak at a care facility. A Zenbo robot, a companion Android app, and a smart thermostat were all active in the timeframe. Describe how you would forensically correlate evidence across these devices to determine whether Zenbo or its associated apps were used in the breach.
6. During a criminal investigation, investigators suspect that a Zenbo robot was used to covertly monitor a victim using modified storytelling scripts. Outline how you would locate, validate, and analyze forensic artifacts that support or refute this claim.
7. Misty II robots operate on both Android and Windows systems. Discuss the forensic challenges of synchronizing evidence between these environments, and explain how you would acquire and validate artifacts from each without compromising evidentiary integrity.
8. A suspect claims that unauthorized applications were uploaded to Zenbo using Zenbo App Builder from a public network. What forensic procedures would you implement to investigate this claim, and how would you handle the limitations imposed by the current version of the Zenbo App Builder?
9. A cyberstalker may have used the Zenbo Master app to trigger video calls with the victim. Describe how you would reconstruct and authenticate call activity using both Zenbo and the companion smartphone.
10. You recover an Android smartphone suspected of having previously interacted with a Misty II robot during a corporate espionage case. Describe your approach to identifying artifacts that confirm the interaction and tie the device to specific Misty II robot actions.

11. Describe how changes between initial and final forensic images of a social robot can help isolate user actions or malicious behavior. Provide examples based on Zenbo's logging and user interaction databases.

12. In a crime scene, a Zenbo robot and a smartwatch belonging to the victim are found. Explain how voice interaction logs, user profile data, and wearable telemetry can be integrated to build a timeline of the victim's final activities.

13. What security risks are introduced by the Zenbo App Builder's allowance for uploading executable files, and how can forensic investigators detect abuse of this functionality during an incident investigation?

14. Discuss the forensic implications of not being able to correlate Zenbo-installed apps with smartphone IP addresses. What investigative workarounds can be employed when direct attribution is not feasible?

15. A social robot was discovered in a suspected surveillance incident. Investigators need to determine whether unauthorized audio or video was recorded via the storytelling feature. Outline a complete forensic strategy to investigate this.

16. You are asked to compare the forensic readiness of Zenbo and Misty II robots in terms of data accessibility, operating system support, and forensic tool compatibility. Which robot presents more complexity and why?

17. A hacker exploited the ROS environment on a Zenbo robot to execute malware through system apps. Discuss how you would examine the /system/app and /system/priv-app directories for signs of tampering, and validate the findings.

18. A Zenbo robot's voice interaction logs show no user commands, but its TTS response logs suggest otherwise. How would you reconcile these logs and validate whether commands were locally or remotely triggered?

19. What limitations exist in the forensic acquisition of Zenbo's voice command history, and how can indirect artifacts (like response logs or scheduled reminders) be leveraged to infer user intent?

20. How does dual-processor architecture in robots like Misty II influence the strategy for preserving the chain of custody and forensic validation across Android and Windows systems?

21. Discuss the significance of Zenbo's ability to store profile photos, birthdays, and email addresses. How can these artifacts be leveraged in forensic identity correlation or social relationship mapping?

22. Explain how you would validate whether a specific media file originated from Zenbo. Include discussion of camera profile, file path, and metadata analysis.

23. During a forensic review of Misty II, suspicious system event logs are found in the Windows environment. How would you correlate these logs with Android-based interaction logs to uncover coordinated attacks or actions?

24. Examine the Misty II log data (below), as viewed via Autopsy. Determine and list at least five forensic artifacts from the SS, along with the metadata for each artifact.

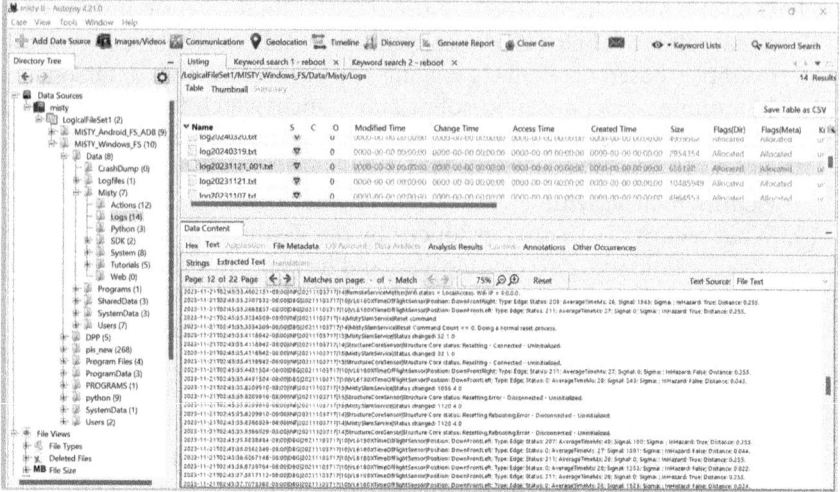

25. How could extracting the application packages list from a social robot be deemed important in a forensic investigation? Discuss in detail.

```
com.android.cts.priv.ctsshim 10005 0 /data/user/0/com.android.cts.priv.ctsshim default:privapp none
com.android.providers.telephony 1001 0 /data/user_de/0/com.android.providers.telephony platform:privapp 3002,3003,3001
com.android.providers.calendar 10002 0 /data/user/0/com.android.providers.calendar platform:privapp 3003
com.android.providers.media 10008 0 /data/user/0/com.android.providers.media platform:privapp 2001,1023,1015,3003,1024,3007
com.android.wallpapercropper 10024 0 /data/user/0/com.android.wallpapercropper platform:privapp none
com.android.documentsui 10007 0 /data/user/0/com.android.documentsui platform:privapp none
com.android.externalstorage 10010 0 /data/user/0/com.android.externalstorage platform:privapp 1023,1015
com.android.htmlviewer 10037 0 /data/user/0/com.android.htmlviewer platform none
com.android.mms.service 1001 0 /data/user/0/com.android.mms.service platform:privapp 3002,3003,3001
com.android.providers.downloads 10008 0 /data/user/0/com.android.providers.downloads platform:privapp 2001,1023,1015,3003,1024,3007
com.android.browser 10029 0 /data/user/0/com.android.browser platform 3003
com.android.inputmethod.pinyin 1000 0 /data/user/0/com.android.inputmethod.pinyin platform 3002,1023,1015,3003,3001
com.android.defcontainer 10006 0 /data/user_de/0/com.android.defcontainer platform:privapp 2001,1023,1015
com.android.vending 10015 0 /data/user/0/com.android.vending default:privapp 3002,3003,3001
com.android.certinstaller 10032 0 /data/user/0/com.android.certinstaller platform none
com.android.carrierconfig 10003 0 /data/user/0/com.android.carrierconfig platform:privapp none
com.android.contacts 10004 0 /data/user/0/com.android.contacts platform:privapp 3003
com.android.camera2 10030 0 /data/user/0/com.android.camera2 platform 3003
com.pekall.fmradio 1000 1 /data/user/0/com.pekall.fmradio platform 3002,1023,1015,3003,3001
com.android.egg 10034 0 /data/user/0/com.android.egg platform none
com.android.mtp 10008 0 /data/user/0/com.android.mtp platform:privapp 2001,1023,1015,3003,1024,3007
com.android.launcher3 1000 0 /data/user/0/com.android.launcher3 platform 3002,1023,1015,3003,3001
com.android.backupconfirm 10000 0 /data/user/0/com.android.backupconfirm platform:privapp none
com.android.provision 10017 0 /data/user/0/com.android.provision platform:privapp none
com.android.statementservice 10020 0 /data/user/0/com.android.statementservice platform:privapp 3003
com.android.Calendar 10043 0 /data/user/0/com.android.Calendar platform 3003
com.android.providers.settings 1000 0 /data/user_de/0/com.android.providers.settings platform:privapp 3002,1023,1015,3003,3001
com.android.sharedstoragebackup 10019 0 /data/user/0/com.android.sharedstoragebackup platform:privapp 1023,1015
com.android.printspooler 10040 0 /data/user/0/com.android.printspooler platform none
com.android.dreams.basic 10026 0 /data/user/0/com.android.dreams.basic platform none
com.android.inputdevices 1000 0 /data/user_de/0/com.android.inputdevices platform:privapp 3002,1023,1015,3003,3001
com.google.android.webview 10041 0 /data/user/0/com.google.android.webview default 3003
android.ext.shared 10035 0 /data/user_de/0/android.ext.shared platform none
com.android.onetimeinitializer 10013 0 /data/user/0/com.android.onetimeinitializer platform:privapp none
com.android.server.telecom 1000 0 /data/user/0/com.android.server.telecom platform:privapp 3002,1023,1015,3003,3001
com.android.keychain 1000 0 /data/user/0/com.android.keychain platform 3002,1023,1015,3003,3001
com.android.printservice.recommendation 10039 0 /data/user/0/com.android.printservice.recommendation platform 3003
com.android.gallery3d 10036 0 /data/user/0/com.android.gallery3d platform 3003
com.google.android.gms 10011 0 /data/user/0/com.google.android.gms default:privapp 2001,1005,3002,3003,3001,1007,3006,3007
com.google.android.gsf 10011 0 /data/user/0/com.google.android.gsf default:privapp 2001,1005,3002,3003,3001,1007,3006,3007
```

26. You have extracted kernel logs from a Zenbo social robot involved in a forensic investigation. Analyze both log segments and discuss: (a) What critical system events can be identified and their forensic significance? (b) How can the hardware enumeration data assist in the investigation? (c) What timeline can be established from the power management events?

```
[    0.910432] usbcore: registered new interface driver sierra_net
[    0.910575] usbcore: registered new interface driver cdc_ncm
[    0.911374] intel-cht-otg intel-cht-otg.0: failed to register extcon notifier
[    0.911382] EM:OEM1  table found, size=64
[    0.911386] cht_otg_probe : usb none_compliance mode selected
[    0.911595] usb_phy_gen_xceiv.1 supply vcc not found, using dummy regulator
[    0.911628] usb_phy_gen_xceiv usb_phy_gen_xceiv.1: No RESET GPIO is available
[    0.911634] usb_phy_gen_xceiv usb_phy_gen_xceiv.1: No CS GPIO is available
[    1.112354] dwc3 dwc3.0.auto: dwc3_suspend_common
[    1.112871] ehci_hcd: USB 2.0 'Enhanced' Host Controller (EHCI) Driver
[    1.112885] ehci-pci: EHCI PCI platform driver
[    1.113472] ohci_hcd: USB 1.1 'Open' Host Controller (OHCI) Driver
[    1.113487] uhci_hcd: USB Universal Host Controller Interface driver
[    1.113959] xhci_hcd 0000:00:14.0: xHCI Host Controller
[    1.114162] xhci_hcd 0000:00:14.0: new USB bus registered, assigned bus number 1
[    1.114326] xhci_hcd 0000:00:14.0: ssic_device_present[0] ssic_port_number[5]
[    1.114337] no xhci or phy_mux_regs
[    1.115597] xhci_hcd 0000:00:14.0: cache line size of 64 is not supported
[    1.115660] xhci_hcd 0000:00:14.0: irq 136 for MSI/MSI-X
[    1.115865] usb usb1: New USB device found, idVendor=1d6b, idProduct=0002
[    1.115872] usb usb1: New USB device strings: Mfr=3, Product=2, SerialNumber=1
[    1.115877] usb usb1: Product: xHCI Host Controller
[    1.115883] usb usb1: Manufacturer: Linux 3.14.64-x86_64 xhci_hcd
[    1.115889] usb usb1: SerialNumber: 0000:00:14.0
[    1.116529] hub 1-0:1.0: USB hub found
[    1.116569] hub 1-0:1.0: 7 ports detected
[    1.118754] xhci_hcd 0000:00:14.0: xHCI Host Controller
[    1.118945] xhci_hcd 0000:00:14.0: new USB bus registered, assigned bus number 2
[    1.119080] usb usb2: New USB device found, idVendor=1d6b, idProduct=0003
[    1.119087] usb usb2: New USB device strings: Mfr=3, Product=2, SerialNumber=1
[    1.119092] usb usb2: Product: xHCI Host Controller
[    1.119097] usb usb2: Manufacturer: Linux 3.14.64-x86_64 xhci_hcd
[    1.119102] usb usb2: SerialNumber: 0000:00:14.0
[    1.119827] hub 2-0:1.0: USB hub found
[    1.119860] hub 2-0:1.0: 6 ports detected
[    1.123163] usbcore: registered new interface driver cdc_acm
[    1.123170] cdc_acm: USB Abstract Control Model driver for USB modems and ISDN adapters
[    1.123344] usbcore: registered new interface driver usb-storage
[    1.123470] usbcore: registered new interface driver ums-realtek
```

```
[   11.568433] bq30z55_get_prop_status: battery_status 0x00C0
[   11.570818] bq30z55_get_prop_status: Charging.
[   11.575592] healthd: battery l=62 v=14817 t=22.2 h=2 st=2 c=-322 chg=ac 2012-01-01 00:00:16.964214522 UTC
[   11.576372] charger: [11563] animation starting
[   11.576444] charger: temp_level -1, capacity 62
[   11.576505] charger: show_leds battery_level 62
[   11.689042] pmic_ccsm wcove_ccsm: VDCIN Detected. Notifying charger framework
[   12.336082] bq30z55_get_prop_status: battery_status 0x0080
[   12.339109] bq30z55_get_prop_status: Charging.
[   12.344754] healthd: battery l=62 v=14969 t=22.2 h=2 st=2 c=1035 chg=ac 2012-01-01 00:00:17.733508637 UTC
[   12.653809] iTCO_wdt: iTCO_wdt_ping
[   13.105036] bq30z55_get_prop_status: battery_status 0x0080
[   13.107905] bq30z55_get_prop_status: Charging.
[   13.113598] healthd: battery l=62 v=15031 t=22.2 h=2 st=2 c=1955 chg=ac 2012-01-01 00:00:18.502496554 UTC
[   13.872454] bq30z55_get_prop_status: battery_status 0x0080
[   13.875405] bq30z55_get_prop_status: Charging.
[   13.880687] healthd: battery l=62 v=15046 t=22.2 h=2 st=2 c=1951 chg=ac 2012-01-01 00:00:19.269732813 UTC
[   14.639552] bq30z55_get_prop_status: battery_status 0x0080
[   14.642636] bq30z55_get_prop_status: Charging.
[   14.648171] healthd: battery l=62 v=15053 t=22.2 h=2 st=2 c=1954 chg=ac 2012-01-01 00:00:20.037364298 UTC
[   15.407776] bq30z55_get_prop_status: battery_status 0x0080
[   15.410445] bq30z55_get_prop_status: Charging.
[   15.416208] healthd: battery l=62 v=15057 t=22.2 h=2 st=2 c=1957 chg=ac 2012-01-01 00:00:20.805542164 UTC
[   15.806085] bq30z55_get_prop_status: battery_status 0x0080
[   15.808932] bq30z55_get_prop_status: Charging.
[   15.814355] healthd: battery l=62 v=15059 t=22.2 h=2 st=2 c=1956 chg=ac 2012-01-01 00:00:21.203802647 UTC
[   15.814412] charger: [15802] rebooting
[   15.814556] SysRq : Emergency Remount R/O
[   15.862927] Emergency Remount complete
[   16.146153] LEDS-WHEEL: leds_wheel_shutdown: power off leds
[   16.152421] CY8C4014SXI: [cy8c_capsense_shutdown] keep CAP_VEN_GPIO low
[   16.202555] bq30z55_shutdown: +++
[   16.205994] bq30z55_shutdown: 1 ---
[   16.206048] bq24725a_shutdown: +++
[   16.206112] bq24725a_shutdown: ---
[   16.326250] reboot: Restarting system
[   16.370236] reboot: machine restart
[   16.372580] ACPI MEMORY or I/O RESET_REG.
```

27. What ethical considerations must be accounted for when conducting forensic analysis on social robots used in private home or healthcare settings? How should investigators balance evidentiary needs with user privacy?

REFERENCES

[1] A. IDC. "Worldwide spending on robotics will reach $188 billion in 2020 fueled by new use cases and expanding market acceptance," 2020. https://www.idc.com/getdoc.jsp?containerId=prUS45800320

[2] Saracino, Andrea, Sgandurra, Daniele, Dini, Gianluca, and Martinelli, Fabio. "Madam: Effective and efficient behavior-based android malware detection and prevention," *IEEE Transactions on Dependable and Secure Computing*, vol. 15, no. 1, pp. 83–97, 2016.

Chapter 7

Gaming consoles forensics

Gaming consoles like Sony's PlayStation, Microsoft's Xbox, and Nintendo's Wii have steadily made their place in the consumer market. Their basic architecture is similar to any PC; they contain a hard drive, OSs, and associated memory. Apart from the conventional gaming capabilities, today's consoles also provide improved features that include Internet-enabled activities (including Web browsing and multiplayer chat features), file storage, and movie players [1]. Gaming consoles can be directly connected to a router of the network via a LAN segment.

Gaming consoles also allow a secondary OS to be installed on the hard disk. While these features provide an advanced user experience, access to the Internet renders the gaming consoles vulnerable to malicious attacks, like PCs, raising security concerns [2]. In such a case of violation, forensic practitioners must be prepared to analyze gaming consoles with efficient methods tailored to the device; however, gaming console forensics remains an under-researched domain [3, 4]. This is primarily because the majority of gaming console file systems are heterogeneous and proprietary, so forensics becomes tricky. Nonetheless, gaming consoles may prove to be of key evidential value, storing important information. For example, there is an option in gaming consoles to send emails about the performance of a player during the match upon the completion of a game. Information like this may seem irrelevant, but it can help the investigator to collect data and time stamps. Therefore, full access to the consoles may be established using methods such as jailbreaking or by using a write blocker and then performing a live analysis [2].

7.1 VULNERABILITIES IN GAMING CONSOLES

The red hats can sabotage gaming consoles in a few steps. The first thing a hacker would do is find out what software runs on the console. For example, if the target console is PS4, it is established that it runs on a custom AMD x86-64 CPU with 8 cores. This CPU architecture is very well documented with research paper resources available on the Internet. PS4 console runs

DOI: 10.1201/9781003644255-7

Orbis OS which is based on Freebase 9.0. Particularly interesting is WebKit. It is an open-source layout engine that is used on the PS4 to render web pages on the browser. However, WebKit has some documented vulnerabilities that can be exploited. For example, CVE-2012–3748 is a heap-based buffer overflow in the JSArray::sort(...) method. This vulnerability can be exploited to give read-and-write access to everything the WebKit process can read and write to. This can be used to overwrite return addresses on the stack and take control of the Register Instruction Pointer (RIP), which holds the address of the next instruction that the CPU will execute. The next step is to copy a payload to memory and use RIP to execute it.

PS4 has a kernel that controls the properties of different parts of memory. The kernel has Data Execution Prevention (DEP), so a payload cannot be copied into memory and executed. However, a code can be executed that is already loaded into memory and marked as *executable*. To write their code and mark it as *executable*, hackers use stack smashing. Particularly, Return-Oriented Programming (ROP), where one can overwrite a chain of memory addresses where the RIP will jump to in sequence. These chains are called gadgets. A gadget is a single desired instruction followed by a *ret*. In the x86_64 assembly, when a ret instruction is reached, a 64-bit value is popped off the stack, and RIP jumps to it. And now that the stack is in control, one can make every ret instruction jump to the intended gadget. For example, 0x80000 contains instructions, then 0x90000 contains instructions.

If a hacker overwrites a return address on the stack to contain 0x80000 followed by 0x90000, then as soon as the first ret instruction is reached, execution will jump to mov rax, 0, and immediately afterward, the next ret instruction will pop 0x90000 off the stack and jump to mov rbx, 0. Therefore, the hacker now has a way to exploit the vulnerability.

The PS4 has Address Space Layout Randomization (ASLR) implemented. This is a security technique that causes the base addresses of modules to be different every time the PS4 is started, which means that the hacker would have no idea what addresses their gadgets reside on. So, they will not know what to write to the stack. For this purpose, they can stay away from static ROP chains. When all modules are loaded, their base addresses are populated in the modules table. If the hacker can read the modules table, they can easily calculate the addresses of ROP gadgets before they trigger execution. This can be done using JavaScript.

System calls can help interact with the kernel. FreeBSD uses the UNIX convention of calling for system calls with arguments stored in the stack. But on the PS4, the LINUX convention is used where arguments are stored in registers. This way, a list of system calls can be obtained.

PID tells important information about the running processes. The WebKit core parses HTML and CSS, executes JavaScript, and decodes images, and another one handles user input, graphics, history, bookmarks, and everything else. Next, system calls can be analyzed by reverse-engineering module dumps. Some system calls are not referenced in the module dumps, so they are analyzed using brute force. If a guess can be made that a certain system call might take a particular set of arguments, brute force can be performed on all system calls that return a certain value (0 for success) with the arguments that were chosen, and ignore all that returned an error.

Zeros (0s) can also be passed for all arguments, and brute force all system calls which return useful errors such as 0xe, *bad address*, which would indicate that they take at least one pointer. To find the vulnerability associated with the system calls, the data manipulated on disk before and after the system call can be analyzed. If the data have not changed, it could be an input prompt. A long string can be fed as an argument to look for a buffer overflow. Or a NULL truncator to limit the length and prevent an overflow. This is a very long process, but it is necessary to identify the system calls. After the system call, the file system can be analyzed for vulnerabilities. Unfortunately, due to sandboxing, one cannot have access to the entire file system. The files that can only be accessed include encrypted saved data and account information. So, these files can also be exploited. For digital forensics, RAM can also be of help by analyzing the system calls and file systems etc. to find any problem or vulnerability.

7.2 GAMING CONSOLE FORENSICS

The need for gaming console forensics has grown significantly in recent years as gaming consoles have become increasingly connected to the internet and integrated into our digital lives. These devices store a wealth of data, including user profiles, chat logs, downloaded content, and even financial information. LEAs, cybersecurity experts, and digital forensic investigators are recognizing the importance of gaming console forensics to uncover evidence in cases involving cybercrimes, hacking, online harassment, and even child exploitation. Understanding how to extract and analyze data from gaming consoles is crucial for investigating and prosecuting criminal activities that may have digital footprints within these gaming ecosystems. Moreover, it highlights the evolving landscape of digital forensics, where investigators must adapt their skills to new and emerging technologies.

7.2.1 Acquisition

Before acquisition, the gaming console is identified and documented. This includes noting the make, model, serial number, and any physical damage or modifications. Detailed images may be taken to record the console's condition. The console is carefully seized following legal and chain of custody protocols. It is essential to prevent any potential tampering or data alteration during this process. Forensic experts identify the various data sources within the gaming console: the device storage, RAM, network, and cloud. In addition, these may also include removable storage devices. Finally, specialized tools (such as FTK Imager, Dumpit, Magnet Axiom, Magnet IEF Forensics, Belkasoft RAM Capturer, Autopsy) and techniques are used to extract data from the identified sources. This can involve connecting the console to a computer, using proprietary software, or extracting data from removable storage media. Given different OSs of gaming consoles, existing tools can be modified to cater to the heterogeneity. For example, the Sleuth Kit can be modified to support recognizing the Xbox file system FATX, which does resemble the FAT entries [3, 4].

7.2.2 Analysis

Extracted data are processed to make it accessible for analysis. This may involve decrypting encrypted files, parsing file structures, and organizing data into a usable format. Forensic experts search for digital artifacts that may indicate illegal activities or unauthorized modifications to the console. This can include the presence of hacking tools, cheat codes, or unauthorized software.

1. **User Profiles and Activities:** Investigators examine user profiles, saved game progress, login history, and user interactions. This can help establish the identity of users, their gaming habits, and potential associations with other individuals.
2. **Chat Logs and Messages:** Gaming consoles often support messaging and chat features. Forensic experts analyze chat logs to look for conversations that may be relevant to the investigation. This can include communication related to cybercrimes, harassment, or illegal activities.
3. **Internet History:** If the console has a web browsing capability, internet history is scrutinized for evidence of online activities, websites visited, and potentially malicious actions.
4. **File Metadata:** File metadata, such as creation and modification dates, can provide valuable insights into when certain actions or interactions occurred on the console.
5. **Deleted Data Recovery:** Deleted files and data are examined and, if possible, recovered. Deleted information may still be relevant to the investigation.
6. **Timeline Reconstruction:** Investigators reconstruct a timeline of events based on the extracted data. This helps establish the sequence of actions and interactions on the gaming console.

Throughout the acquisition and analysis phases, forensic experts must adhere to strict ethical and legal standards, respecting privacy laws and ensuring that evidence is handled and presented correctly in a court of law.

7.3 DIGITAL SURVEILLANCE FOR XBOX KIT (XFT DEVICE)

Although tools from computer and network forensics can be used to perform digital forensics on gaming consoles, there is an increasing need for specialized tools that can directly report data from gaming consoles like Xbox and others. When LEAs collect evidence, they usually overlook a gaming console as an important source of evidence. The XFT Device allows cyber forensics teams to retrieve hidden data from a gaming console hard drive that might have previously gone unnoticed. Hardware and software can be analyzed with this tool, and it is opening a whole new door to cyber forensics that investigation teams are excited to take advantage of.

7.4 FORENSIC ACQUISITION OF AN *XBOX ONE S* GAMING CONSOLE USING FTK

In this guide, we will demonstrate how to use the Forensic Toolkit (FTK) to perform a forensic acquisition of an Xbox One S gaming console. To begin the forensic process, follow the structured steps provided below:

1. **Remove the Hard Drive from the Xbox One S**
   - Power off the Xbox One S and disconnect it from any network connections to prevent data alteration.
   - Carefully open the Xbox One S casing to access the internal hard drive.
   - Safely remove the hard drive from the Xbox One S. Be sure to follow proper handling procedures to avoid damaging the drive.

Figure 7.1 Xbox One S gaming console.

2. Connect the Hard Drive to the Forensic Workstation
- Use the appropriate cables to connect the Xbox One S hard drive to the forensic workstation through a write blocker. This ensures the integrity of the evidence by preventing any writes to the drive during the acquisition process.

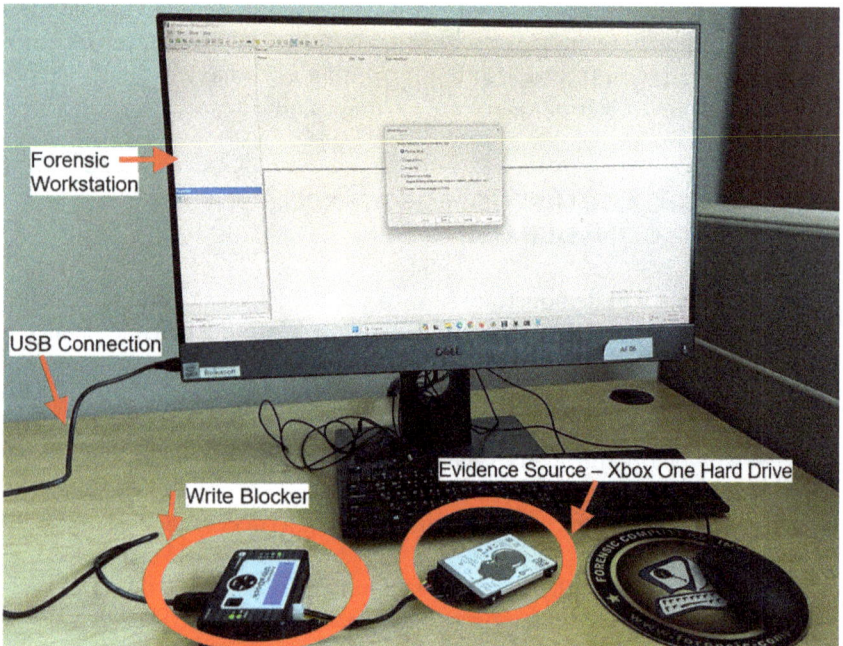

Figure 7.2 Forensic workstation with connected hard drive.

3. Launch FTK Imager, Select the Source Drive, and Configure the Image Destination
- Select *File > Create Disk Image* to start the acquisition process.
- Choose the *Physical Drive* option and select the Xbox One S hard drive from the list of available drives.
- Specify the destination for the acquired image. This could be an external storage device or a designated folder on your forensic workstation.
- Choose the image type (e.g., *Raw (dd)*, *E01*, or *AD1*) based on your requirements. The *E01* format is recommended for its compression and verification features.

4. **Enter Case Information and Start the Acquisition Process**
   - Enter relevant case details, review the settings, and start the acquisition process.
   - FTK Imager will create a bit-by-bit copy of the Xbox One S hard drive, ensuring all data, including deleted files and slack space, is captured.
5. **Analyze the Acquired Image**
   - Use any forensic tool to load the acquired image and perform a detailed analysis.

7.5 DIGITAL FORENSIC ANALYSIS OF PS4 GAMING CONSOLE USING SAVE WIZARD

The PlayStation 4 (PS4), a widely used gaming console developed by Sony, has emerged as a multifaceted platform for digital interaction. Beyond gaming, it supports web browsing, social networking, messaging, and media playback, enabling users to communicate, share content, and store substantial personal data. These capabilities make it a valuable target in forensic investigations involving digital evidence such as communication records, user profiles, gameplay metadata, screenshots, trophies, and saved game data. However, extracting digital evidence from PS4 systems presents substantial challenges due to the proprietary nature of the PlayStation operating system, rigorous encryption protocols, and limitations imposed by Sony's security infrastructure. In this context, tools such as *Save Wizard*, a commercially available game save editor, have emerged as unconventional yet valuable aids for forensic examiners seeking access to encrypted user data. In this section, we explore the forensic acquisition and analysis of PS4 data using *Save Wizard*.

7.5.1 Overview of PS4 architecture and associated forensic challenges

The PS4 architecture comprises several components relevant to digital forensics. The **System-on-Chip (SoC)** integrates the CPU and GPU, managing all processing tasks, including game rendering and system operations. The **internal hard drive (HDD)** stores operating system files, game installations, patches, user profiles, saved games, screenshots, and activity logs. **Removable storage** such as USB drives can be used for backing up data, transferring game saves, or saving media, which is crucial for forensic access. The **network interface** facilitates connectivity to PlayStation Network (PSN), allowing online gameplay, messaging, and digital purchases, with much of this communication potentially being logged or resulting in cached data.

PS4 data are heavily encrypted and tied to the console's firmware and individual user accounts. Accessing forensic data directly from the console's internal hard drive without authorization or custom firmware is exceedingly difficult due to encryption and system integrity checks. As such, investigators often turn to backup-based or save-data-based forensic approaches when conducting digital investigations on these gaming systems. In summary, the PS4's architecture poses multiple barriers to forensic access:

- **Proprietary file system** and operating system (Orbis OS, based on FreeBSD) restrict low-level access.
- **Encrypted storage,** including saved data and application files, hinders conventional extraction and interpretation.
- **Cloud-stored game saves,** inaccessible without the original user account credentials and session tokens.
- **Continuous firmware updates** often render previous forensic techniques obsolete or unstable.
- **Digital Rights Management (DRM)** mechanisms further obfuscate user and system data.

Traditional forensic tools like FTK or Autopsy can sometimes be ineffective for extracting and interpreting PS4 internal storage without hardware-level manipulation or jailbreaks, which in themselves raise legal and evidentiary concerns. To circumvent these limitations, forensic analysts may consider a "dead acquisition" strategy, that is, non-invasive data collection from a powered-off console using built-in utilities and external tools.

7.5.2 Save Wizard: role in PS4 forensics

Originally intended for gaming enthusiasts to apply cheats or transfer game saves, *Save Wizard* supports over 1,000 games and offers several features with direct forensic value. Key features that make Save Wizard useful for forensic purposes include:

- **Decryption of Saved Game Files:** Save Wizard accesses encrypted .bin files, extracting readable content such as progress logs, configuration states, and gameplay outcomes.
- **Hex Editing (Advanced Mode):** This mode exposes the raw byte structure of save files, enabling examiners to interpret underlying data formats and metadata.
- **User Reassignment (Re-Sign Feature):** Enables reassignment of a save file to a different user, facilitating cross-account analysis and ownership verification.
- **Metadata Extraction:** Analysts can retrieve timestamps, file modification history, and session durations—valuable in reconstructing a timeline of user activity.
- **USB-based Access:** Save Wizard works with game saves exported to a USB device, allowing acquisition without dismantling the PS4 or modifying its firmware.

Table 7.1 Types of forensic artifacts recovered from Save Wizard

Artifact type	Description
User Identifiers	PSN IDs or offline profile names linked to saved games.
Timestamps	Save file creation/modification dates.
Geolocation (Game-specific)	In some RPGs, coordinates of in-game locations.
Narrative Context	Active missions, unlocked achievements, and inventory status.
Behavioral Patterns	Frequency and timing of saves, indicating usage habits.

These capabilities allow forensic practitioners to gain visibility into game-related data that may reflect user intent, behavior, or communication (in multiplayer games). While the scope of data accessible through Save Wizard is inherently limited to saved game files, the decrypted content can still yield a rich spectrum of forensic artifacts (see Table 7.1). Such artifacts may enable user behavior modelling by revealing patterns suggestive of compulsive gaming, irregular usage spikes, or abnormal in-game activity that deviates from expected norms. In multiplayer contexts, forensic investigators may cross-reference player identifiers, session metadata, or collaborative gameplay actions to reconstruct online interactions and trace social connections. Save Wizard's profile registration system also facilitates ownership confirmation by verifying the association between specific save files and registered PlayStation Network (PSN) accounts. Moreover, by conducting hex-level comparisons of save files before and after known user interactions, analysts can detect modifications that suggest manual tampering or the use of automation tools such as bots or game trainers. This level of analysis becomes particularly relevant in legal proceedings involving harassment, cyberstalking, or digital rights disputes, where understanding the origin, authenticity, and modification history of game saves may help establish timelines, intent, and account ownership.

These artifacts may be correlated with other external evidence (e.g., online account logs, suspect alibis) to support or refute claims in a criminal investigation.

7.5.3 Forensic acquisition process using Save Wizard

This study employs a five-phase forensic methodology leveraging the PS4's *Backup and Restore feature* and *Save Wizard* software for analysis:

1. **Tool Preparation:** A PlayStation 4 console with user-created save data is paired with a USB 3.0 drive, Save Wizard software, a hex editor (e.g., HxD), and forensic utilities (e.g., Autopsy).
2. **Data Acquisition:** A system backup is created via *Settings > System > Backup and Restore* and copied to the USB device. This backup

includes saved games, screenshots, and settings, though system logs and chat messages are excluded.

3. **Decryption Phase:** Save Wizard is installed in the forensic workstation and used to decrypt individual saved game files. Its *Re-Sign* function allows reassignment of game saves to different user profiles, and its *Advanced Mode* provides access to hex-level editing.

4. **Forensic Analysis:** Analysts inspect decrypted files for metadata (e.g., timestamps, usernames, level progression), in-game behavior (e.g., item use, mission completion), and patterns of interaction. Modified files are compared against original states to detect tampering.

5. **Validation and Replication:** The technique is validated across different game titles and PSN user profiles to evaluate reproducibility and consistency of results.

The effectiveness of the analysis depends heavily on the type of game and the developer's save format.

7.5.4 Legal and ethical considerations

Despite its utility in digital investigations, Save Wizard presents several notable limitations that must be carefully considered by forensic practitioners. As a consumer-grade application, it lacks essential forensic safeguards such as verifiable logging, cryptographic hashing mechanisms, and write-protection features. This absence of forensic soundness means that any evidence acquired using the tool may face heightened scrutiny in court, particularly if the acquisition process is not thoroughly documented, validated, and corroborated through secondary methods. Moreover, Save Wizard's functional scope is restricted to the processing of saved game files—it does not provide access to broader system artifacts such as logs, system messages, or data stored in Sony's cloud infrastructure. The tool's usability is further limited by encryption boundaries, as it only works on saved data tied to registered PlayStation Network (PSN) accounts, and each license supports a maximum of two accounts. This significantly constrains the scope of potential investigations, especially in multi-user environments. In addition, the legal status of Save Wizard remains ambiguous; its usage may infringe upon Sony's terms of service, and the tool's core features, such as game save modification and cheat injection, raise ethical concerns, especially when considered in a forensic or evidentiary context. There is also an inherent risk of data alteration: features like "Re-Sign" and hexadecimal editing, while powerful for investigative purposes, simultaneously introduce possibilities for inadvertent or intentional manipulation of evidence if not tightly controlled.

In conclusion, while Save Wizard is not a forensically certified tool, its unique ability to decrypt and modify PS4 saved game data offers a viable workaround for specific evidence recovery scenarios. When combined with careful documentation, rigorous control, and an understanding of its limitations, Save Wizard can contribute valuable artifacts to forensic investigations involving PlayStation 4 consoles. However, forensic professionals must remain cautious, prioritizing evidentiary integrity, legal compliance, and methodological transparency when leveraging such non-traditional tools.

END OF CHAPTER QUESTIONS

1. What is the primary challenge in acquiring data from a gaming console during a forensic investigation?
2. What kind of data can be critical in a forensic investigation on a PlayStation console?
3. Explain the importance of acquiring volatile memory (RAM) during a forensic investigation on a gaming console. What kind of information can be retrieved?
4. How does the proprietary nature of gaming console file systems affect the forensic analysis of stored data? Provide examples of file systems and challenges.
5. Discuss the significance of user profiles, saved games, and messaging data in a forensic investigation on gaming consoles like the Xbox and PlayStation.
6. In forensic investigations involving gaming consoles, why is it important to extract and analyze network logs? How can these data help reconstruct user activity?
7. Describe the steps involved in acquiring data from a PS4 during a forensic investigation. What tools would you use, and which types of data would you prioritize?
8. How can Return-Oriented Programming (ROP) be identified and used as evidence in a forensic investigation involving console hacking?
9. How do the heterogeneous and proprietary file systems of gaming consoles impact the forensic process, and what strategies can be employed to overcome these obstacles during analysis?
10. Given the PS4's use of WebKit and known vulnerabilities like CVE-2012–3748, how can forensic experts leverage publicly known exploits during an investigation without violating ethical and legal standards?
11. Compare the implications of jailbreaking a console versus using a write blocker for live analysis. How do both approaches affect evidence integrity, admissibility, and access depth?
12. Explain how Return-Oriented Programming (ROP) and Address Space Layout Randomization (ASLR) interact during exploitation of a gaming console like PS4. How might these concepts be relevant in a forensic investigation?

13. Evaluate the forensic significance of email notifications and time-stamps generated during gameplay sessions. How can this indirect data be correlated with user profiles to reconstruct user behavior?

14. Discuss the challenges of conducting system call analysis on gaming consoles that use hybrid kernel architectures. What are the forensic risks associated with brute-forcing undocumented system calls?

15. Describe a scenario in which stack smashing is discovered post-incident. What forensic artifacts would indicate its presence, and how should investigators interpret such findings?

16. What are the limitations of analyzing sandboxed environments on consoles, and how can forensic experts work around restricted file system access?

17. Assess the role of RAM acquisition during forensic analysis of gaming consoles. What types of data can be expected, and how should volatility be managed?

18. In what ways can gaming consoles serve as platforms for illicit communication or cybercrime? Propose a forensic workflow to uncover such activities.

19. How can modifications to the gaming console's OS, such as installation of secondary systems, be detected and verified during a forensic investigation?

20. Analyze the forensic utility of chat logs and messaging features within gaming consoles. How might these logs differ in structure or storage across platforms like PlayStation, Xbox, and Nintendo?

21. Outline the forensic relevance of the Xbox FATX file system. What steps would you take to customize a tool like Sleuth Kit to parse this format effectively?

22. Critique the current toolsets available for console forensics (e.g., FTK Imager, Magnet Axiom, XFT). What enhancements would you recommend for better support of console-specific artifacts?

23. Discuss how file metadata (e.g., creation, access, and modification times) on a console can be used to challenge or validate an alibi provided during a forensic investigation.

24. What are the ethical considerations and legal constraints of using low-level forensic techniques (e.g., chip-off, ROP-chain tracing) when dealing with encrypted or proprietary gaming platforms?

25. Develop a technical procedure for reconstructing a timeline of activity on a console using data such as internet history, saved games, and downloaded content.

26. What benefits does the Digital Surveillance Xbox Forensics Toolkit (XFT) offer over general-purpose forensic tools in console investigations? How would you validate its reliability?

27. Using the FTK acquisition procedure described for the Xbox One S, explain how bit-level imaging ensures data preservation. What potential data remnants can be captured that would be missed in logical acquisitions?

28. During a forensic investigation of a PS4 console, you discover that the suspect has deleted their messaging data. What steps would you take to attempt to recover this data, and which forensic tools would be most useful?

29. You are conducting a forensic analysis on an Xbox One console. The suspect has tampered with the system and installed unauthorized firmware. Explain how you would handle the investigation and retrieve forensic data.

30. An investigator finds an encrypted external USB drive connected to a gaming console. What forensic techniques would you employ to extract and analyze the data, considering that it might contain key evidence?

31. A suspect's gaming console is linked to cloud storage, where game saves and personal data are stored. How would you approach the acquisition of cloud-based data in compliance with digital forensics protocols?

32. During a forensic investigation, you need to prove that a particular gaming console was used for online harassment via chat logs. Explain how you would collect, verify, and present this evidence in court.

REFERENCES

[1] Davies, Matthew, Read, Huw, Xynos, Konstantinos, and Sutherland, Iain, "Forensic analysis of a Sony PlayStation 4: A first look," *Digital Investigation*, vol. 12, no. 1, pp. S81–S89, 2015, ISSN 1742-2876, doi:10.1016/j.diin.2015.01.013

[2] Conrad, S., Dorn, G., and Craiger, P. "Forensic analysis of a playstation 3 console," In Chow, K.P., Shenoi, S. (eds) *Advances in Digital Forensics VI. DigitalForensics 2010. IFIP Advances in Information and Communication Technology*, vol. 337. Springer, Berlin, Heidelberg, 2010. doi:10.1007/978-3-642-15506-2_5

[3] Khanji, Salam, Jabir, Raja, Iqbal, Farkhund, and Marrington, Andrew, "Forensic analysis of xbox one and playstation 4 gaming consoles," 2017. All Works. 1708. https://zuscholars.zu.ac.ae/works/1708

[4] Khanji, S., Jabir, R., Iqbal, F. and Marrington, A., "Forensic analysis of xbox one and playstation 4 gaming consoles," *2016 IEEE International Workshop on Information Forensics and Security (WIFS)*, pp. 1–6, 2016, doi:10.1109/WIFS.2016.7823917

Chapter 8

Smart wearables forensics

The adoption of smart wearables like fitness trackers, smartwatches, and Augmented Reality (AR) glasses continues to increase, fueled by several key factors, including the increasing demand for IoT-based connected health monitoring devices with higher accessibility, preference for sleek and compact devices for easy handling, and the popularity of biosensor-based devices. Key industry players, including Samsung, LG, and Motorola, have been actively contributing to the landscape of smartwatches, with Apple's highly anticipated iWatch entering the market in April 2015, poised to make a significant impact [1]. These devices have become a treasure trove of data that can offer invaluable insight into criminal investigations, cybersecurity incidents, and civil disputes. This emerging discipline involves the extraction, analysis, and interpretation of digital artifacts from these wearable devices, including a person's activities, location history, health metrics, and even interactions, thereby providing forensic experts with powerful tools to uncover critical information and solve complex cases.

8.1 SMART WEARABLES

Wrist-based wearables like health-oriented devices go a step (or two) beyond what regular fitness trackers offer these days. One such device is one Amazon has reportedly patented: A voice-activated wearable device that can recognize human emotions, or Empatica's Embrace, a medically approved advanced seizure monitoring device.

Healthcare is undergoing huge changes driven by the rising adoption and integration of voice technology, which makes it particularly appealing to tech firms. A company, audEERING has achieved a 92% classification accuracy in identifying early symptoms of Parkinson's disease through voice analysis. By detecting tiny changes in a person's voice, voice technology cannot only detect a person's emotional state from the sound of his/her voice but also mental abilities and critical diseases. This is a commendable development that will have the most impact on the early detection and estimation of disease progression to deliver prompt and effective treatment.

 DOI: 10.1201/9781003644255-8

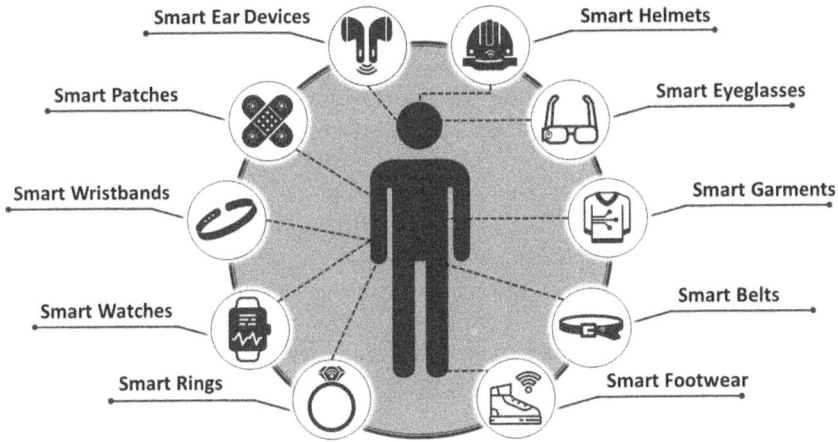

Figure 8.1 Smart wearable devices [2].

The focus of voice AI in a healthcare environment will be facilitating real-time data to improve patient care and make it more personal. There can be a streamlined medical experience with the added convenience of online check-ups and faster response (certainly beats going multiple times to a doctor).

Smart glasses, in particular, are already being developed, with products like Vuzix Blades that are powered by AR and come with *Alexa*, Amazon's virtual assistant.

Some smart earbuds effectively combine wireless listening with the capabilities of voice assistants and a wide range of smart devices. For instance, Bragi Dash Pro has real-time translation, automatic activity training, and Alexa support. Figure 8.1 illustrates a number of common smart wearables.

8.2 SMART WEARABLES FORENSICS

Smart wearables forensics can be a complex process, and it requires expertise in both digital forensics and the specific technology involved. These devices are function-based, performing particular tasks and in turn collecting data about an individual, which is critical. Smart wearables can provide a great source of evidence for the digital forensics process. Activities conducted on smart wearables and connected networks routinely leave some kind of digital fingerprint. For the security professionals protecting an enterprise—or the investigators working to trace the origins of a breach—any or all of the aspects of forensic digital evidence might be key in documenting an incident, formulating a response, or building a strategy for future operations.

8.2.1 Evidence sources

The specific sources of evidence and their accessibility may vary depending on the make and model of the wearable device and its associated ecosystem. In a usual smart wearables' forensics case, the evidence sources may include:

1. **Wearable Device Storage:** Internal storage on the wearable device itself can contain data such as health and fitness logs, sensor readings, user settings, and sometimes even multimedia files (e.g., photos or videos).
2. **Companion Applications:** Many smart wearables are paired with companion applications on smartphones or computers. These apps often store additional data, including user profiles, activity history, and settings. Investigating these apps can provide valuable insights.
3. **Bluetooth Connections:** Smart wearables often communicate with paired devices via Bluetooth. Logs of these connections and associated data transfers may be available for analysis.
4. **Sensor Data:** Wearable devices often have various sensors (e.g., GPS, accelerometer, heart rate monitor) that continuously collect data. These data can be crucial for establishing timelines, tracking movements, or corroborating alibis.
5. **Cloud Services:** If the wearable device syncs data with cloud services (e.g., Apple Health, Google Fit, Fitbit Cloud), investigators may need to access cloud-stored data, if relevant and accessible, through proper legal channels.
6. **Geolocation Data:** If the wearable has GPS capabilities or connects to a paired smartphone with GPS functionality, it may record location data. This can be important for tracking the movements of the device wearer.
7. **Biometric Data:** Biometric data like heart rate, sleep patterns, and step counts can provide insights into the wearer's health and activity patterns. This information may be relevant to a forensic investigation.
8. **Communication Logs:** Some smart wearables can receive notifications or messages from paired smartphones. Investigating communication logs can help establish digital interactions related to the case.

8.2.2 Forensic analysis procedure

Smart wearable devices are not similar to complex computers or smartphones, where there is proper circuitry and memory, etc. These devices can be as simple as an embedded chip. They have a small memory/RAM and storage, which means they cannot store much data, and they try to transfer it to the cloud as soon as possible [3]. These devices may also overwrite memory to compensate. In addition, metadata such as any temporal information like the time of creation, accessed time, etc., may not be stored because of limited storage [4]. Subsequently, when forensic investigators try to capture data from these devices, they may find it a challenge to collect complete data.

The acquisition and analysis steps of the general forensic frameworks need to cater to smart wearables based on the devices' conditions.

Data Acquisition: First, the data sources on the wearable device need to be identified. Common sources include sensors, internal storage, and companion applications on a smartphone or computer. Forensic tools and techniques such as ADB and Smart Debug Bridge (SDB) can be used to acquire data from the device and associated sources, ensuring that the original data remains unchanged during the process. However, the devices may need to be meddled with to enable debug modes and gain root access for ADB/SDB methods to work. These will only give logical acquisitions, however. Physical extraction of data through specialized cables or software-based extraction via Bluetooth or USB connections may also be done. In order to take a bit-level image of the hard drive or storage media of the system involved, a write-blocker may also be used. On occasions where it is necessary to examine a device and read information from it while it is still in operation (e.g., turning off the device would cause valuable evidence to disappear from memory, or cause damage to the owner), a live acquisition may be performed. This involves running a small diagnostic program on the target system, which copies information over to the forensic examiner's hard drive. For legal purposes, such a live acquisition may still produce digital forensic evidence that is admissible in court—so long as the examiner can adequately prove that their intrusive intervention was necessary.

Data Analysis: The acquired data are then examined for relevant information. This may include health and fitness data, location information, messages, call logs, and app usage. Forensic software and techniques may be used to parse and interpret the data, looking for evidence related to the case. Data from the wearable device must be cross-referenced with data from other sources, such as smartphones or cloud accounts, if applicable.

8.3 CHALLENGES IN SMART WEARABLES FORENSICS

Smart wearables forensics presents several unique challenges that forensic investigators must address to effectively collect and analyze digital evidence from these devices. Adherence to established forensic procedures is essential to overcome these challenges and ensure the integrity of the evidence collected. Some of the key challenges include [5, 6]:

1. **Diversity of Devices:** There is a wide range of smart wearables available, each with its own operating system, storage mechanisms, and data formats. Forensic investigators need to be familiar with the specific device they are dealing with and adapt their methods accordingly.

2. **Forensic Tools and Expertise:** Digital forensic tools and techniques may not always be readily available or compatible with all wearables. Forensic experts must continually update their skills and tools to keep up with evolving technology.

3. **Cross-Platform Integration:** Investigating wearable devices often requires integrating data from multiple sources, including the wearable itself, smartphones, and cloud services. Ensuring data consistency and integrity across platforms can be challenging.

4. **Data Loss:** If the device is damaged or reset, data may be lost irretrievably. Careful handling and preservation of the device are crucial to prevent data loss.

5. **Data Fragmentation:** Data from wearable devices may be fragmented across different sources, including the device itself, companion apps, and cloud storage. Reassembling a complete picture of the user's activities can be complex.

END OF CHAPTER QUESTIONS

1. Identify three advanced forensic techniques that could be applied to analyze the data obtained from a fitness tracker.
2. Explore the significance of ethical considerations when conducting a forensic analysis of smart wearables, particularly regarding user consent.
3. Discuss the implications of data loss in smart wearables forensics and the steps that can be taken to prevent it.
4. Explain the role of voice recognition technology in the context of smart wearables and how it may be relevant in forensic investigations.
5. Evaluate the impact of device resets or damage on the integrity of forensic evidence collected from smart wearables.
6. Discuss how wearable technology could aid in real-time crime scene analysis.
7. How does the limited memory and storage design of smart wearables impact the integrity and completeness of forensic acquisition, especially in live investigations? Moreover, given the overwrite behavior in low-memory wearables, how might investigators recover partially deleted evidence, and what acquisition methods best support this effort?
8. Discuss the implications of cloud-sync behavior in wearables for forensic timeline reconstruction. How should investigators manage inconsistencies across local and cloud-stored data?
9. Compare and contrast the forensic utility of sensor data (e.g., heart rate, GPS, accelerometer) versus biometric logs (e.g., sleep patterns, step counts) when used as digital evidence in criminal investigations.
10. How can investigators ensure forensic soundness while enabling debugging or rooting on smart wearables that require invasive access techniques?

11. In what investigative scenarios might live acquisition be favored over traditional offline methods, and what technical and legal safeguards must be in place for admissibility?

12. Design a cross-platform forensic strategy that integrates data from a smartwatch, its companion smartphone app, and its cloud account to validate the user's movements and interactions on a specific date.

13. What are the technical limitations of using tools like ADB for logical acquisition on smart wearables, and how might these affect the ability to extract deleted or volatile data?

14. Evaluate the evidential value of Bluetooth connection logs in a forensic case involving multiple wearable devices. How can these logs be used to determine device-user association?

15. Given the fragmentation of data across a wearable, a smartphone app, and cloud services, what challenges might arise in correlating time-stamps and maintaining data integrity across platforms?

16. How can geolocation artifacts from wearable devices be used to corroborate or challenge a suspect's alibi? What validation steps must be taken before presenting such evidence in court?

17. Analyze how device diversity among smart wearables (different brands, OSs, data structures) affects the scalability and generalizability of forensic tools and methodologies.

18. What risks are associated with conducting physical extraction on fragile smart wearable devices, and what methods could be employed to mitigate potential data loss or device failure?

19. How would you handle a case where a smart wearable device is fully operational, but its paired smartphone is unavailable for analysis? What limitations would this pose?

20. What are the key differences in forensic acquisition approaches between a consumer fitness tracker (e.g., Fitbit) and a medically approved wearable (e.g., Empatica's Embrace)?

21. How can forensic experts maintain legal compliance when acquiring and analyzing data from wearable-cloud platforms that may store information in multiple jurisdictions?

22. Critically assess the potential forensic contribution of voice-based smart wearables in mental health or emotion detection applications. What ethical dilemmas might this raise?

23. In what ways might step count, heart rate variability, or sleep patterns be used as circumstantial evidence in a legal case? How should such physiological data be validated and contextualized?

24. In a multi-user household where wearable devices are frequently paired and unpaired with shared smartphones or tablets, how can forensic analysts establish definitive user-device associations and ownership timelines?

REFERENCES

[1] Baggili, I., Oduro, J., Anthony, K., Breitinger, F., and McGee, G. "Watch what you wear: Preliminary forensic analysis of smart watches," In *2015 10th International Conference on Availability, Reliability and Security*, Aug. 2015, pp. 303–311. IEEE.

[2] Moshawrab, M., Adda, M., Bouzouane, A., Ibrahim, H., & Raad, A. (2022). Smart Wearables for the Detection of Occupational Physical Fatigue: A Literature Review, *Sensors*, 22(19), 7472. doi: 10.3390/s22197472

[3] MacDermott, T. Baker and Shi, Q., "Iot forensics: Challenges for the Ioa era," *2018 9th IFIP International Conference on New Technologies, Mobility and Security (NTMS)*, 2018, pp. 1–5, doi: 10.1109/NTMS.2018.8328748

[4] Servida, F. and Casey, E., "IoT forensic challenges and opportunities for digital traces," *Digital Investigation*, vol. 28, pp. S22–S29, Apr. 2019, doi: 10.1016/j.diin.2019.01.012

[5] Kim, M., Shin, Y., Jo, W. et al. "Digital forensic analysis of intelligent and smart IoT devices," *J Supercomput*, 2022. doi: 10.1007/s11227-022-04639-5

[6] Stoyanova, M., Nikoloudakis, Y., Panagiotakis, S., Pallis, E., and Markakis, E. K. "A survey on the internet of things (IoT) forensics: Challenges, approaches, and open issues," *IEEE Communications Surveys & Tutorials*, vol. 22, no. 2, pp. 1191–1221, 2020.

Chapter 9

Application forensics

Various digital devices and the Internet provide services through application architecture. Applications are enabled via operating systems on client devices and Service Oriented Architecture (SOA) powering the Web. A client device operating system manages computer software (or applications), among other operations. On the other hand, Internet software is based on SOA, which enables a dynamic Web infrastructure that deploys Web Services (WS) and applications reliant on WS. These applications use dynamic connections to communicate with and request services that already exist on the Web. This essentially achieves an agile software arrangement that is economical, independent of vendors, interoperable, and reconfigurable on the Web, based on continuously changing software needs of users [1].

Operating Systems (OSs) and SOA implement strong security mechanisms to prevent rogue agents from attacking/compromising applications for their malicious agendas. While OSs may implement standardized security controls that work efficiently on regular application software, the dynamic nature of Web applications makes it harder to implement such security controls. Web applications communicate large amounts of sensitive data regularly, and threat actors may explore their complex interdependencies to find vulnerabilities to exploit [1]. Also, WS may be invoked from different locations, which adds a layer of complexity in terms of security and digital forensics as well [1]. With a unique attack surface, Web applications have and continue to experience their fair share of exploitation attempts. The Open Web Application Security Project (OWASP) lists injection, broken authentication, and sensitive data exposure among the top 10 Web application security risks [2].

Both client and Web applications may experience security breaches at some point in time, no matter the sophistication of their security posture. Applications may be breached to gain access to a user's personal data or a corporation's trade secrets, etc. CSO Online reported that in 2016, Yahoo revealed that 3 billion user accounts' information was compromised by a hacker group when it was being acquired by Verizon [3]. Another account of breach was reported in 2019; two Facebook datasets containing user account information (including account names, phone numbers, and

DOI: 10.1201/9781003644255-9

Facebook IDs) of more than 530 million users were disclosed. This information was posted freely, two years later in 2021, and was openly available on the dark Web [3].

It is consequently pivotal to perform application-specific forensic analysis in the wake of an application compromise, to have research-backed resources detailing forensic artifacts left behind by various applications to support insider attack investigations and malware investigations stemming from an attacker's malicious use of application vulnerabilities, among other examinations [4].

9.1 APPLICATION HETEROGENEITY

Applications, by nature of their build and/or use case, are inherently heterogeneous. Client device applications are developed to operate specifically in OS environments, whereas Web applications function in a more dynamic (SOA) environment. In addition, several variables, such as front-end/backend programming languages (like JavaScript and PHP) employed for an application's development, and the different data representation formats (including binary, XML, and JSON) utilized for data storage/transfer, may contribute to the subject heterogeneity [5].

Application heterogeneity poses a challenge in following a common digital forensics model in research and investigations. To this effect, very limited forensic tools exist that perform application-specific automated forensic analysis. The Volatility Framework[1] serves as an example, providing plugins for targeted analyses of several applications such as Notes, Notepad, Adium, and Calendar [4].

Since every application may leave behind entirely different pieces of information (artifacts), analysis automation may only be achieved through forensic investigation of individual applications separately and developing tools based on artifacts extracted for each application. The process must be replicated for every critical application. It is pertinent to note that with successive updates of application software, the extracted artifacts (and therefore, the tools developed) may become obsolete. Consequently, to maintain the validity of forensic artifacts and tools, research must constantly incorporate changes in successive updates of applications.

9.2 DATA (ARTIFACT) LOCALITIES

Application data and digital artifacts can be found across multiple computing environments, each with distinct characteristics that influence forensic investigation approaches. The locality of data significantly impacts the complexity of acquisition procedures, available analysis techniques, and the types of evidence that can be recovered during digital investigations.

9.2.1 Client device applications

Client device applications are installed and operated in a more traditional OS environment, which makes pertaining artifact localities less complicated, as opposed to Web applications. A forensic analyst typically inspects (1) the disk storage (or hard drive), (2) volatile Random Access Memory (RAM) (if it is available at a given instance, that is,, the device is not shut down), and (3) the network for clues of *who-what-how-when-where* while connecting the dots in investigative scenarios.

9.2.1.1 Disk forensics

Forensic artifacts about an installed application may be carved from several locations on a device's disk space, such as:

1. A **client application** folder, automatically created in the client's data directory (usually the *AppData* folder) upon an application's installation, is employed to store application and user-specific data about the application. The files and information stored in the client application folder are necessary for its smooth operation. This may include configuration files, user account information, etc., and is deleted if the application is uninstalled.
2. The **AppData** folder contains the *Local*, *Locallow*, and *Roaming* application folders. Information stored in the Roaming folder is a server's copy of the account data and is loaded into any device that the user account is logged into, as opposed to the information stored in the Local folder, which is information that is specific to the device concerning the application (temporary files, caches, configuration settings, etc.).
3. The **Windows Registry (WR)** is a central hierarchical database that houses configuration data for the Microsoft OS. User(s)' information, installed apps, hardware, and past user activities are all recorded by WR. On the client desktop, details about recently and previously installed applications are also stored, including timestamps and the locations and widths of their application windows and dialogue boxes. Registry keys (and their values) related to an application of interest may divulge incriminating information critical to a forensic investigation.
4. **Event logs** record application, hardware, security, and system events like login attempts, application activity, and timestamps of such activities that may be of interest to investigators.
5. **Windows Prefetch files** (located at C:\Windows\Prefetch) are inherently used to speed up the process of loading applications and running them efficiently. A forensic analyst may parse an application's Prefetch files, particularly for information about the run times of executables and related timestamps.

Data and artifacts found on the disk are particularly useful since they are retained even after a device is shut down or if it abruptly crashes.

9.2.1.1.1 Challenges in disk forensics

A prominent challenge faced by investigators during disk forensic analysis is encryption, which may include: (1) Application folder encryption, (2) Volume Encryption, and (3) Full disk encryption.

Encryption is usually found to be more common at the file system level (or application folder level) [6]. For example, user databases in Zoom's data directory, such as *zoommeeting.enc, zoomus.enc,* and *zoomus.tmp.enc* at C:\Users\[username]\AppData\Roaming\Zoom\data were encrypted with successive updates of the application shortly after incidences of *zoom-bombing* and *zoom-raiding*. It was a primary priority to achieve optimal privacy and security of users' accounts and data.

At the file system level, encryption may not cause as much hindrance in investigations since there may be other unencrypted sources of forensic artifacts on disk to be explored. However, if volume and full disk encryption are encountered, there is little room left for analysis.

9.2.1.2 Memory forensics

Memory forensics, typically focused on rootkit detection and retrieval of traces of malware from the system's volatile memory, has seen advancement in the development of techniques for carving and analyzing application-specific artifacts. The memory stores information about running applications and processes in the OS. Data are often stored unencrypted in memory, making it an interesting location for information that serves as digital evidence [7, 8]. Several application-specific forensic artifacts can be extracted from memory, such as running processes with Process Identifiers (PID), encryption keys, profile photos and other media, passwords, email addresses, user account information, user activity information, and network connections.

Major challenges in memory forensics are listed below.

1. Memory analysis for application-specific artifacts greatly relies on *unstructured* analysis
2. Closed-source or proprietary applications' data structures must be reverse-engineered without source code, producing error-prone results
3. Application heterogeneity requires analysis to be performed separately for each application
4. Extractable forensic artifacts must be updated with every software update
5. Page smearing[2]
6. Page swapping[3]

9.2.1.3 Network forensics

Monitoring network traffic to collect and analyze raw network packets to identify how an attack/event was carried out on a network, to identify intrusions, or to detect malware is a usual motivation. Additionally, an application's network traffic may be analyzed to identify patterns in its network activity.

Most network traffic is encrypted in the current Internet architecture using HTTPS, which presents solid challenges in network forensics. While novel Artificial Intelligence (AI) and Machine Learning (ML) are being used in network forensics research today, the encrypted network traffic may still be analyzed, as it is, to extract useful information, which includes client–server connections and vice versa, IP addresses, and related event timestamps [7, 9–10].

Major challenges in network forensic analysis are listed as follow.

1. Encryption
2. Storage constraints for enormous volumes of network packets/logs
3. Time limitation on storage of network logs
4. Services running on atypical ports

9.2.2 Web applications

Unlike traditional desktop client applications that are contained within a single OS, the files that together comprise a Web application are distributed over several computer systems. These include the host machine that runs the Web browser, Web server(s), and application server(s).

9.2.2.1 Host running the web browser

Web applications may not create dedicated application folders on the client device. However, *"residual data generated on devices can also be used as a proxy to data that is being stored in cloud environments"* [11] This residual data may be carved from the Web browser's data directory on the machine's disk to identify and extract artifacts such as traces of the application's usage, favorite websites/bookmarks, history (with timestamps of websites visited), downloads, email addresses, cache, cookies (including their creation and expiry dates), logs, the www directory, and configuration files.

9.2.2.2 Web servers and application servers

Web servers typically keep logs of requests they receive, including a timestamp, IP address, Web browser version, and OS of the host making the request, the type of request (GET/POST), the resource requested, and the status code (indicates success/failure of request). Relevant artifacts include web server and application server logs and configuration files, server-side scripts used by the Web application, third-party installed software logs and vital files, and OS logs and vital system files.

9.3 STATE-OF-THE-ART

With technology undergoing significant evolution over the past decade, from social media to Artificial Intelligence (AI) being incorporated into workflows, achieving mainstream status, it is worth noting how state-of-the-art in application forensics has evolved. A comprehensive understanding of existing digital forensic approaches is essential for contextualizing the developments. In particular, research has extensively examined the forensic artifacts left by messaging applications such as WhatsApp, Signal, and Skype for Business, as well as the challenges of extracting evidentiary data from encrypted or cloud-based sources. More recently, AI applications, particularly those developed by platforms such as OpenAI,[4] have introduced new dimensions to forensic inquiry. These tools, while transformative in domains like Natural Language Processing (NLP) and automation, also present novel challenges for evidence preservation, attribution, and accountability. This section reviews foundational studies, current methodologies, and technological advances relevant to the forensic investigation of modern communication and AI-driven systems, highlighting both achievements and persistent challenges that motivate the need for further innovation.

Wijnberg and Le-Khac explore forensic strategies to extract WhatsApp data from Android devices despite the platform's end-to-end encryption [12]. They assess both rooted and non-rooted methods for acquiring communications, focusing on device-resident data such as logs, databases, and memory dumps. The study also evaluates interception through network monitoring and discusses challenges posed by encryption and Android's evolving security model. It concludes with implications for lawful access and highlights key artefacts of forensic interest.

Son et al. present a comprehensive forensic analysis of three encrypted instant messaging applications—Signal, Wickr, and Threema—focusing on their database structures and the feasibility of decrypting stored data [13]. The authors examine the use of SQLCipher, a library that provides transparent AES-256 encryption for SQLite databases, which these applications utilize to secure user data. The study highlights the challenges forensic investigators face when attempting to access encrypted data without the necessary decryption keys. The research emphasizes that, in many cases, the encryption keys are stored within the applications themselves, making it difficult to decrypt the data without access to the original device or user credentials. This limitation underscores the importance of obtaining physical access to the device or leveraging legal avenues to compel users to provide decryption keys. The paper also discusses the implications of these encryption practices on digital forensics, particularly in legal contexts where access to communication data is crucial. It suggests that while encryption enhances user privacy, it also poses significant challenges for forensic investigations, necessitating the development of new tools and methodologies to address these issues.

Nicoletti and Bernaschi explore a comprehensive forensic analysis of communication artifacts generated by the software [14]. Their research focuses on examining the communication architecture, protocols, and the VoIP codec to extract artifacts. They investigate the recovery of important data such as chat logs, user contacts, and call records while examining the persistent storage locations in both local and cloud-based systems. The study highlights various forensic acquisition methods, including analyzing event logs, the Windows Registry, and databases, emphasizing the reconstruction of conversations and the identification of deleted data. Additionally, it addresses challenges posed by enterprise configurations and the necessity for specialized tools to manage the evolving security measures of Skype for Business, particularly in corporate settings where integration with cloud services can complicate data retrieval.

Ghafarian and Fredy explore the application of memory forensics to analyze Instagram activities on Windows 10 systems [15]. The researchers accessed Instagram accounts via web browsers and employed memory forensic techniques to retrieve and examine artifacts left in the system's memory. Their findings indicate that memory forensics can effectively uncover sensitive information such as login credentials, usernames, phone numbers, email addresses, and details of user interactions like posts, comments, likes, and tags. The paper underscores the significance of volatile memory as a rich source of digital evidence, especially when persistent storage may not retain such data. By analyzing the system's memory, investigators can access transient information that might otherwise be inaccessible through traditional forensic methods. The authors also propose a systematic process for conducting memory forensics to retrieve traces of Instagram activities, highlighting its potential in digital investigations involving social media platforms.

Dragonas et al. present a comprehensive forensic investigation into the ChatGPT mobile application developed by OpenAI, analyzing both Android and iOS platforms [16]. The study focuses on identifying residual artifacts generated through user interaction with the application, including prompt history, responses, session tokens, timestamps, and cached data. Using forensic acquisition techniques, the authors examine file system structures, application directories, and memory snapshots to extract evidentiary data. The research highlights key differences between the two mobile operating systems. Android devices, due to their more accessible file systems, reveal more recoverable artefacts than iOS, where stricter sandboxing limits visibility. Investigators were able to recover traces of user queries, authentication logs, and local cache that could serve as valuable evidence in scenarios involving user intent, digital footprints, or even misuse of generative AI systems. Importantly, the study emphasizes that although ChatGPT does not store conversation history locally by default, certain application behaviors (such as application-level caching or background logs) can still leave behind retrievable traces. The study concludes that forensic awareness of generative AI applications like ChatGPT is essential in modern investigations, particularly as these tools become integrated into our everyday digital workflows. Table 9.1 provides a comparative analysis of the current state-of-the-art in application forensics.

9.4 CASE STUDIES

The following Cisco WebEx, Google Meet, and Microsoft Teams case studies in (video conferencing) application forensics demonstrate how forensic artifacts specific to a client device/Web application may be extracted and analyzed for relevance in investigations for the court of Law. The case studies detail various data (artifact) localities, including memory, disk, network, and the browser, as discussed in previous sections.

9.4.1 Forensic methodology

A general forensic methodology was followed to perform forensic analysis of the applications consisted of the following steps:

1. **Experimental setup:** Creation of test data in Virtual Machines (VMs) for forensic analysis by imitating activities of a typical (video conference) user, based on the features/functions of the application, to create forensic artifacts to be analyzed in later stages.
2. **Acquisition:** Capture of memory and disk forensic images of the VMs after completion of periodic test activity runs using AccessData FTK Imager.
3. **Examination:** Interpret acquired images to determine data objects of value to the subject investigation.
4. **Analysis:** Concluding artifacts extracted during the examination phase.

The stipulated forensic methodology is illustrated in Figure 9.1. Table 9.2 lists the tools used in the analysis.

9.4.2 Cisco WebEx

Cisco WebEx is a *desktop client* video-conferencing application. Upon installation, it assigns *personal meeting room IDs* to users. Users can invite

Table 9.1 State-of-the-art studies—comparative analysis

Existing study	Application(s) analyzed	Focus of analysis	Methods/tools used	Key findings	Challenges/limitations
Wijnberg & Le-Khac (2019)	WhatsApp (Android)	Extraction of forensic artifacts from encrypted messaging app	Rooted/non-rooted device acquisition, network monitoring, memory dumps	Identified device-resident artifacts (logs, databases); insights into interception potential	End-to-end encryption; evolving Android security; legal access complexity
Son et al. (2021)	Signal, Wickr, Threema	Encrypted messaging app forensics and decryption feasibility	Database analysis, SQLCipher, encrypted SQLite databases	Encryption keys are often stored within apps; physical device access is crucial for decryption	Strong AES-256 encryption; difficulty in acquiring decryption keys; legal/ethical barriers
Nicoletti & Bernaschi (2020)	Skype for Business	Communication artifact recovery, VoIP protocol analysis	Event logs, Windows Registry, cloud/local storage, forensic tools	Recovered chat logs, contacts, and call records; demonstrated conversation reconstruction	Enterprise environments and cloud integration complicate acquisition; need for specialized tools
Ghafarian & Fredy (2022)	Instagram (Web on Windows 10)	Memory forensics of social media usage	Memory dumps, volatile memory analysis	Retrieved sensitive user data (credentials, interactions); showed the value of RAM in social media investigations	Data is transient; requires timely acquisition; dependent on browser/app behavior
Dragonas et al. (2023)	ChatGPT (Android & iOS)	Forensics of AI-based mobile application (Generative AI)	File system, app directories, memory snapshots	Recovered prompt history, session tokens, and cached data; Android provided more artifacts than iOS	iOS sandboxing restricts access; minimal local data by default; app behaviors vary by platform

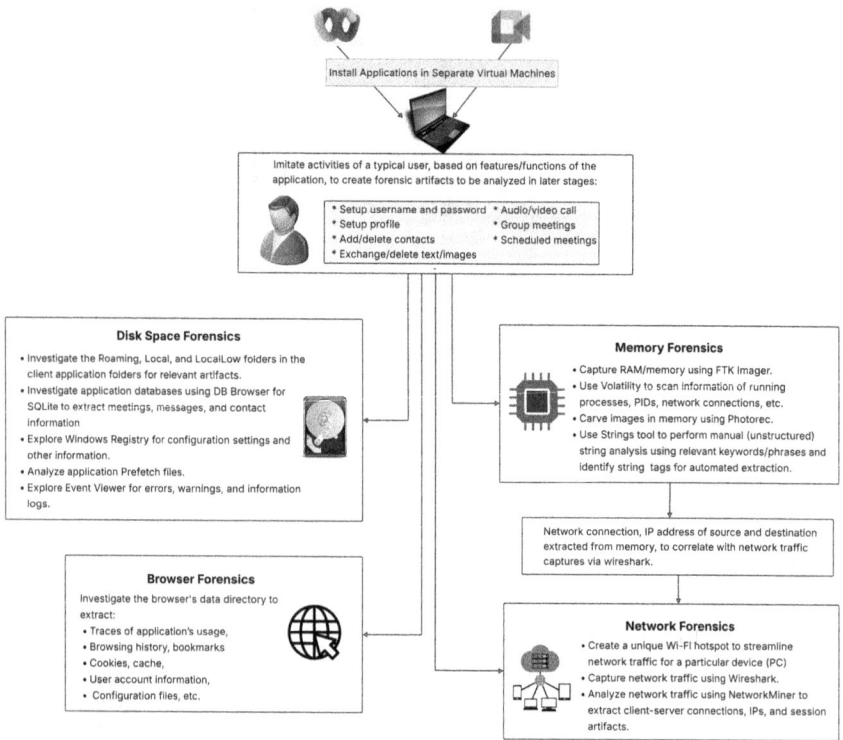

Figure 9.1 Application forensics methodology.

Table 9.2 Tools used for forensic analysis

Tool/Device	Software version	Usage
Windows 10 Virtual Machine (VM)	10	Test environment
Cisco WebEx desktop application	41.3.0.18191	Videoconferencing (desktop) application to test for forensic artifacts
Google Meet Web application	2021.5.1.1	Videoconferencing (Web) application to test for forensic artifacts
AccessData FTK Imager	4.5.0.3	Creation and analysis of forensic images
Volatility	2.6	Analysis of memory dumps
Autopsy	4.19.1	Analysis of forensic images
Strings	2.53	Manual string searching
Bulk Extractor	1.6.0	Analysis of image dumps
Photorec	7.2	Carve .jpeg images

(Continued)

Table 9.2 (Continued)

Tool/Device	Software version	Usage
DB Browser for SQLite	3.12.1	Browse application databases in the client application folder
Regedit	6.1.7600.16385	View Windows Registry
PECmd, Eric Zimmerman	1.5.0.0	Parse prefetch files
Wireshark	3.4.3	Capture/analyze network traffic
NetworkMiner	2.6	Analyze network traffic
Chromecacheview	2.27	View WebEx cache
Chromecookiesview	1.66	View WebEx cookies
DCode	5.5.21194.40	Timestamp decoding

other guests to join them in their personal meeting rooms by sharing their meeting links. This way, videoconferencing meetings may be set up instantly or scheduled at given times.

Cisco WebEx provides several features, including one-to-one and group meetings, creating groups, in-app and in-meeting messages exchanged between users, screen sharing, recording meetings, and finding friends/acquaintances using keyword search. Forensic artifacts about Cisco WebEx (resulting from test activities performed using the given features) identified during the extraction and analysis phases are described in detail.

9.4.2.1 Disk artifacts

Cisco WebEx client application folders in the Local, Locallow, and Roaming folders in the AppData directory revealed user account data and meeting records.

In \AppData\Roaming\webex\Avatar, WebEx saved the avatar of the logged-in user account. Information regarding the last joined location was stored in \AppData\Roaming\webex\Avatar\latestjoinedlocation.ini. The database, \AppData\Local\WebEx\CiscoMeeting.db, revealed information about meetings and their timestamps, along with default WebEx sites of previous and current logged-in accounts. \AppData\Local\CiscoSpark\media\calls stored call logs of the logged-in user.

Registry keys identified for Cisco WebEx are illustrated in Table 9.3.

9.4.2.2 Memory artifacts

Memory artifacts were extracted via automated analysis using tools such as Volatility, Bulk Extractor, and Photorec, as well as manual analysis using string searching to identify *string tags* that may be employed recursively to carve detailed communication artifacts (including meeting records and in-call communication records). Table 9.4 details the memory artifacts extracted for Cisco WebEx.

Table 9.3 Registry keys for Cisco WebEx

Registry key—value explanation
HKCU\SOFTWARE\Microsoft\Installer\Products\[Product ID]\SourceList—Package name of the application (WebEx.msi) and path to installer application.
HKCU\SOFTWARE\Microsoft\Installer\Products\[Product ID]—Information regarding the WebEx application, that is, Version, Product name, Icon, Package code, etc.
HKCU\SOFTWARE\RegisteredApplications—List of registered applications in the client desktop (WebEx inclusive).
HKCU\SOFTWARE\Cisco\Spark—Paths to client application folders.
HKCU\SOFTWARE\Cisco Spark Native—Application settings (e.g., block WebEx desktop app after meeting ends).
HKCU\SOFTWARE\CiscoSystems, Inc.\WebexTeams\Capabilities\URLAssociations— URL associations of the application.
HKCU\SOFTWARE\WebEx\Config—Configuration information (show panelist name, show attendee name, show timestamp, current theme type, etc.).
HKCU\SOFTWARE\WebEx\FeaturePayloads—Default WebEx sites and their configuration information. For example, the *"EnableAES256GCM": true* setting enables AES encryption. 141 such configuration settings are stored in the key.
HKCU\SOFTWARE\WebEx\ProdTools\Logon\[Default WebEx Site]—Credential and folder path with saved profile avatar.
HKCU\SOFTWARE\WebEx\UCF\Components\meetings—Support for Audio, Video, Recording, and WebEx Web, etc., and other related settings such as audio/video file type extensions that are supported by the application.
HKCU\SOFTWARE\WebEx\Framework\RecordPlayback—Path to the folder with saved meeting recordings.
HKCU\SOFTWARE\WebEx\Framework\RecentlyCall—Meeting settings from the last meeting.

9.4.2.3 Network artifacts

Network traffic about various Cisco WebEx activities, such as login, chat messages/files/URLs exchange events, and meeting events, was captured and analyzed (using Wireshark and NetworkMiner) for distinguishing traffic patterns. It was observed that upon login, the application establishes sessions with Amazon, Inc. to employ its cloud services. After authenticating the host to the cloud, it retrieves relevant user account information (including contacts, previous meeting records, etc.) from servers. The captured network traffic is mainly analyzed to establish client–server connections, determine their IP addresses, and timestamps of events that occurred. Table 9.5 details the IP addresses and server addresses that the client communicated with during meetings.

9.4.3 Google Meet

Google Meet is a video conferencing *Web* application; users can conduct quick meetings without having to download/install a desktop application. No records of previous meetings/messages are seemingly kept on the Web

Table 9.4 Summary of memory artifacts extracted for Cisco WebEx

Artifacts	Cisco WebEx
Running processes	[*CiscoCollabHost.exe, Ciscowebexstar.exe, washost.exe, atmgr. exe, webexapplaunch.exe, webexmta.exe*] via Volatility
User Account Information	Username, email address, default WebEx site, personal room number, video address
Encryption keys	AES Keys via Bulk Extractor
Password	×
Profile Photo	×
Keyword Search Terms	**<query> string tag**
Exchanged Text Files	**<sparkShareInfo> string tag** File name, file size
Exchanged Image Files	**<sparkShareInfo> string tag** Image name, image size
URLs – Exchanged	**<a href> string tag**
URLs – Deleted	**<[]> string tag**
Chat Messages – Exchanged	**<sparkMessageGroup> string tag** Chat message body, time of the message, message ID
Chat Messages – deleted	**<p></p> string tag** Chat message body
Scheduled Meetings	**<WebExMeetingData> string tag** Meeting password, meeting key, meeting name, scheduler's username, and default WebEx site, in-meeting messages

Table 9.5 Cisco WebEx network connections

Cisco WebEx LLC.	
global-idbroker-eu.webex.com, idbroker-eu.webex. com, identity-eu.webex.com, global-nebulab.webex. com, meet68.webex.com [user's default WebEx site].	62.109.208.10, 206.197.206.43.
Amazon.com. Inc.	
afra-sni.wbx2.com, ha-k-3az-sni.wbx2.com, u2c.wbx2. com, metrics-k.wbx2.com, ocsp.quovadisglobal.com, ds.ciscospark.com, wdm.k1.ciscospark.com, conv-k. wbx2.com, jabber-integration-k.wbx2.com, meet- wbx2-3az-[id].elb.eu-central-1.amazonaws.com, calliope-k.wbx2.com, contacts-service-k.wbx2.com, avatar-k.wbx2.com, files-api-k.wbx2.com, people. webex.com, hydra-k.wbx2.com, janus-k.wbx2.com, calendar-k.wbx2.com.	18.156.21.71, 18.156.21.15, 18.156.9.248, 34.249.165.103, 18.157.51.3, 35.158.159.116, 3.126.199.220, 3.125.194.2, 35.158.159.125, 52.12.48.103.
Akamai Technologies, Inc.	
e11070.b.akamaiedge.net, query.prod.cms.rt.microsoft. com.edgekey.net, crl.certum.pl, crl.certum. pl.edgekey.net.	23.12.98.160, 88.221.196.113.
Highwinds Network Group, Inc.	
crl.usertrust.com, crl.comodoca.com.	151.139.128.14.

application (except for scheduled meetings via Google Calendar). This is an attractive feature for users with privacy concerns. Since it does not need to be downloaded, Google Meet users can create meetings using a link and share them with individuals they want to *meet* with.

Other Google Meet features, in addition to meetings and in-call messages, include screensharing, captioning, and a whiteboard feature, which uses another Google application called *Jamboard*.

9.4.3.1 Browser artifacts

The disk images captured after test user activity were analyzed to extract target artifacts in browser forensics, which included traces of the application's usage, history, downloads, bookmarks, cache, cookies, profile pictures, email addresses, meeting links, and in-call messages.

Browser artifacts identified for Google Meet with respect to different browsers, including Google Chrome, Microsoft Edge, and Mozilla Firefox, are detailed in Table 9.6.

9.4.3.2 Memory artifacts

The memory dumps captured after test user activity were examined using tools such as Volatility, Bulk Extractor, and Photorec. Manual analysis using string searching was also performed for forensic artifacts related to Google Meet. Table 9.7 details the memory artifacts extracted for Google Meet.

9.4.3.3 Network artifacts

Network traffic about various Google Meet activities was captured and analyzed to distinguish traffic patterns. When Google Meet was accessed, the lh3.googleusercontect.com domain was accessed to load the cache about Google Meet. apis.google.com was accessed then for smooth interaction between Google services. Google LLC servers, contacts.google.com, chat.google.com, meetings.googleapis.com, and jamboard.google.com, etc., were contacted depending on the services required by the user. Another important point to highlight is that Google Meet accessed Microsoft's servers: location-inference-soutneastasia2.cloudapp.net, inference-location-livenet.trafficmanager.net to employ *location inference* services, which essentially identify location profiles of users based on other linked social media apps. User profiling done by applications may have several agendas, such as targeted advertising. Microsoft's Azure was also used for cloud services during Google Meet meetings (onedscolprduks02.uksouth.cloudapp.azure.com).

IP addresses, server domains, timestamps of communication, and digital certificates extracted from packet captures may be used to identify/flag Google Meet traffic or reconstruct events on a timeline chronologically. Table 9.8 records the IP addresses and server domains contacted during meetings.

Table 9.6 Google Meet browser artifacts

Artifact	Google Chrome	Mozilla Firefox	Microsoft Edge
History	...\AppData\Local\Google\Chrome\ User Data\Default\History	...\AppData\Roaming\Mozilla\ Firefox\Profiles\[#].default-release\ places	...\AppData\Local\Microsoft\ Edge\User Data\Default\ History
Bookmarks	...\AppData\Local\Google\Chrome\ User Data\Default\Bookmarks	...\AppData\Roaming\Mozilla\ Firefox\Profiles\[#].default-release\ places	...\AppData\Local\Microsoft\ Edge\User Data\Default\ Bookmarks
Cache	...\AppData\Local\Google\Chrome\ User Data\Default\Cache	...\AppData\Local\Mozilla\Firefox\ Profiles\[#].default-release\cache2 ...\AppData\Local\Mozilla\Firefox\ Profiles\[#].default-release\ jumpListCache	...\AppData\Local\Microsoft\ Edge\User Data\Default\Cache\ Cache_Data
Cookies	...\AppData\Local\Google\Chrome\ UserData\Default\Network\ Cookies	...\AppData\Roaming\Mozilla\ Firefox\Profiles\[#].default-release\ cookies	...\AppData\Local\Microsoft\Edge\ User Data\Default\Cookies
IndexedDB-levelDB	...\AppData\Local\Google\Chrome\ UserData\Default\IndexedDB\ https_meet.google.com_0. indexeddb.leveldb	–	...\AppData\Local\Microsoft\ Edge\UserData\Default\ IndexedDB\https_meet.google. com_0.indexeddb.leveldb
Downloads	...\AppData\Local\Google\Chrome\ User Data\Default\Download Metadata	...\AppData\Roaming\Mozilla\ Firefox\Profiles\[#].default-release\ storage\default\https+++jamboard. google.com	...\AppData\Local\Microsoft\ Edge\User Data\Default\ History
Profile picture	...\AppData\Local\Google\Chrome\ UserData\Default\Accounts\ Avatar Images	...\AppData\Local\Mozilla\Firefox\ Profiles\[#].default-release\ jumpListCache	...\AppData\Local\Microsoft\ Edge\UserData\Default\Cache\ Cache_Data

(Continued)

Table 9.6 (Continued)

Artifact	Google Chrome	Mozilla Firefox	Microsoft Edge
Email address	...\AppData\Local\Google\Chrome\User Data\Default\Login Data	–	...\AppData\Local\Microsoft\Edge\User Data\Default\Web Data
Traces of usage	...\AppData\Local\Google\Chrome\User Data\Default\Web Applications\[.*]	...\AppData\Roaming\Mozilla\Firefox\Profiles\[#].default-release\favicons	...\AppData\Local\Microsoft\Edge\User Data\Default\JumpListIconsRecentClosed
	...\AppData\Local\Google\Chrome\User Data\Default\JumpListIconsRecentClosed	...\AppData\Roaming\Mozilla\Firefox\Profiles\[#].default-release\storage\default	...\AppData\Local\Microsoft\Edge\User Data\Default\Service Worker\Database
	...\AppData\Local\Google\Chrome\User Data\Default\JumpListIconsMostVisited	...\AppData\Roaming\Mozilla\Firefox\Profiles\[#].default-release\AlternateServices	...\AppData\Local\Microsoft\Edge\User Data\Default\Favicons
	...\AppData\Local\Google\Chrome\User Data\Default\Top Sites	...\AppData\Roaming\Mozilla\Firefox\Profiles\[#].default-release\enumerate_devices	...\AppData\Local\Microsoft\Edge\User Data\Default\Network Action Predictor
		...\AppData\Roaming\Mozilla\Firefox\Profiles\[#].default-release\SiteSecurityServiceState	...\AppData\Local\Microsoft\Edge\User Data\Default\Shortcuts
			...\AppData\Local\Microsoft\Edge\User Data\Default\Top Sites

Table 9.7 Summary of memory artifacts extracted for Google Meet

Artifacts	Google Meet
Running processes	[*chrome.exe*] via Volatility
User Account Information	Email address
Encryption keys	AES Keys via Bulk Extractor
Password	×
Profile Photo	Profile photo via Photorec
Keyword Search Terms	Search terms entered in the browser via Bulk Extractor
URLs – Exchanged	**<l, #, null, ["[message]"], l> string tag** Message body, timestamp
Chat Messages – Exchanged	**<l, #, null, ["[message]"], l> string tag** Message body, timestamp
Scheduled Meetings	**{} string tag** Meeting name, downloaded files

Table 9.8 Google Meet network connections

Google LLC.	
clientservices.googleapis.com, www.googleapis.com, accounts. google.com, ssl.gstatic.com, www.gstatic.com, clients.l.google. com, clients4.google.com, meet.google.com, www3.l.google.com, hangouts.google.com, ogs.google.com, play.google.com, chat. google.com, addons-pa.clients6.google.com, hangouts.clients6. google.com, meetings.googleapis.com, people-pa.clients6.google. com, chat-pa.clients6.google.com, contacts.google.com, 14.client-channel.google.com.	142.250.185.36, 172.217.169.227, 172.217.169.234, 172.217.18.141, 142.250.180.35, 216.58.210.78, 172.217.18.142, 142.250.180.42, 216.58.210.74, 172.217.18.138, 142.250.180.46, 108.177.119.189.
Microsoft Corporation.	
location-inference-soutneastasia2.cloudapp.net, inference-location-livenet.trafficmanager.net, inference.location.live.net, onedscolprduks02.uksouth.cloudapp.azure.com, array502.prod. do.dsp.mp.microsoft.com, geo.prod.do.dsp.trafficmanager.net.	13.76.219.184, 52.179.216.235, 51.132.193.104.
Telecom Italia Sparkle S.p.A	
e12437.g.akamaiedge.net, kv801.prod.do.dsp.mp.microsoft.com. edgekey.net.	23.50.147.123.

9.4.4 Microsoft Teams

Microsoft Teams is a *desktop client* video conferencing application that supports meetings, instant messaging, file sharing, and team collaboration. Upon installation and user authentication (typically via Microsoft 365 accounts), users are assigned unique identifiers and can create or join teams and channels to facilitate communication and project coordination. Teams meetings can be initiated instantly or scheduled through integrated calendar functionalities.

Microsoft Teams offers a variety of features, including one-to-one and group video/audio meetings, threaded conversations, private and group chat, screen sharing, meeting recording, file storage, and collaboration via SharePoint/OneDrive integration, and contact discovery using organizational directories or keyword search. Forensic artifacts related to Microsoft Teams—resulting from activities such as messaging, meetings, file transfers, and user interactions—can be extracted and analyzed to reveal valuable digital evidence.

9.4.4.1 Disk artifacts

Although the Microsoft Teams client folder revealed limited critical artifacts, several useful registry keys were identified. These include user-related data such as email addresses, login info, meeting settings, installation source, and web account IDs stored under HKCU\SOFTWARE\Microsoft\Office\Teams. Additionally, Teams' URL associations (e.g., sip, callto, msteams) are recorded under *Capabilities\URLAssociations*, while Outlook integration details appear under *Outlook\Addins\TeamsAddin.FastConnect*. Uninstallation timestamps are stored in UserData\UninstallTimes, although no credentials or sensitive authentication data were found.

Registry keys identified for Microsoft Teams are illustrated in Table 9.9.

Table 9.9 Registry keys for Microsoft Teams

Registry key—value explanation
HKCU\SOFTWARE\RegisteredApplications—List of registered applications in the client desktop (Microsoft Teams inclusive).
HKCU\SOFTWARE\Microsoft\Office\Teams—User account information, including email address, private meeting settings, installation source, web account ID, and login information, etc.
HKCU\SOFTWARE\Microsoft\Office\Teams\Capabilities\URLAssociations—URL associations of Microsoft Teams (e.g., sip, IM, callto, etc.).
HKCU\SOFTWARE\Microsoft\Office\Outlook\Addins\TeamsAddin.FastConnect—Microsoft Teams add-in for Outlook.
HKCU\SOFTWARE\Microsoft\UserData\UninstallTimes—Microsoft Teams is listed if it is uninstalled.

Table 9.10 Summary of memory artifacts extracted for Microsoft Teams

Artifacts	Microsoft Teams
Running Teams' processes	(pslist/pstree) volatility
Network connections	(netscan) volatility
AES keys	Bulk extractor
Profile photos	Image carving against memory dumps via Photorec
User account details (user display name, email address, user ID, etc.)	\<unique_name>/\<userId>String tag
Keywords searched	\<QueryString>String tag
Media/text files exchanged (+deleted)	**\<Microsoft Teams Chat Files>String tag**
Chat/URLs exchanged (+deleted)	**\<skypexspaces-[user ID]>String tag**
Scheduled meetings' details	**\<scheduledmeetinginfo>String tag**

9.4.4.2 Memory artifacts

Memory dumps collected after test user activity were analyzed using tools like Volatility, Bulk Extractor, and PhotoRec. Additionally, manual string searches were conducted to identify forensic artifacts associated with Microsoft Teams. Table 9.10 details the memory artifacts extracted for Microsoft Teams.

9.4.4.3 Network artifacts

The network forensic analysis of Microsoft Teams involved capturing and analyzing traffic using tools like Wireshark and Network Miner. Netscan outputs revealed connections to Microsoft servers over UDP and TLS during meetings, though Volatility missed some PIDs and IPs—a common issue with newer Windows versions. Despite memory volatility and disk manipulation risks, network traffic proved a reliable artifact source. All traffic was encrypted, with no plaintext credentials or media observed. Encryption used the ECDH protocol with TLS (v1.2/HTTP2), and JA3/JA3S hashes fingerprinted TLS handshakes. Teams primarily connects to Microsoft-owned infrastructure but also uses Akamai for content delivery. Login and configuration requests involved domains like "login.microsoftonline.com" and several Skype-associated servers. While packet content remained encrypted, extracted digital certificates confirmed authenticated communication between hosts.

Table 9.11 records the IP addresses and server domains contacted during meetings.

Table 9.11 Microsoft Teams network connections

Microsoft Corporation	
skypedataprdcolneu04.cloudapp.net, mobile.events.data. trafficmanager.net,	52.114.77.33 52.113.195.132
mobile.pip.aria.microsoft.com, teams-office-com.s-0005.s-msedge.net,	52.109.112.104
teams.microsoft.com, asia.configsvc1.live.com.akadns.net,	52.109.124.127
officeclient.microsoft.com, config.officeapps.live.com,	52.114.159.33
asia.odcsm1.live.com.akadns.net, odc.officeapps.live.com,	40.174.108.123
settingsfd-geo.trafficmanager.net, settings-win.data.microsoft.com,	52.114.14.177
sa1-api.nonazsc-teams.cloudapp.net,	52.114.36.126
asm-api-golocal-geo-as-teams.trafficmanager.net, asm.skype.com,	52.114.15.135
as-prod.asyncgw.teams.microsoft.com,	52.114.77.164
apac.ng.msg.teams-msgapi.trafficmanager.net, msgapi.teams.microsoft. com,	138.91.140.216 20.190.175.23
asm-api-prod-geo-as-skype.trafficmanager.net, as-api.asm.skype.com,	52.114.128.9
teams.events.data.microsoft.com, mobile.pipe.aria.microsoft.com,	52.113.194.132
login.microsoftonline.com, stamp2.login.microsoftonline	52.114.16.138 52.114.14.237
Akamai Technologies	
e12370.g.akamaiedge.net, cdn.odc.officeapps.live.com.edgekey.net, cdn.odc.officeapps.live.com.	104.120.112.79

END OF CHAPTER QUESTIONS

1. In disk forensics, what type of data is particularly useful because it is retained even after a device is shut down?
2. What is "page smearing" in the context of memory forensics?
3. Discuss the importance of updating forensic artifacts and tools with successive application updates.
4. How does network encryption impact the strategies used in network forensics?
5. Explain the steps involved in the general forensic methodology outlined for application analysis.
6. Describe the types of forensic artifacts that can be extracted from memory during an investigation.
7. What challenges do investigators face when dealing with closed-source or proprietary applications in memory forensics?
8. A company's web application has been compromised, and sensitive customer data have been leaked. As a forensic analyst, outline the steps you would take to investigate this breach.
9. During a forensic analysis, you discover that the suspect's device uses full disk encryption. What strategies could you employ to access the necessary data?
10. While analyzing memory dumps, you encounter data structures from a proprietary application with no available documentation. How would you proceed to extract useful information?

11. How does the architectural divergence between client device applications and SOA-based Web applications impact the design and execution of a forensic investigation?

12. Compare the evidentiary implications of artifacts retrieved from volatile memory versus persistent disk storage in the context of video conferencing applications like WebEx or Teams.

13. Discuss the limitations and benefits of conducting forensic analysis within virtualized environments (VMs) when investigating application artifacts across memory, disk, and network layers.

14. Design a layered forensic methodology to correlate artifacts retrieved from a browser, memory, and disk image when analyzing a Web application like Google Meet.

15. Encryption poses serious challenges in application forensics. How would you adapt your acquisition and analysis approach when investigating a client application that utilizes volume-level encryption?

16. In application forensics, what role does the Windows Registry play in timeline construction and user activity reconstruction? Illustrate with examples based on the forensic features discussed.

17. Discuss the challenges associated with using volatile memory artifacts (e.g., running processes, PIDs, temporary keys) for evidentiary purposes in applications that aggressively manage memory and employ page smearing or swapping.

18. How can forensic investigators analyze encrypted HTTPS traffic when inspecting application behavior on the network layer? What can still be inferred even without decryption? Describe how you might still extract useful forensic information from this traffic.

19. What challenges do ephemeral artifacts (e.g., cookies, cache, prefetch files) present in the forensic analysis of browser-based Web applications? How can investigators enhance artifact recovery in such contexts?

20. How might closed-source or proprietary application structures affect the extraction and interpretation of forensic artifacts in memory forensics? What reverse engineering strategies can be ethically and legally employed?

21. Explain how residual browser artifacts on a host system can be used as a proxy for cloud-stored Web application data. What are the risks in misinterpreting these artifacts?

22. Application logs are often deleted or manipulated by attackers. How can investigators use indirect or redundant system artifacts (e.g., swap files, RAM, WR) to reconstruct deleted application data?

23. Considering the volatility of RAM, how would you justify the admissibility of recovered memory-resident artifacts (e.g., credentials, tokens, profile images) in a court of law?

24. Examine the application data directory (below), as viewed via Autopsy, of an application after being used for work meetings. Determine and

list at least five forensic artifacts from the figure along with the meta-data for each artifact and discuss in detail of their forensic relevance.

25. Analyze the role of open-source forensic frameworks like Volatility in application-specific memory forensics. What are the advantages and what limitations must be addressed in future plugin development?

26. In what ways might forensic investigators accidentally contaminate or overwrite evidence during memory acquisition for Web applications running in browsers? How can such risks be minimized?

27. Propose an end-to-end forensic strategy to investigate data breaches stemming from JavaScript injection in a Web application. Which system artifacts would be most valuable, and how would they be extracted and correlated?

NOTES

1 https://www.volatilityfoundation.org/.
2 Page smearing occurs during memory acquisition, specifically when the contents of memory pages change while the acquisition process is in progress.
3 Page swapping is a memory management process where pages of memory are moved between RAM and the disk (swap space) to free up RAM for active processes.
4 https://openai.com/.

REFERENCES

[1] Akremi, A., Sallay, H., Rouached, M., and Bouaziz, R., "Applying digital forensics to service oriented architecture," *International Journal of Web Services Research*, vol. 17, no. 1, pp. 17–42, Jan. 2020.

[2] OWASP, "OWASP Top Ten," Owasp.org. https://owasp.org/www-project-top-ten/. [Online], Accessed Jan 10, 2022.

[3] Swinhoe, D. and Hill, M., "The 15 biggest data breaches of the 21st century," *CSO Online*, Jul. 16, 2021. https://www.csoonline.com/article/2130877/the-biggest-data-breaches-of-the-21st-century.html

[4] Case, Andrew and Richard, Golden G., "Memory forensics: The path forward", *Digital Investigation*, vol. 20, pp. 23–33, 2017. ISSN 1742-2876, doi:10.1016/j.diin.2016.12.004

[5] Barradas, D., Brito, T., Duarte, D., Santos, N., and Rodrigues, L., "Forensic analysis of communication records of messaging applications from physical memory," *Computers and Security*, vol. 86, pp. 484–497, 2019. https://www.sciencedirect.com/science/article/pii/S0167404818311313

[6] Casey, Eoghan, Fellows, Geoff, Geiger, Matthew, and Stellatos, Gerasimos, "The growing impact of full disk encryption on digital forensics," *Digital Investigation*, vol. 8, no. 2, pp. 129–134, 2011, ISSN 1742-2876, doi:10.1016/j.diin.2011.09.005

[7] Khalid, Z., Iqbal, F., Kamoun, F., Hussain, M., and Khan, L. A., "Forensic analysis of the Cisco WebEx application," *2021 5th Cyber Security in Networking Conference (CSNet)*, pp. 90–97, 2021, doi:10.1109/CSNet52717.2021.9614647

[8] Khalid, Z., Iqbal, F., Al-Hussaeni, K., MacDermott, A., and Hussain, M. "Forensic analysis of Microsoft Teams: Investigating memory, disk and network," In Paiva, X. Li, S. I. Lopes, N. Gupta, D. B. Rawat, A. Patel, H. R. Karimi *Science and Technologies for Smart Cities – 7th EAI International Conference, SmartCity360°*, 2021, 360. Lecture Notes of the Institute for Computer Sciences, Social Informatics and Telecommunications Engineering, vol 442, 583–601. Springer, Cham. doi:10.1007/978-3-031-06371-8_37

[9] Shahzad, F., Javed, A.R., Jalil, Z., and Iqbal, F. "Cyber forensics with machine learning," In: Phung D., Webb G.I., Sammut C. (eds) *Encyclopedia of Machine Learning and Data Science*. Springer, New York, NY, 2022. doi:10.1007/978-1-4899-7502-7_987-1

[10] Solanke, A.A. and Biasiotti, M.A. "Digital forensics AI: Evaluating, standardizing and optimizing digital evidence mining techniques," *Künstl Intell*, 2022. doi:10.1007/s13218-022-00763-9

[11] Cloyd, T., Osborn, T., Ellingboe, B., Glisson, W. B., and Choo, K. R., "Browser analysis of residual facebook data," In *2018 17th IEEE International Conference on Trust, Security and Privacy in Computing and Communications/12th IEEE International Conference on Big Data Science and Engineering (TrustCom/BigDataSE)*, pp. 1440–1445, 2018, doi:10.1109/TrustCom/BigDataSE.2018.00200

[12] Wijnberg, D., and Le-Khac, N.-A., "Identifying interception possibilities for WhatsApp communication," *Forensic Science International: Digital Investigation*, vol. 38, p. 301132, 2021. doi:10.1016/j.fsidi.2021.301132

[13] Son, J., Kim, Y.W., Oh, D.B., and Kim, K., "Forensic analysis of instant messengers: Decrypt Signal, Wickr, and Threema,' *Forensic Science International: Digital Investigation*, vol. 40, p. 301347, 2022. doi:10.1016/j.fsidi.2022.301347

[14] Nicoletti, M., and Bernaschi, M., "Forensic analysis of Microsoft Skype for business,' *Digital Investigation*, vol. 29, pp. 159–179, 2019. doi:10.1016/j.diin.2019.03.012

[15] Ghafarian, A. and Fredy, J., "Investigating instagram privacy through memory forensics," *Lecture Notes in Networks and Systems*, 1263–1273, 2023. doi:10.1007/978-3-031-37717-4_84

[16] Dragonas, Evangelos, Lambrinoudakis, Costas, and Nakoutis, Panagiotis, "Forensic analysis of OpenAI's ChatGPT mobile application," *Forensic Science International Digital Investigation*, voll. 50, pp. 301801–301801, 2024. doi:10.1016/j.fsidi.2024.301801

Chapter 10

Autonomous vehicle forensics

The advent of digital (/electric) vehicles, and self-driving (autonomous) cars, equipped with a multitude of digital features and functionalities, has significantly elevated their role as crucial repositories of digital evidence in both technical issues and criminal investigations. In the contemporary landscape, digital forensics has emerged as a versatile solution, particularly in contexts such as analyzing warranty claims in the realm of digital vehicles, investigating automobile accidents, scrutinizing security-related implementations, and more. Among these applications, crime investigation within the automotive industry stands out as the most promiGhaidanent and pivotal use case for digital forensics.

Traditionally, in the course of a criminal investigation involving vehicles, evidence collection primarily centered around physical elements like fingerprints and DNA, which were inherently non-digital in nature. However, today's autonomous vehicles have evolved into intelligent entities that store an extensive array of digital data, encompassing information such as travel routes, destinations, frequently visited locations, call logs, videos, music libraries, and more. Consequently, the field of digital vehicle forensics has arisen as a sub-discipline, enabling investigators to systematically preserve and extract a diverse spectrum of digital evidence from modern-day vehicles.

Digital vehicles are invaluable sources of digital evidence. The predominant approaches in vehicle forensics revolve around the acquisition and analysis of this digital evidence [1]. Nevertheless, navigating the intricacies of digital vehicle forensics poses its own set of challenges, which this chapter aims to discuss. It will delve into the intricacies of the digital vehicle forensics process, shed light on the significance of telematics systems, and elucidate the challenges that investigators may encounter throughout the forensic investigation process

DOI: 10.1201/9781003644255-10

10.1 AUTONOMOUS VEHICLE COMPONENTS

Modern-day autonomous vehicles may encompass the following components (Figure 10.1):

1. **Telematics and Infotainment Systems:** These systems represent a significant source of digital evidence related to vehicles. Nearly all vehicle manufacturers incorporate telematics systems into their vehicle designs. It is anticipated that by 2025, virtually every vehicle will be equipped with this technology. Telematics systems facilitate the transmission of data through telecommunication channels.
2. **Event Data Recorders (EDR):** It is also known as black boxes, EDRs were introduced in North America in the late 20th century. These devices primarily activate during vehicle collisions and serve as valuable sources of evidence for various scenarios, including accidents, vehicle theft, forgery, and fraud [2].
3. **Front and Rear Dash Cameras:** Some front and rear dash cameras come equipped with data storage capabilities, making them useful for forensic purposes by providing recorded data.
4. **Electronic Control Units (ECUs) in Autonomous Vehicles:** ECUs, sometimes referred to as Engine Control Modules (ECMs), are small, embedded devices within vehicles responsible for controlling various electrical systems. They also possess data storage capabilities, as microcontrollers are integrated into these devices.
5. **Key Fobs for Keyless Entry:** Key Fobs have become commonplace for accessing vehicles. They hold vital information such as the Vehicle Identification Number (VIN), odometer readings, time stamps, and more. Extracting data from key fobs often requires specialized forensic software or cooperation with local vehicle dealerships.

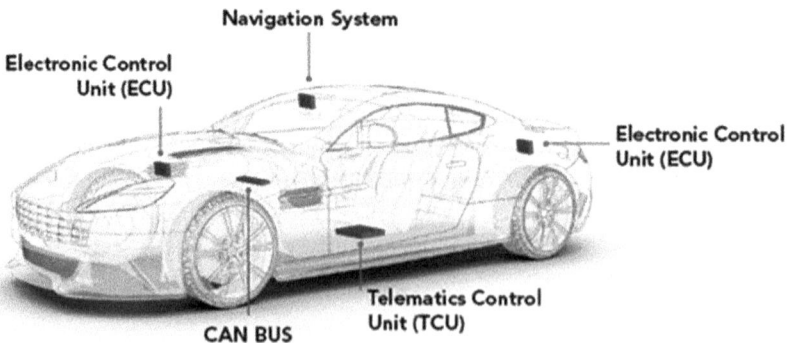

Figure 10.1 Components of an autonomous vehicle.

6. **Controller Area Network (CAN) Bus:** The CAN bus protocol is designed to facilitate communication between ECUs and other vehicle devices in a prioritized manner. It plays a crucial role in enabling various components of a vehicle to exchange information effectively.

10.1.1 Autonomous vehicle telematics

A digital vehicle telematics system is a combination of informatics, telecommunication, electronics, and software that functions to collect and analyze data and, as a result, improve the safety and efficiency standards of the overall driving experience. Global Positioning System (GPS), vehicle diagnostic systems, wireless devices, and black box technologies combine for vehicle telematics to collect and transmit the vehicle data, like location, speed, service, maintenance, etc. The information can be used to improve safety and performance by doing real-time analysis. Today, the general practice is to embed vehicle telematics directly into fleet vehicles. Other telematics devices, like GPS, are also available separately for aftermarket installation. A telematics system consists of three blocks that work together to provide beneficial services (see Figure 10.2):

1. **Telematics Control Unit (TCU):** The TCU is a hardware module installed in modern digital vehicles that is equipped with telecommunication interfaces such as CAN Bus and General Packet Radio Service (GPRS), among others. Its primary function is to gather vehicle data and transmit it wirelessly to a telematics cloud server. TCU relies on technologies like GPRS or cellular systems like 3G, 4G, Edge, 5G, and LTE for data transmission.

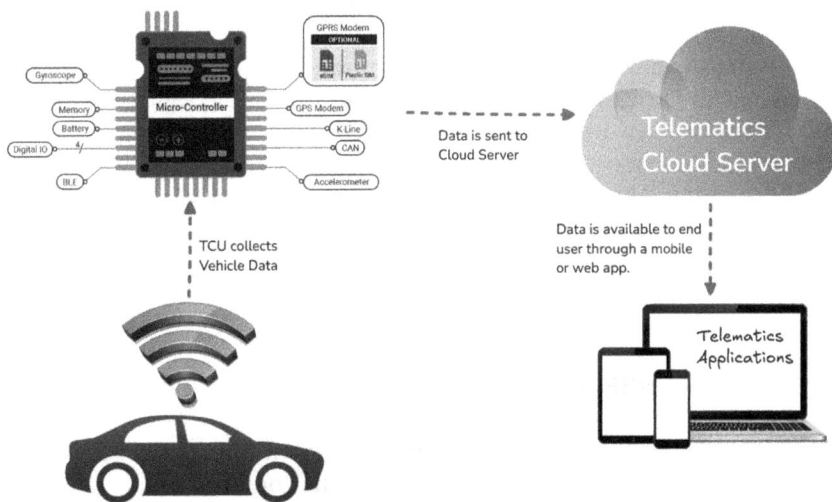

Figure 10.2 Working of telematics system.

2. **Telematics Cloud Server:** Data collected by the TCU is transferred to a cloud server via a wireless network, which can include GPRS and other cellular networks. To enhance security, data packets are encrypted before transmission. Once in the cloud, the data are initially extracted and then stored within a database for further processing.

3. **Web Browser or Mobile App for Data Presentation:** Users can access the vehicle telematics system's data through a web browser or a dedicated smartphone application. These interfaces allow users to interact with the information stored on the server. Additionally, these data can be integrated into third-party software or applications, such as mapping software, for various purposes.

10.1.2 Applications of vehicle telematics

The vehicle telematics system is a beneficial addition to digital cars. The following are some of its applications:

1. **Telematics Vehicle Tracking:** GPS combined with GPRS is used for tracking purposes. A GPRS modem is installed with the user's device. That collects and transmits data from the GPS.

2. **Fleet Vehicle Telematics System Management:** The telematics system is usually embedded with the fleet vehicle to perform management services like vehicle scheduling, maintenance, financing, diagnostics, safety management, fuel consumption, engine health, etc.

3. **Standard Adherence by Telematics System:** Standards by the Association of Equipment Management Professionals are adhered to that deliver data in .xml format.

4. **Car Sharing:** The system helps to keep track of members who use the car or drive the car, and hence can help a digital investigator to figure out the user of the vehicle.

5. **Wireless Vehicle Safety Communications:** Sensors are installed in the vehicle that can help to predict traffic congestion, signal lights, etc. These sensors are connected to the telematics system and hence can record this information too, and optimize the routes.

6. **Insurance:** The insurance companies record the driver's vehicle and calculate the risk assessments. These data from insurance companies can also be helpful for forensic investigators.

10.2 DIGITAL VEHICLE FORENSICS

Digital vehicle forensics is the utilization of digital forensics practices and techniques on automotive vehicle systems. The forensics process answers questions about accidents, forgery, fraud, vehicle manipulation, hit and run, etc. As with any other forensics process, digital vehicle forensics involves the acquisition, preservation, and analysis of resident information. For vehicle forensics, two types of forensics can be considered: (1) *live forensics*, where data are collected in a run-time scenario, which is mostly useful to collect data from volatile memory, and (2) *post-mortem forensics*, where the system is stopped to acquire the data. Between live and post-mortem forensics, the latter eliminates any risk of evidence loss. However, the disadvantage is, it does not acquire volatile data that can have a lot of useful information regarding the crime scene.

10.2.1 Data classes for digital vehicle forensics

Data evidence from digital vehicles can be categorized into five distinct classes, as illustrated in Figure 10.3, each serving a unique purpose [3]. Firstly, firmware refers to the software embedded in the ECU, and analyzing it is crucial for detecting any modifications made to the ECU. Communication data encompass the information exchanged between vehicle components and the cloud server, providing insights into the vehicle's connectivity and communication. User data encompass information that is written, read, deleted, or modified when external devices like USB drives connect with vehicle components, reflecting interactions initiated by third parties. Safety-related data originates from the EDR and focuses on a vehicle's condition during safety-critical moments, offering crucial information about its safety state. Lastly, security-related data provides implicit insights into device security, shedding light on the security measures and vulnerabilities associated with the vehicle's systems and components. These five categories collectively contribute to a comprehensive understanding of digital evidence in the context of vehicle forensics.

10.2.2 Forensics process for digital vehicles

The general forensics process involves forensic readiness, data acquisition, data analysis, and documentation. To perform vehicle data forensics, several components are necessary, including the targeted vehicle, an acquisition computer for communication with in-vehicle systems, an accompanying tool-set to facilitate communication, and a suitable cable that corresponds to the chosen connection interface, such as OBD-II to Bluetooth, OBD-II to Ethernet, or JTAG to USB, ensuring that once all components are set up, data acquisition can proceed. The forensic steps are discussed in detail below [4]:

1. **Forensic Readiness:** The concept of forensic readiness emphasizes an organization's ability to maximize the use of digital evidence while minimizing investigation costs. This readiness entails analyzing firmware software, particularly in ECUs, to detect modifications. The phase

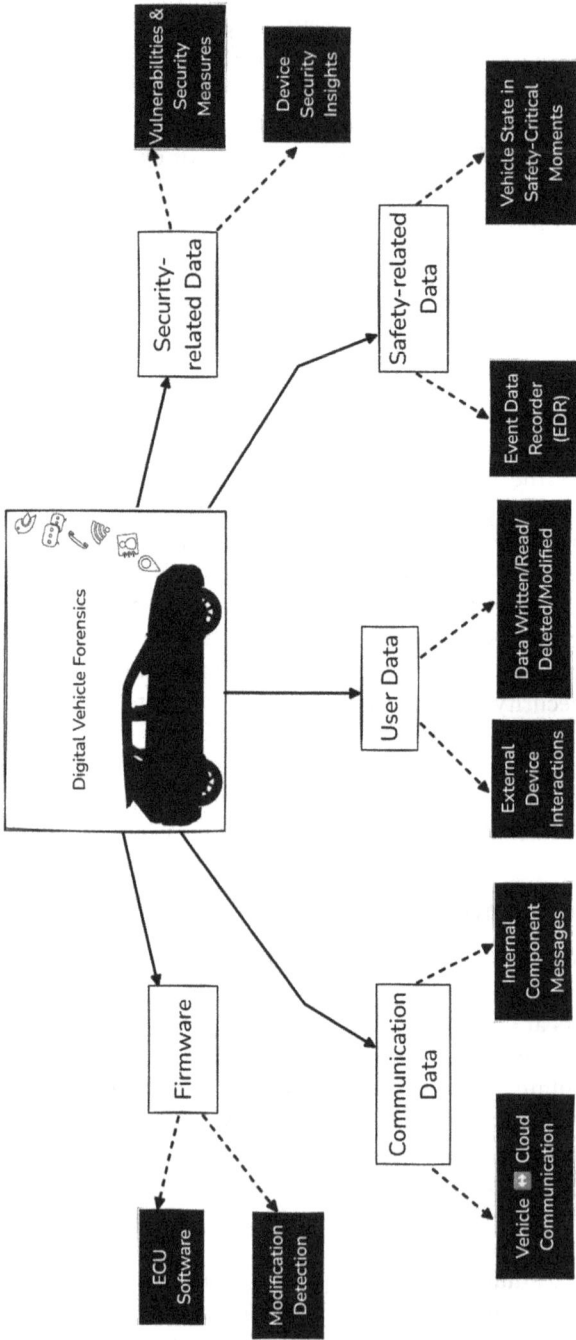

Figure 10.3 Data classes for vehicle forensics.

involves documentation, data source (components) analysis, interface determination, and assessing the level of development in automotive forensics and tool availability. It concludes with selecting a connection interface for data acquisition. Positive examples include EDRs and accessible ECU data via OBD-II connection interface,[1] while challenges arise when no connection interface is present or documentation is insufficient, affecting forensic analysis feasibility. Ultimately, forensic readiness serves as a pivotal foundation for cost-effective and thorough forensic investigations.

2. **Data Acquisition:** It is crucial for ensuring the integrity of data collection, and it involves several key considerations. To maintain data integrity, one-way communication (write-only) is emphasized, which can be achieved using write-blocker devices. Trustworthiness of collected data and the functionality of the toolset used are also vital. Duplicating original data and creating mirror (copy) images are essential to prevent accidental manipulation. This phase is just as critical for automotive systems as it is for general IT systems. The phase includes determining the vehicle's model variant, as in the first phase. The evaluation of chosen data sources depends on the specific investigation requirements, with general and standardized sources easily acquired by reviewing the forensic readiness phase, while more specific and non-standardized sources (like a vehicle black box) may necessitate additional resources, such as internal documentation or reverse engineering of identical vehicle models. Next is selecting an interface (includes OBD-II, JTAG, and actual soldering of chips), followed by checking tools, implementing data acquisition, and ensuring data integrity. Results include comprehensive documentation, original data, and copies for further analysis.

3. **Data Analysis:** In the analysis phase, the primary objective is to reconstruct events comprehensively and logically, creating evidence timelines. To maintain data integrity, a copy of the original data is used for analysis, and logs need to be correlated in a manner that ensures consistency and handles errors. Vehicles present numerous data sources, including ECUs, gateways, and bus systems, allowing for the correlation of data from various other sources (like smartphones) to build evidence trails. The detailed analysis involves an initial inspection of acquired data, filtering for relevant events, and the creation of time lines and evidence trails, all documented for reproducibility. Positive examples include successful reconstruction of events based on network traffic analysis, while negative examples involve misinterpretation of data from an ECU leading to unreliable conclusions that may not be accepted in legal proceedings due to shortcomings in robustness, integrity, and consistency. Tools such as Wireshark, SANS SIFT, and Plasos log2timeline may be used for analysis.

4. **Documentation:** In this step, the reports are collected from the forensic readiness, data acquisition, and data analysis steps. A final report containing all the results is created to be presented in court or to any other relevant body.

10.2.3 Data acquisition from embedded telematics

Data acquisition is an important step in digital forensics; in the case of vehicle forensics, an important source is telematics. Forensic data that can be acquired from the digital vehicles' telematics system involves idling time, location, fuel consumption, maintenance and services, speed, vehicle faults, and braking, etc. Hence, telematics data are of great importance because it helps to improve the driving experience, productivity, etc. The telematics system ranges differently with different models of cars. The data can be stored in many different types, depicting a broad categorization of the vehicle:

- Vehicle information system (Serial Number, Engine Number, Part Number, Vehicle identification number, build number)
- Navigation data (saved locations, recent destinations, track logs, routes followed, speed logs)
- Connected devices (smartphones, media players, USB drivers, hard drives, SD cards, Wireless Access Points (WAPs)
- Application data (traffic apps, weather apps, Facebook, etc.)
- Events (lights on/off, doors open or close, Wi-Fi connection, Bluetooth connection, GPS data sync, odometer readings, braking, gear shifts, acceleration, and other events)
- Device basic information (call logs, contacts, media, Access Point Information, Device IDs)

Till the year 2014, these telematics systems were useless for forensic investigators as the data collected remained inaccessible. Physical data acquisition of data can be done on the telematics or infotainment system. This is the most beneficial and detailed data acquisition. Investigators can acquire all the information bit by bit from the hard drive (even the deleted files). The only drawback is that it takes a much longer time compared to logical extraction. The acquisition can also be done by de-mounting the memory chip, which is known as the chip-off method, but this technique is a very difficult way to acquire data without any damage. FTK Imager and Sleuth kit autopsy can be the best option available. Physical acquisition is a reliable source of data retrieval from a smartphone, but the method faces some issues in digital vehicle forensics due to the lack of forensic tools that are specific to vehicles.

US-based company Berla Corporation released a forensic toolkit, iVe, for digital vehicle forensics in 2014 [5]. It is the first of its kind, with a database to determine if the vehicle is supported for data acquisition, along with instructions for the data acquisition and a data analysis algorithm. Depending on the type and model of the vehicle, the data acquisition can be as big as 25 GB. The data acquired can potentially store information from last year, and all current and previously connected devices. Consequently, these logs can provide essential information to the investigator.

END OF CHAPTER QUESTIONS

1. A forensic investigator is examining a modern autonomous vehicle involved in a fatal accident. The vehicle has advanced driver-assistance systems (ADAS) and was reportedly operating in semi-autonomous mode at the time of the crash. The investigator needs to determine whether the vehicle's systems malfunctioned or if human error was involved. (a). Identify the key vehicle components and data sources the investigator should focus on to reconstruct the events leading to the accident. (b). Discuss the challenges the investigator might face in extracting and analyzing data from these sources, considering proprietary systems and data encryption. (c). Propose a methodology for correlating data from multiple systems to establish a reliable timeline of events.
2. Discuss the impact of vehicle telematics on privacy and how forensic investigators can balance the need for evidence with respecting individuals' privacy rights. Include considerations of legal frameworks and ethical guidelines.
3. Explain why physical data acquisition in vehicle forensics might be preferred over logical extraction, despite being more time-consuming.
4. Describe the importance of the chain-of-custody in digital vehicle forensics and the potential consequences of failing to maintain it properly.
5. How has the shift from physical to digital evidence in vehicles transformed the investigative landscape? What implications does this shift have for forensic methodology and evidence admissibility?
6. Given the integration of telematics, ECUs, and CAN bus communication, how would you structure a multi-source forensic acquisition strategy that preserves evidence integrity while enabling deep analysis?
7. In what ways might vehicle firmware manipulation affect the reliability of digital evidence retrieved from an ECU? How can forensic experts detect and validate such manipulations?
8. Compare the evidentiary value of Event Data Recorders (EDRs) with that of infotainment systems. In what types of investigations would one be prioritized over the other?
9. Evaluate how international variations in laws and regulations might affect digital vehicle forensics, especially in cross-border investigations. Discuss how forensic investigators can navigate these legal complexities while conducting their analyses.

10. How can event correlation from ECUs, dashcam video logs, sensor data as well as braking, GPS, and gear shift events retrieved from telematics logs be used to prove or disprove tampering in a suspected staged accident?

11. Discuss the technical and legal implications of extracting data from key fobs. What challenges might arise in ensuring forensic soundness and lawful access?

12. Evaluate the trade-offs between live and post-mortem forensic acquisition in autonomous vehicle investigations. What types of volatile data might be lost in post-mortem modes, and how can this impact legal proceedings?

13. Design a forensic validation approach to distinguish between legitimate system errors and manipulated error logs in a telematics dataset, particularly in the context of warranty fraud.

14. Telematics cloud servers often store sensitive vehicle data across jurisdictions. How should investigators handle cross-border data access while maintaining compliance with digital evidence and privacy laws?

15. What are the limitations of applying traditional forensic tools like FTK Imager and Sleuth Kit in digital vehicle environments? How does a tool like iVe address some of these limitations?

16. In a car-sharing scenario involving multiple authenticated users, how would you correlate user account activity across telematics logs, infotainment system usage, and smartphone pairings?

17. Discuss how the analysis of application data (e.g., Facebook or weather apps) on a vehicle's infotainment system could reveal behavioral patterns or support timeline reconstruction.

18. How can artifacts related to wireless connections (e.g., Bluetooth pairings, Wi-Fi logs) be used to identify previously connected devices or infer the physical presence of individuals?

19. What are the ethical and investigative concerns involved in performing a chip-off acquisition on automotive components like infotainment memory? How can damage and data loss be minimized?

20. Explain how network forensics tools (e.g., Wireshark) can be adapted to analyze intra-vehicle communication, and what unique challenges vehicle bus protocols pose compared to traditional IP networks.

21. What technical factors determine whether a forensic analyst can extract useful telematics data from an older vehicle model? How might reverse engineering assist in such cases?

22. What challenges do investigators face in distinguishing between vehicle behavior controlled by a user versus autonomous system decision-making? How should forensic analysis be adapted to resolve this?

23. Assume you are examining a fleet telematics system to identify internal sabotage where a driver repeatedly tampered with vehicle software to create false maintenance alerts. What technical approach would you use to correlate CAN bus anomalies, EDR logs, and driver authentication artifacts across multiple vehicles?

24. In a case of alleged insurance fraud, a car crash was staged. You have obtained dashcam footage, TCU logs (telematics), and mobile app activity records from the driver's cloud-synced profile. How would you validate the authenticity of crash data versus spoofed input signals or log manipulation? Discuss methods of timeline alignment, sensor correlation, and anomaly detection. Considering the rapid advancement of autonomous vehicle technology, predict and discuss future challenges that digital vehicle forensics might face, particularly regarding new data sources and increased system complexities. Propose solutions or areas of research that could address these challenges.

NOTE

1 OBD-II allows acquisition of data without physical access to an ECU, unlike JTAG which needs direct access.

REFERENCES

[1] Lacroix, J., El-Khatib, K., and Akalu, R., "Vehicular digital forensics: What does my vehicle know about me?" In *Proceedings of the 6th ACM Symposium on Development and Analysis of Intelligent Vehicular Networks and Applications (DIVANet '16)*, Nov., 2016, pp. 59–66. Association for Computing Machinery, Malta, Malta. https://doi.org/10.1145/2989275.2989282

[2] Daily, J.S., Singleton, N., Downing, B., and Manes, G.W., "Light vehicle event data recorder forensics," In Sobh, T. (eds) *Advances in Computer and Information Sciences and Engineering.* Springer, Dordrecht, 2008. doi:10.1007/978-1-4020-8741-7_31

[3] Buquerin, K. K. G., Corbett, C., and Hof, H. J., "A generalized approach to automotive forensics," *Forensic Science International: Digital Investigation*, vol. 36, p. 301111, 2021.

[4] Gomez Buquerin, K. K., and Corbett, M. "Analysis of digital forensics capabilities on state-of-the-art vehicles," *Forensic Science International: Digital Investigation*, vol. 36, p. 301111, 2021. https://doi.org/10.1016/j.fsidi.2021.301111

[5] "iVe – Berla.co." [Online]. https://berla.co/tag/ive/

Chapter 11

AI, ML, and computer vision in modern digital forensic workflows

The increasing volume, velocity, and variety of digital data in contemporary cyber environments have introduced unprecedented challenges for digital forensic practitioners. Traditional manual techniques for evidence acquisition, analysis, and interpretation are becoming increasingly inadequate when confronted with sophisticated attack vectors, large-scale data breaches, and the widespread use of encryption and obfuscation techniques. In response to these growing complexities, the integration of intelligent computational paradigms, specifically Artificial Intelligence (AI), Machine Learning (ML), Deep Learning (DL), and Computer Vision (CV), has emerged as a critical enhancement to modern digital forensic workflows.

This chapter introduces the foundational concepts of these technologies and examines their relevance and application within digital forensic contexts. It outlines the progression from general AI principles to specialized machine learning techniques and deep neural networks, as well as the role of visual intelligence in the analysis of digital artifacts. The subsequent sections analyze these paradigms in detail, focusing on their operational utility, emerging use cases, and transformative impact on the field of digital forensics.

11.1 ARTIFICIAL INTELLIGENCE

AI embodies the concept of imparting machines with human-like intelligence, enabling them to think and act in a manner akin to humans. AI is meticulously programmed to exhibit traits such as learning and problem-solving, mirroring the cognitive processes of human beings. ML is a subset of AI, with a focus on machines learning from datasets and adapting to new information without human intervention. Further down the hierarchy, Deep Learning represents another facet of ML, leveraging neural networks to facilitate learning from vast, unstructured datasets. AI is rooted in the fundamental premise that machines can emulate human thought and behavior, tackling a wide spectrum of challenges, from simple to highly complex. Its objectives span the emulation of human cognitive functions across various

DOI: 10.1201/9781003644255-11

domains, including mathematics, linguistics, psychology, and computer science. The evolution of AI has been nothing short of remarkable, equipping machines with heightened intelligence. The applications of AI are virtually boundless, transcending numerous industries. From healthcare and innovative surgical procedures to the advent of smart cars, toys, and homes, AI's influence is pervasive. In the financial sector, AI plays a pivotal role in identifying and combating fraudulent activities, enhancing security and efficiency. Digital forensics, too, harnesses the capabilities of AI to streamline the investigative process. The automation of procedures significantly improves the management of large datasets, leading to more efficient and effective results. This synergy between AI and digital forensics holds great promise in the ever-expanding landscape of data analysis and investigation.

11.1.1 Applications of AI in digital forensics

AI and its specialized subfields, such as ML and Deep Learning, exhibit a myriad of practical applications within the domain of digital forensics. Across various facets of this discipline, from malware analysis to memory forensics, image and video forensics to IoT forensics, AI plays a pivotal role.

1. **Malware Analysis**: AI offers invaluable support in the detection and analysis of malware within computer systems. Researchers employ diverse algorithms, including C4.5, k-NN, and Support Vector Machines (SVM), drawing upon accessible datasets like Virus Share and Kaggle to enhance their malware analysis capabilities.
2. **Image/Video Forensics**: The realm of image and video forensics benefits significantly from AI. Datasets can be sourced from platforms like Pascal VOC and ImageNet. Among the array of AI algorithms, Neural Networks and SVM emerge as particularly effective tools for image and video forensics.
3. **IoT Forensics**: The intricacies of the IoT necessitate a comprehensive approach encompassing network forensics, device forensics, and cloud forensics. The inherently time-consuming nature of IoT forensics makes AI a vital asset, expediting the investigative process.
4. **Cyber Forensics**: In the realm of cyber forensics, evidence is gathered both locally and from cloud-based sources. Here, the Random Forest (RF) algorithm stands out as a potent AI tool, aiding investigators in their pursuit of digital evidence.
5. **Network Forensics**: The field of network forensics grapples with the challenges posed by the ever-increasing volume of network packets. The utilization of AI applications plays a vital role in the extraction of relevant information while filtering out redundancy from extensive datasets associated with network traffic analysis. Numerous researchers have employed a variety of algorithms, including Random Forest (RF), K-Nearest Neighbor (KNN), Decision Tree (DT), Random Tree

(RT), and Regression, to automate and streamline this intricate process [1, 2]. This approach not only enhances the efficiency of network traffic analysis but also ensures that valuable insights can be extracted from the vast volumes of data, optimizing the management of network resources and security.

6. **File System Forensics:** The potential for recovering deleted files from file systems often hinges on the presence of remaining metadata. However, there are scenarios in which deleted files lose their metadata, and their contents end up residing in unallocated portions of storage. To facilitate the recovery of these data files, two common approaches are employed: file carving and disk fragmentation. The latter method involves the creation of a large number of file fragments, which can pose a significant challenge when it comes to manual searching. Hence, an automated solution becomes imperative such as leveraging Natural Language Processing (NLP) in the file fragmentation process by combining SVM with a bag-of-words model, effectively harnessing ML techniques. In this context, file fragments are treated as collections of bytes, and the analysis involves the calculation of unigrams and bigrams, along with other statistical measurements [3]. This innovative method not only automates the process of file fragmentation but also enhances the efficiency and accuracy of data recovery from fragmented and metadata-deprived files.

7. **Event Reconstruction:** In the digital forensics process, event reconstruction is an important step and requires great care. With the spread of the internet and other networks, evidence collection is a time-consuming task. AI can help to collect the evidence from every node and hence reconstruct the criminal event with greater accuracy for analysis purposes [4].

Moreover, a wealth of open-source AI tools, especially those related to ML and deep learning, are readily accessible, with many being primarily written in Python. Other programming languages, including R, also offer considerable utility in the pursuit of AI-driven solutions. This diverse toolkit empowers digital forensic professionals to leverage AI's capabilities effectively across a wide spectrum of investigative tasks. Table 11.1 shows the important open-source tools for AI that can help automate the process of digital forensics. Table 11.2 provides information about some of the famous dataset sources that can be used for applying intelligent algorithms to digital forensics.

11.1.2 Potential impacts of AI on digital forensics

AI serves as a solution to numerous challenges in the field of digital forensics, offering a wide range of potential impacts that can ease the investigative process:

Table 11.1 Open-source tools for AI, ML, and deep learning

Tools	Written in language	Algorithm	Features and unique aspects
WEKA	JAVA	• Data preparation • Classification • Regression • Clustering • Visualization • Association rules mining	A comprehensive suite known for its easy-to-use GUI, extensive collection of algorithms, and built-in machine learning libraries. Supports association rules mining.
Shogun	C++	• Regression • Classification • Clustering • Support vector machines. • Dimensionality reduction	Specializes in large-scale learning with support for a wide range of machine learning algorithms. Known for its efficient handling of high-dimensional data and integration with various programming languages like Python, Octave, and R.
LIBSVM	C++	• Support Vector Machine	Provides a simple and efficient implementation of SVM for classification and regression tasks. Known for its speed and effectiveness in handling SVM models, widely used in academia and industry.
RapidMiner	JAVA	• Preprocessing • classification	Offers a robust platform for data preprocessing, classification, and model building with an intuitive drag-and-drop interface. Known for its flexibility in integrating data science workflows, extensive plugin ecosystem, and support for various data formats.
Scikit Learn	C, C++, Python	• Classification • Regression • Clustering • Preprocessing • Model Selection • Dimensionality reduction.	Versatile machine learning library known for its simplicity, comprehensive documentation, and ease of integration with Python-based data science workflows. Strong support for integration with other scientific computing libraries like NumPy and SciPy.

Table 11.2 Datasets for different digital forensics types

Digital forensic types	Malware analysis	Image forensics	Video forensics	Network forensics	Memory/ File system forensics
Datasets	Virus Share, VX Heaven, Comodo Cloud Security Center	Pascal VOC 2012, MS-COCO ImageNet	Karina	CAIDA	Real Data Corpus, 2007 INEX Wikipedia

1. **Enhanced Cybercrime Detection**: AI facilitates the identification and investigation of cybercrimes with greater accuracy and efficiency, significantly improving the probability of successful outcomes.
2. **Cost-Effective and Time-Saving**: AI's ability to process and sift through unstructured data from digital evidence translates to cost-effective and time-efficient forensic investigations, benefiting both law enforcement agencies and organizations.
3. **Cognitive Data Analysis**: AI's cognitive properties enable data analysis without contradiction, contributing to the production of consistent and reliable results.
4. **Criminal Suspect Identification**: AI aids in identifying potential suspects by examining and analyzing relevant records, streamlining the process of narrowing down leads and persons of interest.
5. **Metadata Extraction**: AI can efficiently extract metadata from photos and videos, providing valuable information that can be crucial in forensic investigations.
6. **Commonality Identification**: AI assists in identifying commonalities among evidence, such as timestamps, geographic locations, and other patterns, offering insights that can be used to predict potential criminal activities or trends.
7. **Efficient Data Analysis**: AI's ability to analyze large volumes of evidence data and calculate statistical results ensures that forensic investigations are conducted with greater efficiency and accuracy, minimizing the risk of oversight or error.

In essence, AI not only streamlines the process of digital forensics but also enhances its effectiveness, ultimately contributing to the successful resolution of cybercrime cases and the safeguarding of digital systems and data.

11.2 MACHINE LEARNING (ML) IN DIGITAL FORENSICS

Machine Learning (ML) is a branch of artificial intelligence (AI) that enables computers to learn from data and make decisions or predictions based on that data. Unlike traditional programming, where explicit instructions are given to the machine, ML relies on patterns and inference. The fundamental idea is to build algorithms that can receive input data and use statistical analysis to predict an output while updating outputs as new data become available. ML is broadly categorized into three types: Supervised learning, unsupervised learning, and reinforcement learning.

Supervised Learning: Supervised learning involves training a model on a labeled dataset. Each training example is a pair consisting of an input object (typically a vector) and a desired output value (also called the supervisory signal). A supervised learning algorithm analyzes the training data and produces an inferred function, which can be used for mapping new examples. Common tasks include classification (identifying the category to which an object belongs, such as spam detection or image recognition) and regression (predicting a continuous-valued output, such as stock prices or house values).

In supervised learning, the algorithm is provided with a dataset that includes input-output pairs. For example, in email spam detection, the inputs could be features extracted from the emails (such as word frequency, presence of certain keywords, and sender information), and the outputs could be labels indicating whether an email is spam or not. The learning process involves finding a function that maps inputs to outputs with high accuracy. This is achieved by minimizing a loss function that measures the difference between the predicted output and the actual output.

Unsupervised Learning: Unsupervised learning involves training a model on data without labeled responses. The system tries to learn patterns and structures from the input data. It is used for tasks like clustering (grouping data points with similar characteristics) and association (finding rules that describe large portions of the data, such as market basket analysis). In unsupervised learning, the algorithm is provided with data that does not have explicit instructions on what to do with it. For instance, in clustering, the algorithm will group data points that are similar to each other. An example could be segmenting customers based on their purchasing behavior. The algorithm analyzes the data and finds patterns that distinguish different groups of customers, which can then be used for targeted marketing strategies.

Reinforcement Learning: This type of learning involves training an agent to make a sequence of decisions by rewarding desired behaviors and punishing undesired ones. The agent learns to achieve a goal in an uncertain, potentially complex environment. In reinforcement learning, the agent interacts with the environment by performing actions and receiving feedback in the form of rewards or penalties. The objective is to learn a policy that maximizes the cumulative reward over time. For example, in a game, the agent learns to make moves that increase its chances of winning. This involves exploring different actions and learning from the outcomes, balancing the trade-off between exploration (trying new actions) and exploitation (using known actions that yield high rewards).

11.2.1 Advancements in machine learning

11.2.1.1 Enhanced data processing and analysis

Deep Learning, a subset of ML, involves neural networks with many layers (hence "deep"). These networks can model complex patterns in data. The development of convolutional neural networks (CNNs) for image processing and recurrent neural networks (RNNs) for sequential data has been particularly influential. CNNs are used in image recognition systems, such as those for facial recognition, object detection, and autonomous driving. RNNs are used for tasks involving sequential data, such as language modeling and time series prediction.

Support Vector Machines (SVMs) are effective for high-dimensional spaces and are used for classification and regression tasks. They work by finding the hyperplane that best separates different classes in the feature space. SVMs are commonly used in text categorization, where documents are classified into categories like sports, politics, and technology.

Ensemble Methods combine multiple models to improve accuracy. Examples include Random Forests and Gradient Boosting Machines. For example, Random Forests, which use multiple decision trees to make a prediction, are used in applications like medical diagnosis and credit scoring.

11.2.2 Big data integration

ML algorithms have evolved to handle and process vast amounts of data efficiently. Traditional digital forensic methods often struggle with the sheer volume of data generated in investigations, especially in cases involving multiple digital devices or extensive network logs. ML algorithms have been developed to process these large datasets rapidly, enabling investigators to focus on the most relevant pieces of evidence. Techniques such as distributed computing and cloud-based platforms enable the processing of large datasets. Google's TensorFlow and Apache Spark are platforms that support large-scale machine learning. These platforms allow for the distributed processing of data, making it possible to analyze datasets that were previously too large to handle.

Moreover, the ability to process data in real-time has opened up new possibilities for ML applications. Real-time analysis allows for immediate insights and actions. For example, in fraud detection, real-time analysis can flag suspicious transactions as they occur, allowing for immediate investigation and intervention.

11.2.2.1 Transfer learning

Transfer learning involves leveraging pre-trained models on new but related tasks. This approach can save significant time and computational resources, as the pre-trained models have already learned useful features from a large dataset. An example is using a pre-trained image recognition model (such as VGG or ResNet) for specific tasks like medical image analysis or using pre-trained language models (such as BERT or GPT) for natural language processing tasks.

In transfer learning, a model trained on a large, general dataset (such as ImageNet for images or a large text corpus for language models) is fine-tuned on a smaller, specific dataset. For example, a pre-trained model on general image recognition can be fine-tuned to detect specific types of medical anomalies in radiology images. This approach significantly reduces the amount of labeled data required for training and accelerates the deployment of ML models in specialized domains.

11.2.2.2 AutoML

Automated Machine Learning (AutoML) simplifies the process of model selection, hyperparameter tuning, and deployment. AutoML tools aim to make machine learning accessible to non-experts by automating the end-to-end process of applying machine learning to real-world problems (e.g., Google AutoML, H2O.ai, and Auto-sklearn).

AutoML platforms provide tools that automate the process of selecting the best algorithm, tuning its hyperparameters, and deploying the model. This involves using techniques like hyperparameter optimization, neural architecture search, and automated feature engineering. For instance, Google AutoML allows users to upload their data and automatically generates a machine learning model tailored to their needs, without requiring in-depth knowledge of ML techniques.

11.2.3 Applications of machine learning in digital forensics

Machine learning has a wide range of applications in digital forensics, where it can be used to enhance the efficiency and accuracy of forensic investigations. Digital forensics involves the identification, preservation, extraction, and documentation of digital evidence from various sources. The following sections describe specific applications of machine learning in digital forensics, along with detailed explanations of how these applications can be performed and their applicability in digital forensics.

11.2.3.1 Pattern recognition

Pattern recognition involves identifying patterns and regularities in data. In digital forensics, this can be used to analyze network traffic, user behavior, and system logs to identify abnormal patterns that may indicate malicious activities. The process can be detailed as follows:

- *Data Collection*: Collect data from various sources such as network logs, system logs, and user activity logs. These data can include information like login times, IP addresses, accessed resources, and data transfer volumes.
- *Feature Extraction*: Identify relevant features that can help in recognizing patterns. For example, in analyzing login behavior, features could include the time of login, the IP address, and the resources accessed during the session.
- *Model Training*: Use supervised learning techniques to train models on historical data where patterns are labeled. For instance, a dataset containing both normal and malicious login patterns can be used to train a classification model.
- *Pattern Matching*: Apply the trained model to new data to identify matching patterns or deviations. The model can flag unusual patterns for further investigation.
- *Investigation*: Investigate identified patterns to determine if they represent normal behavior or potential threats. For example, if a login pattern deviates significantly from a user's typical behavior, it can be flagged for a detailed investigation to determine if it represents unauthorized access.

Example: Detecting unusual login patterns that may signify unauthorized access. For instance, if a user typically logs in from one location but suddenly logs in from a different country, this anomaly can be flagged for investigation.

11.2.3.2 Anomaly detection

Anomaly detection involves identifying outliers or deviations from normal behavior that may indicate malicious activity. This can be used to monitor network traffic, file system changes, and application behavior to detect anomalies that may signify security breaches or cyber-attacks.

- *Data Collection*: Collect continuous data streams from network traffic, system logs, and application logs. These data can include information like the volume of network traffic, the types of files accessed, and the behavior of applications.

- *Baseline Modeling*: Use unsupervised learning techniques to model normal behavior from the collected data. This involves creating a baseline model that captures the typical patterns and behaviors observed in the data.
- *Anomaly Scoring*: Assign anomaly scores to new data points based on their deviation from the baseline model. Data points that deviate significantly from the expected behavior are assigned higher anomaly scores.
- *Threshold Setting*: Define thresholds for anomaly scores to trigger alerts. For instance, data points with anomaly scores above a certain threshold can be flagged for investigation.
- *Response*: Investigate and respond to anomalies that exceed the defined thresholds. This involves analyzing the flagged data points to determine if they represent malicious activities and taking appropriate actions to mitigate the threats.

Example: Identifying abnormal network traffic patterns that could signify a Distributed Denial of Service (DDoS) attack. ML models can be trained on historical network data to recognize normal traffic patterns and detect deviations that indicate an ongoing attack.

11.2.3.3 Predictive analysis

Predictive analysis involves using historical data to predict future events or behaviors. In digital forensics, this can be used to forecast potential security threats and vulnerabilities based on past incidents, allowing for proactive measures to be taken.

- *Historical Data Analysis*: Analyze past incidents to identify common features and trends. This involves examining historical data to understand the characteristics and patterns associated with past security breaches or cyber-attacks.
- *Feature Engineering*: Create features that capture relevant aspects of historical incidents. For example, features could include the time of day, the attack vector, the affected systems, and the response actions taken.
- *Model Training*: Train predictive models using supervised learning techniques on the engineered features. This involves using historical data with known outcomes to train models that can predict future incidents.
- *Forecasting*: Apply the trained model to current data to predict future incidents. The model analyzes the current data and generates predictions about potential security threats and vulnerabilities.
- *Proactive Measures*: Implement preventive measures based on the predictions to mitigate potential threats. This involves taking actions such

as strengthening defenses for systems that are predicted to be targeted, implementing additional security measures, and preparing response plans for predicted incidents.

Example: Predicting which systems or applications are likely to be targeted by cybercriminals based on historical attack patterns. This helps in proactively strengthening defenses for those systems, reducing the likelihood of successful attacks.

11.2.3.4 Classification

Classification involves automatically categorizing data into predefined classes. In digital forensics, this can be used to classify emails, documents, and files to streamline the forensic analysis process.

- *Data Labeling*: Manually label a dataset with relevant categories. For example, emails can be labeled as spam or legitimate, and files can be labeled as malware or benign.
- *Feature Selection*: Select features that are indicative of each category. For instance, in email classification, features could include the presence of certain keywords, the frequency of certain words, the sender information, and the structure of the email.
- *Model Training*: Train classification models using supervised learning techniques on the labeled dataset. This involves using labeled data to train models that can automatically classify new data.
- *Automated Classification*: Apply the trained model to new data to automatically assign categories. The model analyzes the features of the new data and assigns it to the appropriate category.
- *Verification*: Validate the classified data and refine the model as necessary. This involves periodically reviewing the classifications to ensure accuracy and making adjustments to the model as needed.

Example: Automatically categorizing emails as spam or legitimate, identifying phishing emails, or classifying files as malware or benign. This aids in quickly narrowing down relevant evidence and focusing on critical areas of the investigation.

11.2.3.5 Clustering

Clustering involves grouping similar data points together based on their features. In digital forensics, this can be used to identify coordinated attacks or fraud rings by clustering related activities.

- *Data Aggregation*: Aggregate related data points. For example, in a cyber-attack investigation, data points could include IP addresses, timestamps, and activity logs related to the attack.

- *Feature Extraction*: Extract features that can help in identifying similarities. For instance, features could include the geographical location of IP addresses, the frequency of access, the types of resources accessed, and the patterns of activity.
- *Clustering Algorithm*: Apply clustering algorithms such as K-means or DBSCAN to group similar data points. These algorithms analyze the features of the data points and group them into clusters based on their similarities.
- *Analysis*: Analyze the clusters to identify coordinated activities or commonalities. This involves examining the clusters to understand the patterns and relationships among the grouped data points.
- *Investigation*: Investigate the identified clusters to understand their significance and potential impact. This involves following up on the clustered data points to uncover the details of the coordinated activities or fraud rings.

Example: Clustering IP addresses involved in a cyber-attack to identify the sources and patterns of the attack. This can help in tracing the origin of the attack and understanding the scope of the coordinated activities.

11.2.4 Machine learning digital forensics framework

Creating a Machine Learning Digital Forensics Framework involves designing a structured approach that systematically incorporates ML methods into the key phases of a digital investigation. This framework should address all critical stages, from data acquisition and preprocessing to evidence analysis and presentation, ensuring that each phase is optimized for the unique challenges posed by different forensic scenarios. Figure 11.1 provides a conceptual methodology that can be adapted and customized to fit a wide range of digital forensic applications, providing a comprehensive guide to integrating ML in a structured and effective manner.

Two notable frameworks exemplify the use of ML in digital forensics: the Smart Digital Forensic Framework for Crime Analysis and Prediction using AutoML, proposed by Sajith A Johnson and S Ananthakumaran, and the Network Forensic Framework Based on Deep Learning for IoT Networks, proposed by Nikos Koroniotis et. al [5, 6]. These frameworks leverage ML techniques to enhance the capability of forensic investigations, particularly in handling large datasets and detecting complex patterns.

11.2.4.1 Smart digital forensic framework for crime analysis and prediction using AutoML

This framework leverages Automated Machine Learning (AutoML) to enhance the efficiency of digital forensic investigations [7]. The core objective is to automate the analysis of vast amounts of forensic data, thereby accelerating crime analysis and prediction. Its key Components include:

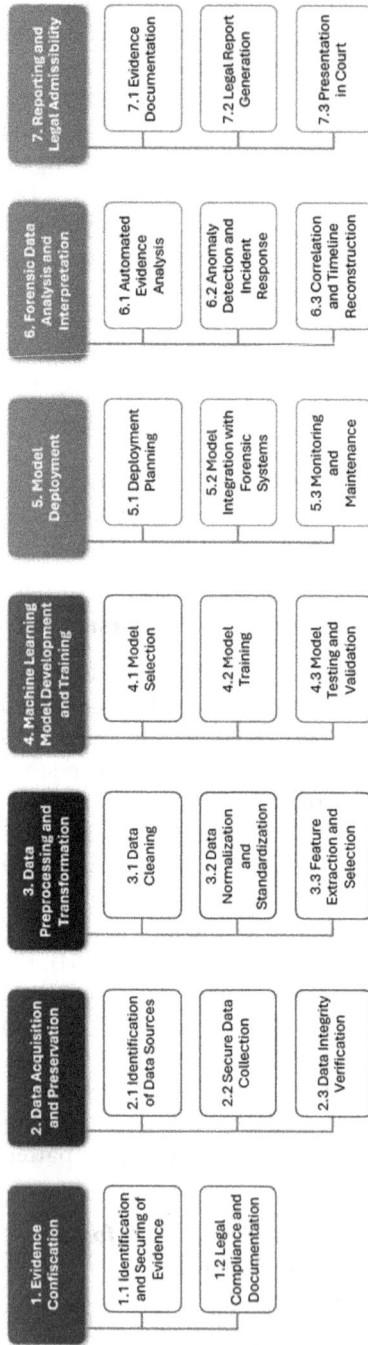

Figure 11.1 Machine learning digital forensics conceptual methodology.

1. **Data Collection and Preprocessing:** The framework begins with the systematic collection of digital evidence from various sources, like computers, mobile devices, and network logs. The data is preprocessed to remove noise, normalize formats, and extract relevant features, ensuring suitability for ML algorithms.
2. **Automated Model Training:** Utilizing AutoML, the framework automatically selects and optimizes the best ML models based on the characteristics of the forensic data. This process includes hyperparameter tuning, model validation, and performance evaluation to ensure that the models are well-suited for forensic tasks.
3. **Crime Prediction and Analysis:** Trained ML models analyze the collected data, identifying patterns that could indicate criminal activities. The framework supports applications such as anomaly detection, classification of digital evidence, and prediction of criminal behavior based on historical data.
4. **Evaluation and Reporting:** The results of the analysis are evaluated against forensic criteria. The framework generates detailed reports that can support forensic findings in legal contexts. The use of AutoML ensures continuous improvement of models as new data becomes available.

This framework is particularly effective in investigations involving cyber-crimes, fraud detection, and other cases where predictive modeling can provide valuable insights into criminal behavior.

11.2.4.2 Network forensic framework based on deep learning for IoT networks

This framework is specifically tailored for forensic investigations within IoT (Internet of Things) environments [8]. It employs deep learning techniques to detect and analyze network anomalies, which are indicative of malicious activities. Its key components include:

1. **Data Acquisition:** The framework collects data from various IoT devices and network logs, ensuring that the data are comprehensive and representative of the entire network.
2. **Feature Extraction and Transformation:** Raw network data are transformed into a suitable format for deep learning analysis. This involves extracting features such as packet headers, traffic patterns, and device behavior, which are then used to train the deep learning models.
3. **Deep Learning Model Training:** The framework employs deep learning models, such as Convolutional Neural Networks (CNNs) and Recurrent Neural Networks (RNNs), to analyze the extracted features. These models are trained to detect anomalies in network traffic, indicating security breaches or other malicious activities.

4. **Anomaly Detection and Forensic Analysis:** The trained models monitor the IoT network in real-time, flagging suspicious activities for further investigation. The framework also provides tools for detailed forensic analysis of flagged events, aiding investigators in tracing the origin and impact of the detected anomalies.
5. **Reporting and Visualization:** The results of the forensic analysis are presented visually, allowing investigators to easily interpret the data. The framework also generates reports that can be used in legal proceedings to substantiate findings.

11.2.4.3 NIST cybersecurity framework (CSF)

The NIST Cybersecurity Framework (CSF) provides comprehensive guidelines for managing and reducing cybersecurity risks, focusing on detecting, responding to, and recovering from cyber incidents [9]. It is widely adopted across various industries to improve the security and resilience of critical infrastructure. Here are the key components included in the framework.

1. **Identify:** This helps organizations develop an understanding of cybersecurity risks to systems, assets, data, and capabilities. This component involves activities such as asset management, risk assessment, and risk management strategy. Machine learning can be integrated here to continuously assess and monitor assets, identify vulnerabilities, and prioritize risks.
2. **Protect:** The "Protect" function outlines safeguards to ensure the delivery of critical infrastructure services. Activities include access control, data security, and protective technology. Machine learning enhances protection by automating access controls, detecting unauthorized access attempts, and safeguarding sensitive data.
3. **Detect:** This function enables the timely discovery of cybersecurity events through continuous monitoring of networks and systems. Machine learning is particularly powerful in this area, as it can automatically detect anomalies and suspicious activities in real-time, improving detection accuracy based on historical data.
4. **Respond:** This involves taking action regarding a detected cybersecurity event, focusing on response planning, analysis, and mitigation. Machine learning can automate response actions, prioritize incidents, and provide actionable insights for mitigation, enhancing the effectiveness of response efforts.
5. **Recover:** The "Recover" function focuses on restoring capabilities or services that were impaired due to a cybersecurity incident. Machine learning can be used to predict recovery timelines, optimize resource allocation, and improve recovery processes for future incidents.

The NIST CSF, when integrated with machine learning techniques, is particularly effective in enhancing forensic investigations by automating threat detection and analysis, thereby improving the accuracy and efficiency of detecting and responding to cybersecurity incidents. This integration strengthens the cybersecurity posture of organizations and supports robust forensic processes.

11.2.5 Potential impacts of machine learning on digital forensics

Machine learning has the potential to transform digital forensics by enhancing efficiency, accuracy, and scalability in investigations. One of its key benefits is the improvement in efficiency through automated analysis. Machine learning (ML) algorithms are capable of analyzing vast amounts of data more quickly and accurately than human analysts, which significantly reduces the time needed to process and assess digital evidence. This allows forensic investigators to dedicate their attention to more complex aspects of investigations. Additionally, ML models enhance detection by improving pattern recognition. They can identify subtle patterns and anomalies that traditional rule-based systems might overlook, enhancing the ability to detect security breaches and other malicious activities.

Furthermore, ML contributes to scalability by enabling the handling of large-scale investigations with data from diverse sources without sacrificing accuracy or speed. This scalability is essential for examining complex cyberattacks that generate large volumes of data. Another advantage is the automation of routine tasks, allowing forensic experts to focus on more critical aspects of investigations, thus increasing the overall efficiency and effectiveness of forensic processes.

Machine learning models also offer adaptability through continuous learning. They can be updated with new data to stay effective against evolving threats, which is crucial in the constantly changing landscape of cybersecurity. For example, an ML-based intrusion detection system can learn from new attack patterns and update its models to detect emerging threats, offering ongoing protection against cyberattacks. Additionally, automated analysis minimizes the likelihood of errors that can occur with manual investigation methods. ML algorithms consistently apply the same criteria during analysis, reducing the risk of oversight or bias. Finally, machine learning offers cost-effectiveness and resource optimization. By automating routine tasks and increasing the efficiency of investigations, organizations can save on labor costs and better allocate their resources, which is particularly valuable for organizations with limited forensic resources.

11.2.6 Additional considerations and challenges

While the potential benefits of machine learning in digital forensics are significant, there are also several considerations and challenges that must be addressed to fully realize these benefits.

1. **High Data Quality and Availability**: ML models require high-quality data for training and evaluation. In digital forensics, collecting and maintaining high-quality data can be challenging due to the diverse and often unstructured nature of digital evidence. Moreover, access to sufficient and relevant data is crucial for effective model training. In some cases, sensitive or classified information may be restricted, limiting the availability of training data.

2. **Model Interpretability:**
   - Understanding Model Decisions: Forensic investigators must be able to understand and explain the decisions made by ML models. This is particularly important in legal contexts where the results of forensic analysis may be used as evidence in court.
   - Explainable AI: Developing explainable AI techniques that make the decision-making processes of ML models transparent and understandable is essential for their adoption in digital forensics.

3. **Avoiding Bias and Ensuring Fairness**: ML models can inadvertently learn and propagate biases present in the training data. In digital forensics, biased models can lead to unfair or incorrect conclusions, potentially impacting the outcomes of investigations. Moreover, efforts must be made to ensure that ML models are fair and unbiased, and that their use does not lead to discrimination or injustice.

4. **Security and Privacy**: The sensitive nature of digital evidence requires robust security measures to protect data from unauthorized access and tampering. The use of ML in digital forensics must balance the need for effective investigation with respect for individual privacy rights. Ensuring compliance with privacy regulations and ethical standards is critical.

5. **Integration with Existing Tools and Workflows**: ML-based forensic tools must be compatible with existing forensic tools and workflows to be effectively integrated into the investigative process. Forensic investigators require training to effectively use ML-based tools. Organizations must invest in training programs to ensure that their personnel can leverage the full potential of these technologies.

In December 2020, a significant cyberattack was uncovered that affected several U.S. government agencies and private companies. This attack involved the insertion of malicious code into SolarWinds' Orion software updates. SolarWinds, a key provider of IT management software, unknowingly distributed these compromised updates to its clients, including federal agencies and Fortune 500 companies [10]. The breach remained undetected for months, allowing the attackers to conduct espionage and access sensitive information.

Once the breach was discovered, affected organizations collected extensive data, including network traffic logs and system logs, to understand the scope of the attack. Machine learning models were employed to establish baselines of normal network and user behavior by analyzing historical data. These models were crucial in detecting deviations that indicated malicious activities. Anomaly detection systems continuously monitored real-time data, flagging suspicious activities for further investigation.

Security teams used these tools to identify unusual network traffic patterns, unauthorized access attempts, and abnormal data transfers. The machine learning models helped trace the attackers' paths and identify instances of malicious code execution within the compromised networks. This technology enabled rapid identification of the breach's scope and facilitated a more effective response, including patching vulnerabilities, notifying affected parties, and enhancing security measures to prevent future incidents.

The use of machine learning in the SolarWinds investigation demonstrated its vital role in modern cybersecurity and digital forensics, improving the detection and response to sophisticated cyber threats.

11.2.7 Deep learning in digital forensics

Deep learning is a specialized branch of machine learning that utilizes neural networks with many layers to analyze complex data. These networks, known as deep neural networks, are designed to mimic the human brain's structure and function, enabling them to model intricate patterns in data (see Figure 11.2). Deep learning has significantly impacted fields such as

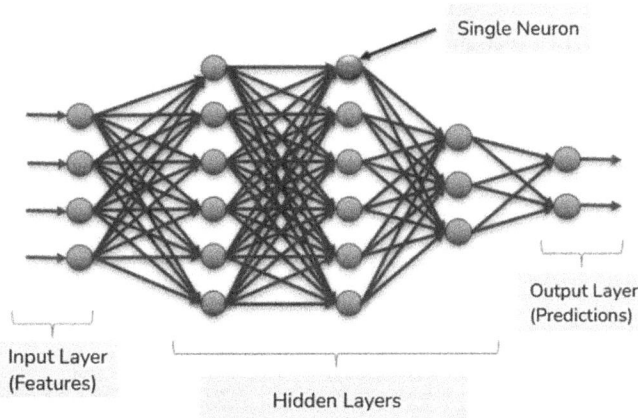

Figure 11.2 Deep learning—input and hidden layers.

computer vision, natural language processing, and autonomous systems due to its ability to learn features directly from raw data without requiring manual feature extraction.

Convolutional Neural Networks (CNNs), Recurrent Neural Networks (RNNs), and Generative Adversarial Networks (GANs) are foundational elements of deep learning, each excelling in different applications. CNNs, with their multiple layers including convolutional, pooling, and fully connected layers, are crucial for image and video analysis. They capture spatial hierarchies of features through convolutional layers, reduce data dimensionality via pooling layers, and perform final classifications using fully connected layers, making them ideal for tasks like image recognition, object detection, facial recognition, and medical image analysis. RNNs, designed for sequential data, excel in language modeling, speech recognition, and time series prediction by maintaining a hidden state that captures information about previous elements in the sequence, making them suitable for language translation and sentiment analysis. GANs consist of two neural networks, a generator and a discriminator, which compete to create and evaluate synthetic data. This adversarial process enhances the generator's ability to produce realistic data, making GANs powerful for image and video generation, as well as data augmentation.

11.2.7.1 Why deep learning is needed in digital forensics

While traditional machine learning models are effective for structured data, they often struggle with unstructured or high-dimensional data, such as images, audio, and video files, which are common in digital forensic investigations. Deep learning models, particularly Convolutional Neural Networks (CNNs), Recurrent Neural Networks (RNNs), and Generative Adversarial Networks (GANs), excel in handling these types of data. For instance, CNNs can effectively analyze visual data, making them ideal for tasks such as facial recognition, object detection, and tampered image detection. RNNs, which are well-suited for sequential data, are critical for tasks involving text analysis, such as detecting phishing emails or analyzing chat logs in investigations.

Digital forensic investigations frequently involve vast amounts of data, making it challenging for traditional ML models to scale efficiently. Deep learning models can manage these large datasets more effectively, particularly when deployed on distributed computing frameworks. This scalability is crucial in processing and analyzing the massive amounts of data generated during forensic investigations, such as network traffic logs or social media content.

Moreover, traditional ML models often require extensive feature engineering, which is both time-consuming and prone to human error. In contrast, deep learning models can automatically learn and extract relevant features from raw data, improving the accuracy of tasks such as pattern recognition, anomaly detection, and classification. For example, deep learning-based models can identify sophisticated malware variants that use evasion techniques to bypass traditional signature-based detection methods, enhancing the detection of security breaches.

11.2.8 What machine learning lacks that deep learning solves

Traditional ML models rely heavily on manually crafted features, which can limit their ability to generalize across different types of data. Deep learning models, however, are capable of automatic feature extraction, learning from raw data without requiring explicit feature selection. This capability is particularly advantageous in digital forensics, where the nature of the data can vary widely, from text and images to network traffic and audio recordings. In addition, traditional ML models typically perform well with structured data but struggle with unstructured data, such as natural language text, images, or videos. Deep learning models, particularly CNNs and RNNs, are designed to process unstructured data directly. For example, CNNs can analyze images pixel by pixel to detect objects or facial features, while RNNs can process sequences of text or audio, making them invaluable for tasks like voice recognition or sentiment analysis in forensic investigations. Another difference they have is in their performance with large datasets. As the dataset size increases, traditional ML algorithms often reach a point of diminishing returns, leading to overfitting or underfitting. Deep learning models, on the other hand, typically benefit from larger datasets, as they can learn more complex patterns. This scalability is critical in digital forensics, where the volume of data can be immense, and the ability to learn from extensive datasets is necessary to uncover subtle or hidden patterns. Refer to the below Table 11.3, for the comparison between the two.

11.2.9 Applications of deep learning in digital forensics

Deep learning has significantly advanced the field of digital forensics by providing powerful tools for analyzing complex data and automating forensic processes. Table 11.4 below shows some applications of deep learning in Digital Forensics.

A real-life example of the application of deep learning in digital forensics is the use of facial recognition technology by law enforcement agencies. One notable case is the use of Amazon's Rekognition software by the Washington County Sheriff's Office in Oregon [11]. The agency faced challenges in identifying suspects from surveillance footage due to the poor quality of the images and the manual effort required for matching faces. To address these challenges, the agency decided to implement a deep learning-based facial recognition system using Amazon's Rekognition software.

Table 11.3 Machine learning versus deep learning

Aspect	Machine learning	Deep learning
Data Requirements	Requires less data to perform well. Effective with small to medium-sized datasets.	Requires large amounts of data for effective training. Performs better with big data.
Feature Engineering	Relies heavily on manual feature extraction and selection by domain experts.	Automatically learns features from raw data through multiple layers of neural networks.
Architecture	Uses simpler models like decision trees, linear regression, and support vector machines.	Uses complex neural networks with many layers, such as CNNs, RNNs, and GANs.
Processing Power	Generally requires less computational power and resources.	Requires significant computational power, often utilizing GPUs and specialized hardware.
Interpretability	More interpretable; models, like decision trees and linear regressions, provide clear decision paths.	Less interpretable; often considered a "black box" due to the complexity of neural networks.
Scalability	Less scalable for very large datasets or unstructured data.	Highly scalable; performs well with large-scale data and complex tasks.
Use Cases	Suitable for simpler tasks such as basic classification, regression, and clustering.	Excels in complex tasks like image recognition, natural language processing, and autonomous systems.
Training Time	Typically, faster training times, especially with smaller datasets.	Training can be time-consuming due to the depth of the networks and large datasets.
Model Flexibility	Models can struggle with unstructured data and complex patterns.	Highly flexible in handling unstructured data such as images, text, and audio.
Error Handling	More prone to manual errors in feature engineering.	Less prone to manual errors due to automated feature learning.
Typical Applications	Spam detection, basic predictive analytics, and recommendation systems.	Advanced image and video analysis, speech recognition, deepfake detection, and autonomous driving.

Table 11.4 Applications of deep learning in DF

Tasks	Deep learning technologies used
Image and Video Analysis	Deep learning models, especially CNNs, are crucial in forensic investigations involving images and videos. For instance, CNNs can be trained to detect tampered images or identify individuals in video footage, tasks that are essential in verifying the authenticity of digital evidence.
Text and Document Analysis	RNNs and transformer models, such as BERT and GPT, are used to analyze large volumes of text from emails, documents, and social media. These models can be trained to detect patterns related to forensic analysis, such as identifying the authorship of a document, detecting sentiment, or recognizing entities mentioned in the text, providing critical insights for investigations.
Malware Detection and Analysis	Deep learning models can be trained to detect and analyze malware by examining patterns in bytecode or network behavior. These models can identify novel malware variants that may evade traditional detection methods, making them invaluable in protecting systems from sophisticated cyber threats.
Audio and Speech Analysis	Deep learning models, particularly RNNs, are employed in audio forensics to identify speakers, transcribe conversations, and analyze emotional content in speech. This capability is critical for verifying the authenticity of audio recordings or analyzing communications in criminal investigations.
Network Forensics	Applying deep learning models to network traffic analysis enables forensic investigators to detect anomalies indicative of malicious activities. CNNs and RNNs can be used to model network behavior and detect deviations from normal patterns, helping to identify potential security breaches or cyberattacks.

The process began with collecting a large dataset of facial images from various sources, including mugshots, driver's license photos, and images from social media. The dataset included both known individuals and unknown faces from surveillance footage. Using a pre-trained CNN model for facial recognition, the agency fine-tuned the model on their collected dataset. The model was trained to recognize and match faces based on features such as facial landmarks, expressions, and angles.

Once trained, the model was applied to new surveillance footage to identify suspects. The system analyzed the faces in the footage, extracting features and matching them with known individuals in the database. The implementation of the deep learning-based facial recognition system significantly improved the agency's ability to identify suspects from surveillance footage. The automated system reduced the manual effort required for facial matching, increased the accuracy of identifications, and provided valuable leads for criminal investigations.

In conclusion, deep learning addresses several limitations of traditional machine learning in digital forensics, particularly in handling complex and unstructured data, scaling to large datasets, and improving accuracy in detecting subtle patterns. The integration of deep learning into digital forensics is not just an enhancement but a necessary evolution to tackle the increasingly sophisticated challenges posed by modern digital crimes. As digital evidence becomes more complex and voluminous, deep learning will play an essential role in ensuring that forensic investigations are both thorough and accurate.

11.3 COMPUTER VISION IN DIGITAL FORENSICS

Computer vision is a field of artificial intelligence that enables computers to interpret and understand visual information from the world. By using digital images and videos from cameras and deep learning models, computer vision systems can identify and classify objects, detect anomalies, and even recognize faces. The goal of computer vision is to mimic human vision, allowing machines to process, analyze, and make decisions based on visual data.

Image recognition involves identifying objects, people, places, and actions in images by training models on large datasets of labeled images. Once trained, these models can recognize and classify objects in new images, making them useful for various applications, including digital forensics. Object detection goes beyond image recognition by locating and identifying multiple objects within an image, drawing bounding boxes around them, and classifying them. This is crucial for tasks that require identifying multiple items or tracking objects over time. Facial recognition is a specialized application of computer vision that identifies individuals based on their facial features. Widely used in security and surveillance, it also plays a key role in digital forensics for identifying suspects and victims. Video analysis extends the capabilities of computer vision to moving images, performing tasks such as tracking objects, detecting activities, and recognizing patterns over time. It is essential for monitoring security footage, investigating incidents, and reconstructing events.

11.3.1 Advancements in computer vision

Computer vision has seen significant advancements due to the development of sophisticated algorithms, the availability of large datasets, and improvements in computational power.

1. **Deep Learning and Convolutional Neural Networks (CNNs):** The introduction of deep learning, particularly CNNs, has revolutionized computer vision. CNNs are designed to automatically and adaptively learn spatial hierarchies of features from images. They have outperformed traditional computer vision methods in various tasks such as image classification, object detection, and facial recognition.
2. **Transfer Learning:** Transfer learning involves using pre-trained models on new tasks, which has become a common practice in computer vision. Models like VGG, ResNet, and Inception are pre-trained on large datasets such as ImageNet and can be fine-tuned for specific applications. This approach reduces the need for large amounts of labeled data and shortens the training time.
3. **Generative Adversarial Networks (GANs):** GANs have been used to generate realistic images and improve the quality of image data. They are employed in tasks such as image super-resolution, image-to-image translation, and data augmentation, enhancing the robustness and performance of computer vision models.
4. **Recurrent Neural Networks (RNNs) and Long Short-Term Memory (LSTM):** For video analysis, RNNs and LSTMs are used to model temporal dependencies. These models can analyze sequences of frames, making them suitable for activity recognition, video summarization, and anomaly detection in videos.
5. **Neural Rendering and Augmented Reality (AR):** Neural rendering combines computer graphics with deep learning to create highly realistic synthetic images and videos. Augmented reality applications use computer vision to overlay digital information onto the real world, enhancing the user's perception and interaction with their environment.

11.3.1.1 Applications of computer vision in digital forensics

Computer vision has a wide range of applications in digital forensics (as shown in Table 11.5), providing powerful tools for evidence analysis, crime scene investigation, and suspect identification.

A real-life example of the application of computer vision in digital forensics is the use of facial recognition technology by law enforcement agencies. In 2020, the New York Police Department (NYPD) implemented a facial recognition system to aid in the identification of suspects and enhance public safety [12]. This technology was used to analyze surveillance footage from public spaces and identify individuals involved in criminal activities.

The facial recognition system utilized advanced algorithms to compare facial features captured in surveillance footage with a database of known individuals, including suspects and persons of interest. The system successfully

Table 11.5 Applications of CV in digital forensics

Task	Application
Image and Video Analysis	Forensic investigators can use computer vision techniques to enhance images, detect objects, and analyze activities captured in surveillance footage. This includes tasks such as identifying suspects in security camera footage, analyzing crime scenes from photos, and reconstructing events from video evidence. Advanced algorithms can enhance low-quality images, making it easier to identify critical details and evidence.
Facial Recognition	Facial recognition technology is widely used in digital forensics to identify suspects, victims, and witnesses. By comparing facial features in images or videos with a database of known individuals, forensic investigators can quickly and accurately identify persons of interest. This technology is invaluable in cases of missing persons, criminal investigations, and security breaches. For example, facial recognition can be used to identify suspects from security camera footage at crime scenes or to match photos of unidentified victims with missing person databases.
Object Detection and Scene Analysis	Object detection models can identify and locate objects within an image or video, providing valuable information about the scene. This is useful for analyzing crime scenes, identifying weapons or stolen items, and detecting suspicious activities. Scene analysis can also help investigators understand the context of an incident, such as determining the location of a crime or reconstructing the sequence of events leading up to an incident.
Automated License Plate Recognition (ALPR)	ALPR systems use computer vision to read and recognize vehicle license plates from images or videos. This technology is used in law enforcement for tracking stolen vehicles, identifying suspects' cars, and monitoring traffic violations. ALPR systems can automatically capture and log license plate numbers, providing a valuable tool for forensic investigations involving vehicles.
Image and Video Authentication	Computer vision techniques can detect tampering or manipulation in digital images and videos, ensuring the authenticity of visual evidence. By analyzing inconsistencies in lighting, shadows, and pixel patterns, forensic tools can identify edited or fabricated media. This is crucial for verifying the integrity of evidence in legal proceedings and preventing the use of doctored images or videos to mislead investigations.
Crime Scene Reconstruction	Computer vision can be used to create 3D models of crime scenes from photographs or video footage. These models provide a detailed and accurate representation of the scene, allowing investigators to analyze the spatial relationships between objects and reconstruct the sequence of events. Crime scene reconstruction can help identify key pieces of evidence, understand how a crime was committed, and present a visual representation of the scene in court.

(Continued)

Table 11.5 (Continued)

Task	Application
Activity Recognition	In video analysis, activity recognition involves identifying specific actions or behaviors captured in footage. This can include detecting suspicious activities, such as a person loitering near a restricted area, or recognizing violent behavior in surveillance videos. Activity recognition helps forensic investigators monitor and analyze large volumes of video data, identifying critical events that require further investigation.
Forensic Facial Reconstruction	Computer vision can be used to reconstruct the facial features of unidentified victims from skeletal remains. By analyzing the skull and other anatomical features, forensic tools can create a digital representation of the individual's face, aiding in identification. This technique is valuable in cases where traditional identification methods are not possible, such as in cases of severe decomposition or skeletal remains.
Document Analysis and Forgery Detection	Computer vision can analyze documents to detect signs of forgery or tampering. This includes identifying alterations in text, detecting signatures that have been copied or forged, and analyzing the consistency of fonts and ink patterns. Document analysis tools help forensic investigators verify the authenticity of critical documents, such as legal contracts, financial records, and identification papers.

identified several suspects, leading to their arrest and aiding in ongoing investigations. For example, the technology was used to identify a suspect involved in a violent assault, leading to a swift apprehension. The use of facial recognition technology demonstrated the potential of computer vision to enhance law enforcement capabilities and improve the efficiency of forensic investigations.

Beyond the above, another significant application lies with Closed-circuit television (CCTV) systems. CCTVs are increasingly ubiquitous and serve as vital evidence sources for both physical crimes like assault and digital crimes, where their footage might reveal individuals interacting with digital devices or committing cyber-physical offenses. The digital evidence derived from CCTV footage can be meticulously analyzed using a variety of digital forensic methods. This involves the extraction, preservation, and analysis of video files, often requiring specialized tools to recover deleted footage, enhance image quality, or verify the authenticity of the recordings.

Computer vision plays a crucial role in this analysis, automating tasks that would be painstakingly manual for human analysts. The sheer prevalence of CCTV cameras means an enormous volume of video data is generated daily, making manual review impractical for investigations. Computer vision algorithms can automatically process this footage, identifying suspicious activities, tracking individuals, and even pinpointing digital interactions captured by cameras. This automation significantly enhances the efficiency and effectiveness of forensic investigations.

11.3.1.2 Potential impacts of computer vision on digital forensics

The integration of computer vision in digital forensics has the potential to significantly enhance the capabilities of forensic investigators, improve the efficiency of investigations, and increase the accuracy of forensic findings. Computer vision provides advanced tools for analyzing visual evidence, enabling forensic investigators to extract critical information from images and videos more efficiently and accurately. Techniques such as facial recognition, object detection, and activity recognition help identify suspects, analyze crime scenes, and reconstruct events, providing valuable insights for investigations.

The use of computer vision allows forensic investigators to explore new investigative techniques and approaches. For example, 3D crime scene reconstruction and automated license plate recognition offer innovative ways to analyze and interpret evidence, improving the accuracy and effectiveness of investigations. Additionally, computer vision can automate many routine tasks in digital forensics, such as image enhancement, object detection, and video analysis. This automation saves time and resources, allowing forensic investigators to focus on more complex and critical aspects of their work. Automated tools can quickly process large volumes of visual data, identifying relevant evidence and reducing the workload for human analysts.

Computer vision models can continuously learn from new data, ensuring they remain effective against evolving threats. As new methods of image manipulation and forgery emerge, computer vision tools can be updated to detect these techniques, keeping pace with the latest advancements in cybercrime and digital fraud. Moreover, automated analysis reduces the likelihood of human error in forensic investigations. Computer vision models apply consistent analysis criteria, reducing the risk of oversight or bias. For instance, automated facial recognition systems can consistently identify individuals with high accuracy, ensuring reliable and objective results.

By automating routine tasks and enhancing the efficiency of forensic investigations, computer vision can help organizations save on labor costs and allocate resources more efficiently. This cost-effectiveness is particularly beneficial for organizations with limited forensic resources. Implementing computer vision-based forensic tools minimizes the need for extensive manual analysis, allowing organizations to optimize their forensic capabilities and reduce overall investigation costs.

11.3.1.3 Additional considerations and challenges

While the potential benefits of computer vision in digital forensics are significant, several considerations and challenges must be addressed to fully realize these benefits. The use of computer vision requires handling large amounts of sensitive visual data, necessitating robust security measures to protect this data from unauthorized access and tampering. Ensuring data privacy and security is crucial to maintaining the integrity of forensic investigations and protecting the rights of individuals involved. Forensic investigators must understand and explain the decisions made by computer vision models, especially in legal contexts where the results of forensic analysis may be used as evidence in court. Developing explainable AI techniques that make the decision-making processes of computer vision models transparent and understandable is essential for their adoption in digital forensics.

Moreover, computer vision models can inadvertently learn and propagate biases present in the training data, leading to unfair or incorrect conclusions. Ensuring that these models are fair and unbiased is critical to avoid discrimination and injustice. Ethical considerations, particularly regarding privacy and surveillance, are also important; while computer vision tools can enhance forensic investigations, they must be used responsibly to avoid infringing on individuals' privacy rights. Integration with existing forensic tools and workflows is essential for effective use, requiring organizations to invest in training programs to ensure their personnel can leverage these technologies. Additionally, implementing computer vision in digital forensics can be technically challenging, requiring significant computational resources and expertise. Ensuring that forensic organizations have access to the necessary infrastructure and expertise is crucial for successful deployment. The use of computer vision must also comply with legal and regulatory standards, ensuring that the collection, processing, and analysis of visual data are conducted within the bounds of the law and that the evidence obtained is admissible in court. Lastly, ensuring the accuracy and reliability of computer vision models through rigorous testing, continuous monitoring, and error mitigation is essential for maintaining the credibility and trustworthiness of forensic evidence.

END OF CHAPTER QUESTIONS

1. What is a primary risk of employing AutoML in the deployment of machine learning models for forensic investigations?
2. In cases of forensic analysis of encrypted data, how does AI provide an advantage over traditional decryption methods?
3. When analyzing large-scale cyber-attacks involving numerous endpoints, how can machine learning be applied to prioritize evidence without compromising investigation accuracy?
4. Describe a scenario in which machine learning models could unintentionally introduce bias into forensic investigations. How can these biases impact the outcome of a forensic analysis, and what measures can be taken to mitigate them?

5. Explain how unsupervised learning algorithms can be applied in cyber forensics to detect previously unknown attack vectors or behaviors within a dataset that lacks labeled examples. How would this approach differ from supervised learning in its application?

6. Discuss the role of AI and machine learning in the reconstruction of digital crime scenes. How can these technologies help piece together fragmented or partially deleted data, and what are the challenges associated with this process?

7. You are leading a forensics investigation involving a large corporate entity that has experienced a significant data breach. You have access to their entire email archive and want to prioritize investigating communications that suggest insider threats. How would you leverage AI-powered anomaly detection to focus your investigation?

8. During a forensic investigation of a sophisticated malware attack, you are tasked with recovering deleted logs from a compromised IoT device. Describe how you would apply deep learning techniques to recover and analyze the partially deleted data, considering that the device's metadata is damaged.

9. A law enforcement agency is investigating a cyber espionage case involving the exfiltration of sensitive government data. The agency needs to identify the origin of the attack by analyzing network traffic data across several nodes. What AI and machine learning techniques could you implement to identify patterns, anomalies, and commonalities in this network traffic to pinpoint the attack source?

10. You are part of a digital forensics team investigating a ransomware attack. The criminals have encrypted crucial data, leaving only a small amount of metadata untouched. How would you use machine learning models to aid in recovering any valuable insights from the remaining metadata?

11. AI systems can support various stages of the forensic investigation process. Discuss the benefits and limitations of using AI in triage, evidence prioritization, and predictive threat modeling in digital forensics.

12. Discuss the potential ethical risks and legal implications of using AI-based decision systems in forensic settings, particularly when AI outputs are presented as courtroom evidence.

13. What forensic problems remain difficult to solve using traditional machine learning approaches, and how does deep learning address these shortcomings? Illustrate with examples from malware detection, log analysis, or image forensics.

14. You are tasked with designing a deep learning model to detect image tampering in social media posts. What architecture would you choose and why? What data preparation and forensic validation steps must be included?

15. What role does transfer learning play in digital forensics, especially when working with limited labeled datasets (e.g., rare cyberattack patterns or forensic traces)?

16. Propose a forensic scenario where computer vision could be used to automate a normally manual process (e.g., analyzing surveillance footage, screen recordings, or GUI interaction). How would accuracy be measured?

17. Given the rise of deepfake content, how can forensic analysts use computer vision to detect manipulated facial expressions or voice-sync mismatches in video evidence?

18. What are the trade-offs between interpretability and performance in deep learning models used for forensic applications? How should investigators balance explainability with model accuracy?

19. How can forensic experts validate the outputs of ML models when ground truth is unavailable or ambiguous? Discuss model testing strategies under uncertainty.

20. Discuss the limitations of relying on AI-driven tools for real-time decision-making in critical digital forensics cases. What procedural safeguards should be in place?

21. In the context of live digital forensics, how can computer vision be applied to analyze user behavior from screen captures or keystroke recordings?

22. As AI systems evolve, attackers are increasingly using adversarial techniques. How can digital forensics researchers develop robust AI models that resist adversarial inputs or spoofing?

23. Explore the concept of forensic model drift—how the performance of a deployed ML model might degrade over time due to changing data environments. How should forensic tools be updated?

24. In what ways does the integration of edge AI (AI computation on-device) into IoT environments influence the future of digital forensics? Consider both the forensic opportunities and risks.

25. How can explainable AI (XAI) frameworks be applied to forensic models used in legal cases to improve transparency, accountability, and trustworthiness?

26. Reflect on the "black box problem" in AI. Should forensic analysts trust highly accurate deep learning systems that provide little to no transparency? Justify your answer in the context of forensic validation.

27. You are assisting in a national cyber fraud case involving hundreds of phishing emails, each subtly different in language. Law enforcement has asked you to identify common behavioral patterns in writing across suspect accounts. Propose a machine learning–based forensic workflow to cluster, analyze, and attribute these emails to specific threat actors. Explain your feature extraction, model selection (ML or DL), and validation steps.

28. During an insider threat investigation in a financial firm, forensic analysts find system logs with timestamp anomalies and missing metadata. The system uses AI-driven behavior monitoring. Explain how adversarial machine learning might have been used to bypass behavioral detection. How would you reverse-engineer the attacker's manipulation and validate detection blind spots?

29. Your forensic unit is given 100 TB of encrypted logs, with no prior labels, from a smart city grid AI. Explain how you would use unsupervised ML for anomaly detection to identify rare but suspicious behavior, and how you would verify and label events for further investigation.

30. A complex fraud case involves the use of AI-generated voice deepfakes to manipulate banking authentication systems. How would you apply forensic audio analysis, ML classifiers, and cross-device correlation to prove voice synthesis and attribute the synthetic content to an originating system?

REFERENCES

[1] Usman, N., Usman, S., Khan, F., Jan, M. A., Sajid, A., Alazab, M., and Watters, P., "Intelligent dynamic malware detection using machine learning in IP reputation for forensics data analytics", *Future Generation Computer Systems*, vol. 118, pp. 124–141, 2021.

[2] Naviq, Mohammed, Azwar, Hassan, Baqir BaqirAli, Syed, and Rehman, Saad. "A framework for Android Malware detection and classification," In *2018 IEEE 5th International Conference on Engineering Technologies and Applied Sciences (ICETAS)*, pp. 1–5, 2018. doi: 10.1109/ICETAS.2018.8629270

[3] Fitzgerald, Simran, Mathews, George, Morris, Colin Colin, and Zhulyn, Oles. "Using NLP techniques for file fragment classification," *Digital Investigation*, vol. 9, pp. S44–S49, 2012.

[4] Du, X. *et al.*, "SoK: Exploring the state of the art and the future potential of artificial intelligence in digital forensic investigation," *Proceedings of the 15th International Conference on Availability, Reliability and Security*, pp. 1–10, Aug. 2020, doi: 10.1145/3407023.3407068

[5] Johnson, Sajith and Ananthakumaran, S. "Smart digital forensic framework for crime analysis and prediction using AutoML," *International Journal of Advanced Computer Science and Applications*, vol. 12, 2021. doi:10.14569/IJACSA.2021.0120349

[6] Koroniotis, N., Moustafa, N., and Sitnikova, E. "A new network forensic framework based on deep learning for Internet of Things networks: A particle deep framework," *Future Generation Computer Systems*, vol. 110, pp. 91–106, 2020, doi:10.1016/j.future.2020.03.042

[7] Johnson, Sajith A. and Ananthakumaran, S. "Smart digital forensic framework for crime analysis and prediction using AutoML," *International Journal of Advanced Computer Science and Applications*, vol. 12, no. 3, pp. 416–423, 2021. doi: 10.14569/IJACSA.2021.0120349

[8] Koroniotis, Nikos, Moustafa, Nour, and Sitnikova, Eleonora. "A new network forensic framework based on deep learning for IoT networks," *Future Generation Computer Systems*, vol. 110, pp. 91–106, 2020.

[9] National Institute of Standards and Technology. *Framework for Improving Critical Infrastructure Cybersecurity*. NIST, 2018.

[10] Sanger, D. E., Perlroth, N., and Barnes, J. E., "As understanding of Russian hacking grows, so does alarm," *The New York Times*, Dec., 13, 2020. https://www.nytimes.com/2020/12/13/us/politics/russian-hackers-us-government-treasury-commerce.html

[11] Harwell, D. "Amazon is selling facial recognition to law enforcement — for a fistful of dollars," *The Washington Post*, May 22, 2018. https://www.washingtonpost.com/news/the-switch/wp/2018/05/22/amazon-is-selling-facial-recognition-to-law-enforcement-for-a-fistful-of-dollars/

[12] New York City Police Department. *YPD announces facial recognition policy*, 2020. https://www.nyc.gov/site/nypd/news/pr0313/press-release---nypd-facial-recognition-policy

Chapter 12

Advanced computational paradigms in digital forensics

Big data, NLP, and GenAI

Building upon the foundational integration of artificial intelligence, machine learning, and visual computing introduced in the previous chapter, this chapter extends the discussion to a set of advanced computational paradigms that are reshaping the analytical capabilities of digital forensics(DF). As digital investigations increasingly contend with vast, heterogeneous, and dynamic data environments, traditional analytic models alone are no longer sufficient. Instead, scalable and semantically aware systems are becoming essential to extract actionable intelligence from complex datasets.

This chapter focuses on three interrelated domains—Big Data, Natural Language Processing (NLP), and Generative AI—that have become instrumental in addressing these demands. It begins by exploring how Big Data frameworks offer scalable solutions for ingesting and analyzing high-volume, high-velocity evidence streams, often in real-time or near real-time. It then examines the growing role of NLP in interpreting unstructured textual evidence, such as communications, logs, and social media content, with increasing accuracy and contextual sensitivity. Finally, it investigates the emergence of Generative AI as both a forensic tool and a source of novel evidentiary challenges, including content synthesis, manipulation detection, and the forensic verification of AI-generated media.

Together, these technologies not only expand the functional scope of digital forensics but also introduce new considerations around evidence integrity, model interpretability, and adversarial resilience. The chapter critically evaluates the potential and limitations of these paradigms, laying the groundwork for the subsequent exploration of explainable AI, blockchain-integrated forensics, and adaptive forensic frameworks in Chapter 13.

12.1 BIG DATA

Big data, a term coined to describe datasets of extraordinary size and complexity, presents a unique challenge for traditional data-processing software. These vast repositories of information exhibit distinct characteristics, often summarized by the 3Vs: Volume, velocity, and variety (see Figure 12.1). Volume

DOI: 10.1201/9781003644255-12

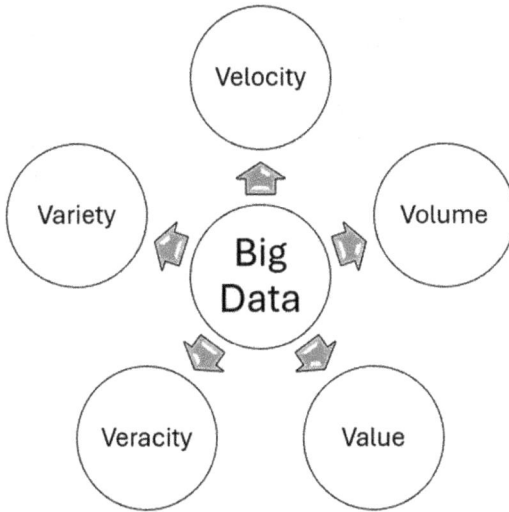

Figure 12.1 Five Vs of big data.

denotes the sheer magnitude of data, often characterized by a proliferation of low-density, unstructured information. Examples include Facebook data feeds, which can amass to tens of terabytes or even hundreds of petabytes. The volume of data has surged in the modern era, especially with the advent of IoT devices, smart technologies that operate in real-time, and the prolific generation of data through platforms like Facebook, YouTube, and Orkut, which emerged around 2005. Velocity reflects the speed at which data is generated and transferred. In today's technological landscape, real-time data transmission has become paramount, a necessity driven by the demand for immediate insights and responses. Internet-enabled smart devices are prime examples of this need for swift data processing. Variety encompasses the diverse formats of data. While structured data adheres to predefined formats and is highly specific, unstructured data takes the form of text, audio, video, and more, often stored in their native formats. The increasing complexity and diversity of data types have led to a demand for additional preprocessing and analysis.

In the realm of big data, two more "Vs" come into play. Veracity pertains to the quality and accuracy of data. Inadequate attention to data quality can lead to risks and excessive costs, making veracity a critical concern for organizations dealing with large datasets. This aspect holds significant importance in digital forensics, where data accuracy is vital for investigations.

The fifth "V," Value, underscores the significance of the information gathered. The value of data is determined by its usefulness and relevance, a concept applicable to all domains handling large datasets.

In the context of digital forensics, the surge in big data presents a double-edged sword. While it offers invaluable insights and evidence, the sheer volume, velocity, variety, and veracity of data pose formidable challenges to investigators. Effectively navigating this multifaceted landscape is essential for leveraging the potential of big data while upholding the standards of veracity and deriving meaningful value from the information at hand.

With the continuous proliferation of data, the definition of what constitutes big data lacks a fixed threshold. However, literature generally acknowledges datasets exceeding 1 terabyte as fitting the description of big data. In 2020, as reported by the International Data Corporation, each online user was generating an average of 1.7 megabytes of data every second [1]. Astonishingly, merely 37% of this avalanche of information was being effectively analyzed, leaving a substantial volume of data largely unattended. Consequently, the foremost challenge faced by big data revolves around storage capabilities. While storage applications and software boast significant capacities, the exponential growth in data volumes poses a pressing risk to the existing storage resources.

One of the key distinctions in data processing lies in the categorization of data into two fundamental types: structured and unstructured. Each necessitates a distinct approach to data processing, thereby presenting a significant challenge for forensic investigators. Structured data adheres to defined formats, often organized in binary trees or string queues, and can be processed through traditional search methods. Conversely, unstructured data exhibits a lack of predefined structure, with examples ranging from text messages, emails, audio recordings, and video files to web pages and social media content. Effectively extracting evidence from this unstructured data demands the utilization of search queries, enabling investigators to navigate the intricate terrain of unstructured datasets. This distinction underscores the importance of adapting investigative techniques to the specific nature of the data being examined.

12.1.1 Potential solution to big data challenges for DF

The burgeoning influx of information, commonly referred to as big data, presents a formidable challenge to the field of digital forensics. This challenge, however, can be addressed through a variety of solutions, as discussed below:

1. **Data Volume Reduction and Classification**: One approach involves the reduction of data volume. Prior to commencing the digital forensic process, it is prudent to filter out extraneous and by-product data. By minimizing data volume, the subsequent analysis can be significantly more efficient.

2. **Data Classification**: An integral step in managing big data involves the classification of unstructured data based on its format and type. This classification streamlines the digital forensic investigator's task, allowing for a more straightforward analysis of data evidence that adheres to uniform standards.

3. **Utilizing AI, ML, or Deep Learning for Forensic Analysis:** The advent of AI, ML, and deep learning has ushered in new possibilities across numerous domains, including digital forensics. These advanced techniques offer a practical means of coping with the escalating data volumes. In particular, ML and deep learning facilitate automation within the digital forensic process, enhancing the capacity to process big data for analytical purposes [2]. Their implementation empowers investigators to navigate the complexities of substantial datasets more effectively.

12.2 NATURAL LANGUAGE PROCESSING (NLP) IN DF

Natural Language Processing (NLP) is an interdisciplinary field at the intersection of computer science, artificial intelligence, and linguistics. It focuses on the interaction between computers and human language, aiming to enable computers to understand, interpret, and generate human language. NLP combines computational linguistics with machine learning and deep learning techniques to process and analyze large amounts of natural language data, making it possible for machines to perform tasks such as translation, sentiment analysis, text summarization, and question answering.

NLP techniques can be broadly categorized into several key areas:

- **Text Mining and Information Retrieval:** Text mining involves extracting useful information from unstructured text data. This includes tasks like identifying key phrases, extracting entities, and summarizing documents. Information retrieval focuses on finding relevant documents or pieces of information from a large corpus based on a query, employing techniques such as keyword matching, vector space models, and semantic search.
- **Text Classification and Sentiment Analysis:** Text classification categorizes text into predefined classes, which can be used for tasks such as spam detection, topic categorization, and sentiment analysis. Sentiment analysis specifically aims to determine the sentiment expressed in a text—whether positive, negative, or neutral, providing valuable insights into public opinion and customer feedback.
- **Named Entity Recognition (NER):** NER identifies and classifies named entities in text, such as people, organizations, locations, dates, and quantities. This is crucial for structuring unstructured text data, enabling the extraction of meaningful information from large volumes of text.
- **Machine Translation and Language Modeling:** Machine translation automatically translates text from one language to another, utilizing advanced neural machine translation systems to achieve high accuracy. Language modeling involves predicting the next word or sequence of words in a text, which is fundamental to many NLP tasks, including text generation and autocompletion.

12.2.1 Advancements in NLP

NLP has witnessed remarkable advancements in recent years, primarily driven by developments in deep learning and the availability of large-scale datasets.

Transformer Models: The introduction of transformer models by Vaswani et al. in 2017 revolutionized NLP [3]. Transformers use self-attention mechanisms to process and generate text, allowing for parallel processing and improved performance. Notable transformer models include BERT (Bidirectional Encoder Representations from Transformers) and GPT (Generative Pre-trained Transformer). BERT is designed for tasks requiring a deep understanding of text, such as question answering and language inference, while GPT excels at text generation and language modeling.

Pre-trained Language Models: Pre-trained language models have become a cornerstone of modern NLP. These models are trained on massive datasets to learn general language representations, which can then be fine-tuned for specific tasks with smaller datasets. This approach significantly reduces the amount of labeled data required for training and improves performance across various NLP tasks. Examples of pre-trained models include BERT, GPT-3, and RoBERTa.

Transfer Learning and Fine-Tuning: Transfer learning involves using pre-trained models on new tasks to save time and computational resources. Fine-tuning is the process of adapting a pre-trained model to a specific task by training it further on a smaller, task-specific dataset. This technique has been widely adopted in NLP, allowing models to achieve state-of-the-art performance on tasks such as sentiment analysis, text classification, and named entity recognition.

Neural Machine Translation (NMT): NMT has made significant strides in recent years, surpassing traditional statistical machine translation methods in accuracy and fluency. NMT systems use deep learning techniques to model the translation process, capturing context and nuances better than previous approaches. Models like Google Translate and DeepL have set new standards in machine translation quality.

12.2.2 Applications of NLP in DF

NLP's capabilities have extensive applications in digital forensics, enhancing the ability to process and analyze large volumes of textual data efficiently and accurately. Here are several applications in detail:

1. Text Mining and Information Retrieval: NLP techniques can mine and retrieve relevant information from vast amounts of textual data. Forensic investigators can use text mining to extract key phrases,

entities, and summaries from emails, documents, and chat logs. Information retrieval systems can help investigators find relevant documents or pieces of information based on specific queries, significantly speeding up the investigation process. For instance, in a corporate fraud investigation, NLP can analyze millions of emails to identify patterns, detect collusion, and extract critical communications that may indicate fraudulent activity.

2. **Text Classification and Sentiment Analysis:** Text classification can categorize documents and communications into relevant classes, such as identifying phishing emails, categorizing types of fraud, or detecting spam messages. Sentiment analysis can analyze the tone and sentiment expressed in communications, helping investigators understand the context and emotional state of the individuals involved. For example, sentiment analysis of social media posts and customer reviews can provide insights into cases of cyberbullying or harassment by identifying negative sentiments and distress signals.

3. **Named Entity Recognition (NER):** NER is crucial for extracting structured information from unstructured text data. In digital forensics, NER can identify and extract names of individuals, organizations, locations, and other entities from emails, documents, and social media posts. This information can establish relationships between entities, track movements, and identify key players in an investigation. For example, identifying mentions of specific locations in communications can help trace the movements of suspects in a criminal investigation, providing vital clues about their whereabouts and activities.

4. **Machine Translation:** In cases involving multiple languages, machine translation can translate communications and documents into a common language for analysis. This is particularly useful in investigations involving international suspects or victims. Modern neural machine translation systems can achieve high levels of accuracy and fluency, making it easier for investigators to understand and analyze foreign language texts. For instance, translating communications between international crime syndicates can reveal plans, strategies, and operational details crucial to the investigation.

5. **Authorship Attribution:** NLP techniques can determine the authorship of anonymous or disputed texts by analyzing writing style, vocabulary, and linguistic patterns. This can be particularly useful in cases of plagiarism, fraud, or online harassment where the identity of the author is in question. Forensic linguists can use NLP to attribute texts to specific individuals with a high degree of confidence, providing crucial evidence in legal proceedings.

6. **Speech-to-Text Conversion:** NLP can convert audio recordings into text, enabling forensic investigators to analyze spoken communications. This is useful in cases where voice recordings are available but need to be transcribed for further analysis. Speech-to-text systems can

automatically transcribe conversations, phone calls, and voice messages, making it easier to search and analyze the content. For example, transcribing intercepted phone calls between suspects can reveal incriminating evidence and help build a timeline of events.

7. **Language Modeling and Contextual Analysis:** Advanced NLP models can analyze the context and content of communications to identify hidden meanings, code words, or linguistic patterns indicative of criminal activity. Language modeling can help detect covert communication strategies used by criminals to evade detection. For instance, analyzing chat logs of organized crime groups can uncover coded language used to plan illegal activities, providing valuable intelligence for law enforcement.

8. **Social Network Analysis:** NLP can analyze social media posts, comments, and interactions to map social networks and identify key influencers or conspirators. By examining patterns of communication, investigators can uncover relationships and connections that are not immediately apparent. This can be particularly useful in counter-terrorism and organized crime investigations, where understanding the network dynamics is crucial for disrupting criminal operations.

9. **Behavioral Profiling:** NLP can assist in creating behavioral profiles of suspects based on their communication patterns, language use, and online activity. By analyzing how individuals communicate, forensic experts can infer personality traits, emotional states, and potential motives. This can help prioritize suspects, guide interrogation strategies, and provide insights into the psychological aspects of criminal behavior.

10. **Cyber Threat Intelligence:** NLP can be used to analyze threat intelligence reports, cybersecurity alerts, and dark web communications to identify emerging threats and attack vectors. By monitoring and analyzing textual data from various sources, NLP can provide early warnings of cyber threats and help organizations proactively defend against cyber-attacks.

A real-life example of the application of NLP in digital forensics is the investigation of the Panama Papers. The Panama Papers were a massive leak of documents from the Panamanian law firm Mossack Fonseca, revealing how wealthy individuals and public officials used offshore entities to conceal their wealth [4]. The leak comprised 11.5 million documents, including emails, financial spreadsheets, passports, and corporate records, totaling 2.6 terabytes of data.

The International Consortium of Investigative Journalists (ICIJ) used advanced NLP techniques to process and analyze the vast amount of data. Text mining and information retrieval systems were employed to extract key phrases, entities, and relationships from the documents. Named entity recognition was used to identify and categorize entities such as individuals, companies, and locations. This helped the investigators establish connections between entities and trace the flow of money. Machine translation was also used to translate documents in multiple languages into a common language for analysis. This enabled the investigators to understand and analyze foreign language texts, uncovering important information that would have been missed otherwise.

The NLP models were continuously updated with new data as the investigation progressed, ensuring that the analysis remained effective against evolving leads and new information. The automated analysis reduced the time required for manual review and allowed the investigators to focus on more complex aspects of the investigation. The use of NLP in the Panama Papers investigation significantly enhanced the efficiency and effectiveness of the forensic analysis. The automated systems were able to quickly process and analyze the massive amount of data, uncovering critical evidence and revealing the complex network of offshore entities used to conceal wealth. The findings from the investigation led to significant political and legal repercussions worldwide, demonstrating the power of NLP in uncovering hidden information and bringing about justice.

12.2.3 Potential impacts of NLP on DF

The integration of NLP in digital forensics has the potential to significantly enhance the efficiency and effectiveness of forensic investigations.

NLP specializes in analyzing text-based evidence, such as emails, chat logs, or social media interactions. This capability allows for the extraction of meaningful information, sentiment analysis, and even the detection of hidden or coded messages in vast amounts of text. NLP can also identify languages and translate text, which is critical in multinational investigations where digital evidence might include communications in various languages. This ensures that all relevant information is accessible, regardless of language barriers.

NLP techniques can automate the analysis of large volumes of textual data, reducing the time required for manual review and allowing investigators to focus on more complex aspects of the investigation. For example, automated text classification and information retrieval can quickly sort through thousands of emails or documents, identifying relevant information and reducing the workload for human analysts. In addition, NLP models can detect patterns and anomalies in text data that may be missed by traditional methods, enhancing the ability to identify malicious activities, fraudulent communications, and security breaches. For example, sentiment analysis can detect signs of distress or anger in social media posts, indicating potential cases of cyberbullying or harassment.

Scalability is another beneficial factor of NLP models, as they can handle large-scale investigations involving vast amounts of textual data from diverse sources. This scalability is crucial for investigating complex cyber-attacks or fraud schemes that generate significant amounts of data. For example, NLP-based information retrieval systems can process and analyze large volumes of documents and communications, enabling comprehensive investigations of large-scale cyber intrusions. Many routine forensic tasks can be automated using NLP, increasing the overall efficiency and effectiveness of forensic investigations. For example, automated entity extraction and text summarization can quickly extract and summarize key information from lengthy documents, reducing the need for manual review. Automated analysis reduces the likelihood of errors that can occur with manual investigation methods. NLP models can consistently apply the same analysis criteria, reducing the risk of oversight or bias. For example, automated text classification systems can consistently categorize emails as spam or legitimate, reducing the risk of human error and ensuring accurate and reliable results.

NLP models can be continuously updated with new data, ensuring they remain effective against evolving threats. This adaptability is essential for keeping pace with the rapidly changing landscape of cybercrime and digital fraud. For example, an NLP-based spam detection system can continuously learn from new spam patterns and update its models to detect emerging threats.

Additionally, by automating routine tasks and enhancing the efficiency of forensic investigations, organizations can save on labor costs and allocate resources more efficiently. This cost-effectiveness is particularly important for organizations with limited forensic resources. For example, implementing NLP-based forensic tools can reduce the need for extensive manual analysis, allowing organizations to optimize their forensic resources and reduce overall investigation costs.

12.2.4 Additional considerations and challenges

While the potential benefits of NLP in digital forensics are significant, several considerations and challenges must be addressed to fully realize these benefits. NLP models require high-quality data for training and evaluation, which can be challenging in digital forensics due to the diverse and often unstructured nature of textual evidence. Access to sufficient and relevant data is crucial for effective model training, but sensitive or classified information may be restricted, limiting data availability. Forensic investigators must understand and explain the decisions made by NLP models, especially in legal contexts where forensic analysis results may be used as evidence in court. Developing explainable AI techniques to make NLP models' decision-making processes transparent and understandable is essential for their adoption. Additionally, NLP models can inadvertently learn and propagate biases present in the training data, leading to unfair or incorrect conclusions. Ensuring these models are fair and unbiased is critical to avoid discrimination and injustice. The sensitive nature of textual evidence also requires robust security measures to protect data from unauthorized access and tampering. The use of NLP in digital forensics must balance effective investigation with respect for individual privacy rights, ensuring compliance with privacy regulations and ethical standards. Furthermore, NLP-based forensic tools must be compatible with existing forensic tools and workflows for effective integration into the investigative process, necessitating organizations to invest in training programs to ensure their personnel can leverage these technologies.

12.3 GENERATIVE AI IN DIGITAL FORENSICS

Generative AI represents a significant advancement in artificial intelligence, focusing on the creation of new content by learning from existing data. Unlike traditional AI, which primarily analyzes and makes decisions based on patterns, generative AI models produce data that mirrors the underlying patterns and structures of the training data. These models are designed to generate a variety of content, including text, images, audio, and video, by modeling the probability distributions of datasets.

Generative Adversarial Networks (GANs), introduced by Ian Goodfellow in 2014, have revolutionized the field by pitting two neural networks against each other: The generator and the discriminator. The generator creates synthetic data, while the discriminator evaluates its authenticity. This adversarial process continues until the generator produces data that is nearly indistinguishable from real data. Variational Autoencoders (VAEs) are another crucial development, encoding data into a latent space and then decoding it to generate new data, particularly effective in producing high-quality images. Transformer-based models, such as GPT-3 and GPT-4, utilize attention mechanisms to handle sequential data, excelling in generating coherent and contextually relevant text for tasks like language translation, summarization, and content creation. Diffusion models iteratively refine an initial random noise input to generate high-fidelity images and videos, using multiple stages of denoising to produce remarkably high-quality outputs. Cross-modal models like DALL-E generate images from textual descriptions, while CLIP integrates visual and textual data, enabling advanced applications in image captioning and visual question answering.

12.3.1 Advancements in generative AI

Generative AI has made significant strides in recent years, with several key advancements that have pushed the boundaries of what AI can achieve. These advancements have significant implications across various industries, providing tools and solutions that were previously unimaginable.

1. **High-Fidelity Image Generation**: GANs and diffusion models have achieved unprecedented success in generating realistic images, with applications ranging from creating human faces to designing art and fashion. These models have pushed the boundaries of what is possible, allowing for the creation of high-quality images that are nearly indistinguishable from real photographs. This has significant implications for industries such as advertising, entertainment, and fashion, where the ability to generate realistic images on demand can save time and resources.

2. **Advanced Text Generation**: Transformer models have revolutionized natural language processing, enabling the generation of human-like text for diverse applications. From chatbots to automated content creation, these models can produce coherent, contextually relevant text that mimics human writing. This has wide-ranging applications in customer service, marketing, and even creative writing, where AI can assist in generating new content quickly and efficiently.

3. **Audio and Music Synthesis**: Generative models can produce lifelike speech and music, enhancing virtual assistants, entertainment, and accessibility tools. By learning the patterns of speech and music, these models can create audio that is indistinguishable from human-produced content. This is particularly valuable in creating voice-overs, synthesizing new music, and providing accessible content for individuals with disabilities.

4. **Cross-Modal Applications**: Models like DALL-E and CLIP bridge the gap between text and images, opening up new possibilities for creative and practical applications. DALL-E can generate unique images from textual descriptions, making it a powerful tool for artists and designers. CLIP, on the other hand, can understand and integrate visual and textual data, enabling advanced applications in image captioning, visual question answering, and more.

5. **Pre-trained Generative Models**: Similar to the advancements in natural language processing, generative models have benefited from transfer learning and pre-training. Models like GPT-3, which are pre-trained on vast amounts of data, can generate highly coherent and contextually relevant text. These models can be fine-tuned for specific tasks, making them versatile tools for various generative applications.

6. **Neural Rendering**: This technique combines generative models with computer graphics to create highly realistic synthetic images and videos. Neural rendering is used in applications such as virtual reality, video game design, and special effects in movies.

12.3.2 Application of generative AI in DF

Generative AI has emerged as a transformative technology within the realm of digital forensics, offering novel solutions and enhancing existing methodologies. By leveraging its ability to create, analyze, and reconstruct data, generative AI significantly improves the efficiency and accuracy of forensic investigations, enhancing the capabilities of forensic investigators and cybersecurity professionals:

1. **Data Augmentation for Forensic Analysis:** Generative AI can create synthetic datasets to augment limited forensic data, improving the training of machine learning models for identifying and analyzing digital evidence. This is particularly useful in scenarios where real forensic data are scarce or sensitive. By generating synthetic yet realistic data, forensic tools can be trained more effectively, enhancing their ability to detect and analyze digital evidence.
2. **Anomaly Detection:** By modeling normal digital behaviors, generative models can identify anomalies indicative of malicious activities. This capability is crucial for detecting unauthorized access, data breaches, and other cyber threats. Generative AI can analyze vast amounts of data to establish what constitutes normal behavior and then flag any deviations for further investigation.
3. **Reconstruction of Digital Evidence:** Generative AI can reconstruct corrupted or incomplete digital evidence, such as restoring missing parts of images or videos. This can be invaluable in forensic investigations where critical evidence has been damaged or is partially missing. Generative models can fill in the gaps, providing investigators with more complete and usable evidence.
4. **Deepfake Detection:** As generative AI advances in creating realistic deepfakes, it also provides tools to detect them. Models trained to identify subtle inconsistencies and artifacts in deepfake media can be essential in verifying the authenticity of digital evidence. This is increasingly important as deepfake technology becomes more sophisticated and widely used for malicious purposes.
5. **Language Modeling for Text Analysis:** Transformer models like GPT-4 can analyze vast amounts of textual data, such as emails, chat logs, and social media posts, identifying key patterns and generating summaries to support forensic analysis. This capability streamlines the process of sifting through large volumes of text, allowing forensic investigators to focus on the most relevant information.
6. **Automated Report Generation:** Generative AI can automate the creation of forensic reports, summarizing findings and generating coherent narratives from analyzed data. This enhances the efficiency and effectiveness of forensic investigations by reducing the time and effort required to produce detailed reports, allowing investigators to focus on analysis rather than documentation.
7. **Crime Scene Simulation:** Generative models can create realistic simulations of crime scenes, which can be used for training forensic investigators or for reconstructing events based on available evidence. These

simulations can help investigators visualize the crime scene and test different hypotheses about how the crime might have occurred.

8. **Natural Language Generation for Threat Analysis:** Generative models like GPT-3 can be used to simulate communications in cyber threat analysis. By generating realistic phishing emails or social engineering attacks, these models can help train cybersecurity professionals to recognize and respond to such threats. Additionally, generative models can assist in the automated generation of reports and summaries of forensic findings, saving time and improving the efficiency of forensic investigations.

9. **Voice Cloning and Speaker Identification:** Generative AI can be used for voice cloning and speaker identification, where synthetic voices can be generated to match the vocal characteristics of individuals. This can be useful for verifying the authenticity of voice recordings or for training systems to recognize specific speakers in audio data. In forensic investigations, this can help identify or confirm the identity of suspects based on voice evidence.

Table 12.1 outlines various applications of generative AI in digital forensics, detailing specific use cases, the models and techniques employed, and the benefits they bring to forensic practices. This comprehensive overview illustrates how generative AI can address some of the most pressing challenges in the field, providing forensic professionals with advanced tools and capabilities to better manage and analyze digital evidence.

A real-life example of the application of generative AI in digital forensics is the use of deepfake detection technology by law enforcement agencies. Deepfakes are realistic manipulated videos or images generated using GANs, posing significant challenges for digital forensics. To address this issue, law enforcement agencies have adopted generative AI-based tools to detect deepfakes and ensure the integrity of digital evidence.

In 2019, researchers at the University of California, Berkeley, developed a deepfake detection system using GANs [5]. The system was trained on a large dataset of both real and deepfake videos, learning to identify subtle inconsistencies and artifacts indicative of manipulation. The model analyzed facial movements, audio-visual synchronization, and other features to detect deepfakes with high accuracy. Law enforcement agencies, such as the FBI, have since adopted this technology to analyze digital evidence in criminal investigations. The deepfake detection system has been used to verify the authenticity of video evidence, ensuring that manipulated media does not compromise the integrity of investigations. The system has also been employed in counter-terrorism efforts to identify deepfake videos used for propaganda and misinformation campaigns.

The use of generative AI for deepfake detection has significantly enhanced the capabilities of law enforcement agencies, providing advanced tools for evidence analysis and improving the accuracy of forensic findings. This case

Table 12.1 Applications of generative AI in digital forensics

Application	Description	Example models/ Techniques	Benefits
Data Augmentation	Creation of synthetic datasets to supplement limited forensic data, improving the machine learning model training	GANs, VAEs	Enhances model robustness, reduces overfitting, and provides more diverse training data
Anomaly Detection	Identification of deviations from normal digital behavior, indicating potential malicious activities	VAEs, Autoencoders, Transformer models	Early detection of cyber threats improves accuracy in identifying unauthorized activities
Reconstruction of Digital Evidence	Rebuilding corrupted or incomplete digital evidence, such as images, videos, and audio	GANs, Diffusion Models	Restores critical evidence, aids in comprehensive analysis
Deepfake Detection	Identifying and verifying the authenticity of media to detect deepfakes	GANs, Transformer-based models	Maintains the integrity of digital evidence, prevents misinformation
Text Analysis	Analyzing large volumes of textual data to extract key patterns and generate summaries	Transformer models (GPT-3, GPT-4)	Streamlines the analysis process, enabling quick identification of relevant information
Automated Report Generation	Creating detailed forensic reports by summarizing findings from analyzed data	Transformer models	Increases efficiency in report writing, reduces manual workload
Image and Video Analysis	Examining visual content to identify and extract relevant forensic evidence	GANs, CLIP	Facilitates detailed visual investigations, enhances accuracy in image/video content analysis
Synthetic Data Generation	Producing synthetic but realistic data for testing and training purposes	GANs, Diffusion Models	Provides controlled datasets for testing, ensures privacy by not using real sensitive data

(Continued)

Table 12.1 (Continued)

Application	Description	Example models/ Techniques	Benefits
Forensic Tool Enhancement	Improving existing forensic tools by integrating generative AI capabilities	Various generative models	Increases tool effectiveness, offers new functionalities
Scenario Simulation	Generating realistic scenarios for training and evaluating forensic response strategies	GANs, Transformer-based models	Prepares investigators for real-world situations, enhances training quality
Evidence Preservation	Creating backup copies of digital evidence by generating highly accurate replicas	Diffusion Models, VAEs	Ensures the integrity and availability of evidence, and prevents data loss
Pattern Recognition	Detecting patterns and correlations within forensic data that may indicate a coordinated attack or breach	VAEs, GANs, Transformer models	Identifies complex attack patterns, improves threat response strategies
Natural Language Processing (NLP)	Extracting insights from communication data such as emails, chat logs, and social media posts	Transformer models (BERT, GPT)	Enhances understanding of communication context, aids in identifying suspects and motives
Malware Analysis	Generating and analyzing synthetic malware samples to understand new threat vectors	GANs, VAEs	Improves malware detection systems, provides insights into emerging threats
Behavioral Modeling	Creating models of user behavior to detect deviations that may indicate insider threats or compromised accounts	VAEs, Autoencoders, Transformer models	Enhances security by identifying abnormal behavior; protects against insider threats

study demonstrates the potential of generative AI to address emerging challenges in digital forensics and highlights the importance of continued research and development in this field.

12.3.3 Potential impacts of generative AI in DF

Generative AI's integration into digital forensics promises to bring both opportunities and challenges. These impacts will shape the future of forensic investigations, providing new tools and techniques while also presenting new ethical and technical challenges.

1. Creation of Synthetic Data for Testing: Generative AI can create synthetic data that mimics real-world scenarios, allowing forensic tools and models to be tested under controlled conditions. This is particularly useful for training forensic algorithms without compromising actual case data.
2. Reconstruction of Missing Data: Generative models can be used to reconstruct missing or corrupted data, such as filling in missing pieces of a damaged digital file, which is not something traditional ML or DL techniques focus on.
3. Forgery Detection: While ML can detect anomalies, generative AI can specifically model and recognize forgeries, making it uniquely valuable in identifying digitally altered content, such as deepfakes or manipulated documents.
4. Combatting Deepfakes: Generative AI models trained to detect deepfakes can stay ahead of malicious actors, ensuring the integrity of digital evidence and maintaining trust in forensic processes. As deepfake technology becomes more prevalent, the ability to detect and counteract these manipulations will be crucial.
5. Ethical and Legal Considerations: The use of generative AI in forensics raises important ethical and legal issues. The creation of synthetic data and reconstruction of evidence must be carefully managed to avoid biases and ensure admissibility in court. Clear guidelines and regulations will be needed to address these challenges and ensure the responsible use of generative AI in forensics.
6. New Challenges in Cybersecurity: While generative AI enhances forensic capabilities, it also presents new challenges as malicious actors may use these technologies to create sophisticated attacks. Continuous advancements in forensic techniques are required to counter these threats and stay ahead of cybercriminals. As generative models become more advanced, they could be leveraged by cybercriminals to create more complex and deceptive attacks, making it essential for forensic investigators to stay up-to-date with the latest techniques and tools for countering such threats.

7. Training and Expertise: The integration of generative AI necessitates specialized training for forensic experts. Understanding the capabilities and limitations of generative models is crucial for effectively utilizing these tools in investigations. This will require ongoing education and training programs to keep forensic professionals up-to-date with the latest advancements in generative AI.

12.3.4 Additional considerations and challenges

While the potential benefits of generative AI in digital forensics are significant, several considerations and challenges must be addressed to fully realize these benefits.

Ethical Considerations: The use of generative AI raises ethical concerns, particularly regarding the creation and detection of deepfakes. While generative models can be used to detect manipulated media, they can also be misused to create realistic fake content that can deceive and harm individuals. Ensuring that generative AI is used responsibly and ethically is crucial for maintaining public trust and avoiding potential misuse. This includes establishing guidelines and regulations for the ethical use of generative AI and promoting transparency in the development and deployment of these technologies.

Data Privacy and Security: The sensitive nature of digital evidence requires robust security measures to protect data from unauthorized access and tampering. The use of generative AI in digital forensics must balance the need for effective investigation with respect for individual privacy rights, ensuring compliance with privacy regulations and ethical standards. This includes implementing strong encryption, access controls, and auditing mechanisms to safeguard forensic data and maintain its integrity throughout the investigation process.

Model Interpretability: Forensic investigators must be able to understand and explain the decisions made by generative models, especially in legal contexts where the results of forensic analysis may be used as evidence in court. Developing explainable AI techniques that make the decision-making processes of generative models transparent and understandable is essential for their adoption in digital forensics. This involves creating models that provide insights into their decision-making process and generating explanations that can be easily interpreted by human investigators and legal professionals.

Bias and Fairness: Generative models can inadvertently learn and propagate biases present in the training data, leading to unfair or incorrect conclusions. Ensuring that generative AI models are fair and unbiased is critical to avoid discrimination and injustice. Efforts must be made to ensure that the models used in digital forensics are trained on diverse and representative datasets and that their use does not perpetuate existing biases. This includes regular audits of training data, implementing bias mitigation techniques, and continuously monitoring the performance of generative models to ensure fairness and accuracy.

Integration with Existing Tools and Workflows: Generative AI-based forensic tools must be compatible with existing forensic tools and workflows to be effectively integrated into the investigative process. Forensic investigators also require training to effectively use generative AI-based tools, and organizations must invest in training programs to ensure their personnel can leverage the full potential of these technologies. This includes developing comprehensive training programs, providing hands-on experience with generative AI tools, and fostering a culture of continuous learning and adaptation.

Legal and Regulatory Challenges: The use of generative AI in digital forensics poses legal and regulatory challenges, particularly in the context of evidence admissibility and chain of custody. Ensuring that generative AI tools comply with legal standards and are accepted in court requires collaboration between technologists, legal professionals, and policymakers. Establishing clear guidelines and standards for the use of generative AI in forensic investigations is essential to address these challenges and ensure the credibility and reliability of forensic evidence.

12.4 EXPERT SYSTEMS IN DF

Expert systems are a branch of artificial intelligence designed to mimic the decision-making abilities of a human expert. They operate based on a set of predefined rules and logic, enabling them to provide solutions or recommendations in specialized domains. In digital forensics, expert systems can play a significant role in guiding investigators through complex cases by leveraging codified knowledge and established protocols, as well as assisting non-expert users to make informed analytical decisions, follow standardized investigative procedures, and interpret digital evidence more accurately (see Figure 12.2).

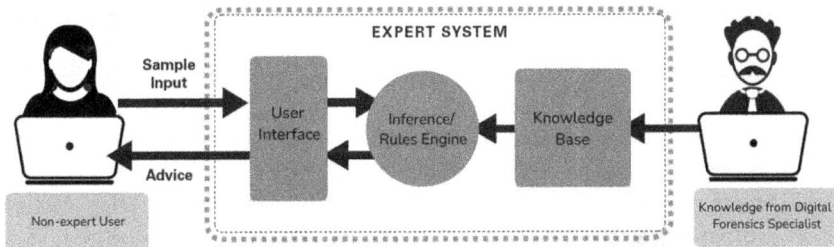

Figure 12.2 Expert systems.

1. **Rule-Based Decision-Making**: Expert systems rely on a comprehensive set of rules derived from expert knowledge in the field of digital forensics. These rules are encoded into the system, allowing it to make decisions or provide recommendations based on the input data. In digital forensics, expert systems can automatically apply legal and procedural guidelines to ensure that investigations adhere to established standards. For instance, an expert system can guide investigators in identifying the correct steps for handling digital evidence, ensuring compliance with chain-of-custody requirements.

2. **Consistency and Predictability**: One of the key advantages of expert systems is their ability to deliver consistent and predictable results. Unlike machine learning models, which may produce varying outcomes based on the data and training process, expert systems follow a fixed set of rules. This consistency is particularly valuable in digital forensics, where uniformity in analysis and reporting is crucial. For example, an expert system could consistently apply the same criteria when assessing the validity of digital evidence, ensuring that every case is evaluated based on the same legal and technical standards.

3. **Legacy System Integration**: Expert systems are often easier to integrate with legacy forensic tools and databases than more advanced AI technologies. This compatibility allows organizations to enhance their existing forensic workflows without the need for extensive system overhauls. In digital forensics, expert systems can be integrated with traditional tools to automate routine tasks, such as verifying the integrity of evidence or cross-referencing data against known databases. This integration helps forensic teams leverage new technology while preserving their investment in established systems.

4. **Automated Decision Support**: Expert systems can provide automated decision support to forensic investigators, offering recommendations or highlighting potential areas of concern based on the evidence at hand. This support is particularly useful in complex cases where the volume of data and the intricacy of the investigation may overwhelm human analysts. For example, an expert system might flag inconsistencies in digital logs that suggest tampering or guide investigators toward potential sources of evidence that may have been overlooked.

5. **Codification of Expert Knowledge**: By encoding the knowledge of experienced forensic professionals into a rule-based system, expert systems ensure that this expertise is preserved and accessible to all members of a forensic team. This codification allows less experienced investigators to benefit from the knowledge of experts, ensuring that critical forensic processes are not dependent on the availability of specific individuals. In digital forensics, this might involve encoding best practices for evidence collection or guidelines for interpreting digital artifacts, enabling even novice investigators to conduct thorough and accurate investigations.

12.4.1 Applications of expert systems in DF

Expert systems offer a range of applications in digital forensics, providing valuable tools for evidence analysis, decision-making, and investigation management.

1. **Automated Evidence Assessment**: Expert systems can be used to automate the assessment of digital evidence, applying predefined rules to evaluate its relevance, integrity, and admissibility. For example, an expert system might automatically verify the metadata of a digital file to confirm its authenticity or assess whether a particular piece of evidence meets legal standards for admissibility in court. This automation speeds up the evidence assessment process and ensures that all evidence is evaluated consistently.

2. **Case Management and Workflow Optimization**: Expert systems can optimize the management of forensic cases by guiding investigators through each step of the investigation. This might involve recommending specific forensic tools based on the nature of the evidence or suggesting the most efficient order of tasks to minimize investigation time. In digital forensics, expert systems can help manage complex cases involving large volumes of data or multiple sources of evidence, ensuring that all aspects of the investigation are covered comprehensively and efficiently.

3. **Knowledge Sharing and Training**: Expert systems can serve as a valuable resource for training and knowledge sharing within forensic teams. By providing automated guidance and explanations, these systems can help train new investigators on best practices and procedures in digital forensics. For instance, an expert system might offer step-by-step instructions for analyzing a particular type of digital artifact, ensuring that all team members have access to the same level of expertise.

4. **Potential Impacts of Expert Systems on Digital Forensics**: The integration of expert systems in digital forensics has the potential to enhance the consistency, accuracy, and efficiency of forensic investigations.

5. **Enhanced Consistency and Accuracy**: Expert systems provide a level of consistency and accuracy that is difficult to achieve with human investigators alone. By applying the same set of rules to every case, expert systems ensure that forensic investigations are conducted according to standardized procedures, reducing the risk of errors or inconsistencies. This consistency is crucial in ensuring that forensic evidence is reliable and admissible in court.

6. **Improved Efficiency in Routine Investigations**: By automating routine tasks and decision-making processes, expert systems can significantly improve the efficiency of forensic investigations. This efficiency allows forensic teams to focus their efforts on more complex and high-priority

aspects of an investigation, reducing the overall time required to process cases. For organizations with limited forensic resources, the use of expert systems can lead to significant cost savings and more effective allocation of personnel.

7. **Preservation and Dissemination of Expertise:** Expert systems ensure that the knowledge and expertise of experienced forensic professionals are preserved and made accessible to all members of a forensic team. This preservation of knowledge is particularly important in organizations with high turnover or limited access to expert personnel. By codifying best practices and expert insights, expert systems help maintain a high standard of forensic investigation, regardless of the experience level of individual investigators.

12.4.2 Additional considerations and challenges

While expert systems offer significant benefits in digital forensics, several considerations and challenges must be addressed to fully realize these benefits. One key challenge is the need for accurate and comprehensive rule sets, as the effectiveness of an expert system is directly tied to the quality of its encoded knowledge. Developing and maintaining these rule sets requires ongoing input from experienced forensic professionals, as well as regular updates to reflect changes in legal standards and forensic technology.

Another challenge is ensuring that expert systems are integrated effectively with existing forensic tools and workflows. This integration may require investments in training and infrastructure to ensure that forensic teams can fully leverage the capabilities of expert systems. Additionally, expert systems must be designed with transparency in mind, as forensic investigators and legal professionals need to understand and trust the decisions made by these systems.

Lastly, the legal and ethical implications of using expert systems in forensic investigations must be carefully considered. Ensuring that expert systems comply with legal standards and are used in a manner that respects the rights of individuals is crucial for their successful adoption in digital forensics.

A real-life example of the application of expert systems in digital forensics is the use of rule-based systems for automated evidence triage. For instance, law enforcement agencies may use expert systems to automatically categorize digital evidence based on its relevance to a case, allowing investigators to quickly identify the most critical pieces of evidence. This automated triage helps streamline the investigation process, ensuring that high-priority evidence is analyzed promptly while less relevant data is set aside for later review.

The use of expert systems in this context demonstrates their potential to enhance the efficiency and accuracy of digital forensic investigations, providing valuable support to forensic teams and ensuring that investigations are conducted according to established standards.

END OF CHAPTER QUESTIONS

1. You are leading a forensics investigation involving a large corporate entity that has experienced a significant data breach. You have access to their entire email archive and want to prioritize investigating communications that suggest insider threats. How would you leverage AI-powered anomaly detection and NLP to focus your investigation?

2. You are leading a forensic team investigating a child exploitation ring that operated via AI-based chatbots on social media. How would you use NLP and ML to differentiate between human and bot conversations in chat logs? What forensic challenges would arise in validating intent or determining authorship?

3. Many digital crimes involve the analysis of massive log files. Describe how NLP and ML can be combined to automate the parsing and clustering of anomalous behaviors in log data.

4. A smartphone has been confiscated with an ML-powered voice assistant that was used to issue commands prior to a physical assault. As a forensic expert, describe how you would extract, process, and analyze voice command logs using NLP and DL models to determine the sequence and intent of user interactions.

5. Investigators suspect that a threat actor used a large generative language model to craft phishing emails. The content lacks the usual grammatical patterns or reuse of known malware phrases. Describe how you would detect AI-generated textual content using forensic NLP and stylometry. What forensic signs distinguish synthetic text from human-written communication?

6. A journalist claims that images used in a whistleblower report were AI-generated fabrications. The defense wants to challenge the authenticity of this visual evidence. Outline a forensic investigation plan using deepfake detection, image forensics, and model inversion to validate or debunk the claim. What would be your legal considerations?

7. During analysis of a deepfake video leak, you suspect a GAN-based image generator was used. Discuss the forensic indicators (e.g., compression artifacts, GAN fingerprints, frequency analysis) that help differentiate synthetic video frames from real ones. What tools or ML models would you apply?

8. You have limited real-world data about a newly discovered malware strain. How would you use Generative AI for data augmentation to train classification models capable of identifying similar attack vectors or obfuscation methods in Big Data environments?

9. Your team needs to review 3 years of encrypted file metadata, including logs from anonymized file-sharing platforms. How would you use Big Data correlation techniques and NLP classifiers to infer intent, file types, and risk levels when the content is inaccessible?

10. A forensic report generated by an AI system includes misclassified evidence, leading to public backlash. How can Explainable AI (XAI) and transparency models be embedded in GenAI forensic pipelines to make outputs traceable, defensible, and verifiable in court?

11. You are auditing an NLP-based system used by a government agency to monitor online radicalization. Bias in predictions has led to disproportionate targeting. Explain how you would forensically evaluate model bias, feature selection, and training corpus, and propose remediation strategies.

12. In a murder trial, forensic investigators retrieve a partial audio file from a smart home device. Voice cloning is suspected. Describe how Generative AI and forensic audio models could be used to verify the authenticity of the voice, identify speaker consistency, and test for tampering.

13. A global cyberattack included automatic report generation using LLMs to confuse investigators. Some logs were synthetically fabricated. How would you build a forensic system to detect LLM-generated narratives, including subtle inconsistencies, hallucinations, or statistical divergences from known communication styles?

14. Investigators suspect that a crime was simulated virtually using generative AI and then staged physically. Discuss how forensic simulation analysis using scene reconstruction and GenAI modeling could help distinguish between synthetic planning and real-world execution.

15. You're training investigators on using GenAI for forensic report automation but face skepticism about its validity. What quality control measures, audit trails, and validation frameworks would you put in place to ensure GenAI-generated forensic reports meet professional and legal standards?

REFERENCES

[1] "IDC: The premier global market intelligence firm," *IDC: The premier global market intelligence company*, 2019. [Online]. https://www.idc.com/

[2] Qadir, S. and Noor, B., "Applications of machine learning in digital forensics," *IEEE Xplore*, May 01, 2021.

[3] Vaswani, A., Shazeer, N., Parmar, N., Uszkoreit, J., Jones, L., Gomez, A. N., Kaiser, Ł. and Polosukhin, I. "Attention is all you need," In *Proceedings of the 31st International Conference on Neural Information Processing Systems (NeurIPS 2017)*, pp. 6000–6010. Curran Associates, Inc, 2017. doi: 10.48550/arXiv.1706.03762.

[4] International Consortium of Investigative Journalists (ICIJ). *How ICIJ deals with massive data leaks like the Panama Papers and Paradise Papers*. ICIJ, Jul., 3, 2018. https://www.icij.org/investigations/panama-papers/wrangling-2-6tb-of-data-the-people-and-the-technology-behind-the-panama-papers/

[5] University of California. "New technology helps media detect 'deepfakes'," Jun., 20, 2019. https://www.universityofcalifornia.edu/news/new-technology-helps-media-detect-deepfakes

Chapter 13

Futuristic technologies and digital forensics

As digital forensics continues to grow alongside intelligent technologies, the need for systems that are not just powerful but also transparent, trustworthy, and resilient is more important than ever. Following the integration of AI, Big Data, and advanced language and generative models, the next phase of innovation necessitates not only performance but accountability, adaptability, and foresight.

Chapter 13 embarks on this trajectory by confronting the challenges and opportunities posed by emerging forensic infrastructures and forward-looking advancements. The growing complexity of cyber environments driven by decentralized architectures, intelligent automation, and pervasive connectivity requires forensic solutions that are not only technically capable but also explainable, verifiable, and resistant to manipulation. This chapter examines how the forensic community is beginning to meet these demands through the adoption of explainable AI, secure evidence chains, and frameworks that anticipate adversarial and obfuscated data environments.

This chapter begins by exploring the integration of blockchain technologies, not merely as tools for securing evidence chains and tamper-proof logging, but as foundational systems for decentralized forensic frameworks. It then transitions into the rapidly evolving field of Explainable Artificial Intelligence (XAI), which addresses one of the most critical limitations of modern AI systems: The opacity of their decision-making processes. It also investigates emerging AI tools and frameworks and addresses futuristic challenges in smart, hyper-connected ecosystems, such as IoT environments, mobile devices, and network forensics.

13.1 BLOCKCHAIN

Blockchain technology is a relatively recent innovation that introduces a shared and immutable ledger for recording transactions and monitoring assets within a business network. This technology offers a robust solution for maintaining transparent and accurate information, which is crucial for many businesses. Assets in a blockchain network can be classified into two main categories: *Tangible*, encompassing physical assets like cars, houses, and real estate, and *intangible*, which includes intellectual property, copyrights, patents, and the like. Businesses often require immediate and dependable access to information, and blockchain technology excels in providing precisely that. It is particularly valuable for tracking various aspects such as payments, account statements, orders, and more. Blockchain networks offer end-to-end visibility into transaction details, ensuring greater efficiency in the management and validation of data. Figure 13.1 illustrates the mechanics of blockchain technology and how it facilitates seamless transactions.

The key components of blockchain technology include:

1. Distributed ledger technology: All users have access to the shared ledger.
2. Immutable records: No user can tamper with the transaction details.
3. Smart contracts: Define conditions for insurance, bond transfers, etc.

Blockchain technology proves advantageous in many ways:

1. **Highly secure blockchain technology**: Uses digital signatures to identify any fraudulent activity. Also, the use of digital signatures makes it impossible for other users to make any changes to the details of a user, except if they have a particular signature with them.
2. **Decentralized system**: In traditional financial systems, approval is required from the regulatory authorities, like banks, etc., for

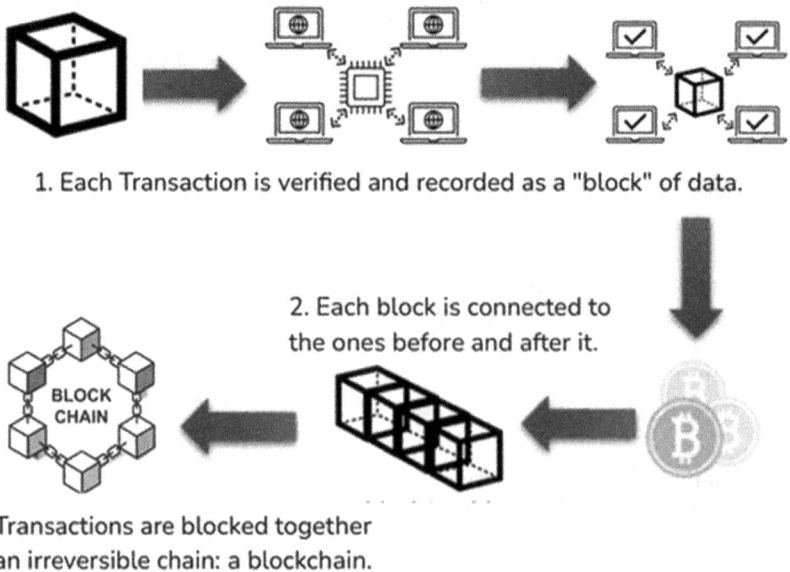

1. Each Transaction is verified and recorded as a "block" of data.

2. Each block is connected to the ones before and after it.

3. Transactions are blocked together in an irreversible chain: a blockchain.

Figure 13.1 Architecture of blockchain technology.

transactions, whereas blockchain technology is based on a decentralized system, which means the transactions are done with the mutual consensus of users.

3. **Automation capability:** Blockchain technology acts immediately when the trigger requirements are met without any outside command.

13.1.1 Blockchain-based digital forensics

Blockchain forensics represents an emerging and advanced technology that harnesses the power of science and technology to combat cybercriminals operating within the cryptocurrency market. Its central objective is to recover and analyze various forms of evidence left on the highly transparent and valuable blockchain digital ledger.

Blockchain is fundamentally a distributed ledger technology, meaning that it operates across a network of nodes rather than being controlled by a single, central entity. Each node in the blockchain network maintains a copy of the entire ledger, and all nodes work together to validate and record transactions through a consensus mechanism. This decentralized structure ensures that no single point of failure exists, making the system highly resilient and secure. The distributed nature of blockchain also enhances transparency, as all participants have access to the same information, which is crucial for maintaining trust within the network.

However, blockchain can be implemented in both centralized and decentralized forms, depending on the specific use case. In a fully decentralized (public) blockchain, like Bitcoin or Ethereum, anyone can participate in the network, contribute to the consensus process, and view the transaction history. This openness ensures maximum transparency and democratizes access to the technology. On the other hand, private or permissioned blockchains, often used by enterprises, are more centralized. These blockchains are still distributed across multiple nodes, but access is restricted to authorized participants, and the consensus process may be controlled by a specific group of entities. This hybrid approach allows organizations to enjoy the benefits of blockchain's distributed nature while maintaining control over who can interact with the network.

The distributed nature of blockchain is particularly useful in various applications, including digital forensics, where it can provide a tamper-proof record of digital evidence. In such cases, the decentralized architecture ensures that once data is recorded on the blockchain, it cannot be altered without consensus from the network, thereby preserving the integrity of the evidence. This makes blockchain a powerful tool for legal and investigative purposes, where the authenticity of records is paramount. By balancing centralization and distribution, blockchain technology can be tailored to meet the needs of diverse applications while maintaining the core benefits of security, transparency, and trust.

13.1.2 Utility and importance of blockchain forensics

The utility of blockchain forensic technology is multifaceted, providing significant benefits in both the prevention and investigation of cybercrimes. One of its primary roles is to bolster user trust in blockchain technology by enhancing its inherent security and transparency. By enabling the meticulous tracking and analysis of blockchain transactions, forensic experts can uncover detailed insights into the flow of digital assets, helping to build confidence among users and stakeholders in the security of blockchain systems.

Moreover, blockchain forensics serves as a powerful tool for detecting and investigating potential cybercrimes. Criminals often leverage the pseudonymous nature of cryptocurrencies to conceal their activities, making traditional forensic methods inadequate. Blockchain forensics, however, allows investigators to trace transactions through the blockchain, uncovering patterns and connections that can reveal the identities of those involved in illegal activities. This capability is crucial in combating a wide range of cybercrimes, from money laundering and tax evasion to fraud and terrorist financing.

13.1.3 Core practices and evidence collection

The core practices of blockchain forensics involve the identification, tracking, and analysis of critical details related to cryptocurrency transactions. These details can include the history of transactions, the origin and destination of assets, the quantities of tokens transferred, ownership records, and other transaction-specific data. For example, forensic analysts can trace the flow of stolen cryptocurrencies across multiple wallets, identify the points of exchange where they are converted into fiat currency, and link these transactions to known criminal entities. This information is invaluable not only for understanding the scope of criminal activities but also for building a strong legal case against the perpetrators.

The evidence gathered through blockchain forensics is highly reliable due to the immutable nature of blockchain technology. Unlike traditional digital evidence, which can be altered or deleted, blockchain records are permanent and unchangeable. This immutability makes blockchain evidence particularly compelling in legal proceedings, as it can provide irrefutable proof of a crime. Courts are increasingly recognizing the validity of blockchain-based evidence in cases involving cryptocurrency crimes, which range from the concealment of assets and embezzlement to more severe offenses like identity fraud, tax evasion, and the financing of terrorism.

13.1.4 Examples of blockchain forensics in action

The practical application of blockchain forensics is already having a significant impact on the investigation and prosecution of cryptocurrency-related crimes. For instance, during the Silk Road investigation, law enforcement agencies used blockchain forensic techniques to trace Bitcoin transactions that led to the identification and arrest of key figures involved in the illegal online marketplace [1]. Similarly, blockchain forensics played a crucial role in the investigation of the Mt. Gox exchange hack, where millions of dollars worth of Bitcoin were stolen. By analyzing the movement of the stolen Bitcoin across the blockchain, investigators were able to recover a portion of the funds and identify the individuals responsible for the hack. In addition to these high-profile cases, blockchain forensic tools are routinely used to investigate a wide array of lesser-known cryptocurrency crimes.

13.1.5 The growing role of open-source blockchain forensic tools

The integration of blockchain technology into digital forensics has led to the development of numerous open-source forensic tools designed to assist investigators in tracking and analyzing cryptocurrency transactions. These tools are crucial for maintaining the integrity and security of the cryptocurrency ecosystem, as they allow law enforcement and forensic experts to keep pace with the evolving tactics of cybercriminals.

For example, Blockchain Explorer[1] is widely used to provide a user-friendly interface for searching and visualizing blockchain data, making it easier to track transactions and identify patterns. Bitcoin Block Explorer and Wallet Explorer[2] offer specialized tools for analyzing Bitcoin transactions and wallets, respectively, helping investigators link transactions to known criminal activities. Blockparser[3] is another valuable tool, capable of parsing large amounts of blockchain data to reveal hidden connections between transactions. ORS CryptoHound,[4] on the other hand, provides advanced analytical capabilities, including the ability to uncover complex relationships between entities on the blockchain.

These tools collectively enhance the ability of forensic experts to investigate cryptocurrency crimes effectively, ensuring that justice can be pursued even in the complex and often opaque world of digital currencies. As the demand for blockchain forensic analysis continues to grow, these tools will play an increasingly pivotal role in the fight against cybercrime.

13.2 EXPLAINABLE ARTIFICIAL INTELLIGENCE (XAI) IN DIGITAL FORENSICS

Explainable Artificial Intelligence (XAI) refers to the methodologies and techniques developed to make AI models' decisions and predictions understandable to humans. Traditional AI models, particularly those employing deep learning techniques, often function as black boxes, producing results without offering insights into their decision-making processes. XAI seeks to bridge this gap by providing clear and comprehensible explanations, enhancing trust, accountability, and transparency in AI systems. This is especially critical in fields like digital forensics, where the stakes are high, and the interpretations of AI models can significantly impact judicial outcomes.

Recent advancements in XAI have led to the development of various tools and frameworks designed to demystify AI models. Techniques such as Local Interpretable Model-agnostic Explanations (LIME)[5] and SHapley Additive exPlanations (SHAP)[6] have been widely adopted to provide both local and global explanations of model behavior. These tools allow forensic analysts to understand the significance of different features in a model's decision, making the AI's reasoning process more transparent. Furthermore, the integration of XAI in digital forensics has led to the creation of comprehensive frameworks, such as the XAI-DF framework, which standardizes the workflow for using XAI in digital forensic investigations.

13.2.1 Application of XAI in DF

The application of XAI in digital forensics is multifaceted, addressing various challenges faced by forensic investigators. Key areas of application include:

1. **Network Forensics**: XAI tools are employed to analyze network traffic and detect anomalies indicative of cyber-attacks. For example, using a dataset, AI models can classify network activities into normal and attack traffic. XAI techniques like LIME can then explain the classification results, highlighting the most influential features in detecting specific types of attacks.

2. **Memory Forensics**: In memory forensics, XAI is used to analyze memory dumps to detect malicious activities. By extracting features such as running processes, network connections, and injected code from memory images, AI models can classify processes as benign or malicious. XAI tools help forensic analysts understand the rationale behind these classifications, making it easier to identify and investigate malicious activities.

3. **Multimedia Forensics**: AI models are used to classify and analyze multimedia content in digital forensics. XAI provides explanations for classifications, ensuring that the models' predictions are based on relevant features rather than spurious correlations. This transparency is crucial for validating the admissibility of digital evidence in court.

4. **IoT Forensics**: With the proliferation of IoT devices, XAI aids in analyzing data from various interconnected devices. AI models can process vast amounts of data from IoT devices, and XAI ensures that the conclusions drawn from these analyses are understandable and justifiable, enhancing their credibility in forensic investigations.

13.2.2 Potential impacts of XAI on DF—the need for Explainable AI (XAI) in DF

In digital forensics, the ability to present clear, understandable, and legally defensible evidence is paramount. The conclusions drawn from forensic investigations often have significant legal implications, meaning that the methods used to arrive at these conclusions must be transparent and easily interpretable. Explainable AI (XAI) addresses this need by ensuring that AI-driven decisions can be understood and justified not only by technical experts but also by non-expert stakeholders such as judges, lawyers, and juries.

- **Transparency in Decision-Making**: XAI focuses on making the outputs of AI systems understandable to humans, which is critical in digital forensics where evidence must be presented in court. Unlike other technologies that focus on accuracy, XAI ensures that forensic investigators can explain how a conclusion was reached.
- **Bias Detection and Correction**: XAI helps identify and mitigate biases in forensic AI models, ensuring that decisions are fair and based on objective data. This is crucial in maintaining the integrity of forensic investigations and ensuring justice.
- **Improved Trust in AI-Based Evidence**: By providing clear explanations for AI decisions, XAI increases the trustworthiness of AI-based evidence in legal contexts, which is a significant challenge with traditional ML models that function as "black boxes."

13.2.3 Existing explainable models and techniques

One of the most widely used AI models in digital forensics is the decision tree. Decision trees are valued for their interpretability, as they provide a clear, step-by-step breakdown of the decision-making process. At each node in the tree, a decision is made based on a comparison of features; such as whether an IP address is known or unknown, or whether a file was accessed during unusual hours. The decision tree then branches off to the next node, continuing this process until a conclusion is reached. This method of decision-making is easily understandable, which is particularly important in a legal context where the reasoning behind forensic conclusions must be clear and defensible.

However, decision trees have inherent limitations. Each decision at a node is based on local information, and only the specific features relevant to that node are considered, without accounting for the broader context. For example, a decision tree might flag network traffic as suspicious based on the IP address and timing alone, without considering other potentially relevant features, such as the overall pattern of network activity or the historical behavior of the user. This focus on local information can lead to a frag-mented view of the evidence, potentially resulting in incomplete or inaccu-rate conclusions.

In contrast to decision trees, more advanced models like neural networks, including deep learning architectures, offer significant power and flexibility in analyzing complex data. Neural networks are capable of identifying intri-cate patterns in large datasets, making them highly effective in tasks such as image recognition, natural language processing, and anomaly detection. In digital forensics, neural networks might be used to analyze large volumes of log data, detect subtle patterns in network traffic, or identify suspicious activities in vast datasets.

However, the power of neural networks comes at the cost of interpret-ability. Unlike decision trees, neural networks operate as "black boxes" and they process input data through multiple layers of interconnected neurons, making complex, nonlinear transformations to produce an output. While the results of these models can be highly accurate, the reasoning behind the decisions is not easily accessible or understandable. This lack of transpar-ency is a significant drawback in digital forensics, where investigators must be able to explain how conclusions were reached.

Support Vector Machines (SVMs) are another powerful tool used in digital forensics, particularly for classification tasks. SVMs work by finding the opti-mal hyperplane that separates different classes of data in a high-dimensional space. While SVMs are effective in distinguishing between classes (e.g., nor-mal vs. suspicious activity), they produce results in the form of numerical values and margins that lack interpretability. Investigators are left with a set of numbers that indicate the classification but provide no insight into the reasoning behind it. This opacity makes it difficult to explain SVM-based decisions to non-expert stakeholders, a crucial requirement in legal contexts.

13.2.3.1 Why we need another framework...

Given the limitations of existing models like decision trees, neural networks, and SVMs, there is a clear need for a new XAI framework tailored specifi-cally for digital forensics. While decision trees offer transparency, they often miss the broader context of the evidence. Neural networks, though power-ful, lack interpretability, and SVMs provide results that are not easily under-standable. An XAI framework for digital forensics would bridge these gaps by offering a balance between transparency and comprehensive analysis, ensuring that forensic investigations are both thorough and understandable.

13.2.4 Scenario analysis: decision trees versus neural networks vs. SVMs

Consider a scenario where an investigator is analyzing network traffic to detect potential security breaches. A decision tree model would clearly show the path taken at each decision node, such as flagging traffic based on a combination of IP address and access time. While this process is transparent and easy to explain, it might miss critical contextual information. Conversely, a neural network might detect more subtle patterns but lacks transparency, making it difficult to explain how conclusions were reached. Similarly, an SVM might effectively classify the traffic, but its outputs are not easily interpretable, complicating the explanation of findings.

For a better understanding, the three of these methodologies and their breadth of their explainability are shown with a forensic scenario.

Figure 13.2 provides a process flow of how a decision tree might classify network traffic into benign or suspicious categories, emphasizing the simplicity and transparency of decision-making. However, it also highlights key issues such as reliance on local decisions, overfitting, ignoring feature correlations, and lack of granularity—challenges that can impact the accuracy and reliability of forensic conclusions.

While the SVM, as shown in Figure 13.3, is effective in separating the two classes, the reasoning behind the classification (e.g., why a specific point falls on one side of the hyperplane) is not easily interpretable. This lack of

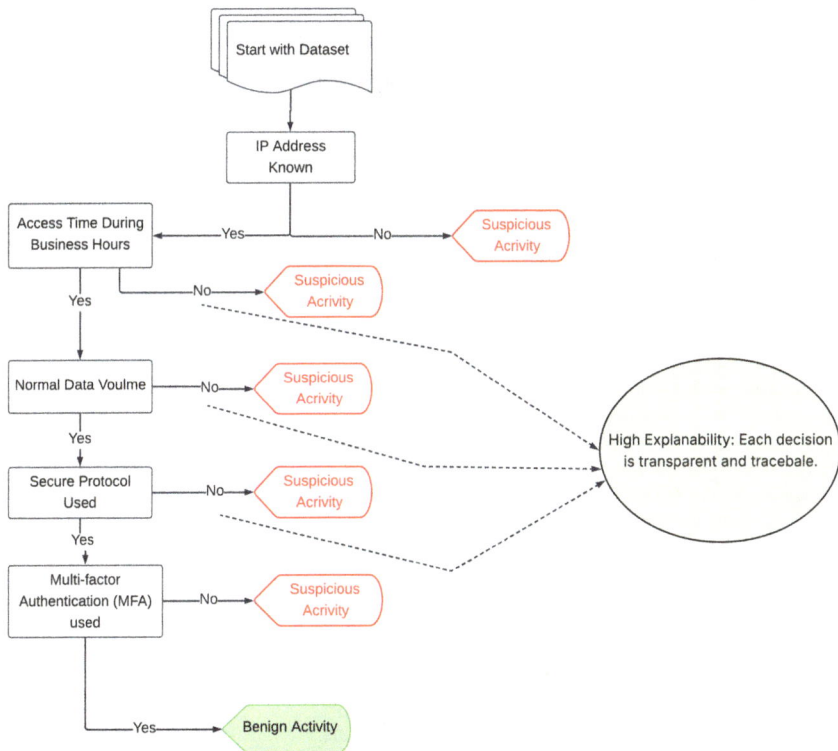

Figure 13.2 Scenario: analyzing suspicious network activity using decision trees.

Classification Output

Low Explainability:
Decisions based on
abstract mathematical
margins

Feature Mapping:

SVM maps the extracted features
into a high-dimensional space

Feature Extraction:

Relevant features are extracted
and converted into numerical
values that SVM can process

For e.g.
* Access Time Score: Numerical value based on
how unusual the access time
* Data Volume Score: Normalized data size (e.g.,
a score based on the amount of data transferred
compared to typical values).

Network traffic Dataset

Features e.g.:

* Source IP Address
* Destination IP Address
* Access Time
* Amount of Data Transferred
* Network Protocol Used
* User Authentication Method

SVM Decision Boundary with Support Vectors

Hyperplane
Support Vectors
Suspicious Region
Benign Region

Feature 1 (e.g., Access Time Score)

Feature 2 (e.g., Data Volume Score)

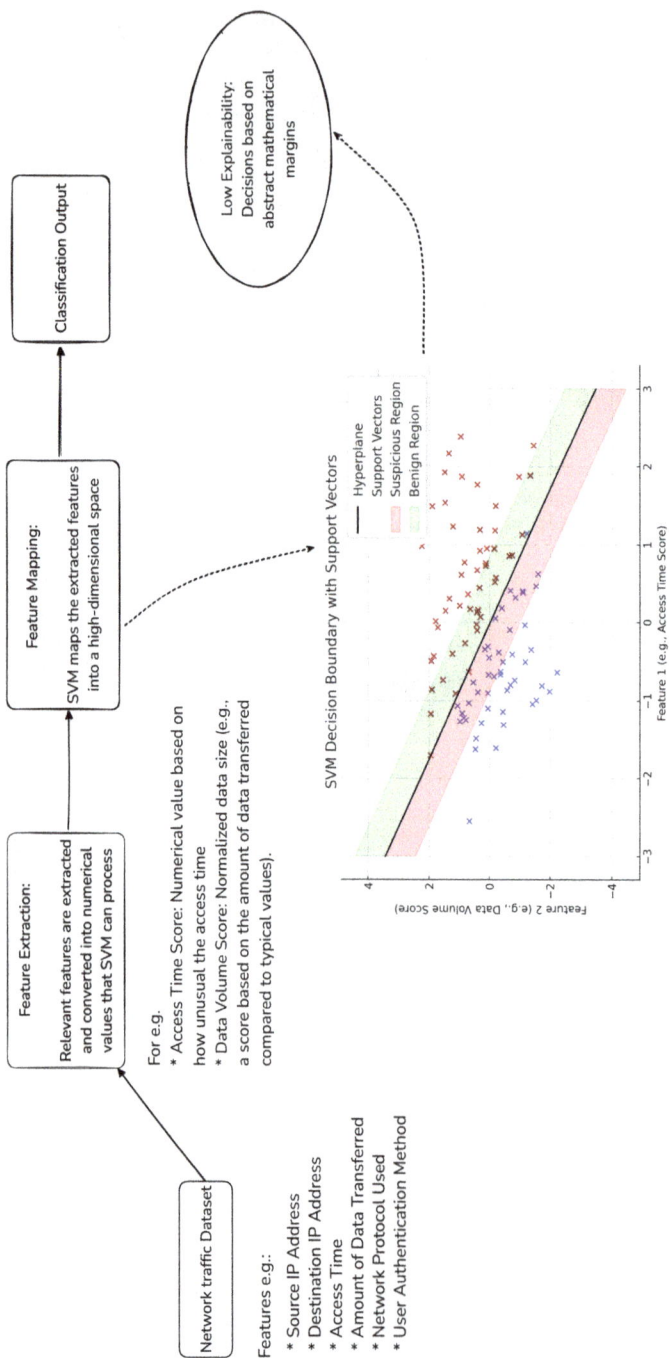

Figure 13.3 Scenario: analyzing suspicious network activity using SVM.

transparency can be problematic in forensic contexts where clear explanations are required.

In Figure 13.4, it can be observed, neural networks, especially with multiple hidden layers, operate as "black boxes." The decisions are based on complex interactions between weights and biases, making it difficult to trace back and understand the reasoning behind each classification.

The XAI framework shown in Figure 13.5 provides a transparent and interpretable process by explaining how each feature contributes to the final decision and considering both local and global contexts, XAI offers a more reliable and defensible approach to digital forensics, addressing the limitations of traditional models like decision trees and neural networks.

13.2.5 Demonstrating the gap and the need for XAI

The limitations of models like decision trees, neural networks, and SVMs highlight the need for an advanced XAI framework in digital forensics. Decision trees, while interpretable, fail to consider the full context. Neural networks are opaque, and SVMs produce results that are hard to explain. An XAI framework designed for digital forensics would provide both transparency and a comprehensive analysis, ensuring that forensic investigations are robust, legally defensible, and easily understood in court. This would enhance the credibility of forensic findings and improve their communication and understanding in legal proceedings.

The significant potential impacts of XAI in digital forensics can be summarized as follows:

1. **Transparency in Decision-Making:** XAI focuses on making the outputs of AI systems understandable to humans, which is critical in digital forensics, where evidence must be presented in court. Unlike other technologies that focus on accuracy, XAI ensures that forensic investigators can explain how a conclusion was reached.
2. **Bias Detection and Correction:** XAI helps identify and mitigate biases in forensic AI models, ensuring that decisions are fair and based on objective data. This is crucial in maintaining the integrity of forensic investigations and ensuring justice.
3. **Improved Trust in AI-Based Evidence:** By providing clear explanations for AI decisions, XAI increases the trustworthiness of AI-based evidence in legal contexts, which is a significant challenge with traditional ML models that function as "black boxes."
4. **Legal and Ethical Compliance:** The use of XAI ensures that AI models comply with legal and ethical standards by providing transparent and interpretable results. This is crucial for the admissibility of AI-generated evidence in court, as it allows legal professionals to scrutinize and understand the evidence presented.

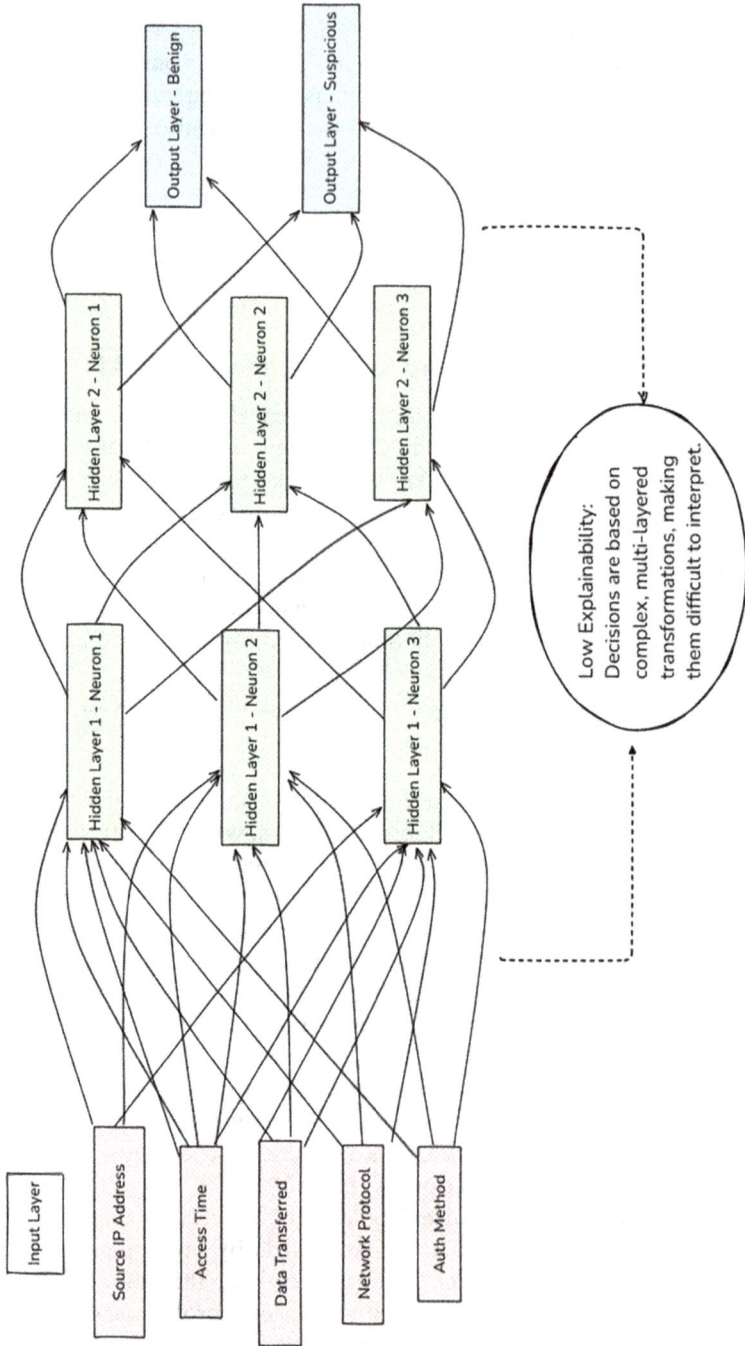

Figure 13.4 Scenario: analyzing suspicious network activity using neural networks.

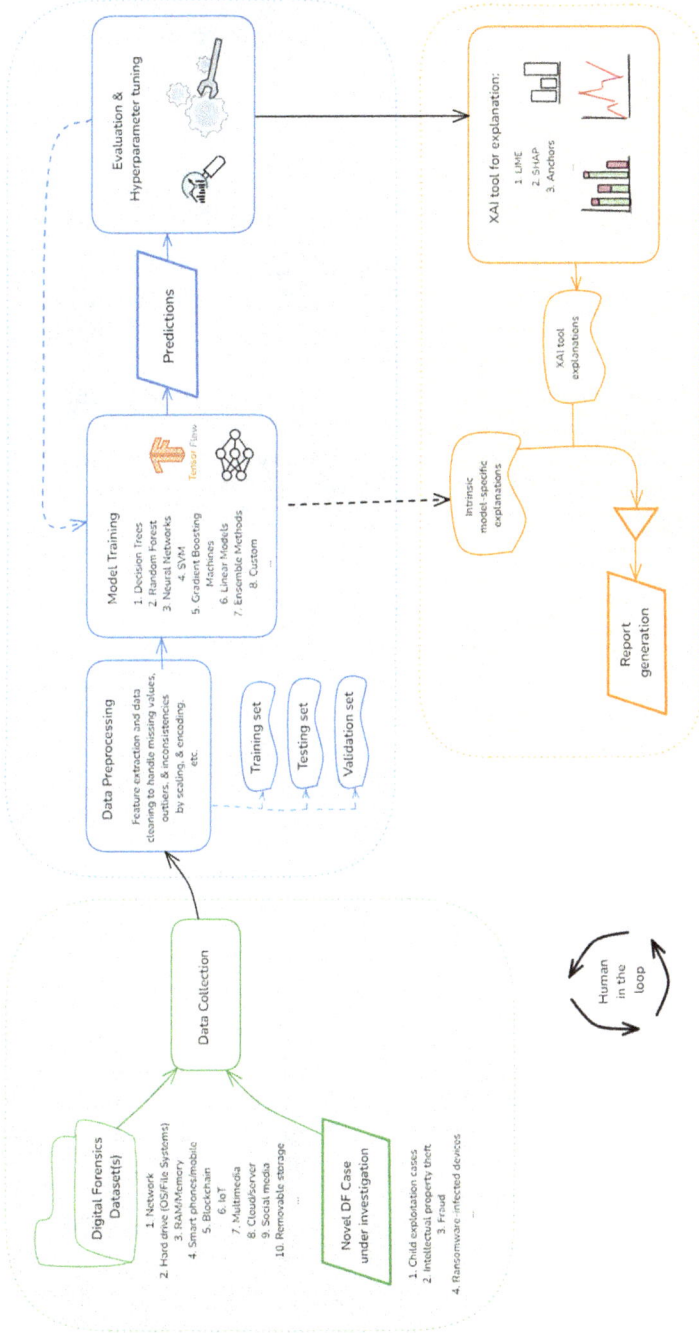

Figure 13.5 Digital forensics implementing explainable AI (XAI).

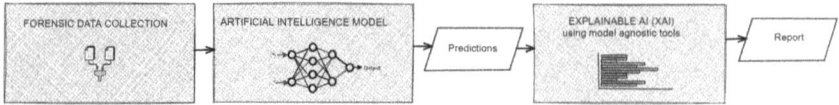

Figure 13.6 Simple digital forensics XAI framework.

13.2.6 A framework for explainable AI in DF

While there is no universally established XAI model specifically for digital forensics, a conceptual framework can be created to integrate XAI techniques throughout the forensic investigation process. This framework ensures that each phase, from data analysis to evidence presentation, is powered by advanced AI models while providing clear, understandable explanations. Figure 13.6 shows a conceptual XAI Digital Forensics Framework, designed to embed explainability within the digital forensics process and adaptable to various investigative scenarios and legal requirements.

13.2.6.1 Problem formulation and data acquisition

The foundation of an effective XAI system in digital forensics lies in clearly defining the forensic problem. This involves specifying the investigative question, the type of digital evidence, and the desired outcome of the AI analysis. For example, the problem might be to automatically detect child sexual abuse material (CSAM) within a large image dataset. Once the problem is defined, the next crucial step is to acquire a representative dataset that accurately reflects real-world forensic scenarios. The dataset should be diverse, encompassing various types of digital artifacts and different crime categories. Data quality is paramount, as inaccurate or incomplete data can significantly impact the model's performance and the reliability of the explanations.

13.2.6.2 Model development and training

The choice of an AI algorithm depends on the nature of the forensic task. For image-based investigations, convolutional neural networks (CNNs) might be suitable, while for text analysis, recurrent neural networks (RNNs) or transformer-based models could be considered. The model is trained on the prepared dataset to learn patterns and correlations within the data that are indicative of forensic relevance. Evaluation metrics are used to assess the model's performance during training, and techniques like cross-validation and hyperparameter tuning help optimize the model's accuracy and generalizability.

13.2.6.3 Explainability integration

To ensure trust and legal admissibility of AI-generated findings, integrating XAI techniques is crucial. Methods like LIME, SHAP, and counterfactual explanations provide insights into the model's decision-making process. These explanations should be presented in a clear and understandable manner, ideally through visualizations.

Key XAI Techniques for Digital Forensics include:

- *Local Interpretable Model-Agnostic Explanations (LIME)*: This technique generates explanations for individual predictions by approximating the complex model with a simpler, interpretable model in the vicinity of the data point of interest.
- *SHapley Additive exPlanations (SHAP)*: By computing the contribution of each feature to the prediction, SHAP attributes feature importance to model outputs.
- *Counterfactual explanations*: These explanations demonstrate how the input data could be modified to produce a different outcome, aiding in understanding the model's decision boundaries.
- *Decision trees*: Owing to their inherent interpretability, decision trees can serve as a baseline or be employed for feature importance analysis

13.2.6.4 Human-in-the-loop integration

Effective human–AI collaboration is essential. A user-friendly interface allows forensic investigators to interact with the AI system, access outputs, explanations, and confidence levels. A feedback mechanism enables investigators to provide input on the model's performance and explanation quality, leading to continuous improvement.

13.2.6.5 Legal and ethical considerations

Transparency, accountability, and fairness are fundamental principles. Clear documentation of the AI system's development, training data, and decision-making processes is crucial for legal compliance. Addressing potential biases in the data and algorithms is essential for fair treatment of individuals. Privacy concerns must also be carefully considered when handling sensitive digital evidence.

13.2.6.6 Evaluation and refinement

Continuous evaluation of the AI system's performance and explainability is vital. Monitoring model accuracy, assessing explanation effectiveness, and gathering user feedback help identify areas for improvement. Model retraining with updated data maintains the system's relevance and accuracy. Staying updated with AI and XAI advancements is crucial for incorporating new techniques and methodologies.

Explainable Artificial Intelligence is revolutionizing the field of digital forensics by making AI models more transparent, interpretable, and trustworthy. The advancements and applications of XAI enhance the efficiency and reliability of forensic investigations, ensuring that AI-driven decisions can be confidently used in legal contexts. As XAI continues to evolve, its role in digital forensics will become increasingly vital, providing forensic analysts with powerful tools to uncover the truth in complex digital investigations.

13.3 EMERGING TOOLS AND FRAMEWORKS IN AI FOR DF

The rapid advancements in AI tools and frameworks have been transforming multiple industries, including digital forensics. Emerging tools are not only enabling seasoned AI developers but are also offering no-code and low-code platforms for beginners. Recent developments such as TensorFlow 2.0 and PyTorch have simplified deep learning model development, making it easier for forensic professionals to deploy AI models at scale. These frameworks are also optimized for distributed computing, which is beneficial when dealing with cloud-based forensic investigations. These tools streamline machine learning (ML) workflows, make it easier to analyze vast amounts of data, and offer solutions that scale to specific needs in forensics. Here's an in-depth look at some of the leading tools and their relevance to digital forensics.

13.3.1 Latest advancements in AI tools and frameworks

Transformers—One of the most important trends in AI is the widespread adoption of Transformer-based models for natural language processing (NLP) and other tasks. Transformers are neural network architectures that have revolutionized tasks like text classification, machine translation, and more. They allow for the processing of sequential data, which is essential in digital forensics for analyzing communication patterns and reconstructing timelines from emails, chat logs, and social media messages.

Hugging Face's Transformers library is one of the most notable frameworks in this space. It provides pre-trained models like BERT (Bidirectional Encoder Representations from Transformers) and GPT (Generative Pretrained Transformers), which can be fine-tuned for forensic applications [2]. BERT is particularly effective at extracting meaning from text, enabling forensic experts to analyze vast amounts of communication data quickly. Similarly, GPT models, like GPT-3 and GPT-4, are used to generate human-like text, which can assist in automating report generation or synthesizing evidence from scattered data points [3].

For digital forensics, these Transformer models are invaluable in classifying large amounts of textual data, identifying key entities, and detecting anomalies in communication logs. The ability to fine-tune pre-trained models for specific forensic use cases makes them a powerful tool for both speed and accuracy in investigations.

TensorFlow—*TensorFlow*, developed by Google, is one of the most widely used open-source machine learning (ML) frameworks [4]. Initially designed for deep learning research, TensorFlow has grown into a versatile tool that supports a wide range of ML tasks. Its ability to scale across distributed computing environments and its support for large datasets make it ideal for handling complex forensic cases where vast amounts of data need to be processed efficiently.

TensorFlow is particularly useful in automating the detection of digital threats such as malware, where AI models trained on millions of data points can rapidly identify suspicious behavior. TensorFlow's ability to integrate with TensorFlow Lite also allows for mobile and embedded device support, making it effective for use in mobile forensics and IoT device investigations. *TensorFlow Lite* allows models to be deployed on mobile devices, making it a key player in mobile forensics and edge computing, where real-time data analysis is required on-site without relying on centralized servers [5]. TensorFlow can also handle image recognition, helping forensic experts analyze digital evidence like surveillance footage.

In the context of digital forensics, TensorFlow models can be trained to detect anomalies in large datasets, identify hidden patterns in user activity, and automate the process of data classification. Its flexibility and the support it receives from an active global community make TensorFlow a popular choice among forensic experts looking to integrate AI into their workflows.

PyTorch—*PyTorch*, developed by Facebook's AI Research lab, is another popular open-source framework, particularly favored by researchers due to its dynamic computational graph and ease of prototyping. Its flexibility is beneficial in forensic investigations where rapid testing and deployment of custom models are necessary. PyTorch is often used for developing models that automate evidence identification and anomaly detection, which accelerates the forensic workflow by reducing the time spent manually sifting through data [6].

Keras—Built on top of TensorFlow, *Keras* is an open-source neural network library designed for fast experimentation and easy model-building. It provides a user-friendly API, making it accessible to both experts and beginners alike [7]. While TensorFlow handles the heavy computational work, Keras focuses on simplifying the process of creating and training models.

Keras is particularly valuable in digital forensics for its ability to quickly prototype machine learning models, enabling investigators to test different approaches to evidence analysis. For example, it can be used to train models that classify images in forensic investigations or categorize logs and text data in a shorter amount of time. Its simplicity also makes it an ideal choice for forensics teams who need to rapidly deploy AI solutions to solve specific forensic challenges, such as identifying suspicious digital behaviors or analyzing large volumes of emails or chat logs.

RapidMiner—*RapidMiner* is a data science platform that offers a no-code environment for building machine learning models [8]. Known for its drag-and-drop interface, RapidMiner allows forensic investigators to create predictive models and perform large-scale data analysis without needing to write code. The platform supports a wide array of machine learning algorithms and provides built-in tools for data preprocessing, transformation, and validation.

In the field of digital forensics, RapidMiner is commonly used for tasks like data mining, anomaly detection, and pattern recognition. Investigators can use RapidMiner to analyze communication patterns, detect irregular transactions, and automate the process of identifying fraud or unauthorized access in large data sets. One of the key advantages of RapidMiner is its ability to integrate with popular forensic databases and file systems, allowing for seamless data import and export during investigations.

No-Code and Low-Code AI Platforms—For investigators who lack extensive AI development expertise, no-code and low-code platforms such as *Google AutoML and IBM Watson Studio* offer a simplified way to build AI models. *Google AutoML* allows non-technical users to train machine learning models for tasks such as image classification, object detection, and natural language processing (NLP) without writing any code. This is particularly useful in digital forensics, where investigators can use AutoML to classify documents, analyze large datasets, or even detect fraudulent activity in communications [9].

Similarly, *IBM Watson Studio* is a visual platform that facilitates the development and deployment of AI models. It offers a suite of AI-powered tools and services that are widely adopted in the enterprise for solving complex business problems, including those related to digital forensics. Watson's capabilities in natural language processing (NLP), image recognition, and machine learning provide forensic investigators with powerful tools to analyze digital evidence, interpret communication logs, and recognize faces in surveillance footage [10].

Watson's ability to process unstructured data makes it ideal for investigations involving emails, chat messages, or large collections of documents. Moreover, its NLP capabilities can automatically flag key entities, such as individuals, locations, and dates, helping investigators quickly identify critical information. IBM Watson's ability to integrate with other forensic tools and systems also makes it a versatile solution for comprehensive forensic investigations.

H2O.ai—*H2O.ai* is an open-source machine learning platform that simplifies AI development. One of its key features is the ability to build and deploy models using AutoML, which automates the machine learning workflow. H2O.ai is used extensively in industries like finance and healthcare, but it is increasingly being adopted in digital forensics due to its ability to handle large datasets and build models quickly [11].

For digital forensic applications, H2O.ai can be employed for predictive modeling, risk assessment, and anomaly detection. Its flexibility in integrating with cloud platforms and enterprise systems makes it a powerful tool for investigating cybercrimes, analyzing communication patterns, and detecting fraudulent activities. The platform's ability to process unstructured data, such as emails or chat logs, also makes it useful in forensic contexts where investigators need to analyze large amounts of textual data.

Apache Spark MLlib—*Apache Spark MLlib* is an open-source library that provides scalable machine learning algorithms. Spark is known for its ability to handle large-scale data processing and real-time data streaming, which makes it highly relevant for forensic investigations that require quick analysis of big datasets. Its integration with Hadoop and other big data technologies allows investigators to perform tasks such as data clustering, regression, classification, and anomaly detection across distributed systems.

Spark MLlib's support for real-time data analysis is particularly useful in cybersecurity investigations, where forensic experts may need to monitor and analyze network traffic or log files in real time. The ability to scale across multiple nodes also ensures that large datasets are processed efficiently, reducing the time it takes to uncover critical evidence in investigations involving large corporations or cloud environments [12].

DataRobot—*DataRobot* is a commercial platform that automates the development and deployment of machine learning models [13]. Its AutoML capabilities allow investigators with limited machine learning knowledge to build sophisticated models for detecting fraud, malware, or network intrusions. DataRobot also offers model explainability features, which are essential in digital forensics when investigators need to understand why a model has flagged certain activities as suspicious.

The platform's ease of use and automated workflow make it highly valuable for digital forensic teams that need to respond quickly to evolving threats. By providing pre-trained models and extensive libraries, DataRobot helps reduce the time spent developing custom models and allows investigators to focus on interpreting the results and gathering actionable insights from digital evidence.

Edge AI Tools—Edge AI frameworks such as *TensorFlow Lite and ONNX Runtime* enable AI models to be deployed directly on devices rather than relying on centralized systems. This capability is particularly useful in mobile forensics and investigations involving Internet of Things (IoT) devices, where data may need to be processed on-site. TensorFlow Lite offers low-latency, real-time inference capabilities on mobile and embedded devices, allowing investigators to analyze digital evidence without transferring data to cloud servers [5]. ONNX Runtime provides similar flexibility, supporting interoperability between frameworks like PyTorch and TensorFlow, making it easier to deploy models across multiple platforms [14].

13.3.2 Comparative analysis of emerging AI tools in DF

Table 13.1 summarizes some of the most significant emerging tools and frameworks that are being applied in digital forensics today, along with their descriptions and specific use cases in forensic investigations.

13.4 FUTURISTIC CHALLENGES IN SMART CONNECTED DEVICE FORENSICS

As we delve deeper into the complexities of smart connected devices, it becomes clear that they present unique and evolving challenges in forensic investigations. With the widespread integration of Internet of Things (IoT) devices into everyday life, from smartphones and wearables to smart home systems, vehicles, and industrial IoT systems, gathering and analyzing digital evidence has become significantly more complex. This chapter focuses on some of the most critical, unresolved issues that forensic professionals are currently grappling with, highlighting the future challenges these technologies will pose.

13.4.1 Mobile device encryption and data protection

Encryption technologies have become increasingly sophisticated, particularly with smart connected devices, making data retrieval a significant hurdle for forensic experts. Many modern devices now come with *Full-Disk Encryption (FDE), File-Based Encryption (FBE), and End-to-End Encryption (E2EE)* to safeguard user data both at rest and in transit. For example, Apple's iPhones employ *Secure Enclave* to encrypt files and biometric data, while Android devices also offer advanced encryption protocols [15]. These encryption methods are designed to protect users, but they also obstruct forensic efforts to retrieve critical evidence.

Table 13.1 Comparative analysis of emerging AI tools and frameworks with respect to DF

Tool/Framework	Description	Type	Use case in digital forensics	Critical analysis
TensorFlow	Versatile ML framework for large-scale model building, offering support for distributed computing.	Open-Source	Building deep learning models for pattern recognition and evidence analysis.	Requires technical expertise to implement; powerful but complex.
PyTorch	Flexible and easy-to-use framework for model development and prototyping.	Open-Source	Developing custom models for log file analysis, evidence classification.	Popular in research but less mature in production environments.
TensorFlow Lite	Lightweight version of TensorFlow designed for real-time inference on mobile devices.	Open-Source	On-device forensic data analysis in mobile and IoT investigations.	Limited to specific hardware and mobile platforms.
Keras	High-level API built on TensorFlow, designed for rapid prototyping of deep learning models.	Open-Source	Simplifying the development of AI models for image classification and data analysis.	Simplified interface but limited control compared to TensorFlow itself.
RapidMiner	Data science platform offering a no-code environment for creating ML models.	Commercial	Automating fraud detection and anomaly identification in large data sets.	Can be limited in flexibility; dependent on pre-built algorithms.
H2O.ai	Open-source platform offering AutoML capabilities for building ML models efficiently.	Open-Source	Predictive modeling and anomaly detection in digital forensics investigations.	Effective for large datasets but lacks support for advanced custom models.
Apache Spark MLlib	Scalable machine learning library designed for big data processing and real-time analysis.	Open-Source	Large-scale data analysis, clustering, and anomaly detection in real-time systems.	Best for large datasets but can be resource-heavy and requires Hadoop integration.
IBM Watson	AI-powered platform with tools for NLP, image recognition, and machine learning.	Commercial	Automating document review, face recognition, and text analysis in forensic cases.	Expensive; requires integration with other tools for forensic workflows.

(Continued)

Table 13.1 (Continued)

Tool/Framework	Description	Type	Use case in digital forensics	Critical analysis
DataRobot	AutoML platform that simplifies the development and deployment of machine learning models.	Commercial	Automated fraud detection and malware classification with model explainability.	High ease of use but relatively expensive.
ONNX Runtime	Cross-platform engine for running machine learning models developed in multiple frameworks.	Open-Source	Deploying forensic AI models across diverse systems and devices.	Limited support for complex forensic models.
Unity ML-Agents	Platform that integrates reinforcement learning into 3D simulations for training AI agents.	Open-Source	Simulating real-world attack scenarios to identify system vulnerabilities.	Limited to specific use cases like simulations and complex to integrate.
Google AutoML	No-code platform for building AI models without requiring programming knowledge.	Commercial	Automating document classification and facial recognition in forensics.	High ease of use but limited in customization and control.
OpenAI's GPT-4	Advanced generative model designed for human-like text generation and understanding.	Commercial	Automating forensic report writing, generating human-like summaries from data logs.	Exceptional text generation but requires high compute resources and oversight.
BERT	NLP models for analyzing unstructured text data, including emails and chat logs.	Open-Source	Extracting key entities from communication data, detecting hidden meaning in text.	High accuracy but computationally intensive for larger datasets.

End-to-end encrypted messaging services like WhatsApp, Signal, and Telegram further complicate investigations, as they make it nearly impossible to retrieve message contents without access to decryption keys. The move to cloud-based storage further exacerbates these issues, as data encryption extends to the cloud with services like iCloud, Google Drive, and proprietary platforms like Tesla's cloud systems. This requires forensic professionals to navigate legal complexities to retrieve data, often needing compliance with international laws like the General Data Protection Regulation (GDPR) or the California Consumer Privacy Act (CCPA) [16]. Additionally, forensic tools such as Cellebrite and GrayKey have limitations, particularly when applied to newer encryption methods in smart connected devices, leaving gaps in forensic investigations.

13.4.1.1 Future solutions and considerations

While the current encryption landscape makes forensics challenging, the future may hold potential solutions, such as *quantum computing*, which could theoretically break modern encryption algorithms. Another viable approach is the creation of lawful access mechanisms in collaboration with device manufacturers, allowing forensic professionals to access encrypted data through legal channels in critical situations.

13.4.2 Network artifacts and location-based forensics

Smart connected devices are constantly generating network artifacts (data logs from GPS, Wi-Fi, and IP addresses) which provide valuable clues for forensic investigations. However, this data is often fragmented across multiple devices, such as smartphones, smartwatches, and IoT sensors, making it difficult to correlate and cross-validate. Moreover, tools that enable *location spoofing* or the use of *Virtual Private Networks (VPNs)* complicate matters further by masking the real location or network activity of a device [17].

Network artifacts are also stored on various cloud services, adding another layer of complexity for investigators. Data stored in the cloud often spans multiple jurisdictions, requiring formal international data access requests, such as Mutual Legal Assistance Treaties (MLATs), which introduce significant delays in investigations. Moreover, forensic investigators must grapple with cloud-based synchronization, where data from smart devices is distributed across multiple cloud systems. Cross-referencing these datasets often reveals inconsistencies or missing data, which makes reconstructing timelines challenging.

Future solutions will likely rely on *data fusion* techniques, which integrate data from multiple sources to improve reliability. Additionally, *AI-based location verification systems* could help distinguish between legitimate and falsified location data. Blockchain technologies might also be explored for creating tamper-evident trails of network activity, ensuring the reliability of digital evidence.

13.4.3 Anti-forensics techniques and evasion tactics

The sophistication of anti-forensics techniques continues to grow, presenting significant obstacles to forensic investigations. These techniques are designed to erase or obscure digital evidence, preventing investigators from accessing critical data. Common methods include the use of secure deletion software, file obfuscation, and remote wiping. For instance, Telegram and Signal allow users to automatically delete messages after a set time, making it difficult to recover conversations post-factum [18].

The use of rootkits and bootkits introduces further challenges, as these malicious tools operate at a deep system level, often undetected by traditional forensic tools. Once triggered, rootkits can hide or manipulate key data, rendering forensic evidence incomplete or misleading. Additionally, remote wiping technologies are now standard features in many smart connected devices, enabling users or attackers to delete all data remotely before it can be extracted.

To counter these anti-forensic tactics, real-time data capture methods and *live memory forensics* must be prioritized. By capturing volatile data before it can be wiped, investigators can retrieve key evidence even when tampering or erasure techniques are employed. Additionally, forensic tools that leverage AI-driven anti-forensic detection capabilities will play a crucial role in identifying and neutralizing these tactics.

13.4.4 Proprietary systems and forensic tool limitations

The explosion of IoT devices has brought about a wide range of proprietary systems and closed-source platforms that make forensic investigations highly challenging. Unlike traditional mobile devices running standardized systems like Android or iOS, IoT devices often run custom-built operating systems and firmware. This problem is especially acute in devices like autonomous vehicles, industrial IoT systems, and medical devices, where manufacturers closely guard proprietary firmware and system architectures. For example, devices like Tesla's autonomous driving system use proprietary software that can only be accessed through manufacturer cooperation.

Proprietary systems often operate on closed-source platforms, meaning that forensic investigators may not have access to the tools required to extract or analyze data. For instance, Tesla's autonomous driving system collects a vast amount of telemetry data, but retrieving and analyzing this data requires specialized tools that are not available to forensic experts without direct cooperation from the manufacturer. The diversity of proprietary systems across the IoT landscape means that forensic investigators must develop specialized tools for each system, which is resource-intensive and often leads to delayed investigations.

13.4.4.1 Future solutions and considerations

To keep pace with the growing diversity of IoT devices, forensic experts may need to invest in *reverse-engineering capabilities* that can deconstruct proprietary systems and extract relevant data. Additionally, advocating for industry-wide standards for data access in IoT devices will be critical for ensuring that forensic tools can keep pace with technological advancements. Partnerships between forensic experts and manufacturers will be necessary to develop universal extraction tools capable of handling a wide range of proprietary systems.

13.4.5 Cloud-based data and remote storage

Smart connected devices increasingly rely on cloud storage for data synchronization and offloading, which presents several new challenges for forensic investigators. For example, data stored on Google Cloud, iCloud, or other proprietary cloud platforms are often subject to *end-to-end encryption*, making it inaccessible without user credentials. Furthermore, cloud-stored data are often scattered across various regions, adding jurisdictional and legal hurdles to data retrieval [19].

Synchronization issues between local devices and cloud servers can also create inconsistencies. Data stored on a device may not fully sync to the cloud, or it may have been altered post-upload, creating inconsistencies in the evidence collection process, and complicating the timeline and integrity of the evidence.

The future of cloud-based forensics will likely require the development of *forensic cloud APIs* that allow investigators to access cloud-stored data in compliance with local laws. *Blockchain-based technologies* could also provide a tamper-evident method for tracking and verifying data stored in the cloud, ensuring that the integrity and authenticity of evidence are preserved.

END OF CHAPTER QUESTIONS

1. Law enforcement uses blockchain to log every forensic acquisition step across distributed crime labs. Midway, a conflict arises: A block hash doesn't match across nodes. How would you validate forensic chain of custody in this decentralized blockchain system? What steps would you take to ensure evidence integrity and defend the log's admissibility in court?

2. Blockchain's immutability makes tampering virtually impossible, yet privacy concerns remain. Discuss the paradox of blockchain's transparency versus forensic privacy in evidence handling. How can zero-knowledge proofs or permissioned blockchains help balance this?

3. Your AI model flags insider activity based on application usage and login times, but the suspect claims bias. The forensic analyst must explain how the model reached this decision. Compare how LIME, SHAP, and counterfactual explanations would each justify the AI model's decision. Which method would you use in a legal setting and why?

4. Decision Trees are transparent, Neural Networks are powerful, SVMs are margin-driven. In the context of digital evidence admissibility, critically compare these models' interpretability versus forensic reliability. When might high accuracy be insufficient?

5. A neural network flags a process in memory for malware, but legal experts require interpretability for court. Explain how SHAP can help dissect feature importance in memory forensics and what its limitations might be in validating behavioral versus signature-based detection.

6. A deep learning model identifies potential CSAM images, but a prosecutor asks whether similar false positives were previously encountered. How can counterfactual explanations help justify why certain borderline images were flagged? How could this impact trial proceedings and expert witness testimony?

7. Explain the role of confidence intervals and model explainability scores in communicating forensic AI findings to non-technical stakeholders, such as judges or jurors.

8. A forensic XAI system used by an agency has a feedback loop where investigators "approve" or "reject" decisions, which are then used to update the model. How does this human-in-the-loop feedback system enhance forensic robustness and reduce model bias? What are the risks of reinforcing human error?

9. You are asked to train an AI model to identify tax fraud behavior from transactional logs. A decision-tree model is interpretable but underperforms; a neural model performs well but lacks transparency. Propose a hybrid forensic AI solution that maintains model explainability without sacrificing performance. Justify your model architecture.

10. Why is XAI not just a technical issue but also a legal and ethical imperative in digital forensics? Provide examples of how lack of XAI has failed in real-world legal settings.

11. You are designing an XAI-based forensic investigation framework for analyzing encrypted traffic data in smart city IoT environments. Based on the Chapter 13 framework, explain how you would implement explainability at each stage of the forensic pipeline (problem formulation, training, integration, human-in-the-loop, legal compliance).

12. In a high-profile case, a model trained on smartphone logs predicts suspicious user activity. The legal team questions the data preparation. How would you ensure forensic soundness of your dataset, and how does data quality impact explainability and model auditability in XAI pipelines?

13. Compare and contrast the following in digital forensics: Model interpretability, Model transparency, and Model accountability. How do they influence digital evidence admissibility?

14. Given the rise of no-code AI tools, how can we ensure that forensic analysts without deep ML training can still trust and explain model outputs?

19. Why is bias explainability as important as prediction explainability in forensic systems? Provide an example where both types must be audited.

20. A criminal cartel is using blockchain-based smart contracts for scheduling criminal transactions and payments in a decentralized system. As a digital forensic analyst, how would you identify, extract, and legally preserve evidence of smart contract execution relevant to criminal activity? What specific blockchain properties and tools would support evidence admissibility?

21. The court challenges a forensic conclusion based on a neural network due to the lack of interpretability. The model correctly predicted a compromised IoT gateway, but cannot show why. Compare the model's behavior with a decision tree or hybrid interpretable model, and explain how you might retrain or substitute the model to improve explainability without compromising performance.

NOTES

1 https://www.blockchain.com/explorer.
2 https://www.walletexplorer.com/.
3 https://github.com/znort987/blockparser.
4 https://poloinnovazioneict.org/en/solutions/ors-cryptohound/.
5 https://github.com/marcotcr/lime.
6 https://github.com/shap/shap.

REFERENCES

[1] Kharif, O. *The hunt for the missing $500 million in the Mt. Gox bitcoin mystery*. Bloomberg, 2019. https://www.bloomberg.com/news/articles/2019-06-19/the-hunt-for-the-missing-500-million-in-the-mt-gox-bitcoin-mystery

[2] Vaswani, A., Shazeer, N., Parmar, N., Uszkoreit, J., Jones, L., Gomez, A. N., Kaiser, L., and Polosukhin, I. "Attention is all you need," *Advances in Neural Information Processing Systems (NeurIPS)*, vol. 30, pp. 5998–6008, 2017.

[3] Brown, T. B., Mann, B., Ryder, N., Subbiah, M., Kaplan, J., Dhariwal, P., Neelakantan, A., Shyam, P., Sastry, G., Askell, A., Agarwal, S., Herbert-Voss, A., Krueger, G., Henighan, T., Child, R., Ramesh, A., Ziegler, D. M., Wu, J., Winter, C., Hesse, C., Chen, M., Sigler, E., Litwin, M., Gray, S., Chess, B., Clark, J., Berner, C., McCandlish, S., Radford, A., Sutskever, I., and Amodei, D. "Language models are few-shot learners,". *arXiv preprint* arXiv:2005.14165. 2020. https://arxiv.org/abs/2005.14165

[4] Abadi, M., Agarwal, A., Barham, P., Brevdo, E., Chen, Z., Citro, C., Corrado, G. S., Davis, A., Dean, J., Devin, M., Ghemawat, S., Goodfellow, I., Harp, A., Irving, G., Isard, M., Jia, Y., Jozefowicz, R., Kaiser, Ł., Kudlur, M., Levenberg, J., Mané, D., Monga, R., Moore, S., Murray, D., Olah, C., Schuster, M., Shlens, J., Steiner, B., Sutskever, I., Talwar, K., Tucker, P., Vanhoucke, V., Vasudevan, V., Viégas, F., Vinyals, O., Warden, P., Wattenberg, M., Wicke, M., Yu, Y., and Zheng, X. et al. "TensorFlow: Large-scale machine learning on heterogeneous distributed systems," *arXiv preprint* arXiv:1603.04467, 2016. https://arxiv. org/abs/1603.04467

[5] TensorFlow. "TensorFlow Lite documentation," 2020. https://www.tensor flow.org/lite

[6] Paszke, A., Gross, S., Massa, F., Lerer, A., Bradbury, J., Chanan, G., Killeen, T., Lin, Z., Gimelshein, N., Antiga, L., Desmaison, A., Köpf, A., Yang, E., DeVito, Z., Raison, M., Tejani, A., Chilamkurthy, S., Steiner, B., Fang, L., Bai, J., Chintala, S., and others. et al. "PyTorch: An imperative style, high-performance deep learning library,". In *Advances in Neural Information Processing Systems* (Vol. 32). Curran Associates, Inc., 2019 https://proceedings.neurips.cc/ paper/2019/hash/bdbca288fee7f92f2bfa9f7012727740-Abstract.html

[7] Chicho, Bahzad and Sallow, Amira. "A comprehensive survey of deep learning models based on Keras framework," *Journal of Soft Computing and Data Mining*, vol. 2. doi:10.30880/jscdm.2021.02.02.005

[8] Hofmann, M. and Klinkenberg, R. *RapidMiner: Data mining use cases and business analytics applications*. Chapman and Hall/CRC, 2013.

[9] Google Cloud. "Google AutoML documentation," 2020. https://cloud.google. com/automl/docs

[10] IBM. "IBM Watson Studio documentation," 2021. https://www.ibm.com/ watson/studio

[11] H2O.ai. "H2O.ai AutoML documentation," 2021. https://www.h2o.ai

[12] Zaharia, M., Xin, R. S., Wendell, P., Das, T., Armbrust, M., Dave, A., Meng, X., Rosen, J., Venkataraman, S., Franklin, M. J., Ghodsi, A., Gonzalez, J., Shenker, S., and Stoica, I. "Apache Spark: A unified engine for big data processing," *Communications of the ACM*, vol. 59, no. 11, pp. 56–65, 2016. doi: 10.1145/2934664

[13] DataRobot. "DataRobot: The AI cloud leader," 2021. https://www.datarobot. com

[14] Microsoft. "ONNX Runtime documentation," 2021. https://onnxruntime.ai

[15] Barmpatsalou, K., Damopoulos, D., Kambourakis, G., and Katos, V. "A critical review of 7 years of mobile device forensics," *Digital Investigation*, vol. 10, no. 4, pp. 323–349, 2013.

[16] Ryder, S., and Le-Khac, N.-A. "The end of effective law enforcement in the cloud? To encrypt, or not to encrypt," *Proceedings of the IEEE 9th International Conference on Cloud Computing (CLOUD 2016)*, pp. 904–907, 2016.

[17] Spiekermann, Daniel and Eggendorfer, Tobias. "Challenges of network forensic investigation in virtual networks," *Journal of Cyber Security and Mobility*, vol. 5, pp. 15–46, 2017. doi:10.13052/jcsm2245-1439.522

[18] MacDermott, Áine, Heath, Howard, and Akinbi, Alex. 'Disappearing messages: Privacy or piracy?" 2022.

[19] Grispos, G., Storer, T., and Glisson, W. B. "Calm before the storm: The challenges of cloud computing in digital forensics," *International Journal of Digital Crime and Forensics*, vol. 4, no. 2, pp. 28–48, 2012.

Glossary of key terms

Address Space Layout Randomization (ASLR): A security technique that randomizes memory addresses to prevent exploitation.

Android Debug Bridge (ADB): A command-line tool used for communication with Android devices to retrieve data during forensic investigations.

Android Forensics: The forensic examination of Android-based smartphones to recover digital evidence.

Anomaly Detection: Identifying outliers or deviations from normal behavior that may indicate malicious activity.

Anti-Forensics Techniques: Methods used to hinder forensic investigations, such as data deletion, encryption, or other evasion tactics.

Application Forensics: The investigation of data related to software applications to recover evidence of user activities.

Application Heterogeneity: The diversity in application development, programming languages, and data formats, posing challenges for forensic analysis.

Artifacts: Digital remnants or traces of user activity or device interactions that can be used as evidence in forensics.

Artificial Intelligence (AI): The concept of machines mimicking human intelligence, including learning and problem-solving.

Augmented Reality (AR) Glasses: Wearable devices that overlay digital information onto the real world.

Authentication Stick Forensics: The analysis of authentication sticks used for secure access to systems or data, often involving cryptographic analysis.

Authorship Attribution: Determining the author of a text by analyzing writing style and linguistic patterns.

Automated Machine Learning (AutoML): Tools and techniques that automate the process of building and deploying machine learning models.

Autonomous Vehicle Forensics: The forensic examination of autonomous vehicles, focusing on extracting data from vehicle systems and sensors.

BERT (Bidirectional Encoder Representations from Transformers): A transformer model designed for tasks requiring a deep understanding of text.

Big Data Forensics: The practice of analyzing large volumes of data to uncover evidence of digital crimes or activities.

Biometric Data: Physiological data collected by wearables, such as heart rate, sleep patterns, and step counts.

Black Box AI: AI models that make decisions without providing explanations.

Blockchain Forensics: The process of investigating transactions and data stored on blockchain systems to uncover evidence related to crimes.

Browser Artifacts: Data remnants from web browsers, including history, bookmarks, cache, cookies, and downloads.

Bulk Extractor: A tool used for analyzing image dumps and extracting data.

CAN (Controller Area Network) Bus: A vehicle communication protocol that allows ECUs and other devices to exchange information.

Chip-off Technology: A technique where memory chips are removed from a device for direct forensic analysis.

Classification: Assigning data points to predefined categories.

Client Application: Software installed and executed on a client device, typically within an OS environment.

Client Device Forensics: The forensic analysis of devices used by individuals, such as computers, smartphones, or tablets.

Cloning (Smart Card): Creating a bit-for-bit copy of a smart card's contents for analysis.

Cloud-Based Forensics: The process of investigating data stored in cloud services, involving challenges related to access and jurisdiction.

Clustering: Grouping similar data points together based on their characteristics.

Computer Vision in Forensics: The use of AI techniques to analyze and interpret visual data, such as images or videos, in forensic investigations.

Confiscation: The act of seizing a device for forensic examination.

Control Device (Drone): A smartphone, tablet, or dedicated remote controller used to operate a drone.

Cookie: A small piece of data stored by a web browser to track user activity and preferences.

Cross-modal Models: Models that integrate different types of data, such as text and images (e.g., DALL-E, CLIP).

Cybercrime: Criminal activities involving computers or networks, including hacking, identity theft, and cyberattacks.

Data Acquisition (Smart Card): The process of creating an exact copy of the data stored on a smart card.

Data Acquisition Tools: Tools used to collect data from digital devices during forensic investigations while maintaining integrity.

Data Execution Prevention (DEP): A security feature that prevents code from being executed in memory regions not designated for execution.

Data Fragmentation: The distribution of data across multiple sources (device, app, cloud), making analysis complex.

Data Locality: The location where application-related data and artifacts are stored.

Data Loss (Wearables): The potential for data loss due to device damage, resets, or limited storage capacity.

Dedicated File (DF): A file type in the SIM card file system that acts as a child directory of the Master File (MF).

Deep Learning: A subset of machine learning that uses neural networks with many layers to analyze complex data patterns.

Deepfake: Realistic manipulated videos or images generated using AI.

Diffusion Models: Generative models that iteratively refine random noise to create high-fidelity images and videos.

Digital Evidence Extraction: The process of recovering data from a digital device that could be used as evidence in an investigation.

Digital Forensics: The process of identifying, preserving, analyzing, and presenting digital evidence for legal purposes.

Digital Forensics Frameworks: Structured methodologies or toolsets used in forensic investigations to ensure thorough analysis and reporting.

Digital Surveillance: Monitoring or tracking activities through digital systems, such as using game consoles or network devices for investigation.

Digital Vehicle Forensics: The forensic process of analyzing data from digital systems within vehicles, such as navigation or engine control units.

Disk Space Forensics: The examination of a device's disk space to recover deleted or hidden files as evidence.

Distributed Ledger Technology (DLT): A decentralized database managed by multiple participants across a network. Blockchain is a type of DLT.

DJI: A leading manufacturer of drones (e.g., Mavic, Phantom, Inspire, Matrice series).

DJI Phantom 3 Forensics: The forensic investigation of DJI Phantom 3 drones, focusing on data extraction and analysis methods.

Drone: An unmanned aerial vehicle (UAV).

Drone Evidence Acquisition: The process of collecting data from drones to be used in forensic investigations.

Drone Forensics: The application of forensic techniques to investigate drone-related incidents and extract digital evidence.

DroneGun: A drone countermeasure tool that can jam signals or force drones to return to their starting point.

DroneShield: A tool used to trace a drone back to its pilot.

DROP (DRone Open source Parser): A tool used to parse encrypted DAT files from DJI drones.

ECU (Electronic Control Unit) / ECM (Engine Control Module): Small embedded devices in vehicles responsible for controlling various electrical systems and storing data.

EDR (Event Data Recorder)/Black Box: A device that records vehicle data during collisions and other events.

EEPROM (Electronically Erasable Programmable Read-Only Memory): A type of non-volatile memory used in SIM cards and other devices to store data.

Edge AI Tools: Tools for running AI models directly on devices (at the "edge"), useful in analyzing real-time data from IoT devices in forensic investigations.

Edge Computing: Processing data at the edge of the network, closer to the source, for faster analysis.

ElcomSoft Distributed Password Recovery: A software tool used for password recovery and decryption of smart cards.

Elementary File (EF): A file type in the SIM card file system that contains the actual data.

Embedded Multi-Media Card (eMMC): A type of internal storage used in smartphones, tablets, and other devices.

Embedded Operating Systems (Drone): The operating systems used in drones, which can be a source of forensic evidence.

Emergency Call Code: A code used to make emergency calls on a SIM card.

Empatica Embrace: A medically approved seizure monitoring device.

EnCase Forensics: A digital forensics tool used to acquire and analyze data from various sources, including SIM cards.

ESI (Electronically Stored Information): Any information stored in a digital format that may be used as evidence.

Event Logs: Records of application, hardware, and system events, including timestamps.

Evidence (Drone): Digital artifacts and physical components of a drone system that can be used in an investigation.

Evidence Collection: The systematic gathering of digital evidence from devices, ensuring it is preserved for legal use.

EXIF Data: Metadata embedded in image files, containing information about the image capture.

Expert System: A branch of AI designed to mimic the decision-making abilities of a human expert, based on predefined rules and logic.

Expert Systems in Forensics: AI systems designed to simulate human expertise in a specific area, used to assist forensic investigations.

Explainable AI (XAI): AI systems designed to provide transparent and interpretable decisions, important for legal and forensic contexts.

Feature Importance: The relative importance of different input variables in an AI model's predictions.

File Systems: The structure used to store and organize data on a storage medium, such as a hard drive or memory card.

First Person View (FPV): A method of controlling drones using video goggles for a more immersive experience.

Fixed Dialing Numbers (FDN): A feature that restricts outgoing calls to pre-configured numbers.

Flasher Box: A specialized device used to read and write data to the flash memory of a device.

Flight Controller Chip (Drone): A chip in the drone that logs flight data, crucial for forensic investigations.

Forbidden Networks (FPLMN): A list of networks that a SIM card is not allowed to connect to.

Forensic Acquisition: The process of collecting digital evidence from a device while ensuring its integrity.

Forensic Analysis and Applets: The process of examining apps or programs stored on a SIM card for evidence of criminal activity.

Forensic Analysis of Smart Cards: Techniques used to analyze data and identify evidence from smart cards.

Forensic Analysis Phases: The stages involved in forensic investigations, including acquisition, analysis, and presentation of evidence.

Forensic Evidence Extraction: The process of extracting digital evidence from devices while maintaining its integrity.

Forensic Investigations: The process of collecting, preserving, and analyzing digital evidence from devices for legal purposes.

Forensic Layers: The different stages or aspects of an IoT device's forensic analysis, from acquisition to reporting.

Forensic Methodologies: Techniques and approaches used to conduct forensic investigations on digital devices.

Forensic Tools: Software or hardware used to conduct forensic analysis and data extraction from digital devices.

Forensic Tools for Smart Cards: Specialized tools used to examine smart cards during forensic investigations.

Firmware (Vehicle): Software embedded in ECUs, crucial for detecting modifications.

FTK (Forensic Tool Kit): A comprehensive digital forensics tool used for the acquisition, analysis, and reporting of digital evidence.

Game Console Forensics: The forensic process of analyzing game consoles to extract digital evidence for legal use.

Gaming Console Forensics: The application of digital forensic techniques to extract and analyze data from gaming consoles.

Gemalto Smart Card Reader: A hardware tool used to read contact and contactless smart cards.

Generative Adversarial Networks (GANs): A type of generative AI model that uses two neural networks (generator and discriminator) competing against each other.

Generative AI: AI systems that generate new data or content, such as images, text, or even synthetic data, relevant in digital forensics.

Geolocation Data: Location data recorded by wearables with GPS capabilities or connected smartphones.

Global System for Mobile Communications (GSM): The standard for mobile communication networks.

Google Meet: A web-based video conferencing application.

GPT (Generative Pre-trained Transformer): A transformer model that excels at text generation and language modeling.

Ground Control Station (GCS): The system used to remotely control a drone, often including a handheld device and/or computer software.

Ground Control Station Evidence: Evidence recovered from the control station used to operate a drone, including logs and communications.

Group Identifier (GID1, GID2): Identifiers used to group SIM cards for specific purposes.

H2O.ai: An AI platform used for data analysis and model building, relevant for digital forensic investigations.

Hash Verification: A method used to ensure data integrity.

Hobbyist Drones: Drones flown for recreational purposes.

Home PLMN Search Period (HPLMN): Specifies how often a device should search for the home network.

Human-Robot Interaction (HRI): The study of how humans interact with robots and how to design robots for optimal interaction.

Humanoid Robot: A robot designed to resemble the human body, often used for tasks that require human-like interaction.

Immutable Records: Records that cannot be altered or deleted, a key feature of blockchain technology.

IndexedDB: A browser API for storing structured data.

Integrated Circuit Card Identifier (ICCID): A unique identifier for a SIM card.

Internal Flash Memory (Drone): Memory built into the drone that stores system files and other data.

International Mobile Subscriber Identity (IMSI): An identifier used for signaling and messaging on a GSM network.

Interpretability: The degree to which a human can understand the reasons behind an AI's decisions.

iOS Forensics: The forensic examination of Apple devices running iOS to extract and analyze data.

IoT Devices: Physical objects embedded with sensors, software, and other technologies to connect and exchange data with other devices or networks.

IoT Forensics: The study and application of digital forensics techniques to Internet of Things (IoT) devices to gather, preserve, and analyze data from them.

IoT Forensics Models: Frameworks and methodologies used to perform forensic investigations on IoT devices.

ISO/IEC 7816 Standard: The standard that defines the physical dimensions and properties of smart cards.

Issuer Identification Number (IIN): A part of the ICCID that identifies the issuer of the SIM card.

Jamboard: A Google application used for the whiteboard feature in Google Meet.

JTAG (Joint Test Action Group): A hardware interface used to access and manipulate device memory.

Keras (AI Tool): A high-level neural networks API that runs on top of TensorFlow, used for rapid development of AI models in forensics.

Key Features: Specific functionalities or characteristics of a forensic tool.

Key Fob: A device used for keyless entry to vehicles, which can store vehicle information.

Language Modeling: Predicting the next word or sequence of words in a text.

LIME (Local Interpretable Model-agnostic Explanations): An XAI technique that explains individual predictions by approximating the model locally.

Live Acquisition: Acquiring data from a running device when necessary to prevent data loss.

Live Analysis: Analyzing a device while it is running, minimizing data alteration.

Local, Locallow, and Roaming Folders: Subfolders within the AppData folder that store different types of application data.

Location Area Identity (LAI): A unique identifier for a location area in a GSM network.

Location Area Information (LOCI): Information related to the location of a SIM card in a GSM network.

Logical Acquisition: The process of acquiring data from a device through standard operating system functions without accessing raw memory.

Machine Learning (ML): A type of artificial intelligence where systems learn from data to make predictions or decisions, relevant in forensic analysis.

Machine Translation: Automatically translating text from one language to another.

Manual Acquisition: A method of evidence acquisition where the investigator manually collects data from the device.

Master File (MF): The root of the SIM card file system.

Memory Chip: A component in smartphones and other devices used to store data, including operating systems, apps, and user files.

Memory Forensics: The process of analyzing volatile memory (RAM) from devices to recover evidence of criminal activity.

Misty Companion App: A mobile app used to interact with and control the Misty II robot.

Misty II Robot: A specific robot model used in forensic studies, including the acquisition of data related to its operation.

MOBILedit: A smartphone forensics tool that can also acquire and analyze SIM card data.

MOBILedit Acquisition Tool: A tool used to acquire data from mobile devices for forensic purposes.

Mobile Country Code (MCC): A code that identifies the country of a mobile network.

Mobile Device Encryption: Security measures that protect data stored on mobile devices, making forensic acquisition more difficult.

Mobile Equipment (ME): The part of a smartphone that remains after the SIM card is removed.

Mobile Network Code (MNC): A code that identifies a specific mobile network within a country.

Mobile Station International Subscriber Directory Number (MSISDN): The full phone number of a subscriber, including the country code.

Murphy's Model: A model used to guide the process of extracting forensic evidence from smartphones and mobile devices.

Named Entity Recognition (NER): Identifying and classifying named entities in text (e.g., people, organizations, locations).

Natural Language Processing (NLP): A branch of AI focused on the interaction between computers and human language, used for analyzing textual data in forensics.

Network Forensics: The analysis of network traffic and logs to investigate crimes involving digital networks.

Omnikey Reader: A hardware tool that interfaces with contact and contactless smart cards.

OSForensics: A digital forensics tool used for analyzing and acquiring data from various devices, including drones and smartphones.

Own Dialing Number: A feature that allows users to retrieve their own phone number.

Page Smearing/Swapping: Memory management techniques that can complicate memory forensics.

Paraben SIM Card Seizure: A forensic tool used for SIM card acquisition and analysis.

Parrot: A manufacturer of drones (e.g., Anafi, Bebop, Disco).

Pattern Recognition: Identifying patterns and regularities in data.

Payload (Drone): The cargo carried by a drone.

Personal Identification Data: Information stored on smart cards used for identification, such as names, addresses, and biometric data.

Photorec: A tool used for recovering deleted files, including images.

Physical Acquisition: A method of acquiring a device's physical memory, often used when the device is inaccessible by logical means.

Physical Evidence (Drone): Physical components of the drone system, such as the drone itself, batteries, and controllers.

PIN (Personal Identification Number): A security code used to access a smart card.

Post-mortem Forensics (Vehicle): Data acquisition from a stopped vehicle, minimizing the risk of evidence loss.

Predictive Analysis: Using historical data to predict future events or behaviors.

Prefetch Files: Windows files that store information about application execution to speed up loading times.

Preferred Languages (PL): Language preferences stored on a SIM card.

Preferred Network List (PLMN): A list of preferred networks for roaming.

Proprietary Systems: Systems that use custom, closed-source technologies, often posing challenges in digital forensics due to a lack of access.

Proxmark3: A hardware tool used to analyze RFID and NFC communications.

PUK (Personal Unlocking Key): A code used to unlock a SIM card after multiple failed PIN attempts.

PyTorch (AI Tool): A machine learning framework used in AI model development, useful for forensic data analysis tasks.

PySim: A software tool used to clone and interact with SIM card data.

Quantaq USIMdetective: A forensic tool specifically designed for analyzing SIM card data.

Radio Controller (Drone): A device used to control a drone remotely.

RapidMiner: A data science platform that can be used in forensic analysis for predictive modeling and data mining.

Registry (Windows): A hierarchical database that stores configuration data for the Windows OS.

Reinforcement Learning: Training an AI agent to make decisions through rewards and punishments.

Remote Storage Forensics: Investigating data stored remotely, such as in cloud storage, and the challenges in acquiring it as evidence.

Removable SD Card (Drone): A memory card used to store data, such as images and videos, captured by the drone.

Return-Oriented Programming (ROP): An exploitation technique that chains together existing code snippets in memory to execute malicious code.

Robot Forensics: The forensic investigation of robots to extract data that can be used as evidence.

Robot Operating System (ROS): A software framework used to control robots, relevant in robotic forensics for extracting evidence.

Rooting and Jailbreaking: The process of removing device restrictions to gain root access, often used to bypass security features for forensic analysis.

Rule-Based Decision-Making: A type of AI where decisions are based on a set of predefined rules.

Safety-Related Data (Vehicle): Data from the EDR related to the vehicle's state during safety-critical moments.

SCDs (Smart Connected Devices): Devices connected to the internet that collect, process, and transmit data.

SD Card Forensics: The process of analyzing data stored on SD cards to extract digital evidence for criminal investigations.

Secure Digital (SD) Card: A portable memory card commonly used in smartphones and other devices to store data.

Security-Related Data (Vehicle): Data providing insights into the security measures and vulnerabilities of vehicle systems.

Sensor Data: Data collected by sensors in wearables, such as GPS, accelerometer, and heart rate monitor.

Sensors (Drone): Components that collect data, such as cameras, GPS sensors, gyroscopes, and accelerometers.

Sentiment Analysis: Determining the sentiment expressed in a text (e.g., positive, negative, neutral).

Serial Number (Drone): A unique identifier for a drone or its components.

Service Dialing Numbers (SDN): Numbers associated with specific services offered by a network provider.

Service Oriented Architecture (SOA): An architectural style that enables dynamic web infrastructure and web services.

Service Provider Name (SPN): The name of the GSM network service provider.

SHAP (SHapley Additive exPlanations): An XAI technique that assigns importance values to features based on game theory.

SIM Card Artifacts: Digital traces and remnants left on a SIM card that can be used as evidence.

SIM Card Forensics: The process of analyzing data stored on a SIM card for evidence related to criminal activities.

SIM Card Security: The mechanisms that protect the data stored on SIM cards, such as encryption and authentication methods.

SIMClone: A software tool used for cloning SIM cards.

SIM Manager: A forensic tool that can acquire SIM card data.

SIMScan: An open-source toolkit for retrieving SIM card information.

SIM Service Table (SST): A file that indicates which services are active on a SIM card.

Sleuth Kit: A collection of command-line tools used for digital forensics analysis.

Smart Card Forensics: The forensic examination of smart cards, which store encrypted data for secure transactions or identification.

Smart Debug Bridge (SDB): A tool potentially used for data acquisition from smart wearables.

Smart Earbuds: Wearable audio devices with smart features like voice assistants and activity tracking.

Smart Glasses: Wearable devices that provide visual information, often with AR capabilities.

Smart Wearable Devices: Devices worn on the body, like smartwatches or fitness trackers, that can store and transmit data, useful for forensics.

Smart Wearable Forensics: The application of forensic techniques to investigate data from smart wearables.

Smartphone Examiner (MPE): A forensic tool from AccessData used for smartphone acquisition and analysis, including SIM card data.

Smartphone Forensics: The forensic investigation of smartphones to extract and analyze digital evidence.

Smartphone Heterogeneity: The variation in smartphone operating systems, hardware, and configurations, which complicates forensic analysis.

Social Robot: A robot designed to interact with humans in a social manner, often used for companionship or assistance.

Sparse Acquisition: A method of evidence acquisition where only partial data are collected, focusing on essential evidence.

Stealth Combat Drones: Highly advanced military drones.

Subscriber Identity Module (SIM): A small card used in mobile phones to store subscriber information and enable network communication.

Subscriber Number (SN): The unique number assigned to a subscriber within a mobile network.

Supervised Learning: Training a model on labeled data with known input–output pairs.

Telematics: A combination of informatics, telecommunications, electronics, and software used to collect and analyze vehicle data.

Telematics Cloud Server: A server that receives and stores data from vehicle telematics systems.

Telematics Control Unit (TCU): A hardware module in vehicles that gathers and transmits data to the cloud.

Telematics Data (Drone): Data transmitted by the drone, including flight parameters and sensor readings.

Telematics Vehicle Tracking: Using GPS and GPRS to track vehicle location.

Temporary Mobile Subscriber Identity (TMSI): A temporary identifier used for communication between a mobile device and the network.

TensorFlow (AI Tool): A machine learning framework used for building and deploying AI models, applied in digital forensics for data analysis.

Text Classification: Categorizing text into predefined classes.

Text Mining: Extracting useful information from unstructured text data.

Thumb Drive Forensics: The process of examining USB thumb drives to extract and analyze data for legal investigations.

Transaction Logs: Records of transactions stored on smart cards, such as banking cards.

TransFlash Card Forensics: The forensic examination of TransFlash cards (a type of microSD card) for evidence extraction.

Transformer Models: A type of deep learning model that uses self-attention mechanisms to process sequential data, such as text.

Transformers (AI Tool): A deep learning model architecture used for tasks like text and image analysis, relevant for AI-based forensic tools.

UAV (Unmanned Aerial Vehicle) Forensics: Forensic techniques applied to drones to recover and analyze data from the devices.

UMTS (Universal Mobile Telecommunications System): The 3G mobile communication standard.

Unmanned Aircraft System (UAS): A system that includes a UAV and its control components.

Unsupervised Learning: Training a model on unlabeled data to discover patterns and structures.

Unstructured Data: Data that does not conform to a predefined data model or schema (e.g., text, images, video).

USB Drive Forensics: The forensic examination of USB drives for digital evidence, such as documents or software.

USIM (Universal Subscriber Identity Module): A type of SIM card used in 3G and later networks.

Variational Autoencoders (VAEs): A type of generative AI model that encodes data into a latent space and then decodes it to generate new data.

Vehicle Information System: Data about the vehicle itself, such as serial number, engine number, and VIN.

Vehicle Telematics: Data generated by vehicle sensors and systems, often used in forensic investigations to track vehicle movements.

Volatility Framework: A tool used for memory forensics, including application-specific analysis.

Vuzix Blades: AR-enabled smart glasses with Alexa integration.

Wearable Device Storage: Internal storage on the wearable device itself, which can contain user data and settings.

Wearable Forensics: The forensic examination of data from wearable devices, such as fitness trackers, to extract personal or health-related evidence.

Web Application: Software accessed and used over the internet, typically within a web browser.

Web Application Forensics: The process of extracting evidence from web-based applications, often used in cybercrime investigations.

Web Services (WS): Software components that provide specific functionalities and can be accessed by other applications.

Windows Smartphone Forensics: The forensic investigation of smartphones running Windows Phone OS.

Wireshark: A tool used for capturing and analyzing network traffic.

Write Blocker: A device that prevents changes to evidence during analysis.

Xbox Forensics: The process of extracting and analyzing digital evidence from Xbox consoles, including account and gameplay data.

XFT Device: A device used for forensic acquisition and analysis of Xbox consoles, crucial in gaming console investigations.

XRY: A comprehensive mobile forensics tool that can acquire and analyze data from smartphones and SIM cards.

Zenbo App Builder: A platform for creating custom applications for the Zenbo robot.

Zenbo Master: A mobile app used to control and interact with the Zenbo robot.

Index

For Product Safety Concerns and Information please contact our EU
representative GPSR@taylorandfrancis.com
Taylor & Francis Verlag GmbH, Kaufingerstraße 24, 80331 München, Germany

9 781041 082033